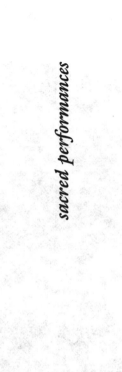

sacred performances

sacred performances

ISLAM, SEXUALITY, AND SACRIFICE

M. E. Combs-Schilling

COLUMBIA UNIVERSITY PRESS
NEW YORK

Frontispiece: Holy men preparing for the sacrifice of the Prophet's Birthday, the High Atlas Mountains.

All photographs by David M. Schilling.

"A Tale of Baghdad" from *Mirror of the Orient* by Roland and Sabrina Michaud is reprinted by permission of Hachette/Editions du Chêne. Copyright © 1980 by Hachette; English translation copyright © 1981 by Little, Brown and Company. "Partisans" by W. S. Di Piero is reprinted by permission of *Carolina Quarterly*.

Columbia University Press
New York   Oxford
Copyright © 1989 M. E. Combs-Schilling
All rights reserved

Library of Congress Cataloging-in-Publication Data
Combs-Schilling, M. E.
    Sacred performances : Islam, sexuality, and sacrifice / M. E. Combs-Schilling.
        p.   cm.
    Bibliography: p.
    Includes index.
    ISBN 0-231-06974-X
    1. Islam and politics—Morocco.   2. Morocco—Politics and government.
3. Monarchy—Morocco.   4. Morocco—Religious life and customs.
5. Marriage customs and rites, Islamic—Morocco.
6. Sacrifice—Morocco.   7. Sacrifice—Islam.
I. Title.
BP64.M6C66 1989
306.2'0964—dc20   89-35800
                                                                              CIP

Casebound editions of Columbia University Press books are Smyth-sewn and are printed on permanent and durable acid-free paper.

Printed in the United States of America
c 10 9 8 7 6 5 4 3 2 1

for Jonathan, David, and Dorothy

contents

Illustrations follow p. 186. Maps appear on pp. 104 and 112.

contents

note on transliteration and pronunciation

In transliterating Arabic, I have kept as much as possible to the classical Arabic spellings of words while nonetheless minimizing diacritical marks in the text in order not to overburden the non-Arabic speaker. Fuller transliterations occur in the glossary, where long vowels are noted by a straight line above (ā) and emphatic consonants by a dot underneath (ṭ).

Written Arabic has twenty-eight consonants. The two consonants that are most unfamiliar to the English speaker are the *hamza,* ', and the *ayn,* '. The hamza, ', is a glottal stop, a cut-off in air flow, as in the Cockney pronunciation of "bottle," which becomes "bo'le." The ayn, ', is a deep sound made in the back of the throat that makes the surrounding vowels deeper also. The Arabic "kh" is like the German "ach." The Arabic "q" is a deep and emphatic "k" sound that takes place far back in the throat.

Written Arabic has three vowels, a, i, and u. They are the only vowels I use in transliteration; thus, for instance, I spell the Prophet of Islam's name as "Muhammad," not "Mohammed." Written Arabic does not have the consonant c; thus I spell the holiest city in Islam as "Makka," not "Mecca."

Like others who have journeyed to Morocco, when walking down local streets I found myself gazing at the face of the central monarch. In mountain hamlets, city markets, and desert camps, the king is powerfully present. Present in words, pictures, and deeds, he is occasionally present in person also. In 1985, King Hasan II passed through the town where I lived. Sporting designer sunglasses and a khaki safari suit, he drove a Winnebago. The townsfolk covered the streets with carpets so that the imperial wheels would not touch ground.

At first, the monarchy appears rife with paradox. Over time one comes to see it as laden with workable synthesis, an unexpected and yet incredibly dynamic adaptation to this age. The paradox and the synthesis are both real. Morocco's Hasan II occupies the millennium-old position of the Islamic caliphate, the position of overarching political authority in the Muslim world established upon Muhammad's death. He is "Prince of the Faithful," the rightful leader of the political community of the faith. He traces his patrilineal blood descent to the Prophet Muhammad, 39 generations removed. He holds a doctorate in law from Bordeaux, wears French suits, and dons long white religious robes. His passions are golf, architecture, women, and Islam.

Morocco's monarchy eludes stereotypical depiction, as does the population's understanding of it. On the whole, Moroccans combine a straightforward realism toward the man in power with deep-seated respect for the ancient institution, much as Americans respect the presidency while diverging in their opinions of a given occupant. Moroccans are often disarmingly pointed in their appraisals of their own system's strengths and weaknesses, at the same time that they are pragmatic about the frailty of power's construction everywhere. Americans tend to view monarchy as an outmoded institution from a distant past. Moroccans tend to view monarchy as a part of themselves and their distinctive identity, and many envision its presence in their future.

The Moroccan monarchy's combination of paradox, dynamism, and synthesis makes it a riveting institution. Physically, one feels its influence; one is visually drawn into its power. It is a symbol of collective identity, the icon of Morocco's great past, viable present, and future hopes.

argument

At first I had no idea why the Moroccan monarchy was so powerful and enduring. My early research focused on the history of the institution, and my early explanations centered on the chronology of events. My opinion about the crucible of the monarch's power changed through time, finally to emerge in the book you are about to read. The core of my argument is that during a great historical crisis of the 1500s, Moroccans used ritual to reformulate the foundations of their central political institution. The reformulations made for a remarkably forceful cultural substratum of power—unquestioned and enduring—that enabled Morocco to surmount five centuries of Western assault and enter the twentieth century with its cultural identity and political integrity intact. The reformulations inscribed the monarchy deep within the popular subconscious, embedding the definition of rule within the definition of self and ultimate hope.

Three rituals were crucial to the reconstruction: the Prophet's Birthday, the popular celebrations of first marriage, and the Great Sacrifice. Innovations in the Prophet's Birthday made the monarch the definition of the nation. Innovations in popular marriage practices made the ruler the definition of the man and the link to successful reproduction. And innovations in the Great Sacrifice made the ruler the collective hope for transcendence—formidable foundations for a formidable institution.

Although *Sacred Performances* draws upon history, it is not a history in the traditional sense of the word: a document that portrays collective life as emerging from the straightforward unfolding of a chronological sequence of events. Rather, it is an interpretive essay that looks to major symbols, themes, and cultural paradigms that help explain why history evolved in the way in which it did.

The argument is novel. The contribution of major Islamic rituals to the stability of the Moroccan monarchy has not been previously analyzed. Current descriptions of these rituals, much less analyses, are hard to find—even for the most important ritual occasions such as the Great Sacrifice, a rite enacted by almost every Moroccan family every year as well as by most of the world's 900 million Muslims. Moroccans as a whole spend more money on the Great Sacrifice than on any other annual event and commonly describe it as the most crucial. Western historians have not taken rituals seriously as undergirders of the monarchy, although some Moroccan historians have, such as al-Fishtali (who wrote in the 1500s) and al-Ifrani (who wrote in the 1700s). Al-Fishtali and al-Ifrani do not analyze the role of rituals in the monarchy but rather simply describe them as part of the history of the institution. I use their descriptions in building my analysis. My emphasis on the importance of ritual in the reconstruction of the Moroccan monarchy first occurred to me while reading al-Ifrani.

The argument of *Sacred Performances* is not exclusivist. Collective reality is everywhere too complex for a single variable to determine all. Multiple factors always enter in. What I argue for is the relative importance of ritual practices in reconstructing and reestablishing the monarchy during an age of radical transition.

Like other interpretative arguments, that of *Sacred Performances* is not amenable to experimental verification. One cannot replay Moroccan history, taking out ritual performances, to see what would occur. Rather, one must do the reverse, start from undeniable givens: in this case, the existence of the oldest still actively ruling monarchy in the world,[1] a twelve-hundred-year-old institution that survived five hundred years of Western assault while much of the rest of what we now call the Third World succumbed to colonial domination. From that starting point, one begins to search for plausible relationships among the multiplicity of variables, seeking to uncover those that most fully account for the history that was produced.

Sacred Performances is a representation of history and culture. As

Paul Friedrich once stated, "All representation is misrepresentation—but there is truth in some misrepresentation."[2] *Sacred Performances* searches for that kind of truth. The test of the argument's worth lies in its ability to highlight crucial dimensions of Moroccan collective life so that overall understanding is enhanced and scholarly inquiry is focused in new directions.

form

Sacred Performances contains five sections and seventeen chapters. The first section (chapters 1 and 2) establishes the essentials: the power of rituals and the problems of the mind/body dichotomy.

The second section (chapters 3 and 4) addresses the consolidation of political and sexual culture in Islam. Chapter 3 concerns the life of Muhammad, the founding of Islam, and the establishment of the basic cultural matrices that became crucial to Islam's spread, including basic ritual performances. Chapter 4 examines the battle over the proper definition of political authority that emerged upon Muhammad's death and the battle over the definition of male and female sexuality that was associated with it.

The third section (chapters 5 and 6) focuses upon the grandeur of Islam's coming to Morocco and the power of the Islamic monarchy that was built. Chapter 5 looks at the advent of Islam and its age of glory. The section then turns to the crisis that nearly caused Morocco's downfall. Chapter 6 examines the role of the bubonic plague in the post-1350s economic plummet.

Section four (chapters 7 through 15) is the book's core. These chapters concentrate upon the role of central cultural definitions and ritual practices in the survival of the Moroccan monarchy. Chapter 7 focuses upon the rise of the Sa'di dynasty and its ability to restore the central monarchy by resting it on the demand for blood descent from the Prophet Muhammad. Chapter 8 examines the role of rituals in that restoration; it explores the way in which Sa'di developed a national celebration of the Prophet's Birthday that communicated and legitimated the new form of monarchy by iconically linking it with the Prophet's light and God's truth. Chapter 9 examines the rise of 'Alawi dynasty, the second blood-descendant dynasty to emerge in the crisis. Chapters 10 and 11 analyze the popular practices which surround first marriage ceremonies, practices that established the new definition of rule as pivotal to the individual's definition of self, to the practice of legitimate sexual intercourse, and to the hope for progeny. Chapters 12 through 15 address the ritual of sacrifice, the most important in the monarchy's repertoire. In it, a great leap is made such that the monarchy is no longer confined to simply earthly things but becomes a channel to eternal being, a pathway to transcendent hope.

The fifth section (chapters 16 and 17) brings the analysis to the present. Chapter 16 examines the twentieth-century French colonial era. It highlights the way in which the French severed political culture from the political apparatus; the political culture remained with the Moroccan population and the Moroccan king, symbol of the national whole, while the political apparatus was taken over and greatly elaborated by the French. Moroccans then used the power of political culture to gain control of the ruling apparatus and to oust the colonists from the land. Chapter 17 examines the unification of culture and apparatus that occurred with political independence. That unification made for a new era in Moroccan rule when the powers of the monarchy were greatly expanded.

The book's multiple concerns—power, legitimacy, and sexuality —are unified by an overarching argument against the mind/body dichotomy. I examine the way in which experiences of the body build categories of the mind. I contend that the most powerful conceptual abstractions are often founded upon a bodily basis, and that the most formidable political entities are those in which the regularities of mind, body, and spirit converge.

research

Given the paucity of ritual descriptions and the absence of in-depth analysis, *Sacred Performances* had to begin from the beginning in addressing the ritual foundations of the Moroccan monarchy. Most anthropological descriptions of ritual in Morocco have focused upon local rituals—for example, rites surrounding local saints and religious brotherhoods—and not upon the great Islamic rituals that unite the Moroccan population as a whole.[3] The basic ritual groundwork had to be built. I have spent four of the last twelve years in Morocco and have been in Morocco for the celebration of six of the last twelve Great Sacrifices and Prophet's Birthdays. Both are annual events that I witnessed in 1976, 1977, 1978, 1985, 1987, and 1988. I have attended thirty-seven marriage ceremonies.

My initial research interests in Morocco (1976–1978) lay in commerce and change, and resulted in "Abiding Constraints: Permanence and Change in a Moroccan Boom Town." But from the beginning, Moroccans insisted on the importance of rituals and persuaded me to attend these events and to record in detail, through notes, tape recordings, and photographs, what happened at them. Once my interests began to focus on rituals, I gathered more precise documentation. I added video recordings to the previous materials and began searching the literature for descriptions of the rituals, using libraries and archives in Morocco, Paris, Aix-en-Provence, and the United States. I began a series of interviews, conducted in Moroccan colloquial Arabic. From 1985 to 1988, I completed sixty-five formal interviews and innumerable informal ones on the role of rituals in Moroccan collective life. Those interviewed represented a wide cross section of the country's population: rural and urban, poor and elite, scholarly and nonscholarly. At the time the interviews were conducted, many of those interviewed had known me for over a decade. Mutual respect had been built over the years, which greatly facilitated the range of allowable questioning and the straightforwardness of the responses. Those interviewed included people from the small southern town of Imi-n-Tanut, where I lived from January 1977 to May 1978 and to which I return on a regular basis, as well as members of the national elite located in Ribat (Rabat) and Dar al-Bayda' (Casablanca). I first lived in Ribat, Morocco's political capital, for six months in 1976, and I regularly return. In 1987 and 1988, I lived there again for a year, and from Ribat commuted to Dar al-Bayda', the economic capital—an hour by the fast train dubbed "The 'Awayta" in honor of Morocco's world champion long-distance runner. During the summer of 1988 I briefly changed my residence to Dar al-Bayda' in order to facilitate research there. The research in Ribat and Dar al-Bayda' was designed to complement the research in the outlying areas that had focused on the rural elite and the middle and lower rungs of rural society. Research in Ribat and Dar al-Bayda' concentrated on the centers of power—key members of government, the top echelon of the economic elite. Yet, in Ribat and Dar al-Bayda', I also interviewed people from the middle and lower strata; I had introductions to many of them through people in Imi-n-Tanut. Moroccans—from the top to the bottom of the political, economic, and social scale—have been consistently gracious and helpful. Open-mindedness and hospitality are striking Moroccan traits.

Moroccans, scholars and others, have been influential in the development of this book. My debt to the centuries-old historians al-Ifrani and al-Fishtali has already been acknowledged. My debt to the living is much greater. Given the frequency of my visits to Morocco, I regularly presented my ideas as they were developing and received valuable input, revising and refining my argument as a result of those exchanges. For instance, it was a group of young men in Ribat who, late one night in a heated conversation in the open air, challenged my original ideas on the father-son relationship depicted in the Great Sacrifice. My interpretation at that point had been highly idealistic. They turned my attention to the underside also—to the demanded submission of the son, submission to his own death.

There are many Moroccans to thank for their contributions, and yet none of these individuals is responsible for the interpretations presented in *Sacred Performances;* rather my ideas were developed through interactions with them and with others to whom my debt is great and whose support has been substantial. My gratitude to the people of Imi-n-Tanut is boundless: they took me in, treated me with respect, and taught me much about Morocco, Islam, and life. Greatest thanks go to Muhammad al-Wali Qaissar, his wife Malika, her sister Fatima, Brahim Baʿali, al-Hajj Belmamoune, al-Hajj Arab, and al-Hajj Muhammad u Hassan. Morocco's intellectual community, especially that of Ribat, Dar al-Baydaʾ, and Marrakush, is enormously fertile and lively, and gracious in letting outsiders in. Especially helpful were Paul Pascon (who tragically died in 1986), Abdallah Hammoudi, Fatima Mernissi, Muhammad al-Mansour, Fatima Harrak, Abdelhad Sebti, and Muhammad Kably. They generously listened to my ideas, reacted to them, and encouraged their development. Morocco's older Qurʾanic scholars and Istiqlal ("Independence") leaders have been equally insightful and helpful. My debt to the wise old al-Hajj Abd al-Latif al-Hajji is straightforwardly acknowledged. Over the last twelve years, he has been the most constant source of exchange and encouragement, serving as benevolent uncle, critic, mentor, and friend. In recent years the greatest debt has been to Si Driss Senoussi. In Ribat, he provided that domain of acknowledged acceptance that allowed me and my ideas to flourish. He listened to my suppositions with serious attention and addressed them with serious critique. Like al-Hajj Abd al-Latif, Si Driss Senoussi epitomizes a strength of self and breadth of vision that is characteristic of many Moroccans. The two of them stand unthreatened by people and ideas different from their own, and neither the wise old Islamic scholar nor the bright young commercialist tolerates mediocrity. It has been an enduring honor to be in Morocco over the last twelve years, and a distinctive honor knowing them.

acknowledgments

for repeated readings and substantial input

Dorothy Combs Hill
Ann Miller
Katherine Newman
David M. Schilling

for important contributions

Alexander Alland, Jr.
al-Hajj Arab
Brahim Baʿali
al-Hajj Belmamoune
Burton Benedict
Mawlay Bih
Richard Bulliet

acknowledgments

Claire Cesareo
Dominique Chabre
Wendy Chamberlin
Robert Clark
Elizabeth Colson
Kenneth Combs
Jennifer Dossin
al-Hajj Abd al-Latif al-Hajji
Abdallah Hammoudi
Fatima Harrak
al-Hajj Muhammad u Hassan
John Hawes
Ira Lapidus
Muhammad al-Mansour
Fatima Mernissi
Robert Murphy
Jack Murrah
Ambassador Thomas Nassif
Zinetta Nassif
Celia Owens
Jean Scandlyn
Jonathan David Combs Schilling
Driss Senoussi
Denise Spellberg
Edward H. Thomas
Muhammad al-Wali Qaissar
Louise Waller
Lucille Walters Combs
Wendy Wilkinson
Neguin Yavari

for generous support that made this work possible

Columbia Council for the Social Sciences
Danforth Foundation
Fulbright Foundation
Islamic Civilization Awards
Moroccan/American Commission for
    Educational and Cultural Exchange
Social Science Research Council

sacred performances

A TALE OF BAGHDAD

There were in Baghdad two advisors in the caliph's service. It was unclear which of the pair was the more refined, so superlative was the taste and splendor of each. The caliph's court urged him to put them to the test: he consented, and decided as the criterion that each should arrange a banquet. He who organized the most elegant display would be the ultimate authority on taste and etiquette. Thus the day arrived for the first of the competitors. Upon entering the banquet hall, what was to be found? Perfection itself. All without flaw: the guest selection, the quality of the menu, the embellishment of the hall uniting fresh elegance with brilliant lighting, all lacking any obvious artifice. There were poems recited, music and dance, edifying but friendly conversation, at times erudite, but always witty. All was truly perfect; to imagine a better presentation was impossible. The other contestant seemed doomed. Some already mourned his defeat. Others, more enterprising, commenced paying their court to the obvious victor.

One week later, the night of the second banquet arrived. There was at first extreme curiosity, then great surprise, finally a profound disappointment. Surprise and disappointment arose because of the nature of this second banquet: it was in every way, point by point, identical to the previous one. The same guests were invited, the hall's arrangement and decoration a repetition. Identical were the poems, the melodies, and dancing. There were the same flowers and the same fragrances. Conversation took up again as a repetition of itself. Echoes and reflections. It was impossible for the frustrated guests to criticize the plagiarist; holding their tongues, they began to enjoy themselves.

After a short while, the caliph announced, "Today's banquet has won. May the Lord's benediction follow its maker always, just as will our delighted appreciation for the exceptional moment he has given us, and which we shall forevermore savor in our memories."

The stunned hall showed no reaction. What if the caliph spoke ironically? That supposition seemed likely, and in fact, was the only possible explanation.

Finally, the great advisor came forth, urged on by the crowd, and dared ask, "Oh great and illustrious caliph! In your unsparing justness, you perhaps wanted to laugh at the impertinence of this unlucky one, or else, in your boundless wisdom, you have seen what our eyes were not capable of seeing. If your limitless indulgence would accept to clear up this matter for us, please share the reasons for your choice."

And the caliph responded, "I do not know what to say, in truth, because the reason is subtle and avoids clear explanation. We had almost forgotten that moment we lived but a week ago. Now, this advisor's art has restored through a dreamlike repetition all the magic that had disappeared, all the evaporated perfume from the shattered flask. What occurred the other night simply occurred. But the reflection we saw this evening was a true act of creation: this reflection has tapped and actually restored our flow of happiness in its spontaneous perfection. In addition, it gave us three other treasures: memory, recognition, and victory over the annihilation of the past. No success is sweeter than this!"

(quoted in Michaud 1981:ii–iii)

ESSENTIALS

*argument
prism*

1

Flickering candles—great shafts of light swathed in the brocade of brides—are borne into small narrow streets aloft on the shoulders of porters. The darkening city at twilight springs into sharp relief as rose-hued adobe walls catch the moving patterns of dark and light. Distinctions between object and silhouette blur and the whole world becomes a shadow play. As the candles move swiftly through the streets, they take on human form—young virgins, carried to the wedding bed. Their gold and silver threads catch the light and shimmer. Drums beat, ghaitas play, crowds applaud—even the women let out their shrill ululations of joy when the candles pass. Then, as suddenly as it came, all disappears. The light is extinguished. Silence holds the city in its grip. Night envelops the land. Just when all hope seems lost, before dawn while night still abides, the great gates open. A king, dressed in shimmering white robes, emerges. The crowds, deprived of light, turn to him, and he leads them in the prayers that break the day. Dawn comes. He is the bringer of the light, this descendant of Muhammad. With the Prophet's blood in his veins, he pushes away the darkness and brings back the Prophet's light. And later he will shed the blood that will secure that light forever.

■   ■   ■

Sacred Performances concerns power, rituals, and sexuality. It examines the durability of the Moroccan monarchy, the power of ritual performances, and the consequences of embedding political authority in sexual and religious understandings, in definitions of male and female and in pathways of human hope.

Power, rituals, and sexuality converge on Morocco's monarchy to create a formidable institution, the world's oldest ruling monarchy. Established in 789, a hundred years before King Alfred instituted the British crown, 1989 marks its twelve hundredth anniversary. The Moroccan monarchy is not just old, it is stunningly potent: Morocco's king oversees political decisions, makes laws, forms governments, and dissolves parliament at will. Old and powerful, the monarchy is also legitimate, by law and by popular consent. The monarchy lays effective claim to the supreme political position in Islam, the caliphate, established over 1,350 years ago upon the death of the Prophet Muhammad. Old, powerful, and legitimate, the monarchy is also deeply valued. It constitutes the heart of the nation, the symbol of self, the link to Islam and to the past. Even the country's most strident critics tend to support it, calling for its reform, not its eradication.

The supports for the monarchy's power are multiple, as are the vantage points from which to explore them. *Sacred Performances* unearths the cultural foundations, focusing upon basic definitions and ritual practices. The cultural emphasis emerges both because this is the nature of the anthropological enterprise and because political culture has played a particularly determinant role in Moroccan political life. The analysis sheds light on the patriarchal foundations of Islam, enabling us to better understand why the systems of political power that have developed in the Muslim world tend to be highly authoritarian and why the majority of the world's ruling monarchies exist there. The analysis also helps us understand the construction of power elsewhere. The case is particular, but the processes are panhuman.

historical conflict and cultural resolution

The strength of Morocco's monarchy during the first six centuries of its rule is not surprising. From the 700s to the 1350s, political, economic, and cultural supports coalesced. Morocco was a part of a great Islamic civilization that dominated much of the known world, and from the 1000s to the 1350s, Islamic Morocco dominated much of the western Mediterranean. Gold flowed, the Qur'an was sung, and armies marched. It was Morocco's age of potent glory.

Then power shifted. Crisis struck. In the 1350s, the bubonic plague swept through the Mediterranean and collapsed Morocco's well-developed economy, while it indirectly sent Europe's less-developed economy spiraling upward. Europe began its ascent to world domination and Morocco began its plummet. From the 1350s to the 1900s, practical crises continued to strike Morocco. The economy faltered, the armies dispersed, and the country's central administration fell apart. Europe began colonizing Morocco's ports. It appeared that Morocco as a distinctive political entity was finished, that it would succumb to the growing power of the West.

Yet, all was not what it seemed. Out of the midst of the turmoil, a family of blood descendants of the Prophet Muhammad came forward and reconstituted Moroccan collective life by reconstituting the Moroccan monarchy, altering its basic foundations. The new form of rule rested on two central pillars of Islam—the acknowledged excellence of blood descendants of the Prophet Muhammad, the sharif, and the properness of the caliphate as the overarching position of political authority in Islam. The monarchy became the sharifi caliphate.

The time was the 1500s, the dynasty the Sa'di. In the 1600s, another family of blood descendants of the Prophet Muhammad came forward, took over Morocco's throne, and remain in power to this day—the 'Alawi, the longest ruling dynasty in Moroccan history. The practical foundations of the monarchy often came undone during the 'Alawi reign, yet the monarchy remained secure through cultural supports; the monarchy had become essential to the basic definitions of self, including the sexual self, and to the basic understandings of the truth of the universe. Rituals built these understandings, and blood was their legitimizing seal. Blood descent from the Prophet Muhammad was made requisite for monarchical rule, and blood sacrifice gave it visible confirmation.

It was a formidable political reconstruction, appropriate to the times in which it arose. Grounded in culture, it became dominant and excelled thanks to ritual's ability to establish the worth of the rulers and the form of rule, even in the absence of practical supports. It is no accident that the sharifi model of rule emerged when more mundane undergirdings of central power were destabilized. Cultural definitions and ritual practices compensated for practical inadequacies, and enabled Morocco and its system of rule to endure through centuries of tumult despite the frequent weakness and occasional absence of military, economic, and administrative supports commonly associated with viable political systems. Great collective performances that emphasized the power of blood became the blood-legitimated monarchy's most reliable means of reproduction, the mechanism for its continual reinsertion into popular practice and consciousness. The performances drove the monarchy ever deeper into the population's ultimate longings and essential concerns.

Reformulations in the Prophet's Birthday, the popular celebrations of first marriage, and the Great Sacrifice were crucial to the establishment and survival of the sharifi caliphate. All three were reworked so that they substantiated the truth of new political construction. In the late 1500s, the Prophet's Birthday ('Id al-Mawlid) was established as an enduring national ritual in which the monarchy literally and figuratively shone. The performance surrounded the king with blazing light and encircled him by the holy words sung from the Qur'an.

Popular wedding practices supported the new form of rule. First marriage became a rite of passage in which the boy-groom became a man by first becoming ruler; the ruler metaphorically lent the groom his identity for the process. The groom's friends ritually transformed him into the ruler Mawlay Sultan, Our Lord the Powerful One, at the beginning of the wedding ceremonies, and the groom remained the ruler until the ceremonies were complete, until the bride's blood was spilled.

Furthermore, and most dramatically, in the late 1600s the Moroccan monarchy instituted the practice—regularly performed nowhere else in the Muslim world—of the Moroccan ruler's ritually sacrificing a ram on the nation's behalf on the occasion of the Great Sacrifice ('Id al-Kabir). It was a dramatic reformulation, modeled on Muhammad's own performance, that placed Morocco's monarch in the position of the great collective sacrificer upon whom the good of the whole depends.

Ritual's fusion of body and mind is the fulcrum of its power. There is no mind/body dichotomy here. Ritual inserts culture's imagination into experiential history. Wedding spirit to matter, Moroccan rituals transformed the caliphal abstraction into tangible substances and visceral actions of which the population could grab hold. The rituals fused the new definitions of the sharifi monarch as "nation," "man," "birth giver," and "transcendent hope" to the central elements of mortal existence: blood and light, male and female form, sexual intercourse, birth and death.

Ritual's convergence of body and mind is blatant. A monarchy whose legitimacy lies in blood descent was, and is, most forcefully renewed through rituals where red flowing blood is present—the blood of the ram on the ground, the blood of the bride on the bed. The most basic physical templates that the monarchy uses to reinforce itself are sexual intercourse and human birth—the thrust of phallic-shaped object into soft white tissue to make lifeblood flow and bring the hope for creation into being. Bolstering the entire political construction is the individual's desire for connection, connection that is at once physical and transcendent, a practical reaffirmation of self, a link to another, and a hope for transcendence beyond the limits of this world. Through the use of such basics, the reformulated rituals inserted the new conceptual abstraction into the collective unconscious, writing it deep within the structure of the universe and within the structure of the self. Upward to God and inward to the psyche: therein lies the foundation of the monarchy's power—and it is awesome.

During the centuries of crisis, rituals became the regenerative prism of Moroccan existence; they passed the sharifi definition of rule through the body of the population, refracting its rich light in full colors. The ritual prism was strong and pure—not an escape from the world, but the means of the world's reconstruction. Carefully faceted crystalline performances offered beauty, integration, and coherency to a world gone awry. For the individual, the rituals were stays against hollowness and confusion; for the collectivity, they were bulwarks against annihilation. Central to the central performances stood the blood-descendant monarch, in long white robes with satin threads that caught the candlelight and shimmered, casting that light all around.

Confronted with nearly lethal assault, Moroccans reconstructed their political system from cultural definitions and ritual performances outward. Life mimicked art. The mundane drew coherency from high drama. Ritual stabilized and renewed collective life even when other institutions failed to uphold it. The power and beauty of the performances—the palpability of the substances and the deep-rooted familiarity of the actions—combined with their intellectual forcefulness to establish the truth of the newfound definition of kingship.

The foundation, the Prophet's blood and the ritual prism, was solid and enabled Morocco and its monarchy not only to survive the tumult of the 1500s to the 1900s, but to reach beyond mere survival to creative renewal. Morocco staved off centuries of Western assault. The first country to be attacked as the West began its age of expansion (in 1415), Morocco was the last North African country to be finally colonized (1912–1933), and the first to break free of the colonial bond (1956). Five hundred years separate Europe's initial attempt at colonization from Morocco's eventual, but brief, capitulation. Political culture was the base of Moroccan resistance. That political culture centered on male and female definitions of self, political definitions of nation, Islamic definitions of faith, and panhuman hopes for immortality. Ritual was its most clarified means of realization.

political economy and political culture

world systems A large body of recent work addresses the relationship between what people value as meaningful (culture) and what they face as critical economic, military, and administrative constraints (political economy), especially during western Europe's age of world domination (post-1500s). An important and influential part of this work has been the examination of the interaction of non-European peoples with processes of history that originated outside their boundaries.

A "world system" approach has guided this debate and has transformed anthropology's vision, lifting its gaze from strictly local variables (the worm's-eye view) to the structures of global economic and military power (the bird's-eye view). In the 1970s, Emmanuel Wallerstein followed Fernand Braudel's lead but went beyond it, refining the world system framework and becoming its most prodigious spokesperson (Braudel 1973, Wallerstein 1974, 1979). Wallerstein argues that with the rise of European mercantile capitalism, the major cities of western Europe (and later of the United States) became the core that dominated the world. So definitive was the economic and military power of the European core that other peoples and cultures stood as more or less passive recipients of processes of history that originated elsewhere and were beyond their control. World system theory has demonstrated that local systems are never strictly local. To understand even the most isolated regions of the world after the 1500s, one must take a European-centered world capitalist economy into account.

Like other major integrative frameworks, world system theory has spurred considerable debate and received resounding support as well as strident criticism. In support, world system theory provides a powerful integrative framework that facilitates the systematic examination of interactions between peoples and cultures in different regions. Its basic suppositions have inspired a fine body of important works. Among these are Eric Wolf's analysis (1982) of the relationship of Europe to the parts of the world whose history Europe denied, Talal Asad's critique (1973) of anthropology's encounter with other peoples from the vantage point of the discipline's own tie to colonialism, and, directly concerning Morocco, J. David Seddon's analysis (1981) of the relationship of northern Morocco to Europe in the late nineteenth and twentieth centuries.

Burton Benedict (1983), Michel Foucault (1972), and Edward Said (1978) pushed world system theory an important step further by emphasizing the relationship of cultural domination to economic control. Said's brilliant exposé *Orientalism* (1978) is particularly pertinent. There Said demonstrates that the Occident's perception of "the Orient" is a self-reflexive construction, derivative of the Occident's interpretive elaborations and political aims rather than of substantive reality as it existed, and exists, in the East. So definitive is the imagined construction that alternative perspectives have difficulty penetrating, and so the Occident's invented Orient keeps regenerating itself as the guiding paradigm through which Westerners perceive the Other. As a result, the Occident continues to view the Orient as inferior, irrational, and threatening—in need of Western control and Western representation—and fails to recognize the Muslim world's formidable achievements, past and present, in many domains, including literature, medicine, agriculture, chemistry, political forms, poetry, and scholarship. Sidney Mintz illustrates the force of the observation when he notes that the West systematically overlooks the fact that it took only seven years for Muslims to originally conquer Iberia, while it took the Christians seven hundred years to regain it; the reasons for this divergence have to do with Muslim vitality (Mintz 1985:23–32).

In terms of weaknesses, world system theory is a parallax of the worm's-eye view and involves equal distortions, but of an opposing sort. It so singly adopts utilitarian and Eurocentric perspectives that it disregards the complexities of cultural and practical dynamics in the rest of the world. Both worms and birds have limited visions; the most complete vista is gained in combining their viewpoints.

A growing body of analyses accepts the basic supposition that non-Western peoples and cultures have been profoundly shaped in the post-1500s era by the West, and yet demonstrates that non-Western existence was far from simply determined by the European core (Bloch

1986, Comaroff 1985, Fischer 1980, Hanks 1986, Lan 1985, Nash 1981, Sahlins 1976 and 1985, Taussig 1980, and Worsley 1980). Indigenous peoples and cultures participated in the construction of history, even in the midst of Western domination. Resiliency, innovation, and determination characterize many such civilizations.

Yet, the critique of world system theory has often been limited by the critics' own methodological stance. This stance has often treated non-Western peoples and cultures as if they existed in relatively small-scale, insulated, and stable social systems prior to the coming of the West. To most fully counter the limitations of the world system framework, anthropologists need to address non-European systems that were international, dynamic, and changing before the Western attack, and for which extensive historical documentation exists. Muslim North Africa provides an ideal case in point.

historical potency and cultural resistance: Islamic Morocco

The Muslim world was hegemonic in the Mediterranean between 700 and 1350, before Europe came into its power; the Muslim world was the core of a world system before Europe became the core (see Schneider 1977 on the existence of a pre-European core). Muslim supremacy, like later European domination, was built on global expansion, commercial monetary exchange, manufacturing superiority, and innovations in agriculture.

When Europe began its attempt at expansion into North Africa, the interactions involved powerholders of comparable strength and dimensions. This was not a situation involving political entities so unequal in size, and so disparate in kind, that it would have been unlikely from the outset for them to have had an equal impact on history—as is the case when a European polity on its way to becoming a world power is compared with a relatively isolated Polynesian or African tribe.

Despite the importance of the Muslim case, it has been largely ignored in Western scholarship, especially during the age of the transference of Mediterranean power (1400–1700). Said helps us understand why. Given the West's construction "the Orient," it is not surprising that the region most effective in resisting western European assault is the one least explored by it. Victories loom larger than defeats in the West's remembrance of its expansionary era. Even the best of scholars—including Wallerstein and Braudel—tend to gloss over Muslim dynamics in this age. If they focus on the Muslim world, they

focus on the Ottoman Empire, a relatively late-coming Muslim political entity, itself centered in Europe.[1] The dynamics of the Muslim
heartland—Muslim North Africa and the Middle East—after the 1400s
remains a great blind spot for the West.

Morocco is a particularly important case in point. Its closeness to
Europe, the frequency of Moroccan-European interactions, and Morocco's own age of European domination make it a crucial contrast.
Morocco was the dominant force in the western Mediterranean from
the 1000s to the 1350s. When European armies began to invade North
Africa, Morocco's response was *not* that of a small-scale, unchanging
local society reacting to international processes derivative of a far-
away Europe. Rather, it was an instance of one part of a formerly
hegemonic transnational culture—Islam—and a transnational economic system—that which governed the Mediterranean before the
West's rise to power—reacting to the great shifts of power that were
taking place. Furthermore, the grandeur of Morocco's Islamic past
contributed to the success of its present, which in large part was built
on the wealth of cultural resources Islam had developed during its
age of domination.

The perspective developed in *Sacred Performances* is complementary to that of *Orientalism*. Whereas Said demonstrates how much
the West's construction of "the Orient" was a Western construction,
I seek to clarify how much the East's construction of itself—with Morocco as the case in point—eluded the West's imagination. While it
is true that the West was convinced of the veracity of its images and
attempted with its formidable economic and military strength to impose its vision on reality, an in-depth exploration of Morocco shows
that, though greatly affected by the West's power, Moroccans refused
the West's vision. The West did monopolize strong-arm power during
much of this era, and through that power brought much of the rest
of the world into its economic, military, and administrative purview,
but nonetheless Moroccans and others continued to participate in the
building of history, and constructed history in their own images, using
the resources they had available. For Moroccans, the resources of Islam were the building blocks, and ritual performances were the means
of reconstruction.

A historical crisis set in motion the reformulation of the Moroccan
monarchy, but the reformulation then affected history. History emerges
as particular peoples with particular cultural understandings and experiences interact with processes that lie beyond culture's control—
droughts, plagues, locusts, fire, ice—and with other peoples who have

different understandings and experiences. Collective life is a never-ceasing interplay of culturally constructed meaning with noncultural variables of history.

alternative approaches to the Moroccan monarchy   The Moroccan monarchy is a complicated institution that has inspired numerous perspectives from which to explore its durability. In *The Commander of the Faithful* (1970), John Waterbury, an American political scientist, offers a social explanation. Adopting a kind of game theory, he argues that the monarchy survived the upheaval of recent decades (1956–1969) because of an entrenched social style of "divide and rule" which enabled the monarch to play various sectors of the political elite off each other and hence keep itself at front stage center. His analysis draws upon the work of William Zartman (1964), the political grandfather of Moroccan studies in the United States, as well as upon his own understanding of segmentary theory. Waterbury has since moved away from the theoretical stance he developed in *The Commander of the Faithful*. Nonetheless, it integrated a large body of Moroccan material in an informative and enduring way.

Remy Leveau, a leading French political scientist, makes a somewhat similar social argument in *Le Fellah Marocain Defenseur du Trone* (1985). Leveau contends that the monarchy survived the conflicts of recent decades because of the wealth of political credit that the position holds in the rural countryside, credit that allows the central ruler to play the countryside off against the urban elite, keeping members of the army and the intelligentsia from becoming too strong.

As political scientists, Waterbury and Leveau naturally center their arguments on recent decades and do not attempt to explain the twelve hundred years of Moroccan monarchy that brought it to its present position. Although they contend that encoded social styles greatly determine political life, they do not focus upon the origins of the social styles nor their means of reproduction through time. Their central concerns lie elsewhere.

Ernest Gellner, the formidable British anthropologist, also develops a social argument for Morocco's system of political rule, but it is of a very different sort. Gellner contends that Morocco's distinctive political reality emerged due to the underlying social principles of the patrilineally organized tribes in the area. He is a functionalist who argues that the tribal organization (which Gellner and others refer to as "segmentation") demanded the existence of overarching "saints" —figures who existed beyond the social organization of the tribe and could maintain a continuity that the tribal organization did not ensure. Hence local areas had their saints (*Saints of the Atlas,* 1969), while the national arena had its monarch (*Muslim Society,* 1981). The functional needs of the tribal organization produced these saints, but imposed limits on them also. When a given tribe managed to occupy the central throne, the egalitarian tribal structure that brought it to power was transformed into an institutionalized hierarchy that reduced the tribe's organizational power, which depended on the operation of egalitarian principles. Thus, the tribe in power became vulnerable to tribes not in power, tribes whose organizational strength had not been adulterated by power's success. This, Gellner argues, is at the base of the circulation of tribal elite that characterized Morocco's monarchy during part of its existence.

Gellner's argument has much in common with that of Ibn Khaldun (1969 [1381]), the father of historical sociology. Their arguments are most informative about Moroccan political life from the 1000s to the 1400s, centuries during which a series of Berber tribes occupied the central throne and in which there was considerable circulation of dynastic elite. Their perspective is also helpful for understanding center-periphery dynamics in the 1800s, when the practical foundations of central rule reached a low point and the monarch increasingly depended upon the organizational strength of the outlying tribes for the implementation of practical tasks (see Burke 1976, Dunn 1977, Gellner 1981, and Hart 1981). Their arguments are less useful for understanding the foundations of the monarchy itself during the 1500s to the 1900s, when urban-based Arab aristocratic descendants of the Prophet, whose origins lay in social groups not organized into tribes, occupied the central throne.

Moroccan social scientist Paul Pascon (1977) and British anthropologist J. David Seddon (1981) stress the political economic foundations of the Moroccan monarchy, which are substantial. The monarch controls the army, navy, and air force, as well as the administrative and economic structures. The central government which he heads authorizes all major economic endeavors, regulates prices, and strictly controls the currency. Furthermore, the king's personal wealth is massive. In 1980, King Hasan II became the prominent stockholder in Omnium Nord-Africain (ONA), the largest private holding company in all of Africa (see *Le Monde Affaires,* January 7, 1989, p. 21). Informed sources estimate that the king's wealth is on the scale of that of Ferdinand Marcos, former president of the Philippines. Yet the king's control of military, administrative, and economic structures has not been a consistent variable in Moroccan history and does not explicate the monarchy's durability during those eras when the administration fell apart, the armies were dispersed, and the central storehouses were empty.

Moroccan historians offer other valuable perspectives on the monarchy. Terasse's *Histoire du Maroc* (1949–1950) and Julien's *Histoire de l'Afrique du Nord* (1951–1952) are recognized by Occidentals as the classic histories of Morocco. Erudite in the sequence of events, they are enormously flawed in terms of interpretation; colonialist perspectives greatly inform both works. Extremely valuable as counterpoints to the Western approach are older Moroccan works such as those of al-Fishtali (reprinted in 1973), al-Ifrani (translated and reprinted in 1889), and al-Nasiri (reprinted in 1954–1956). Julien's more recently published history *Le Maroc face aux imperialismes 1415–1956* (1978) also offers a much more dynamic and multifaceted approach.

Two recent general histories of Morocco written by North Africans, Abun-Nasr (1987) and Laroui (1977a), provide rich insight, as do a series of scholarly works that focus on the dynamics of specific eras, including Cornell (1983, 1986), Harakat (1985), and Kably (1978) on the Saʿdi, and Burke (1976), Cigar (1981), Dunn (1977), al-Mansur (1989), and Sebti (1984, 1986) on the ʿAlawi. For the present political situation, important perspectives are provided by Eickelman (1986), Entelis (1989), Ihrai (1986), Munson (1986), Seddon (1984), Swearington (1987), Tessler (1982), Tozy (1979, 1984), and Zartman (1987). Entelis' (1989) is the most comprehensive work on the present; it is a masterful synthesis of the complex political dynamics of the current situation. Recent historical works allow for the impact of cultural foundations upon history, though it is not their purpose—while it is mine—to uncover these foundations.

comparison with Geertz: anthropological alternatives Clifford Geertz's now classic analysis of the Moroccan monarchy, *Islam Observed*, was perhaps the first book printed in English to emphasize the power of culture in shaping Moroccan political reality and the importance of the 1500s breakpoint in history. Published in 1968, *Islam Observed* inspired a rush of anthropological research in Morocco, some in support, some in dissent, but nearly all in relation to that initial study.

Islam Observed concentrates, as do I, on overarching patterns of national political culture over great stretches of time, thus differing from more focused anthropological studies that illuminate the life of peoples and cultures of a given region during a particular historical era (e.g., al-Boudrari 1984, Crapanzano 1973 and 1980, Eickelman 1976 and 1985, H. Geertz 1979, Gellner 1969, Hammoudi 1980,

Jamous 1981, Maher 1974, Miller 1984, Munson 1984, Rabinow 1975, Rassam 1974, and Rosen 1972 and 1979). Moroccan culture emerges from the interaction of local, national, and international dimensions. There is considerable room for alternative vantage points, which in fact inform each other.

While there are points of similarity between my approach and that of *Islam Observed,* there are differences also. This is not surprising, given the amount of research that has taken place since that book was published and the differing analytical stances we take. Geertz contends that in the 1500s, the Moroccan monarchy managed to rebuild itself and survive the assault by developing a highly parochial form of Moroccan Islam, a saint-centered complex of ruler worship, called "maraboutism." According to this paradigm, Morocco's monarch is a saint writ large, and a myriad of other saints exist in the countryside and reinforce the national complex. Geertz argues that this maraboutic Islam arose in response to a historical crisis, but then was consolidated so effectively on the cultural level that it remained the stable lens through which Moroccans viewed life in the centuries to come. Geertz assumes cultural stability over time.

I argue the reverse—that there was a relative deparochialization of Moroccan political culture in the era of assault, that the supports utilized were central, Islamic, and sustaining, and that the supports had to be continually undergirded over time. When the world fell apart, Moroccans in fact turned more fully towards—not away from—the mainstream supports of mainstream Islam to rebuild a plausible reality. The turn to the Islamic center was direct. Moroccans called upon nothing less than a blood descendant of Muhammad to come and rule, as if through the power of Muhammad's blood the world could be renewed. A blood descendant came forward, the world was renewed, and a blood descendant still rules Morocco's throne.

Not only did Muhammad's blood flow through the new ruler's veins—as direct a link to the Islamic center as possible—but also the position he occupied was the central political position of orthodox Islam, the Islamic caliphate. The maraboutic paradigm, the saint complex, was only one aspect of the reformulated monarchy, one of a great variety of political subimages that the sharifi caliphate gathered under its imperial parasol. More central was the emphasis on patrilineality, the blood criterion of rule, and the caliphal position itself, durable resources of mainstream Islam.

Before the 1500s reconstruction, the Moroccan monarchy had been parochial. It had been occupied by Berber tribesmen (1050–1450) who had no direct links to the Prophet Muhammad and to the Islamic center. Their origins lay in local regions; their mother tongue was Berber, not Arabic. This is the age when Ibn Khaldun's and Gellner's models are most illuminating.

When the 1400s and 1500s assault by the Christian Other came, Moroccans sought more direct links to the heartland of Islam. They began to demand that their monarch be Arabic, Hijazi, Qurashi, and sharifi— that is, that he be a native speaker of Arabic (the holy tongue of God); that his patrilineal origins lie in the Hijaz (the land of the Prophet's birth); that he be a member of the Quraysh (the broad-reaching descent category into which Muhammad was born); and most important, that he be a sharif (a patrilineal descendant of the Prophet himself). In the 1500s, Morocco's national political culture was successfully rebuilt, on central Islamic foundations.

The new template had to be continually revitalized in order to remain popularly convincing. Ritual was the means of revitalization. In the age before telecommunications, great collective rituals served as the mass media forum through which collective reality could be cultivated. The Prophet's Birthday, popular rites of first marriage, and the Great Sacrifice were pivotal.

The sharifi construction and its ritual means of regeneration were not knee-jerk repetitions of the past, but rather dynamic adaptations to a constantly changing present, in which the past played a part. Morocco created history in its own image at the same time that it responded to history's independent creations. That was, and is, the basis of the polity's and the monarchy's survival.

The reconstructed monarchy had deep local resonance, for it combined established meanings of old with meanings that were new. For instance, although the sharifi definition of rule had not been a part of the monarchy in over five hundred years, it was a consistent part of Morocco's rich cultural repertoire. Long before, in the 700s and 800s, a blood-descendant dynasty had ruled part of Morocco, and even after that dynasty's fall, sharifi descent remained a basis for respect, a useful asset in establishing political authority in local areas. What the 1500s reconstruction and the 1600s–1900s renewal accomplished was to move the sharifi criterion of rule from the political peripheries to front stage center, making it the pivotal criterion for central rule.

The monarchy was powerfully local but not simply local, and therein lay further strength. At the base of the Moroccan world view is the notion that what is most important is the truth of Islam, not local practices. That perspective gives the Moroccan population a way to move away from its own formulations, by labeling them as not fully

Islamic. In rebuilding the monarchy, Moroccans turned to the broad-reaching resources of an expansive faith and utilized them in a great variety of ways to construct new and convincing realities—all of which the population firmly believed rested on the life of Muhammad and the truth of the Qur'an.

The cultural foundations of the reconstructed monarchy were local and Islamic, but they were universal also. Moroccans sunk the fence posts of their reformulated monarchy into the foundations of the world. The monarchy rests on universal givens, on basic foundations of human life everywhere: the human longing for connection, for affirmation, for sexual expression, for a plausible means of affecting the ways of the world in favor of those one loves.

There are two incontrovertible facts of human existence, that we are mortal and that we are sexual. Through cultural redefinition and ritual innovation the Moroccan monarchy inserted itself into both, and used mortality and sexuality to reorient the basic parameters of daily life. As culturally reformulated, the monarchy offered order and continuity in the throes of upheaval. The monarchy defined, limited, and dictated collective existence. Yet, equally important, it appeared to free people from those limitations. The ability to simultaneously circumscribe daily life and release people from its bonds is the monarchy's fundamental paradox and fundamental source of strength. As ritually reconstructed, the monarchy became the means of marking and organizing the temporal domain as well as the means of smashing temporal limitations, giving people access to the hope of transcendence. In the end, the sharifi monarchy is not simply a system of worldly power but a conduit to self-definition and human hope.

Culture consists of basic conceptual understandings and physically encoded practices that are unconscious, taken for granted, or consciously highly valued. Culture everywhere affects the construction of political power, but culture affects power to different degrees in different places. Since the 1500s, culture has played a particularly determinant role in the production of Moroccan political life. The cultural resources the Moroccan monarch has at his disposal are formidable. The king is the center of the most important ritual practices of the faith. He is popularly recognized as the blood descendant of the Prophet Muhammad, the rightful occupant of the caliphal throne, and the twenty-first ruler of Morocco's sixth ruling dynasty, the longest ruling dynasty in Moroccan history and the one that brought Morocco through its age of resistance, including its drive for independence. The king is viewed as an archetypal man, the one upon whom other men rely in constructing their own identity. The king is the link to the ultimate hope, the conduit to immortality. He is the popular representation of collective self, the symbol of corporate identity in the present, the means of collectively remembering the greatness of the past. Morocco's monarch relies more extensively on cultural resources than do many world rulers, because he has more resources upon which to rely.

commonalities: Occident and Orient

As is common in anthropology, the more we examine other political systems and cultural paradigms, the greater clarification we find of our own. While gazing at Morocco's kingship, I found myself gazing at the Catholic church, Jewish rabbis, the U.S. presidency, and the power structure of the Ivy League. Many political systems, those of Morocco, the United States, and western Europe included, embed the basic institutions of temporal power in fundamental definitions of self (especially the sexual self), in fundamental acts of humanity (birth, sexual intercourse, and death), and in the fundamental hope for transcendence (which may be envisioned in either religious or secular terms).

Morocco's political reconstruction and the role in it of cultural definitions and ritual practices is, I suggest, a paradigm for the construction of political power that bridges continents, oceans, and years. The commonalities between it and pillars of Western political authority are marked, as are the collective mechanisms for their renewal—including great orienting myths, ritual practices, and individual artistic expressions. There is striking similarity between the Muslim myth of Ibrahim's sacrifice (chapters 12–15) and prominent Occidental myths including Abraham's sacrifice, Jesus' crucifixion, and Ahab's quest for the white whale. There are links between the Moroccan ritual of the Great Sacrifice, Jewish Rosh Hashanah, Catholic communion, and rituals marking the social clubs of the power elite.[2] There is also striking similarity between the Muslim myth of sacrifice and individual literary expressions in the West, including Benjamin Britten's opera War Requiem Opus 9, Sören Kierkegaard's Fear and Trembling, and Ernest Hemingway's The Old Man and the Sea.

Commonalities can be found in unexpected places; for instance, there are links between Muhammad's practice of the Great Sacrifice in the Arabian Peninsula in the year 624 and the poem "Partisans," written in the United States by the contemporary American poet W. S. Di Piero. Both articulate enduring power as male-centered, defining men as links to what is durable and tying women to more ephemeral things. Both legitimate this division of sexuality on the presumption that men have greater capacity to transcend the temporal domain than do women—who, as those who spontaneously bleed and give birth, are more associated with this world and nature.

The Muslim myth and the American poem make striking use of common actors, themes, settings, and symbols. The Muslim myth (chapter 13) defines males as the links to transcendence by depicting them as gathered on mountain peaks for momentous interaction with the divine, a meeting that culminates in the male's performance of blood sacrifice, an act that in turn covenants the male's dominance of durable things, of transcendent questing. Women are entirely absent from the Muslim myth. They are left behind on the plains while males regenerate what is ultimately important and everlasting to humankind. Di Piero's poem, constructed 1,350 years later, and thousands of miles and a whole culture away from the Muslim myth, articulates similar themes through remarkably similar setting and symboling. It presents men on mountains gathered for momentous purposes; women as left behind on the plains, women as "absence," dangerous enticements of temporal existence, "the indecent promise of flesh"; and most stunningly, it presents men spilling blood on rocks on mountaintops in order to affirm their dominion over durable things, particularly their desire to regenerate reality without female aid: "I do not want to need their blood."

If we live, we can find wisdom in debris.
Balloons of smoke and powder
rising from the valley,
eyes tricked by sunlight,
blood on rocks . . .
Men alone together
are pure need.

Sometimes I can't remember
why we are here. I never ask myself
what to do with potatoes and stars.
The noblest places are places to hide,
fear isolating every bone.
That concealment will collapse on my head
like sliding rock, my eyes will ache
with the presence of nothing, my feet
will become another road
leading me deeper into the mountains.

ESSENTIALS

There's a small city in the valley.
Its towers burn in the night, inexhaustible father
of my impoverished camplight, also inexhaustible.
Long ago, I forgot why the city exists
but today, tonight
I remember what I feel,
that I am here only
because I am not there.

Women in the mountains are pure absence,
a song spinning in the dust,
or the air itself, cold and always dawning,
indecent promise of flesh

at the end point of solitude.
I do not want to need their blood,
the heat in the hollow of their necks,
memory of straw twisted in my clothes.
Only when we are with women
do we forget to die.

Waiting, fathering ourselves by firelight.
If only this were merely a beginning.
But I know the miserable pull of things in sequence,
all these generations
thick-skulled, weary, famished for wishes.

And I know myself, sucking my own heart
on the mountain of my blood.
Wherever I stand I stare at my feet
and when blood runs
it does not sing.

(1980:30–31)

Di Piero no doubt considers his poetic reflection to emerge from
deep within his individual consciousness, and no doubt it does, but
it is a consciousness powerfully informed by basic collective cultural
constructions, constructions whose imaging is not shared by all humanity but that has found particularly potent expression in societies
that have grown up within the context of the Mediterranean's three
monotheisms: Islam, Christianity, and Judaism.

The monotheistic development of a God outside of nature, men as the intervening links, and women as dependent on men for transcendence profoundly impacts on the individual structures of self and on the public structures of power in societies informed by these monotheisms' culture. I look at this impact in Morocco, and elsewhere.

When political power is embedded within the individual's psyche and within the collectivity's ultimate hopes, to battle the temporal constructions of power is to battle the self and to damage the readily available means of achieving comfort and assurance. I suggest that systems of power often endure, not because people are blind to their grip, but because the structures of power are so intimately linked to individual identity and the longings for transcendence that people have yet to discover how to loosen the one without losing the others.

Outsiders are often confounded by the continuing power and legitimacy of the Moroccan monarchy. Some point to the monarch's control of administrative, military, and economic resources. Yet to concentrate on the utilitarian sources of the monarchy's power is to miss its regenerative foundation. In Morocco, the monarchy is intrinsic to the definition of self, including sexual self, the definition of power in the world, and the basic understanding of how one can be released from worldly constraints and conjoined to the truth of the universe. These are powerful definitions inscribed through powerful substances on powerful forms; they are ritually written in blood on male and female bodies, in the acts of sacrifice, intercourse, birth, and death. As such, to undercut the monarchy is not only to damage the temporal structures of worldly power, but to undercut oneself, one's basic identity, and the familiar pathways of hope. Hence, the Moroccan monarchy with its particular combination of hope and coercion—built on its particular construction of sexuality and mortality—endures.

2

prism

People often confuse culture with abstract symbolism, failing to recognize the importance of body postures and physical practices in it.
Yet culture reproduces itself as forcefully in and through our bodies
as it does in and through our minds. For instance, culture establishes
its definitions of male and female by creating distinctive patterns of
eye contact as well as by creating distinctive patterns of abstract symbols.[1] The body leads the mind, guides the mind, and creates for the
mind many of its basic templates. Since rituals unite body and mind,
they are potent arenas for culture's construction. In ritual, culture's
imagination is made incarnate and lives among us.

cultural constitution and lived practice

Humans are born, live, and die in collectivities that are systematically informed by shared values and practices—that is, by culture. Culture consists of enduring representations in thought and practice that may be so taken for granted that they are unconscious, or may be acutely realized and highly valued. Culture includes how people conceptualize the universe, hold their bodies, build their houses, structure their economies, envision authority, react to death, and sacrifice to their gods. Whether cultural representations are consciously or unconsciously held, individuals and collectivities tend to reproduce these representations through time.

Any given culture is diverse, and people can participate in more than one culture. Culture consists of a repertoire of representations, rather than a single, unchanging, monolithic whole. The most powerful representations comprise culture's constitution. Given the diversity of representations within any given constitution (e.g., inheritance of name and property from the father's patriline, and affection for mother's kin), a variety of on-the-ground practices and institutions can emerge from it (see Comaroff and Roberts 1981). Furthermore, the constitution changes in time. Old representations fade away, new ones are added, and worn-out representations may be discarded or revitalized.

Broad-reaching cultural systems like Islam and Christianity rest on rich repertoires that manifest themselves in a great variety of ways. There is breadth and diversity within them, room for maneuver—characteristics that have much to do with their popular appeal and historical durability. Yet the diversity and room for maneuver are not endless. Systematic patterns emerge, domains of great clarity and representational integration. Not all representations are malleable. Some are open to rapid change while others are quite durable even in the face of considerable opposition. I will be exploring durable cultural foundations.

Durable foundations are often articulated through diverse means: through public performances, perfumes, art forms, and patterns of joking and laughter, as well as through notions of the deity and economic, political, and familial power structures. Even when some of their means of reproduction falter, others tend to support them.

One of the most durable foundations of Islam and Christianity is their patriarchy. Their myths, symbols, rituals, and systems of domination deeply inscribe that patriarchy on the multiple dimensions of individual and collective being. Islam and Christianity articulate their patriarchy in forms of architecture, physical postures, styles of dress, and forms of speech—embedding it in streets, buildings, and sacred texts, writing it upon the individual's body, etching it upon the individual's mind.

Yet even the most durable elements of culture—such as the patriarchy of Islam and Christianity, and the "Orientalism" of Westerners—can, it appears, be altered, as some Muslims, Christians, and Westerners are attempting to do. But the changes are difficult, demanding not only self-conscious reflection but also self-conscious reconstruction of the practical experiences of daily life and the symbolic elaborations of world view. Such fundamental changes demand the overhaul of subtle, unconscious dimensions of individual identity as well as the overhaul of the overt practices of collective being. It is here that dramatic ritual reformulations can play a definitive role.

Cultural representations channel collective life, but they do not simplistically determine it. There are elements of collective existence that operate beyond the ability of even the most formidable of cultural representations to control: encounters with other people, fluctuations in the world economy, innovations in technology, and natural disasters. Collective life emerges from the interaction of basic cultural givens with the noncultural elements of collective existence. Life is constructed as people work out the practical exigencies of living by combining highly valued and enduring representations with more manifest constraints and opportunities of the day-to-day. Each takes place in the context of the other. Each informs the other, but neither collapses into the other.

Ritual is both cultural constitution and lived practice. To the degree that ritual's actions and attitudes are highly valued and repeated in time, they are a part of the enduring cultural foundation. But since they are also directly experienced in the quotidian, they are manifest practice, a part of a given people's experience on-the-ground. As both enduring representation and on-the-ground practice, ritual performance is a potent channel for the transformation of the one into the other—as when Morocco's new model of political rule was made an enduring part of people's popular ritual expressions and thereby given entry into the culture's constitution. Thenceforth, the ritual was re-performed, its basic representations (physical and mental) upheld, and the newfound monarchy thereby undergirded, even when other dimensions of collective life failed to support it.

ritual defined

For the purposes of this work, I define ritual as a circumscribed, out of the ordinary, multiple media event—recognized by insiders and outsiders as distinctively beyond the mundane—in which prescribed words and actions are repeated and crucial dilemmas of humanity are evoked and brought to systematic resolution. "Ritual is a medium for transmitting meanings, constructing social reality . . . [and] for that matter, creating and bringing to life the cosmological scheme itself" (Tambiah 1985:129).

Form and meaning cannot be separated, for the systematics of form are essential to the meaning that is built. "Certain meaning and effect are intrinsic to the very structure of ritual, and ritual thus may impose, or seem to impose, logical necessity upon the vagrant affairs of the world" (Rappaport 1979:173). Moore and Myerhoff (1977) uncover the systematics of form; they demonstrate that ritual formality produces meaning by conjuring up the great rhythmic processes of the universe, creating an environment of grandeur and seriousness. Tambiah summarizes: "ritual's repetition, stylization, ordering, evocative presentational style, and staging [are] . . . formal features which enable ritual to imitate the rhythmic imperatives and processes of the cosmos and thereby to attach permanence and legitimacy to what are actually temporal social constructions" (1985:132). In high drama, ritual produces a worthy arena where the great issues of human existence can be expressed and can be to a certain degree resolved— life and death, pain and sorrow, hope and heartache.

Ritual formalism accomplishes the double feat of bringing mythic time to the present and projecting the present time onto the level of myth. As such, rituals draw individuals beyond the limits of their lives and tie them to larger processes of humanity and the universe—as when each year individual Muslims participating in the ritual of Ibrahim's sacrifice are united with millions of other Muslims simultaneously sacrificing as well as with the billions of Muslims who have gone before, all of whom on the tenth day of the last month of each year for over 1,350 years have stood before God and slain animals of this world that God might see their faith and grant his favor.

The structured regularity of ritualized actions is important to the individual as well as to the collectivity and the cosmos. It can help build healthy egos. As Erik Erikson argues, rituals, like those between mother and child, provide "persistent, periodical reassurance of familiarity and mutuality" that can countermand feelings of abandonment and isolation, the "chilling sense of not being needed" (Erikson

1966:605). Collective rituals can also countermand the chilling sense of living in a world without meaning. Furthermore, as Kafka (1983) demonstrates, ritual's structured formalism allows individuals to express deep-seated fears and emotions, for the end is known in advance. The security of the process and the assuredness of the outcome create a setting in which individuals can address the awesome unknown with greater ease.

Most of life exists in bits and pieces, torn parts, shattered fragments. Some of the driving force behind the ritual experience lies in the sense of wholeness rituals convey. Rituals mark beginnings and endings and offer systematic internal development, lending a fullness and clarity to life that eludes most of living.

Rituals are totalizing events that involve the whole person and the entire environment (see Rappaport 1979:27–42). They build meaning and inscribe messages on every dimension through which humans experience existence. Radcliffe-Brown highlighted this multiple media quality of rituals in his study of ritual dance when he noted that ritual's musical sounds not only appeal to the ear but also bring to life stored-up, unconscious motor images that are endowed with deep meaning (quoted in Tambiah 1985:130).

Rituals can be finely hewn performances of complexity, durability, and grace that are marked by spectacular beauty and profound evocative appeal. They can mobilize body, heart, and mind—experience, emotion, and imagination—and combine them all into a unified whole in which the essential foundations of a given culture are verified in an environment uncluttered by the confusion of the quotidian. The sounds of solemn assemblies can drown out the noise of everyday life and allow its participants to experience what they perceive as life in its essence.

rituals and theater

Given these characteristics, rituals share many of the qualities of great theatrical performances; they are circumscribed occasions involving multiple media, a total environment, elaborate formalism, and profound human dilemmas that are at one and the same time personal and universal. Yet an important distinction remains. When one compares even the best of classic theatrical performances with ritual enactments, one sees that an inverse relationship holds between what is real and what is not. Theater, especially as understood in the Western world, presents "plays" on life, not real living. The plays may be complete fabrications or "reflections" of the really real, but they are not at the time of their enactment real occurrences, nor are the people performing them being themselves. Rather, theater presents actors and actresses pretending to be others.[2]

The reverse holds for rituals. Those who sincerely participate in ritual are real performers in real-life dramas. In enacting the Muslim ritual of Ibrahim's sacrifice, believers are not pretending to be sacrificing to God; they *are* sacrificing to God (whether or not they create God through the sacrifice is a separate issue). In the ritual drama, they are God's children, facing the dilemma of faith that Ibrahim faced, and their actions have direct consequences for themselves and their children.

Rituals manufacture public and private experiences rich in sight, smell, sound, taste, touch, and imaginative abstractions. At best, they are not simply experiences, but crystalline experiences so vibrant in meaning and medium that they serve as counterpoints to other experiences built in daily life. When persuasive, rituals are experienced by the participants as life at its most profound, and can cast aspersions on the rest of experience as being less than essential. For this reason, great orienting rituals can be as important for the building of collective life as great battles and other dramatic historical events. Rituals propel novel cultural inventions onto the historical stage, creating pristine popular experiences of history in the culture's own image. That is culture's trump card. For rituals are staged cultural expressions that at their best appear neither staged nor cultural but rather evoke life as it exists in its essence. At their most effective, rituals weight the sum total of popular consciousness in their favor. They are shadow plays in reverse: the performers and the performance become real, while everything else becomes the shadow.

anthropology and ritual analysis

Societies mobilize rituals to different extents. Tambiah states; "I am well aware that Balinese life . . . is more ritually patterned, more suffused with aesthetic values than contemporary American life" (1985:125). Moroccan life is also more ritually suffused.

Anthropology, as a discipline, has a long history of respect for ritual performances and has done much to illuminate their foundations. Yet, anthropology has been hindered by the mind/body dichotomy. Anthropologists have tended to view ritual as a collective occasion for the building of culture and society through either the expression of the "collective body" or the "collective mind," instead of as a profound occasion when body and mind constitute each other in constituting collective life.

The body focus first dominated anthropology, and Emile Durkheim was its spokesman. Durkheim (1965 [1912]) argued that the gathering of the social body in ritual builds a collective reality that physically verifies the truth of the social order—the divisions of labor, images of male and female, and constructions of authority. The ritual accomplishes this, Durkheim assumed, by projecting the society's imagination onto the universe, creating through dramatic action a sacred dimension cast in the image of the social structure, but experienced as something beyond the social whole. Durkheim reversed the Genesis myth, in which God created man in his image, by contending that in ritual, social collectivities create God in their image, without noticing the mortal origins of their immortal creation. Durkheim's insight endures.

The British school of social anthropology (1940s–1950s), following closely in Durkheim's footsteps, treated ritual as an occasion for the dramatic reconstitution of the social whole, the collectivity reified by being made manifest by and to its members. For Durkheim and the British, ritual is a collective enactment that serves as a great social glue—by passing itself off as sacred bonding. (Moore and Myerhoff's work, 1977, extends these observations to "secular" rituals such as those of the People's Republic of China, demonstrating that they, like rituals that label themselves as religious, rely on sacred verification. The sacred is somewhat differently constituted in secular rituals but it is no less imagined, no less distant from the mundane and everyday, no less millenarian.)

In reaction to the Durkheimian and British concentration upon the social body and concrete physical practices, two related schools of thought developed, interpretation and structuralism, both of which come under the rubric of "symbolic anthropology." Both stress the power of the collective mind, the importance of the collective imagination in framing social being. Culture becomes a symbolic code to be cracked, an interpretative lens on the world in which lexicalised symbols are the basic elements. Rituals, if examined, are treated as forums for the code's expression—as symbolic texts rather than as physical experiences. While Durkheim and the British school seemed to say that "in the beginning came the collective body which then produced the collective mind," the interpreters and structuralists began with the opposite notion that "in the beginning came the collective mind which then produced the collective body."

The notion of culture as an abstract symbolic system, a codified interpretative framework, dominated anthropology in the 1960s and 1970s. It shook scholarship and fomented much development. There was clearly recognizable truth in it (just as there was, and is, truth in Durkheim's position also). Interpretation put the assumption of "objectivity" on a permanent chopping block as people came to recognize how imaginatively constructed—how idiosyncratically invented—were many of the most basic frameworks with which they dealt with life, such as their construction of the Oriental Other (Said 1978).

The interpretative school of symbolic anthropology was centered in America, and Clifford Geertz became its most eloquent spokesperson. The approach is highly intellectual and idealistic and takes its inspiration from Max Weber, rather than from Durkheim. For interpreters, culture consists of a powerful symbolic structure that filters pragmatic experience so that "reality" comes to fit the culture's symbolic world view. Ritual is an arena for symbolic communication, for the conveyance of the constructed code. The physical movement of the ritual is a way of bringing the population into the domination of the abstract symbolic structure, not a means of creating those structures.

In the 1960s and 1970s, Victor Turner effectively combined interpretative and Durkheimian approaches with forceful results and became anthropology's most prodigious ritual analyst. He stressed the importance of physical actions as well as abstract symbolism, but saw them as alternative poles that were emotionally brought together in the ritual process rather than mutually constitutive dimensions of being.

The structuralist school of symbolic anthropology had at its center the formidable French anthropologist Claude Lévi-Strauss, who looked not so much at particular cultural lenses (the interpretative enterprise) as at the universal processes of lens production. Lévi-Strauss focused upon the deep structure of the abstract symboling process, which he saw as dependent upon the basic conceptualizing capacity of the brain. Lévi-Strauss characterized this capacity as producing meaning through the articulation and resolution of binary oppositions (cold versus hot, raw versus cooked, female versus male). Lévi-Strauss fruitfully used his approach to analyze systems of meaning around the world, especially on the level of myth.

Another formal school of structuralism was semiotics. It concentrated not so much on the formal structure of the brain as on the formal structure of language. Specific texts or whole languages were the foci of analysis, and meaning was characterized as built from the formal interplay of symbol, sign, and signification. At its most refined, semiotics, like Lévi-Strauss' structuralism, left human beings and the sociocultural context behind. Meaning came to be treated as a disembodied, highly formal system of articulation, in which abstract signs bounced off one another in the building of structured symbolic codes. Humans, social life, and rituals vanished from the arena of concern.

Like all productive approaches, the view of culture as an abstract symbolic code reached its limits, and by the late 1970s interpreters and structuralists were critiqued. While Durkheim and the British school could be charged with so overly concentrating on the hands and feet of the ritual process that the human mind and the imagination were lost, interpretation and formalism were vulnerable to the critique that they so solely concentrated on structured abstractions of the mind that the body—social and individual—was forgotten.

As a result, in the late 1970s and throughout the 1980s, the human body and physical practices once again came to the forefront of anthropological analysis, but in a new way—not simply as feeding into the social body, but in terms of building the cultural frameworks that channel how people deal with life. Pierre Bourdieu's *Outline of a Theory of Practice* was crucial in the reformulation. Bourdieu argues that basic representations of culture are acquired through physical practices, through visceral experiences:

> The essential part of the modus operandi [of culture] which defines practical mastery is transmitted in practice . . . without attaining the level of [abstract, symbolic] discourse. The child imitates not [conceptual] "models" but other people's actions. Body *hexis* speaks directly to the motor function, in the form of a pattern of postures that is both individual and systematic . . . [and] charged with a host of social meanings and values.
>
> (1977:87–88)

For instance, Bourdieu argues, children learn what it is to be an adult in their society by paying close attention to gestures and postures, to "everything that goes to make an accomplished adult—a way of walking, a tilt of the head, facial expressions, ways of sitting and of using implements, always associated with a tone of voice, a style of speech, and . . . a certain subjective experience" (1977:87–88).

The point is not that abstract symbolic structures are irrelevant to cultural codification, but rather that in addition to abstract symboling, we need to look at systematic patterns of looking, seeing, standing, gesturing, and laughing that communicate from "body to body, i.e. on the hither side of words and concepts" (Bourdieu 1977:87). We need to examine the way in which physical actions and behavioral postures are directly encoded in the brain so that they become acceptable action schemata that are reproduced from generation to generation and carry with them meaning, assurance, and constraint.

Bourdieu hinges his argument upon daily life and on the physical postures and behavioral practices built there. In *Outline of a Theory of Practice,* he minimizes the role of ritual. From his perspective, ritual is episodic and hence not pivotal to cultural production, a role he reserves for everyday practices.

Yet others, like Gilbert Lewis (1980) and Maurice Bloch (1974), have brought the emphasis on practice to the ritual arena, highlighting the degree to which ritual is practice in particularly vivid form. What ritual lacks in daily repetitiveness, it makes up for in high drama. In analyzing penis-slashing ceremonies of the Gnau of New Guinea (*Day of Shining Red,* 1980), Lewis uses a performative approach to argue that what is first and foremost in ritual, as in stage drama, is common action and aroused emotions, while the complexities of abstract symboling are secondary.

Maurice Bloch systematized and clarified the emphasis on ritual practice by developing it from a neo-Marxist position. In his seminal article "Symbol, Song, Dance, and Features of Articulation" (1974), Bloch argues that while interpreters look to ritual for symbolic integration and conceptual explanation, ritual is in fact the last place to find anything explained, for ritual does not communicate through explanatory forms of reasoning. Drawing from linguistics, Bloch argues that ritual is a form of communication that conveys its messages through "illocutionary force," that is, through the power of visible actions and dramatic presentation, rather than through reasoned propositions. Therefore, Bloch contends, one cannot argue with ritual. One either participates in it and accepts its presentations as true, or one does not. In this view, ritual's stereotypic form, repetitive actions, and collectively elicited emotions communicate through *fait accompli* affirmation which actively blocks the complicated processes of abstract symbolic reasoning. Hence, Bloch contends, ritual serves to hide rather than explain reality and masks the actualities of economic and political might so that established forms of political authority are upheld. (The Marxist argument shares with Durkheim the emphasis on the human body and physical practices, yet with an opposing evaluation. While Durkheim sees ritual as a beneficial societal lubricant, Marxists see it as social bondage. For them, ritual works to obscure economic and political oppression, making it less accessible to critique.)

Although the neo-Marxist emphasis on the power of practice and on ritual's ability to obscure the structures of domination continues to be important, a number of its other suppositions have been critiqued, and Bloch (1986) is one of its critics (as are Comaroff 1985, Sahlins 1976 and 1985, and Silverstein 1981). One can, after all, argue with rituals; innovations in ritual actions are forms of argument. Although rituals may not offer straightforward verbal explanations, they often develop persuasive physical and iconic explanations for the universe and world. Rituals can highlight structures of power as well as obscure them. They can foment rebellions as well as put lids on them. And rituals do more than simply hide, or they would not be able to hide so effectively.

The late 1970s and 1980s reemphasis on practice has refocused ritual analysis on actions, on movements of the body, on physical and aesthetic as well as symbolic means of perception. Yet, thus far, the reemphasis on practice has not often resulted in a dynamic integration of the symbolic and practice perspectives. Rather, the emphasis on practice has tended to replace the symbolic focus, so that once again anthropology's methodological stance itself excludes the multifaceted ways in which meaning is built.

Bourdieu's work is subject to this critique, and in fact to the more serious charge of more basic reductionism. In the end, Bourdieu assumes that an underlying "self-interested" utilitarian substructure determines practice, and that practice in turn determines thought (as if such a substructure could operate outside of, and prior to, collective thoughts and practices). He is a determined Marxist of sorts.

Clearly a combination of approaches is needed. Ritual depends upon that combination. Ritual creates and renews cultural representations through its combination of dramatic actions, physical icons, aroused emotions, and abstract symboling. It cannot be analyzed in isolation from any of its parts.

recent approaches

Several recent works combine approaches, notably Maurice Bloch's *From Blessing to Violence* (1986) and Jean Comaroff's *Body of Power, Spirit of Resistance* (1985). These are important studies that approach creatively the complexities of history and change and the role of ritual in it from symbolic, practice, formalist, historical, and Marxist perspectives. They have gone far in demanding a new look at the body's role in shaping culture and ritual's role in constructing collective life. They provide the most important comparisons to the analysis that follows. Yet even in these exceptionally fine works, the mind/body dichotomy exerts its influence, and the various approaches tend to be used serially—one after another—rather than being pushed into dynamic integrative synthesis. Highly abstract, easily lexicalised symbols still tend to be seen as the ultimate domain of meaning, that which dominates, mediates, and integrates all else; physical practices are seen as feeding into it, rather than as creators and carriers of meaning that need not be translated into abstract verbal symboling in order to be collectively absorbed, codified, and sustained. We have yet to develop an analytical perspective that allows us to look at how the mind and body mutually constitute each other at the same time that they mutually constitute collective life. We still do not have a vantage point that lets us see mind and body as part and parcel of the same process of cultural construction so that they cannot be severed without losing the understanding of what they in combination build, just as hydrogen and oxygen in the construction of water cannot be pulled apart without losing the water.

Recent findings in cognition, however, do aid in addressing the physical as well as the abstract dimensions of human culture in a more mutually constitutive way, especially in the ritual process. Physical practices are themselves symbols, physical icons, a means of cultural encoding.

the body of thought

George Lakoff in his book *Women, Fire, and Dangerous Things* (1987) contends that the mind/body dichotomy has been a part of "the superstructure of Western thought" for over two thousand years. Actually, the dualism did not achieve unrivaled prominence until the 1700s, but it maintains this prominence into the present, despite repeated attempts to move beyond it, despite the fact that the dichotomy is—as Alfred North Whitehead succinctly put it—"quite unbelievable" (1948:56). Thought, especially in the West, still tends to be imagined as a disembodied process of highly abstract symboling in which the human body plays little part. Johnson (1987) and Lakoff (1987) call this view Objectivism. It tends to characterize thought as follows:

■ It is . . . incidental to the nature of meaningful concepts and reason that human beings have the bodies they have and function in their environment in the way they do. Human bodies may play a role in *choosing* which concepts and which modes of transcendental reason human beings actually employ, but they play no essential role in *characterizing* what constitutes a concept and what constitutes reason.

- Thought is *abstract* and *disembodied,* since it is independent of any limitations of the human body, the human perceptual system, and the human nervous system.
- Thought is *logical* in the narrow technical sense used by philosophical logicians; that is, it can be modeled accurately by systems of the sort used in mathematical logic. These are abstract symbol systems defined by general principles of symbol manipulation and mechanisms for interpreting such symbols in terms of "models of the world." . . .
- The mind is separate from, and independent of, the body.
- Emotion has no conceptual content.

(Lakoff 1987:xii, xiii, 9)

The mind/body dichotomy and its associated Objectivist mode of thinking served the physical sciences well through the 1800s, but in the 1900s they lost their usefulness and the physical sciences abandoned them; yet "the rest of us still take mind-matter dualism for granted in many ways, including ways of understanding other people's religion" (Jay 1981:27). The mind/body dualism and the Objectivist mode of thinking are difficult to leave behind, not only because they have dominated Western thinking for so long, but also because they tend to be reproduced in so many dimensions of daily life. Even when consciously rejected in words, the mind/body dualism tends to be reconstituted in daily practice, including the practice of anthropology. Yet recent reformulations, notably those of Johnson and Lakoff and a growing body of cognitive research, can help us self-consciously move beyond the old views. Called "Experientialism," the new view reverses the traditional perspective that placed thought outside the body and instead sees thought as being made possible by the body. It describes embodied imagination:

- Thought is *embodied,* that is, the structures used to put together our conceptual systems grow out of bodily experience and make sense in terms of it; moreover, the core of our conceptual system is directly grounded in perception, body movement, and experience of a physical and social character.
- Thought is *imaginative,* in that those concepts which are not directly grounded in experience employ metaphor, metonymy, and mental imagery—all of which go beyond the literal mirroring, or representation, of external reality. It is this imaginative capacity that allows for "abstract" thought and takes the individual beyond

what [he or she] . . . can see and feel. The imaginative capacity is also embodied—indirectly—since the metaphors, metonymies, and images are based on experience, often bodily experience. . . .

■ Thought has *gestalt properties* and is thus not atomistic; concepts have an overall structure that goes beyond merely putting together conceptual "building blocks" by general rules. . . .

■ Emotion has conceptual content, and emotional concepts are embodied.

(Lakoff 1987:xiv–xv, 9, 14)

Recent findings lead to the perception that human reason is not an instantiation of transcendental reason,

> but rather grows out of the nature of the organism and all that contributes to its individual and collective experience: its genetic inheritance, the nature of the environment it lives in, the way it functions in the environment, the nature of its social functioning, and the like.

(Lakoff 1987:xv)

Four areas of research are particularly relevant to our rethinking the role of the body in human thought and our reevaluation of the role of ritual practice in cultural construction: color perception, basic level categories, kinesthetic image schemata, and the imaginative processes.

color categories

Berlin and Kay's (1969) findings on the role of the human body in the formation of color categories were, in their own quiet way, earthshaking, for those findings underline the way in which the physical dimensions of the body shape the conceptual apparatus of the mind. Berlin and Kay originally set out to test the notion that cultures and languages divide up the color spectrum as they please, which should be the case if color categorization is indeed a purely abstract, symbolic process of cultural designation in which the parameters of the human body do not play a role. What they found was that there are basic regularities in color recognition that are universal, because they depend upon regularities in the way in which the human brain is structured and in how it perceives and codes color information. Brain structure provides basic underlying parameters within which particular cultures elaborate their own variations in color coding and color emphasis, but they are elaborations of universal givens, not purely arbitrary designations. The underlying structure does not simplistically determine a given culture's color categories, but it powerfully informs them. It structures them in systematic ways (see Sahlins 1977).

Berlin and Kay found that people—the world over—conceptually recognize eleven basic color categories, whether or not their languages designate them. (Hence, human beings perceive things that their culture does not mark through abstract symbols; they recognize things for which they have no words, but which their brain nonetheless sees.) The color categories themselves emerge because the human brain "sees" eleven psychologically real "focal colors" around which it clusters the categories. The eleven color categories correspond to what English labels by the terms "black," "white," "red," "yellow," "green," "blue," "brown," "purple," "pink," "orange," and "gray." The boundaries between categories (e.g., where red stops and brown begins) are open to individual and cultural variation, but the eleven focal colors themselves are remarkably consistent for all of humanity. For example, when asked to select "focal red" from a standardized chart of 320 color chips, virtually all people—no matter where they lived—chose precisely the *same hue* of red, as they chose the same hue of blue, green, brown, and so forth, when asked to choose the best-of-category example. The human brain perceives eleven psychologically real colors around which it clusters the eleven color categories, colors that are recognized by the structure of the brain itself; and around these eleven psychologically real focal colors, humans orient primary categories, essential conceptions about color, even if their language does not divide and label the color spectrum in this way.

Although humans perceive eleven focal colors and cluster basic categories around them, not all languages linguistically mark all eleven categories. Many designate fewer. Yet, even then, cultural designation follows a highly systematic pattern. Some languages designate only two basic color terms, and when this occurs, they are *always* "black" and "white," which are perhaps more appropriately called "cool" and "warm." The "cool" color always includes focal black, blue, green, gray, and the hues associated with them, while "warm" includes focal white, yellow, orange, red, and the hues associated with them (Lakoff 1987:25). When a language adds a third category to the first two, it is always red, and so forth (Berlin and Kay 1969, Lakoff 1987: 24–26).

"Black," "white," and "red" are the first three color categories designated by human languages. They are also the colors that dominate many of the world's great ritual performances (Catholic communion, Azande divination, Merina circumcision), including the three

Moroccan rituals to be discussed here. While it is true that a given culture can highlight any given color and endow it with deep meaning (e.g., yellow for the Chinese), it is also true that cultures can play upon the meaning that already inheres in the basic color categories that are themselves related to the basic physical foundations of the world. Colson describes Tonga prophets who approach the spirits concerning rain:

> They wear wristlets of black or dark blue beads, colours associated with rain clouds. Those who approach them for rain take black or blue beads. Those who wish an end to continuous rain take white beads because white is associated with clouds which carry no rain. Red beads or anything red in colour is taboo during consultation because red symbolizes blood. . . . if a prophet announces that the basangu [wild spirits] want an offering carried out at a local shrine, this usually involves slaughter of a black chicken, goat or ox—any trace of white being forbidden since this would bring lightning with the rain.
>
> (1977:126)

A given culture can reinforce its construction of authority by ritually expressing it through the three most basic categories; the culture can have its authorities appear in black and white and dominate red substances, as when black-and-white-cloaked Catholic priests dispense the red "blood" of communion. When this occurs, basic templates of physical perception are being used to undergird that culture's particular invention of power. In reformulating their monarchy, Moroccans used this capacity of color to help support their new system. They articulated a ritual in which their ruler stood in egret-white robes before the nation and sacrificed a ram on its behalf, a ram that was pure white except for thick black markings around its eyes—and the ram's red blood flowed, the people achieved hope, and the authority achieved durability.

basic level categories

The power of the human body in creating human thought is also underlined by recent findings concerning basic level categories. Cognitive theorists have demonstrated that a basic level of categorization exists around which most of human thought is organized. On this level, the body, with its distinctive images and experiences, is crucial to category formation. Rosch, Mervis, Gray et al. (1976) have found that basic level categories are:

- The highest level at which category members have a similarly perceived overall shape.
- The highest level at which a single mental image can reflect the entire category [a chair].
- The highest level at which a person uses similar motor actions for interacting with all category members [e.g., sitting]. . . .
- The level with the most commonly used labels for category members. . . .
- The level at which most of our knowledge is organized.

(cited in Lakoff 1987:46)

"Dog," "chair," "flower," and "ball" are examples of basic level categories. People develop the concept of "dog" by combining the action of dog "patting" with the vivid physical icon of "dog shape." People learn what a flower is by simultaneously smelling it and forming a visual image of its physical construction. They learn what a ball is by bouncing it and forming an icon of it.

From the basic level, more complicated categories are constructed, categories that are less physically and visually accessible, categories that depend on the achievements of the imagination. Superordinate categories (e.g., "furniture") are not characterized by definitive motor action nor by a definitive shape. One does not "sit" on all furniture, nor can all members of the category (e.g., bed, chest of drawers, table, chair, and so forth) be characterized by a single visual image; but after one has learned the basic level category of "chair," one is able to use one's imagination to form the more complicated superordinate category that depends upon broader processes of generalization. As Brown puts it, in time the child learns that the dog he pats is not only a dog, but also "a boxer, a quadruped, an animate being" (1958:14).

Basic level categories are what children learn first and most easily.

FIGURE 2.1. Category Levels

Superordinate Category	animal	furniture	plant	sports equipment
Basic Level Category	dog	chair	flower	ball
motor activity	patting	sitting	smelling	bouncing
Subordinate Category	boxer	desk chair	jonquil	tennis ball

By age three, children are virtually perfect on basic level sorting, while they still have trouble with superordinate and subordinate sorting. Furthermore, the basic level is the one at which people are fastest in identifying category members, and which contains the most commonly used labels for category members. It is also the first level to enter the lexicon of a language and the level with the shortest primary lexemes (the lexeme is the basic vocabulary unit). Additionally, it is the level at which terms can be used in neutral contexts, such as, "There's a dog on the porch," whereas special contexts are needed for "There's a mammal on the porch," or "There's a wire-haired terrier on the porch" (Cruse 1977). Most important, basic level categories are those at which most of human knowledge is organized (Brown 1958, Lakoff 1987:46).

What is important for my analysis of Moroccan political reconstruction is the degree to which ritual can produce basic level categories by manufacturing and combining profound visual icons with distinctive motor actions. For instance, Moroccans reformulated the ritual of Ibrahim's sacrifice so that it defined and linked the basic level category of "man" and the basic level category of "ruler." Men were shown to be those who stand before the community in long white robes (the physical icon) and spill the blood of sacrifice on the community's behalf (the physical action), and of those men, the ruler was shown to be the male *par excellence* because he physically stands before the community as a whole and sacrifices a ram on everyone's behalf.

kinesthetic image schemata

The human body also constitutes thought through kinesthetic image schemata that result from the way the body is physically structured and operates in the world—for instance, the basics of male and female form, sleeping and waking, sexual intercourse, birth, and death. The basics are universal to humankind.

Mark Johnson analyzes these basics in *The Body in the Mind: The Bodily Basis of Reason and Imagination* (1987). Johnson defines kinesthetic image schema as "a recurring, dynamic pattern of our perceptual interactions and motor programs that gives coherence and structure to our experience" (1987:xiv). For instance, "verticality" is an image schema that our bodies make viscerally available to us, and that we then use to decipher and code meaningful structures of experience:

> We grasp this structure of verticality repeatedly in thousands of perceptions and activities we experience every day, such as perceiving a tree, our felt sense of standing upright, the activity of climbing stairs, forming a mental image of a flagpole, measuring our children's heights, and experiencing the level of water rising in the bathtub. The VERTICALITY schema is the abstract structure of these VERTICALITY experiences, images, and perceptions.
>
> (Johnson 1987:xiv)

The body makes physically available to us kinesthetic image schemata which we then use, through the power of imaginative reasoning, to broaden the range of experiences and understandings to which the category applies. We extend the physical perception of verticality to more abstract domains, so that we conceive of "upright men," "tempers rising," "people standing up for their rights," and "the rise of the middle class." Kinesthetic image schemata are crucial to human thought. They build basic action frames of meaning that we then use to discover and codify our world.

In his remarkable book *The Body Silent* (1987), Robert Murphy addresses the problem of locating reality when an individual's own body becomes "the body silent" through paralysis. A myriad of difficulties occur, among them a true dualism of body and mind. The body exists, but the paraplegic has trouble physically experiencing it. Kinesthetic image schemata become less accessible, and the mind must—through abstraction—try to make up for what the body can no longer demonstrate and provide. Reality formation, no easy task for any human, is truly formidable for the paraplegic precisely because of the inaccessibility of physical experience, including the physical experience of the "whole" self—body and mind conjoined. The internal lack of fusion is greatly exacerbated by the outside world that typically refuses to acknowledge the paraplegic's existence. Others often refuse to recognize the paraplegic's presence, keeping eyes averted and avoiding physical contact. Whole institutions systematically deny the existence of paraplegics by not constructing the physical lines of access that would give them entry and concretely acknowledge their importance in the world. All humans need the external environment to confirm the internal self. The difficulty that the paraplegic experiences in creating a plausible reality when mind and body are disjoined underlines how important is the fusion of mind and body.

Like the foundations of color perception, kinesthetic image schemata do not simplistically determine human thought. Rather they establish basic experiences, fundamental visceral categories, and offer

familiar paradigms upon which cultures elaborate. As in color categorization, cultures can arbitrarily invent and highlight certain physical actions and physical forms and endow them with meaning (e.g.,
bowing for the Japanese), but cultures can also take basic physical
forms (male versus female) and basic physical actions (like sexual intercourse) that already are endowed with deep meaning and use them
to build particular cultural inventions, basic divisions of labor, basic
structures of power, and basic understandings of the universe.

In ritually reconstructing its political order, Moroccans used icons
of male physical form, the image schema of verticality, and the action
of sexual intercourse to undergird the power and authority of the
newly established sharifi caliphate. Through the use of these basics,
the rituals inscribed the legitimacy of the reformulated system of rule
upon the structure of people's own bodies—on their basic drives,
emotions, and physical perceptions—in such a way that to rend apart
the monarchy would be to tear apart themselves.

imagination

The body is crucial in the construction of thought, but thought does
not rest on the physical dimensions alone. The imaginative capacity
of the human brain is vast; the use of metaphor, metonomy, and complex mental imagery enables human thinking to go far beyond what
the human body can see and touch. Yet even here the body plays a
role. The human body is the human imagination's most basic template, its most accessible metaphor. We think of "the heart of the
problem," "the head of a state," "the body of the nation," "the wound
in the heel."

In *Body of Power, Spirit of Resistance* (1985), Jean Comaroff il-
luminates the importance of body imagery in human thought, demonstrating how crucial body metaphors have been in the confrontation of native South Africans with western Europeans who dominate
them. "The logic of that universe is itself written into the 'natural'
symbols that the body affords" (1985:7). The Zionist church of South
Africa helps consolidate popular resistance by using "healing" as its
key metaphor. The metaphor emphasizes the need to reintegrate spirit
and matter, to relocate the displaced, to draw back together the body
that was rent asunder by the bleak experience of colonialism and wage
labor (1985:176).

Metaphors we live by often center in the body, by means of which
we also live. Leaps of the imagination are grounded in physical experience, from which they go spiraling off into the domain of as-

cending abstractions. For humans, abstract symboling and physical form—mind and body—interpenetrate to constitute each other while constituting culture, and ritual is a primary arena for their interplay.

The reevaluation of the body's role in human thought enables us to begin an equally dramatic reformulation of the role of ritual in culture. Rituals do not simply communicate abstract thought, they help constitute it. In solemn assemblies—in the convergence of body, mind, and spirit—collective reality is built.

FOUNDATIONS

Muhammad
death and debate

3

Muhammad

To understand the reconstruction of the Moroccan monarchy in the 1500s, we must begin a thousand years before and 3,000 miles away, with the birth of Muhammad in the Arabian Peninsula in about 571. Muhammad was a remarkable man who captured the dynamics of his age and wielded them into creative synthesis, establishing a new faith and a new political order that swept across the face of the earth. Before his death, the Islamic community encompassed the whole of the Arabian Peninsula. Within a hundred years thereafter, Islam had already expanded across three continents, across 5,000 miles, and had brought into systematic connection for the first time in human history the great arc of humanity that inhabits the dry lands of North Africa, the Middle East, and Central Asia. Its western boundary was already the Atlantic, its eastern boundary China's great wall. The expansion continued. As of the twentieth century, one of every five people is Muslim.

During its early era, Islam's cultural repertoire of enduring representations was built. I summarize those representations. This is *not* an examination of the mind of God, nor of the essence of Islamic faith, nor of the diversity of individual believers. It is rather an examination of particular cultural representations—abiding assumptions and implicit practices—that came to dominate collective life as it was historically realized in parts of North Africa and the Middle East.

The early era is cloaked in obscurity. Written records for the most part do not survive. History was transmitted in oral form, carried by word of mouth until later. An early version of the Qur'an was written during the reign of 'Uthman, 644–656; yet its writing was so cryptic that it has been the subject of much debate. The first written biographies of the Prophet occur over a century after his death. The hundreds of thousands of orally transmitted stories and sayings about the Prophet and the life of the early Muslim community began to be systematically collected, evaluated, and written down during the 800s and 900s. These are the sayings, the "traditions"; they are collectively known as the *Hadith*. There is great diversity within them, much room for debate. The Hadith are the secondary source of authority in Islam.

For purposes of my analysis, the historical ambiguities of this age pose no serious problem, for it is remembered history that affects collective consciousness and collective practice. In the foundations of faith, remembrances are the real events, for they are what orient the believer and motivate him or her to action. What follows is an account of common remembrances as well as accepted historical events. Much of it no doubt occurred. Some of it no doubt was invented. As in all cultural traditions, historical event and cultural legend intermingle. It was this intermingling that affected Morocco's political reconstruction and survival from the 1500s to the 1900s.

Makka

Muhammad was born into the thriving commercial city of Makka. His father died before his birth; his mother died when he was young. He was raised first by his grandfather and later by his father's brother, Abu Talib. Muhammad was a part of the Banu Hashim sublineage of the Quraysh. The Quraysh was a large group of people who saw themselves as belonging to a common descent category. All of the Quraysh claimed common relationship through the patriline (the male line of father—grandfather—great-grandfather), even though precise patrilineal connections could not be traced at the higher levels. The Quraysh had taken over the rule of Makka in the 400s.

The decisive move for Muhammad as a young man was his marriage to Khadija, a wealthy tradeswoman for whom Muhammad worked. Khadija proposed the marriage. She was fifteen years older than Muhammad, had been married twice before, and was a formidable, kind, and successful woman. She supported Muhammad emotionally and financially during the early years of his prophecy. Khadija bore the Prophet's only children to survive to adulthood (all were daughters). During the twenty-six-year-long marriage, Muhammad took no other wives (Rodinson 1971:48–52).

Muhammad was a serious and thoughtful man who came to ponder the central issues of humankind: what was the nature of existence? was there life beyond? what of human suffering and what was to be done about it? For these ponderings, he began to journey to the caves outside of Makka to better meditate. There, at about the age of forty, he began to receive the revelations that comprise the Qur'an, the holy book of Islam (Lapidus 1988:25; Rodinson 1971:70–75).

In Islamic understandings, the revelations came from the archangel Jibril (Gabriel) in the form of individual "recitations" or *suras*. In combination they comprise the Qur'an, one hundred and fourteen suras in all. Hence Muhammad did not compose the Qur'an. He simply recited to himself and others what the archangel had recited to him. The words of the Qur'an are God's words—uncreated; like God they have always been and will always be. Many Muslims believe the earthly Qur'an is an exact replica of a Qur'an that has always existed in heaven. (There is some suggestion of this in the Qur'an, Sura 85, The Constellations, 21–23.) Hence, the words and the word order are considered to be sacred, and they are Arabic. Meaning and holiness exist in the Arabic itself, the language of ultimate truth, the language of God. Most Muslims believe that the Qur'an cannot be translated into other languages without losing much of its meaning. Its recitation is one of the highest forms of Islamic art (Nelson 1985).

As the body of recitations began to expand, Muhammad began to consolidate Islamic faith and the Muslim faithful. The new faith centered on the omnipotence of the single God, opposing the error of polytheism. Yet, from the beginning, Islam was not simply a system of belief, it was a system of living, and Muhammad preached the corruption of Makka's powerholders and the need to care for widows and the poor. His wife Khadija and his friend Abu Bakr were two of the first converts.

The Makkan power structure was not pleased with the young up-start. Taunts and insults were followed by an economic boycott (Lapidus 1988:25). Makka's prosperity as a thriving commerical center was linked to the practices of polytheism; people from all of the Arabian Peninsula came to Makka to sacrifice to the multiple gods whose shrines were located there, and to carry out commerce in the peace that Makka's religious-political environment insured.

Yet, the power structure tolerated Muhammad at first, probably both because Islam had few adherents and because Muhammad was a member of the Quraysh, the ruling group that dominated Makka's political life. But in time, Makka's tolerance reached its limits. By 622, Makkans had apparently had their fill and according to tradition planned to take decisive action against Muhammad and his followers. Muhammad did not linger waiting for the omnipotent God to deliver the city to him. Like many other wise strategists who are also faithful believers, Muhammad picked up his beliefs and his community and emigrated to a more receptive environment where the faith and the polity were consolidated.

emigration

The migration away from Makka is central to Islam. A city that lay 200 miles to the north of Makka was Muhammad's destination. That city, then called Yathrib, came with Islam to be called Madina al-Nabi, "the city of the Prophet," or more simply Madina, "the city." Several of its leaders had been in Makka, come in contact with the young politician and prophet, and invited him to become a political arbitrator in their city. At first Muhammad had declined, but when it became apparent that he and the Islamic community could no longer remain in Makka, he decided upon the northerly migration.

Quietly, during the summer of 622, Muhammad sent his small band of followers, seventy some strong, group by group, to Madina. He and Abu Bakr stayed behind. In September, when all who were leaving had gone, Muhammad and Abu Bakr walked out of the city of their birth. Traveling with a guide, they journeyed first in the opposite direction (apparently to confuse any Makkan authorities who might try to follow them) and for three days remained in caves to the south of Makka before finally beginning the ten-day journey across the desert to the north, to the city where Islam as a political entity would be born.

The emigration, the *hijra* in Arabic, is crucial for Muslims. Muslims calculate all of time from it. They number their years according to the length of time since the hijra, *anno Hijrae* (hereafter noted in parentheses as A.H.).[1]

Madina: political success and ritual articulation

Madina was a new world, a "godsend," as Lapidus puts it (1988:26). Muhammad now held an officially recognized position of political authority and was free to organize the community of Muslims. Yet a new problem faced him: how to clarify the boundaries of Islam in the context of other strong monotheisms. Back in Makka, Muslims had been distinctive because the community was largely polytheistic, but in Madina, a large Jewish community was well established and Christianity had had some impact. The distinctive dimensions of the Islamic monotheism had to be clarified for the Muslim community to flourish. Ritual was a means of clarification.

At first, Muhammad sought lines of connection to the other monotheisms. In Islamic perception, there is truth at the core of Judaism and Christianity. Hence, the Qur'an recognizes the people of all three monotheisms as "People of the Book," true believers, and affirms that Christians and Jews are not to be harmed as long as they do not mount armed attacks against Muslims. Although they are seen as people of truth, in Islamic understanding Christians and Jews have strayed somewhat, and hence God sent the Qur'an and the Prophet Muhammad to convey the truth to humanity in final and complete form, one last time—as Islam. Islam sees itself as the clarified culmination of the other two traditions, the unadulterated expression of truth.

At first Muhammad thought that when Jews and Christians heard the words of the Qur'an, they would recognize that it was the final and complete truth of God and would convert spontaneously. Early Madinan preachings and ritual enactments stressed the lines of unity between Islam and the other monotheisms. For instance, Muhammad instituted a fast for Muslims on 'Ashura', the tenth day of Muharram, in echo of the Jewish fast celebrated on the Day of Atonement, the tenth of Tishri. In Makka, Muslims had prayed only twice a day, but in Madina, Muhammad instituted another prayer, so that Muslims prayed three times a day, as did Jews (Brockelemann 1973:21–22). And, at first, Muhammad enjoined Muslims to conduct these prayers like Jews, facing Jerusalem, a city all three monotheisms regard as holy.

Yet when it became clear that there were not going to be mass conversions of Jews and Christians, Muhammad began to use rituals to distinguish Islam, to mark off its sacred boundaries. He dramatically altered the direction of prayer, calling upon Muslims to turn around, to no longer face Jerusalem, which lay to Madina's north, but rather to pray facing Makka, a city which lay in the opposite direction, to Madina's south. Makka was a city that was distinctly Islam's own. The number of prayers was eventually changed so that Muslims were called upon to pray five times a day rather than three. Muhammad instituted a whole month of fasting from dawn to dusk, Ramadan. He distinguished Muslims through the style of prayer. Whereas Christians were summoned by bells and Jews by trumpets, Muslims were summoned by the sound of the human voice crying out "Allah Akbar," "God is great." Furthermore, Muhammad settled upon Friday as the Muslim sabbath (Brockelemann 1973:22).

Hand-in-hand with the ritual distinctions came theological clarification. The Prophet Ibrahim became increasingly important. Muhammad stated that he used Ibrahim as his personal guide to faith, his model, and, at Madina, the Qur'anic revelations increasingly came to center on Ibrahim and clarify his role in the founding of the Muslim faith (*Encyclopedia of Islam* 1927, "Ibrahim," pp. 431–432). Next to Muhammad, Ibrahim is the prophet most frequently discussed in the Qur'an. While all three monotheisms acknowledged Ibrahim (Abraham) as a prophet, many Muslims believe that not only was he the father of all true faith—Judaism, Christianity, and Islam included—but also that he was in fact a Muslim.

The most important ritual event in establishing Ibrahim's authority and linking himself to it was Muhammad's reenactment of Ibrahim's great sacrifice, a ritual through which Muhammad brought to a close the eventful second year of the community's life at Madina, a year in which Muslims spilled blood, gained booty, and won a war—a year in which Muslims politically came of age.

raid In that second year, while traveling in the desert, a group of Muslims had raided a Makkan caravan they came upon, gained considerable booty, and taken it back to Madina where they presented it to Muhammad. To the surprise and consternation of many, Muhammad accepted the proceeds of the raid. The consternation came not because the money had been gained in a raid—raids were a common means of supplying economic needs—but rather, because the raid had taken place in a month of agreed truce, the month of Rajab. This was a month in which the peoples of the Arabian Peninsula had agreed to suspend attacks on one another so that the caravan trade could flow smoothly. It was a sacred month of cease-fire, and there was deep respect for it. Not only had Muslims broken the agreement by participating in the raid, they had spilled blood in carrying it out; a Makkan merchant traveling with the caravan had been killed.

Muhammad had not authorized the raid, but his acceptance of the booty sanctioned the act. It was a statement that the Muslim community stood outside the old rules. Consternation came from within the Muslim community as well as from without, finally causing Muhammad to issue a formal proclamation, which he had received in revelation from God, that outlined the reasons for the raid's propriety. It declared that because the people of the Peninsula were unbelievers, a sacred truce with them was not invariably binding. Agreements with infidels were not to be taken lightly, but if transgression was demanded for the furtherance of the true faith, it was legitimate. Muhammad contended that the transgression was demanded in this case because the funds were needed to further the Islamic cause. Hence, the raid was legitimate. The interpretation seems a remarkable move of self-assertion and self-confidence on the part of the young community whose adherents still numbered no more than several hundred.

Badr Muhammad soon went from accepting the money gained in a raid not authorized by him to organizing his own attack. In 624, the second year at the Madina (A.H. 2), Muhammad set out with 316 men for the wells of Badr, where he planned to ambush a large Makkan caravan that was going to stop there for water. The Makkans, however, got word of the attack, sent the caravan by another route, and to Badr's wells sent an army of some 600 men. Instead of facing a lightly armed caravan guard, the Muslims found themselves facing an organized fighting force twice their size (Hodgson 1974a:176). The battle was fierce and Muslim defeat seemed inevitable. Yet Muhammad led wisely, the Muslims stood firm, and in the end they were victorious. The small group of Islamic followers had defeated the forces sent by the seat of political power of the time. For many Muslims, the victory was a real-world confirmation of the validity of Muhammad's preachings and the worth of Muslims in God's eyes. Badr became a paradigm, a guiding representation, through which many Muslims approached the world. A common Islamic rallying cry became "to fight like the men at Badr," to fight like those who had "converted when Islam was weak and had held firm during its leanest years" (Hodgson 1974a:176). Nearly a thousand years later, in 1578 (A.H. 986/87), when Moroccans faced invading Portuguese troops, they rallied themselves to sacrifice by comparing their fight to Badr. They too urged one another to stand firm even though the forces of opposition seemed overwhelming.

After Badr, the Muslim community at Madina experienced several devastating defeats before beginning the long series of victories that resulted in Islam's phenomenal spread over the next centuries. But Badr was perceived by many as the turning point.

sacrifice According to tradition; Muhammad brought the momentous year to fruition through momentous action. That is, on the tenth day of the year's last month, he gathered the community of faithful outside his home in Madina and had brought to him two pure white rams whose eyes were boldly encircled with black markings. Several men turned the first ram over on its back, positioned with its face towards Makka, and held it fast. Muhammad took a knife in his right hand, called out God's name, and then said, "O Lord, I sacrifice this for my whole people, all those who bear witness to thy unity and to my mission." He then plunged the knife into the ram's throat, causing its blood to fall. Muhammad then sacrificed the second ram in like manner. Before its slaying, he said, "O Lord, this is for Muhammad and for the family of Muhammad" (Hadith, quoted in Sell 1920:435).

The ritual recalled the great myth, told in the Qur'an, in which God demanded that Ibrahim sacrifice his first-born son as a sign of faith. Ibrahim prepared to comply with God's command—though with great sorrow—and stood ready to slay the child. His absolute submission to God's will ("Islam" means "submission"), his willingness to take the life of his child at divine command, gained God's favor, and God spared the child, sending a ram that was then sacrificed as a substitute for the son.

Muhammad's reenactment of the ram sacrifice unified the Muslim community in common action, but equally important, it was a crystalline expression of the theological foundations of the faith. The ritual confirmed the existence of a God outside of nature who holds all power, including the power over life and death. The ritual confirmed that men of faith in connection to God are the community's signposts to eternal life. Furthermore, by performing the sacrifice, and then calling upon Muslim heads of households and communities to perform the ritual of sacrifice every year from thenceforth at the specified time, Muhammad theologically and experientially confirmed Ibrahim's place at the center of Islam and created a mechanism for its continual reaffirmation in the future. Equally important, the ritual enactment verified Muhammad's position as the prophetic inheritor of Ibrahim's faith, for in the ritual, Muhammad stood in Ibrahim's place before God and sacrificed a ram on behalf of the whole community.

The ritual also gave ultimate religious sanctification to the organizational principles of patriarchy and patrilineality. Patriarchy has to do with the male exercise of power in the present. Patrilineality has to do with the genealogical inheritance of position through the male line through time. Both were important idioms in the organizational life of the Arabian Peninsula at the time, but the association with Islam gave them ultimate legitimacy. All faiths, including those that claim to be applicable to all peoples in all times, are articulated in and through the specifics of human culture. This says nothing about the ultimate nature of the divine. It says much about the nature of collective expression. Whether or not the divine exists, existentially speaking, the idea of the divine must enter human communities in forms that humans are capable of understanding, practicing, and communicating with others, and those forms are cultural. The Qur'anic myth of Ibrahim and Muhammad's sacrificial enactment helped establish patrilineality and patriarchy at the center of the cultural matrix of Islam. The specifics of the myth and the ritual are analyzed in considerable depth in later chapters, but here a few of the basic parameters must be mentioned.

The Ibrahim myth powerfully undergirds the rightful domination of father over son, of senior men over junior men, of all males over females and children—of patriarchy. Ibrahim (Islam's archetypal father) submitted to God's demand even to the point of trying to kill his own son, and the son, because he was faithful and loyal (Islam's archetypal son), actively cooperated with the father's attempt at his own sacrifice; the son knowingly submitted to what was to be his death at his father's hands. In reenacting the sacrifice, Muhammad gave the myth lived vitality and profoundly reinforced the patriarchy intrinsic to it, adding to that patriarchy the ritual's own construction. Muhammad stood central and sacrificed on behalf of the community as a whole and on behalf of the women and children directly dependent on him. He then called upon senior men to perform that sacrifice every year thenceforth. Senior men were made the pivot of the sacrifice.

Islam's myth both transcends and reinforces patrilineality, the inheritance of goods and position through the male line. Transcendence comes because, as told in the Qur'an, the prophet Ibrahim had to deny his own father in order to remain faithful to the one God (Ibrahim's father rejected monotheism and forced the fissure between father and son.) Yet the Qur'an also reinforces patrilineality by portraying the ultimate sacrifice that God demands of humans as the sacrifice of the most precious tie on earth—the father's link to his male child—the fundamental patrilineal connection. The myth of sacrifice ennobles that bond over all others. So at the same time that the Qur'an underlines the limits of patrilineal affiliation (Muslims must deny it if it threatens the faith), it reinforces patrilineality, for it was the father in connection with the son that made for connection to the divine and won for father and son—and by extension all of humanity—long life on earth and eternal life thereafter. According to tradition, Ibrahim and his son walked away from the place of sacrifice and went on to establish some of the holiest places in Islam.

Muhammad's ritual performance also both transcends and reinforces patrilineal connections. As remembered, Muhammad sacrificed two rams, the first on behalf of the overarching community of Muslims, brought together by faith, not patriline. But the second ram was slain on behalf of Muhammad's patriline, the children already born to him and the children he hoped still would come, especially on behalf of the son he hoped would be born and live to adulthood.

Islam did not invent patriarchy and patrilineality, but it did make them sacred. Islam's central orienting myth (Ibrahim's sacrifice) and central orienting practice (the yearly performance of Muhammad's rite of sacrifice) are crucial in that sanctification. They provide patriarchy and patrilineality with ultimate legitimacy by making them the pathways of human hope for divine connection.

From the beginning, patriarchy and patrilineality were central to Islam. Patriarchy went unquestioned, while patrilineality was both utilized and transcended. Most early converts were not linked to Islam through patrilineal connections. In fact, many had to deny their patrilineal connections in order to join the Prophet in the pursuit of Islam. Yet as Islam grew and spread, patrilineal organizational principles and patrilineal groups became important. Leaders of whole patrilineal groupings sometimes allied themselves with Muhammad and Islam and brought their patrikin along with them. Tribes throughout the Peninsula allied themselves to Islam in this way. Military units were organized along patrilineal lines. The speed with which Islam expanded over the globe is in part a function of the flexibility and efficiency of this kind of patrilineal organizational schema, especially when combined with the zeal of a universal faith. Early non-Arab converts to Islam were first adopted into Arab patrilines (Bulliet 1979:41). A transcendent God was, and is, the center of Islam, but patrilineality and patriarchy were from the beginning worldly means of connection to him. Islam's patrilineal and patriarchal foundations will be summarized, for they are crucial to the political templates that were built.

proper. They might interfere with men's prayers, men's focus on God. And while the Qur'an assures women of faith that they will go to heaven (for instance, Sura 16, The Bee, 98, and Sura 4, Women, 125), it offers them no insight as to what their place in heaven will be, and in fact does not create a place for them. "When you look . . . at how space is organized and equipped in Paradise, you realise that it is a space equipped . . . solely for the believer of the male sex" (Sabbah 1984:94), "solely for the happiness of men" (Sabbah 1984:93). Islamic women must speculate on where they might spend eternity and how, while men in contrast are provided with bounteous detail on what their place in paradise will be and the pleasures they will receive there—for instance, Sura 56, The Event, 12–41, and Sura 55, The Beneficent:

> Which, then, of the favours of your Lord will ye twain deny?
> Therein will be maidens, good and beautiful.
> Which, then, of the favours of your Lord will ye twain deny?
> Fair maidens with lovely black eyes, guarded in pavilions.
> Which, then, of the favours of your Lord will ye twain deny?
> Whom neither man nor jinn will have touched before them.
> Which, then, of the favours of your Lord will ye twain deny?
> Reclining on green cushions and beautiful carpets.
> Which, then, of the favours of your Lord will ye twain deny?
> Blessed is the name of thy Lord, Master of glory and honour.
>   (Sura 55, 70–79, tr. Farid 1969)

In Islam's cultural imagination, males carry basic sociobiological definition and sacred pleasure. Essential being and essential affiliation pass down through the patriline—that is, from great-grandfather to grandfather to father to son. Enduring biological essence is seen to transfer from father to progeny and creates an inalienable tie, written in the life-blood itself (in much of the Muslim world, patrilineal bonds are known as "blood" ties).

Daughters as well as sons receive their basic definition from their fathers, but only sons are capable of passing it on to future generations. Females are dead ends for their patrilines—important, but ephemeral additions. A female is a member of her father's patriline for as long as she lives (this basic sociobiological affiliation is inalienable; it does not change because of marriage; Muslim women typically maintain their father's name). She provides beauty, nurture, comfort, and pleasure, but she cannot provide for historical continuity or durability. That is a task for men. A female bears children who receive their definition from their father. Hence, a patriline's female members are important while they live, but historically, they tend to be forgotten, for the patriline is carried from generation to generation through the names and bloodlines of men. Sons are the enduring links. To lack sons is to lack the potential for history—hence the enormous value that people operating within this cultural context place on the birth of sons, for that is their hope for the only kind of durability and continuity that this world can provide.

females These basic kinship parameters provide basic understandings of males and females. Men are permanent; women are ephemeral. Those basic understandings inform the organization of collective life. Those dimensions of collective existence of more ultimate concern tend to be allocated to men (notably communal decisionmaking and communal quests for transcendence), while more temporal things are the domain of women (the preparation of food and clothing, the care of small children).

The inheritance system reflects these basic understandings. Within Islamic legal codes, both males and females are recognized as inalienable members of their father's patriline and hence have a right to inheritance from him. But the males are, so to speak, more inalienable. As noted above, the male—the carrier of the patriline from generation to generation—is by law to receive twice the inheritance of the female—the evanescent addition. In practice, it is common for women to receive less than their legal allocation of half of their brother's share. Sometimes they receive nothing. Furthermore, it is common practice among many Muslims for males to receive the durable and reproductive wealth of the patriline as their inheritance—for example land, trees, and commercial enterprises—while daughters typically receive movable property—for instance wool, glassware, and jewelry.

agnation and the collective emphasis The kind of patrilineality that is a part of the cultural matrix of Islam stresses not only the vertical relationships of the direct patriline (grandfather—father—son), but also the lateral relationships of agnation (brothers and cousins). It demands that a person not simply look up to father, grandfather, great-grandfather, but also across and down, to one's brothers (and their children), to father's brothers (and their children), to grandfather's brothers (and their sons and their children), and so forth. Furthermore, the system systematically clusters a hierarchy of rights, duties, and obligations around this broad-reaching organizational schema. One's greatest rights and duties are to one's closest patrikin—one's father and brothers—and then systematically extend out to include the more distant patrikin, all the sons and grandsons of one's grand-father, all the sons, grandsons, and great-grandsons of great-grand-father, all the sons, grandsons, great-grandsons, and great-great-grandsons of great-great-grandfather. Proper affiliation and legitimate action thus depend on the social relationships of those involved, and are situation specific. The relativity is embodied in the oft-quoted Arabic saying, "I against my brothers; my brothers and I against our cousins; my brothers, my cousins, and I against the world."

The system stresses equality of birthright. People who hold the same positions within the patrilineage are considered structural equals; that is, all sons of one's father, all sons of one's grandfather, all sons of one's great-grandfather, and so forth. Within people of the same generation, differences emerge because of differing achievements in historical practice, not because of differing ascriptions at birth. There is no systematic favoritism given to first-born sons or latter-born sons, as exists in systems of primogeniture and ultimogeniture. In terms of constitutive principles, all sons are to inherit equal shares.

The ascribed hierarchy of authority within the system is attached to generation of birth. Authority passes down through the generations. Elders have the ultimate power of decision making over juniors, an authority legitimated because elders give juniors their sociobiological identity.

naming This system of patrilineality is carried through the names of men. Figure 3.1. depicts a patriline. Isma'il's full name is Isma'il ibn Idris ibn Badr al-Din ibn 'Umar ibn Abu Bakr (*ibn* is the Arabic word for "son of"; *banu* is its plural, meaning "sons of"). Each person's name hence summarizes his patriline as well as his systematic incorporation into the increasingly larger nested units designated by all the sons of (*banu*) a given ancestor; for instance, banu Badr al-Din ("sons" is here taken to include sons and grandsons), banu 'Umar (which includes all of his sons, grandsons and great-grandsons) and banu Abu Bakr (which includes all of his sons, grandsons, great-grandsons, and great-great-grandsons). From the standpoint of the individual, his name indicates affiliation into a simple and straightforward series of nested units, as depicted in figure 3.2. From the standpoint of the overarching system, the named designation of patrilineal units is complex. Only a small portion of such a system is depicted in figure 3.3. It is an elaborate, branching organizational schema that can be used to regulate a great number of tasks. What is neat and simple from the individual's perspective is complex from a system's perspective.

The beauty of this organizational model rests on the combination of the ease with which it can be carried and the complexity of the organization it can call into play when the situation demands. Everyone must simply know his own name and operate from a system of loyalty and commitment that begins with the self and is systematically extended back up through the patriline to the apical ancestors and all their descendants.

organizational idioms   The patrilineal genealogical charter is used in many places in the Islamic world to organize a great number of basic tasks of daily living: from whom one receives inheritance, to whom one owes allegiance, with whom one can pasture animals, from whose wells one can expect water, with whom one should share food in time of drought, with whom one should ally in times of war, from whom one can expect aid in the building of large-scale commercial enterprises, to whom one turns in times of personal crisis. It is a flexible and effective system for regularizing certain types of relationships within and between social groupings. No single person needs to be able to specify the whole organizational structure for it to be carried through

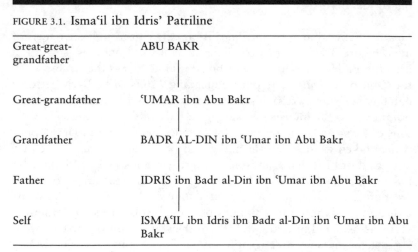

FIGURE 3.1. Isma'il ibn Idris' Patriline

Great-great-grandfather	ABU BAKR
Great-grandfather	'UMAR ibn Abu Bakr
Grandfather	BADR AL-DIN ibn 'Umar ibn Abu Bakr
Father	IDRIS ibn Badr al-Din ibn 'Umar ibn Abu Bakr
Self	ISMA'IL ibn Idris ibn Badr al-Din ibn 'Umar ibn Abu Bakr

NOTE:

First names are indicated by capital letters. The rest of the name is a short history of the person's patriline. In daily speech a man is typically referred to by either his first name (e.g., Isma'il) or by his first name followed by the name of his father (e.g., Isma'il ibn Idris), but the entire name is proper.

time and to be called into play when necessary. Unlike territorial systems (e.g., city, country, state, nation), it requires no grounded structures for its systematic reproduction, and probably for this reason receives its greatest elaboration among nomads whose ground keeps changing, who do not have durable physical structures through which to articulate organizational divisions, and hence spin their organization through the names of men.

For example, using the patrilineal affiliation indicated in figure 3.3., in a large migration of the nomadic descendants of Abu Bakr, the names of the apical ancestors are used to divide the overarching collectivity into appropriately sized subgroups when necessary. If three groups are needed, the great-grandfather level is used, and the banu ʿUmar, for instance, can be told to take the trail to the east, the banu Hamid the trail to the west, while the banu Sulayman, "the sons of Sulayman," take the trail in the center. If more divisions are needed, the grandfather level can be used, which in this case would divide the overarching collectivity into seven distinctive groupings.

If every man simply knows his name, an elaborate organizational structure can be called into play that systematically specifies rights, duties, and loyalty among vast numbers of people. The Tiv of Nigeria, in the past, used patrilineality in the organization of over a million people (Bohannan and Bohannan 1953). But that is an outside limit. The number of people mobilized through patrilineal affiliation is usually smaller, numbering in the thousands or tens of thousands. Beyond that number, loyalty to the descent group tends to be hard to maintain, as Ibn Khaldun (1969 [1381]) and Ernest Gellner (1981) have demonstrated.

In many parts of the Muslim world, the patrilineal charter is used in the selection of political leadership, especially among tribal peoples,

---

FIGURE 3.2. Incorporation into Patrilineal Groupings as a Function of Name

sons of GREAT-GREAT-GRANDFATHER:			banu ABU BAKR
sons of GREAT-GRANDFATHER:		banu ʿUMAR	
sons of GRANDFATHER:	banu BADR AL-DIN		
sons of FATHER:	banu IDRIS		
self	ISMAʿIL		

FIGURE 3.3. The Patrilineal Organizational Schema Viewed from Above

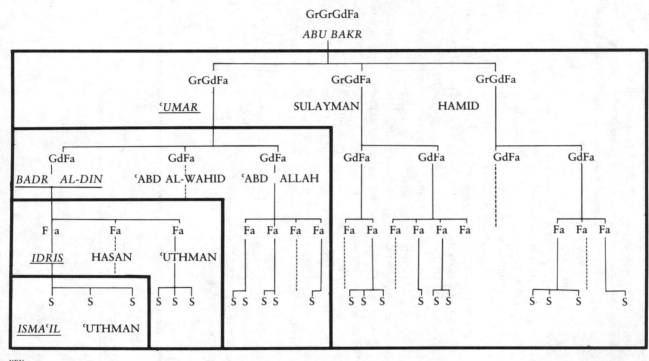

KEY:

GrGdFa great-grandfather   **GdFa** grandfather   **Fa** father   **S** son

NOTE:

The members of the patriline indicated in figures 3.1 and 3.2 are underlined, while the corporate affiliation of figures 3.2 is shown here by the hierarchy of nested rectangles. Dotted lines indicate descendents were too numerous to include.

where it is common for the position of overarching leadership to be gained through a combination of earned right and democratic selection. While this kind of patrilineality invests authority in elder generations, it does not indicate who within a given generation should lead. After all, the system stresses equality by birthright. Hence, authority is often earned in practice; that is, those who show themselves capable are chosen to lead, and the patrilineal schema is often used to organize the choice. Patrilineality clarifies who has a right to vote (senior men), and from which group the leader should come. Often there is a council of elders that selects the leader, and in many places leadership regularly rotates among major patrilineal divisions (Gellner 1969, Hart 1981). For instance, again drawing upon the patrilineal example indicated in figure 3.3 above, to select the overarching leader of "the sons of Abu Bakr," a council of elders representing all the senior men of the banu Abu Bakr would select one man, but leadership would rotate among the three named groupings designated by the great-grandfather level. During the first cycle, the leader would be selected from among the senior men of the banu ʿUmar sublineage (in many places the senior men of that sublineage cannot vote when the leader is to come from their group; this appears to be an attempt at keeping overarching capacity rather than personal loyalty at the forefront of the election). During the next cycle, the leader would be chosen from the senior men of the banu Sulayman, and during the final cycle from among the senior men of the banu Hamid, and then the cycle would begin again (Gellner 1969, Hart 1981).

This system of earned and elected leadership makes much sense for North African and Middle Eastern nomads, who have most developed it. In guiding a nomadic group and their flocks over the harsh, dry terrain that characterizes this region, there is little margin for error, no margin for major mistakes. Leaders must know what they are doing, or the group and their animals will not survive. It is not a land where elaborate cushioning separates decision making and consequences.

enduring values   Patrilineality entered Islam not only in terms of on-the-ground organizational schema, but also in terms of underlying values and understandings, including:

- The notion that sociobiological inheritance passes through the patrilineal *bloodline,* and essential rights and duties are properly organized around it (the blood emphasis leads to the conception of the Prophet's blood descendants as superior).
- The notion that the *father-son* link is the most crucial in human existence.

67

- The evaluation of *men as the links to permanence* and durability and women as links to more temporal things.
- A strong theme of *egalitarianism,* that people are equal by birth, that differences emerge in the living of history and are based on individual achievements, and that these achievements should be communally recognized.
- An emphasis on *senior males' corporate decision making.*
- *Situational loyalty,* that is, loyalty that depends on the social context and alters according to the kinship relationships of those involved.

The diversity of values ensured that Islam's constitutive repertoire would be rich. There is room for considerable breadth and maneuver within the basic principles. For instance, the notion that blood descent determines identity is in some ways the logical opposite of the notion that all people are created equal at birth. Both notions have received play in Islamic political constructions. In some Islamic systems, the leader is selected by election and considered to be an equal of all other men, while in others, some men are thought to be superior because of blood descent from Muhammad and attain their position on that hierarchical basis.

loyalty to God and Islamic community Patrilineality organizes relationships within the named grouping, not beyond it. In forming a universal faith that encompassed all of humanity, Islam stepped outside of patrilineality's boundaries and demanded overarching loyalty to a single God who is invested with all power and all authority and demands ultimate human allegiance because he lies outside of the things of this world, beyond nature and the universe itself; he is in fact the creator of it. This God demands allegiance to himself and to the political community of the faithful that follows him, the Muslim *umma* (the community that marks itself off as God's own by following the leadership of the Prophet Muhammad). God also demands allegiance to the senior men who in any given age oversee the umma and who are invested with considerable authority. According to the Hadith the judgment of the umma, the political community of the Muslim faithful, will not be in error.

From the beginning, Islamic political communities combined the stress on loyalty to the overarching group of the faithful as a whole with other organizational principles relevant to particular times and places (for example, bureaucratic and territorial models), and yet patrilineality remained important. The universal faith of Islam, applicable to all peoples in all times, is presented through myths, stories, recitations, and rituals in which the patrilineal idiom and its under-lying values are deeply imbedded. In Islam, as in Christianity and Judaism, when one ties oneself to a universal God, one uses the ropes of patrilineality and patriarchy.

women and political bonds: the tie that binds

One of those patrilineal ropes involves the practice of giving women in concubinage and marriage as a means of creating and solidifying ties between individual men or between political groups. The practice is a logical derivative of patrilineality's understanding of the female; that is, she is valued for her contribution to the here and now, but she is evanescent, not enduring, and her evanescence makes it plausible to contemplate "giving her away." The gift of a son in contrast would be awesome, for thereby one would give away one's permanence, one's chance for history.

In many ways, the female is the perfect gift—inalienably linked to the father by birth, but transferable for the practice of daily life, and hence able to remain a permanent go-between, a living link between her father and her husband, between the man from whom she derives her ascribed affiliation and the man from who she derives her achieved status in adulthood. Historically speaking, the woman is a dead end for her own patriline, but she can make herself useful to her husband's patriline by serving as the physical conduit for his patriline's children.

Several kinds of strategies are involved in the giving of women, including whether to marry a daughter within the patriline or outside it. There is a high value placed on "ingroup" marriage, particularly the marriage of a daughter to a brother's son (or to a higher-level equivalent, e.g., to a father's brother's son), an act that ideally reinforces the moral obligations of kinship—the imperatives of blood—with the practical obligations of daily life. This form of marriage solidifies ties among a patriline's younger-generation males by linking them through women. For instance, in the kin group depicted in figure 3.3, Idris might give a daughter to Hasan's son, or on the next generational level to Abd al-Wahid's son or grandson, or on the next generation level to Sulayman's son or grandson or great-grandson; in each case, the daughter would be a living link between the men of the patriline's major divisions.

Through this kind of marriage one keeps wealth close to home. Any inheritance that the daughter might receive stays within the greater patriline, for she is marrying her patrilineal cousin, the man who has the greatest right to her father's inheritance if her brothers do not survive (Goody 1976, Murphy and Kasdan 1959, Salzman 1978). Inmarriage prevents the dispersal of the father's emotional wealth as well. Fathers often care deeply for their daughters, both because of "natural" affection and because of the daughter's cultural exclusion from the authority structure of the patriline. In the daughter, a man has a person who is part of his blood essence, but not a competitor for his blood-earned position of patrilineal dominance, as are sons, and not a potential sexual threat, as are wives and concubines. The cultural exclusion from the patriline's authority structure relieves the father-daughter relationship of many of the tensions that characterize father-son ties, and the father-daughter relationship is often one of considerable affection. By marrying his daughter to his brother's son, the father marries her to a man over whom he has considerable authority. Thus he is likely to see her more often and to have more control over her fate.

The second strategy is to extend one's alliances outside the patriline by marrying a daughter "out," thereby creating a living link to a man with whom one has no culturally prescribed durable bond. If one desires a long-term connection to a man outside one's patrikin, a daughter is the most valuable gift, the tie that binds. While inmarriage serves to reinforce patrilineal obligations, outmarriage helps compensate for their absence, and prominent men who are blessed with a sufficiency of daughters often pursue both strategies at once (Combs-Schilling 1985, Jamous 1981, Salzman 1978). Both were used by the Prophet Muhammad, as well as by political leaders who followed him, to consolidate alliances.

Muhammad's marriages   While Jesus took twelve disciples, Muhammad took from nine to thirteen wives—the number varies according to one's definition of wifehood (Ibn Hisham 1955). Muhammad's zest for marriage is often viewed in terms of the Prophet's emotional makeup (Rodinson 1971). Yet, his marriages also need to be seen from a political perspective. The great rush of marriages did not begin until after the migration to Madina when the political community of Muslims was in the process of consolidation. Confirming political alliances and developing clarified lines of political communication were issues, among others, that affected Muhammad's marital exuberance. Several of his wives provided living links to the men who were his most important political confidants. At stake also was Muhammad's desire to have a male heir, a desire that was probably heightened—

like that of Henry VIII—by his political success. Potentates tend to want to leave their male blood descendant on the throne. If Muhammad desired that, he failed; only daughters survived him. (Muhammad had a son born to him at Madina. He named him Ibrahim in honor of the great Prophet. The child died before weaning.)

At Makka, Muhammad had been married to Khadija—merchant, friend, and confidante. During his long marriage to her, Muhammad took no other wives and long grieved for Khadija after her death in 619. Yet practically speaking, Muhammad needed a woman to replace her, to take care of his household and look after his daughters, and soon he married the plump and elderly Sawda, a widow, who had also been an early convert to Islam. Muhammad had no sexual interest in her, a fact he made clear; he wedded her as a housewife and a replacement mother, and honored her for those roles (Rodinson 1971:134).

The political marriages spanned the Prophet's life from the age of fifty-two to sixty-two, his last decade. The first such marriage was to a daughter of Abu Bakr, Muhammad's closest confidant, the one who had stayed behind with him in Makka. Abu Bakr's closeness to Muhammad and the position of respect that he held in the Muslim political community was made clear after Muhammad's death, when he was chosen to be the first political leader of the Muslim community in Muhammad's absence; Abu Bakr was the first caliph of Islam. Abu Bakr's offer of his daughter 'A'isha to the Prophet in marriage solidified the ties between the two men. The offer was formalized when the daughter was only six years old; the marriage was consummated when she was nine; Muhammad died when she was eighteen. 'A'isha was a remarkable girl and young woman. Forceful, dynamic, and assertive, she won the Prophet's heart. She gave him no children but became Muhammad's favorite wife. Tradition says that the Prophet died in her arms.

Muhammad's next political marriage was to a daughter of 'Umar, another close associate, early convert, and advisor. Upon the death of Abu Bakr, 'Umar became the second caliph of Islam. The marriage contract concerned 'Umar's eighteen-year-old daughter Hafsa, whom Muhammad took as wife along with 'A'isha (Islam allows a man four wives if all can be treated equally). For 'Umar as well as for Abu Bakr, the gift of the daughter served as a living bond between himself and the Prophet who was also the head of the political community of Muslims.

In consolidating political ties, Muhammad not only took wives but also gave daughters. Muhammad solidified a tie to 'Uthman, another close advisor, by giving him his daughter Ruqiyya. When she died just two years later, Muhammad gave ʿUthman another of his daughters, Umm Kalthum, a clear indication of Muhammad's desire to maintain a living link to the dynamic young man who was a member of Makka's powerful patrilineage, the Banu Umayya, "the sons of Umayya." ʿUthman followed ʿUmar as supreme authority in Islam; he became Islam's third caliph.

While these marriages were arranged outside of Muhammad's immediate patriline, he also consolidated a marriage within it. He married his daughter Fatima to his father's brother's son, ʿAli. ʿAli followed ʿUmar as political ruler and became the fourth caliph of Islam.

Several years before his death, Muhammad married Umm Habiba, daughter of the powerful leader of Makka, Abu Sufyan, who at that point was still mounting political opposition to Muhammad and the Muslims. But a year later he came to Muhammad and arranged the political compromise that was crucial in clearing the way for Muhammad's triumphant entry into Makka in 630 (A.H. 8) (Rodinson 1971:258–262). Umm Habiba's brother was Muʿawiya, who became Muhammad's *katib*, his writer, during the last two years of the Prophet's life. Muʿawiya became the fifth caliph of Islam and established Islam's first imperial dynasty, the Banu Umayya.

Political marriages and political succession closely followed each other in early Islam (see figure 4.1). Consciously or unconsciously, the Muslim community used Muhammad's decision making concerning political alliances solidified through marriages as a guide to which men were worthy to rule.

success

Through the creative synthesis of a profoundly appealing new faith, a deeply moving holy book, old and new organizational principles, skillful leadership, and military and economic conquest, Islam excelled. Eight years after the emigration, Muhammad marched back into the city of Makka at the head of an army 10,000 strong. The city capitulated with little resistance. Makka joined into the household of faith (Dar al-Islam). Islam promises everlasting life in the hereafter, but from the beginning managed to give its believers a successful political community on earth.

Muhammad codified Islam's political success and religious excellence in ritual performance. Even his entry into Makka was ritually marked. He rode around the Kaʿba seven times (the Kaʿba is an ancient stone structure, an ancient shrine, believed by Muslims to have been built or rebuilt by Ibrahim and Isma'il). More profoundly, Muhammad undertook the rite of pilgrimage to Makka and called upon Muslims to take it forever more. In the spring of the tenth Muslim year after the hijra (A.D. 632), two years after his reentry into Makka, Muhammad solemnly performed the sacred pilgrimage. To history, it is known as the "farewell pilgrimage"—the Prophet of God died soon thereafter.

Muhammad's performance of the pilgrimage established Makka's prominence as the holiest city of Islam, the Ka'ba's place as the holiest structure in Islam, and Ibrahim's position at the faith's center. But, most importantly, it created a single rite that each year unites the whole of the Muslim world in common action before the one God.

Muhammad established the pilgrimage as one of the five pillars of Islam, a duty incumbent on all Muslims who are able to perform it. The other pillars—the statement of faith, prayer, almsgiving, and fasting—must be practiced on a regular basis, but the sacred journey to the center of the faith, the pilgrimage, the *hajj*, is demanded only once in a lifetime. Muhammad placed the great rite of sacrifice into the pilgrimage, making it the pilgrimage's culminating act (see Awn 1984, Bousquet 1949, Partin 1967, Roff 1985).

The pilgrimage draws each Muslim year to a close, for it takes place during the last Muslim month. The seventh through the tenth days of the month are the most important, and involve a series of highly prescribed ritual actions. As of the late twentieth century, the pilgrimage has been celebrated almost every year for over 1,350 years. Over two million Muslims now journey to Makka for the event, and the rest of the Muslim world travels with them, following it through radio, newspaper, and television reporting. In Morocco, the events of the pilgrimage are broadcast on television throughout the day.

The physical journey to the heart of the faith is at the same time a theological journey to the foundations of Islam. Thought and action are not separable. Faith and deed are one. In pilgrimage, Islam's abstract symbolism and its visceral practices are brought together and constantly rebuild each other at the same time that they rebuild the conceptual foundations of the faith.

Individual pilgrims prepare for the rite through acts of purification. Some fast; all fervently pray, carefully clean their bodies, and cut their nails. Men must shave their heads and don a single, unsewn white cloth, which is wrapped loosely around the body. Women, in contrast, wear clean but everyday clothing. The differentiation in dress results from and reinforces the greater sanctity that Islam accords to males. During the performance of the pilgrimage proper (the rites of the seventh to the tenth days), the pilgrim cannot engage in sexual intercourse, which is considered polluting.

Ka'ba   On the seventh day of the month, the communal actions begin. Each pilgrim must make seven circumambulations of the Ka'ba, the stone structure that lies at the center of the vast courtyard of the Great Mosque of Makka. A huge black drape covers the Ka'ba; it is made of velvet and embossed with glittering golden verses from the Qur'an. So numerous are the pilgrims that they cannot simultaneously enter the courtyard and hence there is a continuous flow of people into and out of the swirling mass of thousands upon thousands of pilgrims circling the great stone. Muslim unity is made manifest. Individuals enter and exit, but the community of Muslims remains faithfully together, faithfully moving. If possible, the pilgrims are to kiss a black meteorite that is embedded in the Ka'ba's side, but the masses makes it impossible for most to approach the stone. Those that cannot reach it call out salutations to it from afar.

The pilgrimage ritual of prayer, like the circumambulation of the Ka'ba, also physically confirms the unity of Muslims. Elsewhere in the world, Muslims pray in straight lines facing the direction of Makka. But here, at the heart of the faith, in Makka itself, Muslims gather in a great circle around the great stone foundation to pray as one to the one God.

'Arafat   The rituals of the ninth and tenth days are most important. On the ninth day, the ritual reaches a peak when the pilgrims climb Mount 'Arafat, the Mount of Mercy. The physical action, the visceral experience, helps build conceptual understanding. The pilgrims journey away from the flat plains and climb to one of earth's high pinnacles where interaction with a God who exists beyond earth can most appropriately take place. The physical experience of height accents the theological understanding of a high and abstract divinity.

The action at Mount 'Arafat is a manifest trial. The pilgrims must stand from high noon to sunset seeking repentance for themselves and others. The sun shines hot and they must neither eat nor drink, nor shield their heads—except for the old and weak, and even they must shield them only briefly. Physical steadfastness, not easy verbalizations, must be demonstrated, and in response God forgives pilgrims their sins and the sins of the whole of the Muslim world. At the Mount of Mercy, the Muslim pilgrims represent Muslims everywhere.

slaying With the past wiped clean, the pilgrims are ready to forge a connection with God for the future, and for that purpose they make use of the most powerful means available, the causing of earthly death, the spilling of life's blood. They engage in sacrifice. They must slay a beast of this world as did Ibrahim and Muhammad. God is clear on the need for sacrifice. In the Qur'an, God states:

> We have appointed by every nation
> a holy rite, that they may mention
> God's Name over such beasts of the flocks
> as He has provided them. Your God is One God,
> so to Him surrender. And give thou good tidings unto the
>   humble. . . .
> And the beasts of sacrifice—We have appointed
> them for you as among God's waymarks:
> therein is good for you. So mention
> God's Name over them, standing in ranks;
> then, when their flanks collapse, eat of them
> and feed the beggar and the suppliant. . . .
> So He has subjected them
> to you, that you may magnify God for
> that He has guided you.
>   (Sura 22, The Pilgrimage, 35–37)

The sacrifice takes place after midmorning prayers on the tenth day of the Muslim year's last month. The two million pilgrims stand on the broad plain of Mina and spill the blood of this world in order to connect with the God who exists beyond it. In this rite, the pilgrims cannot take the place of Muslims elsewhere. Every Muslim household throughout the world must at this same time engage in sacrifice. They must each year slay an animal in sacrifice to God, so he can see their faith and grant his favor.[4]

faith and practice Through the sum total of household sacrifices, the Muslim world—divided by language, geography, and ethnic affiliation—is drawn together. The world's 900 million Muslims become one, the single umma connecting with God. From Dar al-Bayda' to Djakarta, Muslim heads of household slay a beast that God may see the fervor of their commitment and continue interacting with them. Many families save for months, sometimes for the whole year, to purchase the sacrificial animal, the spilled blood of which is a sign to God of their willingness to give the most valuable things of earth in order to connect with him. The number of animals sacrificed on this single morning reaches the tens of millions and the amount of spilt blood measures thousands of liters, a forceful sign to an almighty God that the Muslim faithful continue to desire covenant with him. On the plan of Mina alone, over 200,000 animals are slain, and today their carcasses are delivered by refrigerated airplanes to the poor throughout the world.

In creating the ritual, Muhammad created a forceful experience of unity in which the Muslim world could engage, an experience that sealed Muslims' unity with God and with each other in blood. Muhammad's enactment of sacrifice renewed the central paradigm myth of Islam and established a paradigm ritual that held within it the very heart of Islam. It was into this ritual and into this myth that the Moroccan monarchy inserted itself in the crisis of the 1700s (A.H. 1100s), and through the success of that insertion renewed itself into the present.

The ritual performance of ram sacrifice gives physical dimension to the theological foundations of Islam. It confirms that God is in control of death and can overturn death if he will. It recalls the awesome trial of Ibrahim and God's benevolent resolution. It physically connects Ibrahim, the father of faith, and Muhammad, faith's final prophet. It reminds fathers and sons of how close was the call. The closeness continues to elevate father and son in the sacrifice—it is not them by a hair. They are worthy of sacrifice but their worthiness gains their release. The fervor of their faith causes God to provide an animal substitute, while they are allowed to go on living with all privileges. Through sacrifice and the images sacrifice evokes, men earn each year the right to domination.

It is common for scholars to separate ritual practice from theological beliefs, and a few go so far as to say that Islam should be called an "orthopraxy" rather than an "orthodoxy," on the purported grounds that Islam's unity comes in a common set of ritual practices rather than in a set of common theological beliefs (B. Turner 1984). But the dichotomy is false. Mind and body are not severed. Ritual action constitutes theological beliefs, just as theological beliefs constitute ritual action. In slaying a ram of this world a belief in a God beyond nature is built, and the unity of the Muslim world is continually reexperienced.

4

death and debate

In 632 (A.H. 11), Muhammad, Prophet of God and superb politician, died. He had founded a new faith, conveyed a new holy book, and established a powerful political, economic, and sociocultural order. Muhammad endowed the Muslim community with a plethora of rituals, symbols, practices, beliefs, and accomplishments, but was curiously silent on how political authority was to be established in his absence.

battle for political definition

Muhammad's life was to serve as a guide, that was certain, but only in part. The religious-political unification that occurred in his life could not be repeated. Muhammad was the Prophet of God as well as the political head of state, but Muhammad was God's last Prophet. None would follow. The prophetic form of communication between God and humanity has ceased.

Men could step into Muhammad's political role, but none could repeat his religious authority. With his death, supreme religious and political authority in Islam were pulled apart. Supreme religious authority now inhered in the Qur'an, the Hadith, and the umma (the community of the faithful as a whole), while supreme political authority came to rest with a single political leader who would provide the temporal framework within which the belief and the believers could flourish. From early on, the overarching political position in the Muslim world, the caliphate, was an essentially political one. The caliph was not a diviner of faith, not a creator of religious law, no pope, no prophet. He was the worldly overseer of a political-religious community that itself was the upholder of the true faith.

This depiction contrasts with one frequently used. Many scholars say that in Islam political and religious authority are indistinguishable. That characterization rests on the analyst's confusion of the Islamic prescription that religion infuse all of life with a supposed Muslim inability to distinguish between life's domains, resulting in the analytical assumption that political and religious authority have no separation in "the Muslim mind." That is an error. Islam is to inform all of life, not only faith and politics, but also how one washes, what one eats, and how one engages in sex. But mainstream Islam acknowledges the differences. Informing and collapsing are not the same thing, and most Muslims separate the purely political from the quintessentially religious. As one friend ironically put it, "we are, after all, able to tell a mosque from a ballot box."

When it came to who was to become the political leader in Muhammad's absence, the majority of the community of the faithful agreed on two things. First, Muhammad's position could not be repeated, and for that reason his successor was to be called his *khalifa*, his lieutenant (it is from the Arabic word *khalifa* that we derive the English word "caliph"). Second, a single male was to serve as the political head of the community (as opposed to, for instance, a council of men). Beyond that there was much room for debate. A battle of definition ensued that is not yet finished. In this battle, the cultural representations consolidated in the Prophet's era played a part, including ritual practices, patriarchy, blood descent, earned leadership capacity, election by notables, and marriage as a means of solidifying ties.[1]

mainstream   In the mainstream Muslim tradition, the Sunni tradition, the selection of Muhammad's political successor is remembered to have taken place in the following way: On the night of the Prophet's death, a group of knowledgeable elders gathered in his widow 'A'isha's house and elected her father Abu Bakr to head the political community in Muhammad's absence, to be Muhammad's khalifa, his lieutenant on earth. Several factors led to the choice. When Muhammad fell ill, he designated Abu Bakr to replace him as ritual prayer leader. Many interpreted that ritual selection as indicating Muhammad's political preferences. From the beginning, political authority and ritual leadership were closely intertwined. Further in Abu Bakr's favor, he was one of the oldest and most respected companions of the Prophet, one of the first converts to Islam, the man who was at Muhammad's side during the departure from Makka and who remained at the Prophet's side ever after.

Achieved leadership also played a role. Abu Bakr was not wealthy, nor militarily powerful, nor from a prominent patriline within the Quraysh. He was a deeply pious man who had achieved his faith and his position of leadership through sincere effort. Humility played a part. When he was first nominated, tradition remembers Abu Bakr as having declined, having proposed instead the selection of 'Umar. Abu Bakr's hesitancy about occupying Muhammad's political position was taken as a sign of his worthiness.

Abu Bakr's link to the Prophet through 'A'isha also entered in. Muhammad had several wives but 'A'isha had his heart, and it was in 'A'isha's house, at her side, that the great Prophet of God died. It was in that same house that the gathering of respected elders and the election took place. It is not surprising that 'A'isha's father was the man selected to rule.

Of the core cultural criteria highlighted above, only blood descent did not enter into Abu Bakr's selection, but blood descent entered the selection of a competing political authority on that very same night in another household on the Prophet's own compound.

blood dissenters   As remembered by the major alternative tradition, the Shi'i tradition, the selection of proper political authority in Islam took place in this way: a group of men met on the night of the Prophet's death in the house of the Prophet's daughter Fatima and her husband 'Ali, who, in addition to being Muhammad's son-in-law and the father of Muhammad's only grandsons, was Muhammad's close patrilineal cousin, Muhammad's father's brother's son, as indicated in figure 4.1. In fact, ʿAli was Muhammad's closest patrilineal relative, the nearest thing to brother or son that he had. Muhammad and ʿAli had grown up in the same household, that of ʿAli's father, Abu Talib, Muhammad's uncle. In the view of the men gathered in Fatima's house, patrilineal blood descent was the only proper criterion for political selection. Given ʿAli's patrilineal closeness to Muhammad, given the similarity of their blood essence, ʿAli was the proper inheritor of political leadership in Islam. Those who held this view became known as "Shiʿa ʿAli," "the partisans of ʿAli," or the Shiʿi. They are the major subsect within Islam.

Yet, in Shiʿi remembrance, once ʿAli learned of Abu Bakr's selection, to avoid bloodshed among the faithful, he did not contest the choice. Yet it was a wrongful choice in the Shiʿi view, and the cause of much worldly sorrow that followed.

As remembered by two separate communities of Muslims, it was on this first night, in two separate houses on Muhammad's compound, that the foundations were laid for what would become the major political split in Islam, that between mainstream Sunni Muslims, who accept the rightfulness of Abu Bakr's political selection, and the Shiʿi, who do not. The split centers on the nature of political inheritance, not on the nature of God, on which Sunni and Shiʿi agree.

Yet the conflict was not simply political. It was sexual as well, and affected the definition of femaleness that came to dominate Islam. In the first house lived the Prophet's wife ʿA'isha—dynamic, exuberant, sensual, and childless. In the second lived the Prophet's daughter Fatima—the staid and pious mother who is credited by some with having given virgin birth to the Prophet's grandsons.

Rashidun: rightly guided ones and ties of marriage

Abu Bakr reigned for two years, 632–634 (A.H. 11–13), then died of old age. Thereafter, three men succeeded him as caliph: ʿUmar, the great military commander; ʿUthman, the organizational strategist and member of the Quraysh's most powerful sublineage, the Banu Umayya; and ʿAli, the Prophet's patrilineal cousin (figure 4.1). These three men along with Abu Bakr became known to history as the Rashidun, the "Rightly Guided Ones."

The position the men occupied was the caliphate, yet they took on several titles. During the reign of ʿUmar, the proper titular designation for the caliph became *amir al-muʾminin*, which remains the proper title to this day. *Amir al-mu'minin* is translated as both "Commander of the Faithful" (e.g., by Waterbury 1970) and "Prince of the Faithful" (e.g., by Abun-Nasr 1987) and holds something of the semantic valence of both phrases in English. The amir al-mu'minin was the commander of the armed forces, just as today the president of the United States is the Commander-in-Chief; but, like the U.S. president, the amir also handled a great variety of political tasks. Those tasks are better reflected in the word "prince," though at first the office had no connotations of "noble blood" or ruling dynasty. In time, however, both developed.

The title of "Imam" was also taken by some of the early caliphs

---

FIGURE 4.1. Political Successors to Muhammad

FIRST CALIPHS

1. Abu Bakr	632–634 (A.H. 11–13)	distant Quraysh patriline	father-in-law
2. 'Umar	634–644 (A.H. 13–23)	distant Quraysh patriline	father-in-law
3. 'Uthman	644–656 (A.H. 23–35)	close patriline, linked through Muhammad's great-great-grandfather 'Abd al-Manaf	son-in-law
4. 'Ali	656–661 (A.H. 35–41)	closest patriline, linked through Muhammad's grandfather 'Abd al-Muttalib	son-in-law
5. Mu'awiya	661–680 (A.H. 41–60)	close patriline, linked through Muhammad's great-great-grandfather 'Abd al-Manaf	brother-in-law

IMPERIAL DYNASTIES

| 1. Banu Umayya | 661–750 (A.H. 41–132) | close patriline, linked through Muhammad's great-great-grandfather 'Abd al-Manaf | |
| 2. 'Abbasi | 750–1258 (A.H. 132–656) | closest patriline, linked through Muhammad's grandfather 'Abd al-Muttalib | |

NOTES:

Mu'awiya is the last Companion of Muhammad to rule, as well as the founder of the first imperial dynasty.

In genealogical terms, the patrilines of 'Ali and the 'Abbasi are equidistant from that of Muhammad.

and by many Muslim political rulers thereafter. "Imam" stresses the religious legitimacy that inheres in the position of overarching political leader of the Muslims. The role is not that of prophet. But the appelation of Imam accents the necessary spirituality of the man who is responsible for the temporal maintenance of the true faith.

Four characteristics unite the four Rashidun, the four Rightly Guided Ones, as well as Muʿawiya, the caliph who immediately follwed them. (That early Muslim history was written down after Muʿawiya's dynasty, by those who overthrew it, may be why Muʿawiya is not remembered as one of the Rashidun.) The characteristics are membership in the Quraysh, companionship with the Prophet, demonstrated leadership ability, and marriage ties to him. Only the last—the link through women—is a truly distinguishing characteristic, one that marks these five men off from a plethora of other candidates. The Quraysh numbered in the thousands, Muhammad's companions in the hundreds, potential leaders in the tens, but only a handful of men, including the five selected, were directly allied to the Prophet by ties of marriage. That the first five men chosen to rule were five men directly linked to the Prophet through the exchange of women is too consistent a pattern for the selection to have been a matter of happenstance.

Since Muhammad left no sons, the political community had to find another means of selecting his successors. Consciously or unconsciously, they used Muhammad's own decision making concerning marriage alliances as a guide. It was a plausible principle for narrowing the field of candidates, for by using it, the Muslim community selected people that Muhammad too had selected, people in whom he had such confidence that he made them his intimates.

Not only were all five early caliphs linked to Muhammed by ties of marriage, but the order of succession is one with which anthropologists are familiar—first fathers-in-law, then sons-in-law, then brothers-in-law. It is a common hierarchy for men linked through marriage. Fathers-in-law are typically those who derive most authority from the exchange of women. They give part of their blood essence to be the conduit for another patriline's children. A considerable debt is owed. Abu Bakr and ʿUmar were bride givers. Next come the bride takers, who receive the gift of the woman and are directly obligated to their father-in-law for it. ʿUthman and ʿAli were bride takers. And last comes the brother-in-law, whose own father is considered to have given the gift, and who by consequence is linked to the receiver of the bride in a relationship of more or less equality. He is one step removed from the role of bride giver and bride taker, but is still in intimate connection. Muʿawiya was thus linked and was in fact the last man to possess the entire spectrum of traits (that is, membership in the Quraysh, companionship with the Prophet, demonstrated leadership capacity, and a direct tie of marriage to Muhammad). The succession of several of the caliphs, including Muʿawiya, had been contested, but it was not until Muʿawiya's death—when there were no more men directly linked by marriage to the Prophet—that the most violent battle for political succession took place. When Muslims no longer had the Prophet's marriage hand to guide them, the underlying conflicts concerning what constituted proper political authority emerged full blown.

The conflict was bloody. It was waged between Muʿawiya's son, Yazid, and ʿAli's younger son, Husayn. The conflict of sons was a conflict of principles played out on the bleak plains of Karbalaʾ. Yazid claimed the caliphate on the earned leadership right, while Husayn claimed it on the basis of blood tie to the Prophet. Yazid and his practical base of power won, and he became the ruling authority of mainstream Islam. Husayn and blood descent lost. Husayn, the Prophet's own grandson, was beheaded by those who came to rule Dar al-Islam (the House of Islam). The Shiʿi, for whom Husayn was the only proper political authority, recount the battle with great sadness; they tell the stories of how individual members of the Prophet's family died, how Husayn's three-year-old daughter frantically searched the battlefield for her father, and when she finally found his headless body, lay down by him and died. Many of the Prophet's patrikin were there slain. The blood of the Prophet's patriline flowed freely on that unholy ground. For Shiʿi, the battle serves as orienting paradigm through which the world is viewed. It played a part in the twentieth-century Iranian revolution (Fischer 1980). The culture built from it is one of sorrow, cries, and lament. In Shiʿi understanding, history went awry, the wrong people won, and Islam's true political authority died cruelly.

lineal dynasties

Yazid was the first caliph in Islam to succeed his father, and Yazid's own son succeeded him. Hence Yazid's succession signals the transformation from the communal designation of authority to Islam's first lineal dynasty, the Banu Umayya. The patrilineal matrix associated with Islam became the guiding template as to who should rule, including its demand that leadership capacity be demonstrated within the overarching patriline; hence a man might be followed by his uncle or brother rather than by a son. The council of senior men—the spokesmen for the umma—was relegated to a position of affirming the selection that had already been made, rather than making the selection. These men demonstrated their affirmation in a ritual oath of allegiance, the *bayʿa*, which continues to be used in Morocco.

The Banu Umayya right to rule lay in basically secular criteria, and those who later seized power from them criticized them on that basis, labeling them as having ruled through a system of *mulk*, pure earthly kingship, rather than the caliphate. One should not take the succeeding dynasty's critique too seriously, yet the mulk label demonstrates an important dimension of Banu Umayya rule. Their claim to legitimacy lay in worldly success, in military victory, in economic prowess. By definition, any dynasty that comes to power must in some sense be successful on the ground. Yet while some dynasties rest their right to rule solely in the practical domain, others construct alternative foundations of legitimacy that insulate the dynasty from practical failure. The Banu Umayya did not develop that kind of insulation. They did not translate their military, economic, and administrative success into more mystical dimensions, and their reign lasted less than a century, 661–750 (A.H. 41–132).

The Banu Umayya were replaced by the ʿAbbasi as the central political authority of mainstream Islam. The ʿAbbasi dynasty developed a more multifaceted and durable model of rule, one that combined an emphasis upon on-the-ground success with an emphasis upon ritual verification and blood tie to the Prophet. When the former faded, the latter endured, as did the dynasty itself. Its reign lasted for over five hundred years, 750–1258 (A.H. 132–656).[2]

The ʿAbbasi developed an elaborate ritual foundation that supported their leadership through mystery, beauty, and high drama. They were specialists in color and performance. The population's vivid experience of them in ritual affected its valuation of the dynasty in the everyday.

The ʿAbbasi also insulated themselves by reintroducing into mainstream Islam blood link to Muhammad as a criterion of caliphal rule, but in a modified form as compared to the Shiʿi. The ʿAbbasi claimed relationship to the Prophet through Muhammad's patrilineal uncle ʿAbbas, as indicated in appendix a. (The dominant sects of Shiʿi Islam do not recognize the ʿAbbasi claim as legitimate; for them, rightful political authority can pass through the bloodline of Ali-Husayn only.) The ʿAbbasi represent an accommodation of the blood-descent stress with other more worldy criteria. But the accent on blood descent and its ritual elaboration provided the dynasty with durability. It commanded political loyalty to the "ruling" caliphs as rightful members of the Prophet's bloodline, as centers of Islam's performative dramas, even when practical power moved elsewhere.

During the early years of their reign, the 'Abbasi achieved worldly success, and the Islamic empire reached its greatest dimensions. Yet, later, the empire divided, and local and regional authorities began to take the reins of practical power into their hands. Still, much of the empire continued to regard the 'Abbasi as the luminous center—the true caliphate, the true successors to Muhammad—even if they no longer directly controlled the lines of administrative communication and military conquest. Their legitimacy was verified by the blood that flowed through their veins and the ritual experiences that flowed from their court in Baghdad, then queen of cities.

They endured. The 'Abbasi caliphate continued to inform political life in much of the Muslim world from the 750s (A.H. 132) until the Mongol sack of Baghdad in 1258 (A.H. 656). In the nature of the political construction and in its durability in time, the 'Abbasi foreshadowed the model of political authority that emerged in Morocco in the crisis of the 1500s (A.H. 900s) and endures to the present. In both systems, the Prophet's blood and ritual experience insulated the rulers from wayward political winds.

Mainstream Islam, Sunni Islam, recognizes the first four caliphs, as well as the rulers of the Banu Umayya and 'Abbasi imperial dynasties, as proper political successors to Muhammad. A single criterion unites them all—membership in the Quraysh, which is a general nod to the relevance of patrilineal affiliation and biological descent since the Quraysh is considered to be a vast group of patrilineally related kinsmen. Beyond this membership, authority was consolidated by particular rulers and dynasties through distinct combinations of the practices and principles we have highlighted as well as others. Islamic forms of political rule exhibit considerable diversity. Yet the diversity lies within bounds. There are three main forms of Islamic political authority, noted below, and all three of them, through all the ages, have been male. Until the present, patriarchy has reigned supreme in Islam, and patrilineality has often been crucial in political ascent (see appendix a).

Islam's three divisions

piety, election, and egalitarianism: the Khawarij   The Khawarij are the smallest of the three major subsects of Islam. They comprise less than 1 percent of the total Muslim population. They broke off from the mainstream through their doctrinal adherence to the notion of the equality of all believers and the demand that leaders be communally elected. The Khawarij take the Qurʾanic stress on equality and communal legitimacy to its logical conclusion: all Muslims are born equal, only through achievement do distinctions emerge, neither blood relationship to Muhammad nor de facto domination of the structures of power are legitimate reasons for rule. Achieved piety and earned leadership capacity are what matters, and those qualities are best discerned by knowledgeable male elders of the community, who should elect the proper caliph. It is a populist model of rule; responsibility flows from the bottom up. When the system is full blown, there can be no lineal dynasties among the Khawarij, for each ruler must be selected on the basis of his own personal qualities.

The Khawarij departed from the mainstream during the battle of Siffin when Muʿawiyya and ʿAli were fighting for the caliphate (A.D. 657; A.H. 37). In the heat of battle ʿAli agreed to arbitration, demonstrating—from the Khawarij perspective—that he was not the true caliph, because they do not view arbitration to be legitimate in those circumstances. Since they perceived his decision making to be illegitimate, the Khawarij walked out of the battle and away from the mainstream, whence comes their name, which literally means "to walk away, to leave, to go outside." For the Khawarij, the fact that ʿAli was related to Muhammad by ties of blood was no reason to remain with him when he proved, through his own actions, that he was not the proper caliph.

blood relationship to Muhammad: the Shiʿi   The Shiʿi comprise 11 percent of all Muslims. Most live in Iran and Iraq. They are distinguishable from the mainstream through their doctrinal adherence to the view that direct blood link to Muhammad's patriline is the only legitimate criterion of Muslim rule. The dominant forms of Shiʿi Islam specify that only descendants through the direct patriline of ʿAli and Husayn are true leaders of the faith and heads of the political community. These leaders are the Imams. The Shiʿi are divided into subsects according to the number of Imams they accept. The largest subsect, the "Twelvers," accept twelve legitimate inheritors. In their view, the last true Imam did not die, but rather went into occultation (hiding) because of the waywardness of the world. This last rightful ruler, this "Hidden Imam," disappeared in 874 (A.H. 260). Hence, these Shiʿi have been without a rightful ruler, a true Imam, for over a thousand years. Yet, the Shiʿi believe that someday he will return to bring about the reign of justice. In that day, the martyrdom of Husayn and the wrongful decision making of the world will be overturned. In the interim, the Shiʿi accommodate themselves to the world and to the very limited authority of earth's rulers. The Ayatullah Khomeini of Iran was a Shiʿi but he was not *the* Imam; he was only *an* imam, in the lesser sense of a prayer leader. His official title "Ayatullah" literally meant "a sign of God." He was believed by many to be a sign, but he was not the hidden one returned, and his authority was intrinsically limited.

The Shiʿi position is the logical opposite of the Khawarij view. From the Shiʿi perspective, popular selection has no place in determining the proper political authority in Muhammad's absence. This authority is ordained by God and passes down through Muhammad's bloodline to a specified number of descendants, the Imams. These descendants are endowed with special religious capacities; they are ultimate religious authorities. In Shiʿi ideals, political and religious authority merge; yet because the world has failed to recognize the proper authorities, the merger has thus far not been practically realized. For the Shiʿi, when the twelfth Imam returns he will be that combination. They are intrinsically hierarchical.

real-world success, political and economic might: the Sunni The definition of political authority that won out in history—the mainstream—is compromising and pragmatic. It is held by the 88 percent of all Muslims, who are known as Sunni Muslims, that is, the followers of the Sunna, "the Beaten Pathway." Their name reflects their practical stance toward the world. They have always been accommodationist, adopting neither the doctrinaire Khawarij nor the doctrinaire Shiʿi view. The Sunni stand in between, taking the reasonable position that, in terms of political authority, it all depends. Sometimes a blood descendant is legitimate, sometimes not. Sometimes communal election is pivotal, sometimes not. Sometimes a monarchy is appropriate, sometimes not. Sometimes military rule is legitimate, sometimes not. Sunni Muslims do not categorically deny any of the principles or practices that exist within Islam's broad constitutive repertoire of political authority, nor do they accept any single combination of them as inevitable for all time. For the Sunni, what really matters is what works, what successfully establishes Islamic political authority in the world. This politically pragmatist view is theologically legitimated by the conviction that God is supremely concerned about the survival of the Muslim community in the world, and hence what ensures worldly survival is divinely sanctioned.

Morocco is a part of this mainstream. Morocco's emphasis on sharifi descent lies within Sunni parameters. Most Shiʿi do not accept the blood tie that Moroccan rulers claim as legitimizing political authority, since it is through Hasan, not Husayn (see appendix a). Muhammad's grandson Hasan originally challenged Muʿawiya's occupancy of the caliphate, but then acceded to it, accepting the generous pension that Muʿawiya offered and living out his days in comfort in Makka. Morocco's Sunni rulers trace their descent from this politically accommodationist grandson, an appropriate archetypal figure for mainstream Islam, in contradistinction to the uncompromising and martyred Husayn, the Shiʿi archetype, who may well have gained God's glory in heaven but whose life was snuffed out on earth.

definition of women

The definition of political authority that came to dominate Islam's mainstream political culture is related to the definition of women that came to dominate Islam's mainstream sexual culture. Men came to be understood as those who could control their nature, connect to the divine, make hard-nosed collective decisions on behalf of the whole, and consciously carry out life's most difficult actions. Women in contrast came to be defined as those rightfully excluded from those domains because of their closeness to nature and their difficulty in transcending its bounds.

ʿAʾisha versus Fatima

The Islamic definition of female, like the definition of political authority, did not come ready-made but was established in an active battle in history, when particular interpretations won out over others. The battle for political definition pitted the icon of Abu Bakr against the icon of ʿAli, that is, the political ruler selected by achievement against the political ruler selected by claims of blood descent. The battle for sexual definition, as Denise Spellberg demonstrates (1989), pitted the icon of Abu Bakr's daughter ʿAʾisha against the icon of ʿAli's wife Fatima—the dynamic, forceful, and childless female against the obedient and reserved wife and mother. Both were women close to the Prophet, ʿAʾisha his favorite wife, Fatima one of his daughters. In terms of political definition, a compromise was reached between the two male icons and the respective principles they embodied, but in terms of the female definition, the dynamic ʿAʾisha lost and the retiring Fatima won.

'A'isha and political influence 'A'isha was bright and assertive; she gave the Prophet much tenderness but no children. 'A'isha spoke with assurance about herself and confirmed her own favor in the Prophet's eyes:

> Muhammad married no other wife as a virgin except me. He did not marry anyone else whose mother and father were both *muhajirun* [early converts who made the flight from Makka to Madina]. God sent down my innocence from heaven. ['A'isha was charged with adultery when she was fourteen and was later cleared through a Qur'anic revelation.] The angel Gabriel brought Muhammad my picture in silk from heaven saying "Marry her, for she is your wife." I used to wash with Muhammad from a single vessel and he did not do that with any of his wives except me. And he used to pray while I was in his presence. He received a Revelation while he was with me and this did not happen to him when he was with any other of his wives. Muhammad died in my arms. He died on a night which was turned over to me. He was buried in my house.
>
> (From a ninth century Hadith, quoted in Spellberg 1989)

Muhammad died in 'A'isha's arms, her father became the first caliph of Islam, and after his death she was involved in the political battling that decided who would rule. 'A'isha held a position of respect in the early community and then, as well as later, was often referred to as the "Mother of the Faithful." She apparently was involved in the attempt to overthrow the caliph 'Uthman and clearly was involved in the battle against 'Ali, known to history as the Yawm al-Jamal, "the Day of the Camel." She oversaw the battle mounted on camelback (and thus, some argue, gave the battle its name). 'A'isha's forces lost, and she was sent back to Madina and confined to her home. It seems possible that if 'A'isha and those associated with her had won, a different, much more public and political image of the female might have become dominant in the sexual-political matrix of Islam. But her forces lost and the dynamic 'A'isha was secluded within household walls, and by many Muslims in the centuries that followed she was saddled with demeaning interpretations. Many blamed her for inciting political dissent in the early house of Islam, and many continued to call her an adulteress. The undermining of 'A'isha took place despite the fact that she was so clearly valued in Muhammad's eyes, and despite the fact that the Qur'an itself clears her of the charge of adultery. Muslims, like all people, are selective in terms of which of their body of unalterable truths they emphasize.

Fatima and virgin birth ʿAʾisha's competitor for dominant cultural definition was Fatima, Muhammad's daughter, who was nearly a decade older than ʿAʾisha. As Henri Lammens (1912) noted, the figure of Fatima is less "historically" known, for she died soon after the Prophet, and fewer of the generally accepted early Hadith concern her. Yet it is this historically veiled Fatima who won the competition for Muslim womanhood (see Spellberg 1989). She became the archetypal image of the proper female.

Fatima came to be adored especially by the Shiʿi, but the adoration informed the female image that came to dominate all of Islam. The Shiʿi adoration bears similarities to the Christian adoration of the Virgin Mary. Fatima is a Mary-like figure, thought by some to have been a virgin when she conceived Husayn. Fatima is imaged as a quiet and obedient wife who achieves motherhood through piety—not sexuality. This asexual mother became the proper woman in the dominant tradition in Islam, as did Mary in the dominant tradition in Christianity. Her virginity sexually neutralizes her. Through the neutering, the Islamic mother loses her potential hold over men, which Islam considers to lie in her sexuality. Neutered, she is threatening neither to men nor to the faith.

Yet, in truth, even ʿAli, Fatima's husband, seems to have had mixed feelings about her. He wanted to take a second wife while she was still alive, but the Prophet Muhammad forbade it. ʿAli having married the daughter of the Prophet of God, the Prophet would allow him to take no other wives. (What Muhammad himself did and what he would allow the men who married his daughters to do were different things.)

descent Those who argue that Fatima gave virgin birth to Husayn also settle the otherwise problematic issue that in strict cultural terms neither of the Prophet's grandsons, Husayn nor Hasan, is a part of his patriline, nor are any of their descendants—for their father, Ali, not their mother, Fatima, would have given them their lineal association. Hasan and Husayn belong to the patriline that produced Muhammad, the patriline that descended from Muhammad's grandfather ʿAbd al-Muttalib. But they would not be descendants of Muhammad himself, he left no sons to pass on that descent (see appendix a). Rather, as sons of Ali, Hasan and Husayn would be descendants of the ʿAbd al-Muttalib/Abu Talib/ʿAli branch of ʿAbd al-Muttalib's patriline.

It is some Shiʿi who most elaborate the notion of virgin birth, and they naturally concentrate their attention on Husayn. In the case of his miraculous conception, where no human father was involved,

Husayn's "blood" identity would have come from his mother. It would have been constructed from Fatima's own blood substance which she acquired from her father, the Prophet Muhammad. In that case, Husayn would be Muhammad's true descendant.

The majority of mainstream Muslims, the Sunni, do not argue for Fatima's having given virgin birth to Muhammad's grandsons, but simply—without argument—unquestioningly accept that Fatima and no other woman was able to pass on patrilineal descent, to pass on Muhammad's literal blood affiliation. For instance, Moroccan sharif (of which there are many) boldly trace their descent through the bloodline of Muhammad/Fatima/Hasan and claim to be full blood descendants of the great Prophet, allowing a singular female exception in multiple generations of male-carried blood affiliation.

There was a struggle in Muslim history over which image of woman—'A'isha or Fatima—would dominate, and eventually the submissive image of Fatima won on both sides of the Sunni and Shi'i divide. As Spellberg (1989) argues, that victory was not definitively achieved until the 900s and 1000s (A.H. 300s and 400s), but once consolidated, it endured. Patriarchy selects for a submissive image of the female. While politically useful, it is personally inhibiting.

kingdom of mothers

With Fatima's victory the image of the ideal Muslim woman came to be the pious, asexual mother of her husband's children who does her husband's bidding in organizing his household, bearing his descendants, and bringing him honor. Islam, as Bouhdiba (1985) argues, created a kingdom of mothers. The variety of images of the female that are possible for humanity, some of which existed in early Islam, were lost.

Early Islam exhibits much the same trajectory in the definition of the female as does early Christianity (see Pagels 1988 for the Christian definition). Islam has its 'A'isha just as Christianity has its Mary Magdalene. Both are highly charged sexual and sensual females—the one suspected of adultery in the desert, the other confirmed of prostitution—and yet each is valued as somehow intrinsically pure and good in the eyes of the founder of the faith, Muhammad or Jesus. It seems plausible that these founders did not dichotomize sexuality and spirituality in the ways that their followers did, and in fact found them persuasively combined in these women. Yet their esteem for that combination was not to endure. Neither 'A'isha nor Mary Magdalene became the dominant image of the proper female in the respective cultural traditions that arose out of the two faiths. Muslims on the whole find blasphemous the notion that it might have been good for ʿAʾisha to have won at the Battle of the Camel, to have become an important political actor in Islam and a public model for other women, while Christians on the whole find blasphemous the notion that Jesus might have exchanged sexual tenderness with Mary Magdalene (see Nelson 1978:11–13). What is considered blasphemous says much about where the hearts of the two religious traditions lie.

Yet it could be argued that the founders of the two faiths were broader in their understanding of the possible combinations of faith, womanhood, and sexuality than the majority of their followers, and that they made that acceptance clear—Muhammad by dying in ʿAʾisha's arms and Jesus by first appearing after his crucifixion to Mary Magdalene, whom he authorized to go and tell the male disciples the earthshaking news that he still lived. These events are recorded in the hallowed texts. Yet the dominant cultural perspectives that have developed in the contexts of these faiths for the most part leave by the wayside these two women as embodiments of proper womanhood and instead concentrate the collectivity's attention and definitions on immaculate conception and virginal mothers.

Numerous analysts from the Muslim tradition have critically evaluated the image of the female in historical Islam, including Bouhdiba (1985), Mernissi (1987a, 1987b, and 1988), Musallam (1983), Naamane-Guessous (1987), and Sabbah (1984). Boudhiba summarizes their position well:

> Of course everything is expressed in subtle terms and the status of women is certainly ambiguous, even in the Qurʾan itself. . . . Nevertheless, a male-worshipping society [emerged and led] to the negation of women. . . . [the dominant sexual culture in Islam] is nothing less than the sacralization of the masculine and the trivialization of the feminine.
>
> (1985:213)

Islam's dominant sexual culture allocates to women the position of being that part of humanity that is closest to nature and hence least able to transcend its natural drives, including sexual impulses, and therefore least able to connect with the divine who exists beyond the natural realm. Consequently, females are understood to be in need of male supervision, because men—in the culture's imagination—are defined as able to keep their natural inclinations in control.

As Mernissi (1987a) forcefully argues, Islamic sexual culture emphasizes the female as a powerful, seductive temptress who—consciously or unconsciously—is driven to capture the hearts and souls of men and bind them to her, interfering with the male's ability to focus on God. Islam is not, Mernissi argues, so much straightforwardly against women as it is against a strong heterosexual bond that would pose a competition for Islam's cultural construction of a God who exists beyond nature and men who should invest the best of their being in him—above with God, not below with women.

kingdom of sirens

In the Islamic sexual culture that has come to dominate, the woman is conceived as the ultimate *femme fatale*—a nearly irresistible seductress who can bring men earthly pleasure but can cause their downfall also. Islam's kingdom of asexual mothers necessitated a kingdom of sexual sirens. Hence men must be on their guard, careful, controlled, and contained around women, never giving females their essential selves. Women are in Islamic sexual culture seen as natural and powerful, to be feared and physically contained. Mernissi (1987a) compares this image with the Western construction of the female. She argues that the dominant Western image of the female is also marginalizing, but in a different way; the Western image emphasizes passiveness. In the West, women have come to be defined as impotent—natural lightweights who by their nature are marginalized. Their impotency bridges sexual and political domains. Cultural containment is accomplished through psychological cloaking and psychological reclusiveness rather than physical separation. Western women wear their veils inside. In Islam, in contrast, the female is defined as naturally potent in the sexual domain and therefore must be actively controlled through physical veiling and physical seclusion. In fact, Mernissi argues, both images of the female—as sexually potent and as naturally impotent— exist in both places, but in Islam the first image became dominant while the second took the role of subtheme, while in the West the second became dominant and the first became the subtheme (see Mernissi 1987a:30–45).

The Islamic view of woman as the *femme fatale* is well developed in the literature (see Mernissi 1987a:41–45 for a summary). According to the Hadith, Muhammad said:

> After my disappearance there will be no greater source of dissension and sedition for my nation than women.
>
> (Hadith, al-Bukhari, book 67, Nikah, section 18, no. 4;
> 1868:5:554)

When the woman comes towards you, it is Satan who is approaching you. When one of you sees a woman and he feels attracted to her, he should hurry to his wife. With her, it would be the same as with the other one.

     (Hadith, al-Tirmidhi, book 9, Nikah, no. 1167; n.d. 2:413)

Muslim men have reinforced what the Prophet said ever since. For instance:

Never trust in women; nor rely upon their vows;
For their pleasure and displeasure depend upon their passions.
They offer a false affection
         for perfidy lurks within their clothing.
By the tale of Yusuf be admonished, and guard against their
         stratagems.
Does thou not consider that Iblis ejected Adam by means of
         woman?
         (*The Thousand and One Nights* 1889:9)

Women are fleeting wooden vessels
Whose passengers are doomed to destruction.

         (a Moroccan proverb)

Women's intrigues are mighty
To protect myself I run endlessly
Women are belted with serpents
And bejewelled with scorpions.

         (al-Majdhub 1966[1500s]:153)

Love is a complicated matter
If it does not drive you crazy, it kills you.
     (a Moroccan proverb, quoted in Westermarck 1930:330)

Islam considers sexual pleasure, like other human drives, not wrong in and of itself, but rather in need of proper control and channeling. In the Islamic view, the sexual impulse demands satisfaction for psychological health, for the release of nervous tension. It is a biological need that must be satisfied, but men should not invest in the vessels that bring them satisfaction. According to Islam's imagination, it is emotional attachment to the woman, not sexual intercourse with her, that is the real danger to man and faith. What is important and durable is God. On earth, physical satisfaction needs to be kept on a temporal plane.

Women are conceived as possessing a nearly irresistible sexual attractiveness that can capture men's souls. Hence men must be on their guard around women. The Arabic word for a beautiful women is *fitna*, also the word for dissension, sedition (Mernissi 1987a:31). As constructed in Islam's imagination, only in heaven can men finally relax around beautiful women because God creates a heavenly form of woman there for man's use—the great wide-eyed huris, who have no will of their own, but are simply beautiful things designed to satisfy man's sexual longing. They are virgins demurely cloaked in seventy veils (Bouhdiba 1985:72–77 and Sabbah 1984:91–91). In heaven, orgasm becomes a purely male domain, while in Islamic understandings of earthly sexual relationships, the female's craving for orgasm must be satisfied. God creates for male believers the ideal type of Islamic woman in heaven, not an earthly woman who is transformed, but a different creature: physically exquisite, completely passive, solely for the use of man's sexual satisfaction. She is transparent; like a crystal, man can actually see through her. How many huris the believer receives depends on how pious he was on earth. With the huris man's orgasm lasts for twenty-four years:

> Every man who observes the fast during the whole month of ramadan is married by God to a huri of paradise of a special type known as *hur al'ayn* [black-eyed huri] and God sets them in a tent hollowed out of a white pearl. Each huri wears seventy veils. Each man has seventy alcoves, each carved out of a red hyacinth. In each alcove are arranged seventy beds; on each bed is a woman [a huri] awaiting the Chosen One [the male believer]. . . .
>
> One grows more beautiful with every day. One's appetite increases a hundred fold. One eats and drinks to one's heart's content. Man's sexual potency is also multiplied. One makes love as on earth but each climax is extended and extended lasts for twenty-four years.
>
> (Boudhiba 1985:75)

With the huri, sexual satisfaction is neverending, and not marred by fear as it is on earth. Men have nothing to fear from the huris, for they have no personalities, no individual desires, no chance for roaming; the Qur'an guarantees their virginity, that they will not have been touched by man nor jinn when the believing male enters them, and they will be permanently attached to the man to whom they are given. Heaven as portrayed in the Qur'an and Hadith is, among other things, a man's sexual playfield.

The place of flesh and blood women in Islam's envisioned paradise is enormously problematic. Though believing women of earth are guaranteed entry,

> when you look at the spatial logistics . . . in Paradise, you realize
> that it is space equipped, on the level of sexuality, solely for the
> believer of the male sex. Not only does he have a sexual partner,
> the huri, who makes the earthly wife's value to her husband ex-
> tremely marginal, but also nowhere in Paradise are the needs of this
> earthly woman taken into consideration.
>
> (Sabbah 1984:94)

In fact, Sabbah concludes, in Islam's image of paradise, the earthly
wife becomes "more and more a phantom, if not a sour note in the
divine harmony" (Sabbah 1984:95). Of course, in point of fact, the
huri is the real phantom as her transparency shows, but she is central
to Islam's paradise vision, while flesh and blood women are imagined
out of its existence.

Christianity's imagination of paradise is asexual, while Islam's is
one of infinite male orgasm. For those who would ennoble the sexual
act, Islam's imagination has some advantages; it speaks of sexuality
in highly poetic and lyrical terms. Yet this imagination is profoundly
limited, for it does not apply sacrality to sex between partners on
earth. It does not allow the man to have sacred sex with a real woman,
only with the imagined huris in heaven. What is more, that quintessential intercourse—that fundamental orienting frame of heavenly
reference that informs life below—is not a culminating act of unification between two dynamic entities, both of whom have desires, understandings, and insight. It is a male act of sex performed on a heavenly doll, patriarchy *absurdus*. In Islam's imagination, sacred sex is
biased towards the man and towards heaven, so that it profoundly
interferes with the depth of intimacy that males and females can experience on earth. It does not allow the man to spiritually, emotionally, and sexually invest where he plausibly could.

Christianity interferes in other ways. Its dominant tradition denies
sanctity to the sexual act itself and tends to inhibit sex on earth and
deny its existence in heaven. Islam allows sexual intercourse on earth
and in heaven, but it gives ultimate sanctity only to the act in heaven,
sex performed with a nonhuman female. Christianity's sexual culture
encourages sexual abstinence, while Islam's encourages sexual engagement but emotional abstinence.

In Islam's cultural imagination, earthly women are to be feared,
for they have their own personalites, aims, and sexual passions. They
are only once the much-desired untouched virgin whom the man breaks
open. After the breaking, the female loses much of her worth in the

cultural imagination, for her sexual desires, like Pandora's box, have been unleashed, and she is no longer considered pure.

The dominant sexual culture of Islam systematically works against the heterosexual bond (Bouhdiba 1985, Mernissi 1987a). Bouhdiba summarizes:

> There is a progressive decline of the Muhammadan ethic of marital tenderness. . . . Arabo-Muslim . . . practice has led to the enclosure of women in a double role as objects of pleasure and as producers of children. In either case we are dealing with woman-as-objects. A cruel contradiction! On the one hand there is a persistent tendency to sing the praises of sexuality, to celebrate love, to encourage a lyrical view of life. The libidinous forces are exalted, liberated, even unleashed. . . . But, on the other hand, sexual dimorphism ends ultimately to place all positivity on the side of masculinity and to empty femininity of all value. To be more precise, femininity is reduced to being no more than the obverse of masculinity. Woman is the shadow of man, in the literal as well as the figurative sense. Everywhere denied, femininity hides itself and seeks refuge: woman becomes a creature of the home and of night.
>
> (1985:214)

In the mainstream Islamic culture, the female is allocated the role of being the giver of temporal pleasure and the physical producer of the man's children. In each role she earns her worth by and through men, and her worth is inherently transitory. The role of giver of sensual pleasure is especially short-term. The woman's body can provide the man immediate sexual release, but he must not become psychologically attached to her. That would give her an enduring hold over him, and she cannot be trusted. She is both evil and temporal. One should not give valuable, durable things to evanescent creatures. According to the Hadith, the Prophet Muhammad himself said, "God made us love three things in this earthly world of ours: perfume, women, and, that which is most pleasing to me, ritual prayer" (al-Ghazzali 1953[1000s]:33).

The woman satisfies in the moment; that is all. The proper Muslim male is to construct his relationship with a woman taking this into account. He allows her to give him sexual release, which any other woman can also give. Tenderness, the exchange of heart and soul in an act of intercourse that is itself a part of a long-term relationship of mutual commitment and interdependency, does not receive much articulation in the dominant foundations of Islamic sexual culture, though it is not totally denied there either. One could argue that the relationship between Khadija and Muhammad must have been one such as this, but that elaboration has not yet received a prominent place in collective remembrance. Individual exceptions exist, but they remain individual exceptions, not something that collectively emerges from the mainstream culture.

The one role for a proper Islamic woman that has an element of durability and gives her some hold over males is becoming the mother of male children, for they are durable creatures. Their names and their male progeny will carry on their father's bloodline. The mother remains their mother as long as the sons live, and she is honored in that role. Yet the remembrance and the honor die with the sons, while the patriline lives forever.

As Bouhdiba argues, Islam's valorization of the role of mother has as an underside the devaluation of the role of the woman as wife-companion-friend. The constructions that have come to dominate the sexual culture of Islam leave available to women two main options, the kingdom of mothers or the kingdom of sirens. Most women who are able choose the former. Yet, many Muslim women are no longer accepting the rigidity of the formulation and are demanding that Muslim men and the Muslim faith expand its horizons. After all, the Prophet's horizons, even in the constraints of the 600s, were larger. The Prophet Muhammad married and was faithful to the successful commercialist Khadija, and he adored the dynamic and childless 'A'isha, prayed in her midst, received revelations in her presence, washed from the same basin, and died in her arms. The holy book itself reveals 'A'isha's worth and confirms that she controlled her "natural" impulses when left alone with another man in the desert. Muslim women are attempting to expand the options of what they can legitimately be, but they, like Christian and Jewish woman involved in similar expansions, are finding that sexual culture is recalcitrant to change, in part because political culture is so bound to it. Culture's constructions of power are deeply embedded in its constructions of sex.

The Thousand and One Nights

Popular cultural stories both emerge from and reinforce sacred culture. Over the ages, one of the most popular compilations of tales in the Muslim world has been *The Thousand and One Nights*. The overarching context in which the stories are set is itself the logical culmination of two dominant themes that have developed within the sexual culture of Islam: first, that sexual intercourse ideally takes place within the bond of marriage, and second, that women are by definition conniving seductresses whom one cannot trust and to whom one should not become emotionally attached. These themes yield the *ad extremum* of *The Thousand and One Nights*, a book that begins with the premise of a caliph who kills each of his brides on their wedding night after having intercourse with her. As the story goes, the caliph began this violent and unusual practice after discovering his first wife's sexual betrayal of him. He had been deeply attached to her, but caught her and his manservant *in flagrante delicto* and killed them both. Her betrayal, so it is said, revealed to the caliph the true nature of women, and so he began the practice of contracting marriages with young and beautiful virgins (a foretaste of the huris of heaven), having intercourse with them, and then killing them before they had a chance of betraying him—a foolproof way of ensuring legitimate sexual satisfaction within the bond of marriage while simultaneously making certain that the woman would gain no emotional hold over him. The temporal creature was gone by morning; his practice ensured her departure. (Of course, the practice did not address the need for male progeny; one can only assume that the great caliph must have had enough sons already.)

Then in walks Shahrazad, the daughter of the wise *wazir* (advisor), who has inherited not only her father's patrilineal affiliation, but also part of her father's wisdom. Through that wisdom, Shahrazad manages to contain her natural seductress nature and save her own life by telling the great caliph wonderful tales. She still seduces him, but through words rather than sex. This popular folktale portrays the use of words—storytelling—as a more noble and durable means of female seduction. Instead of having sexual intercourse with the caliph, Shahrazad spins stories through the night that bring the caliph so much pleasure that he spares her life until each story is finished. But having finished one story, Shahrazad wisely begins the next. And so Shahrazad tells a thousand and one tales on a thousand and one nights, and in the end softens the caliph's hatred and madness.

Yet *The Thousand and One Nights* is a variation on, not a confrontation of, the major cultural themes. The female remains dependent on the male for her existence, for her life itself. Her ability to bring the man pleasure, to entertain him, can give her a degree of worth in his eyes and therefore some influence on him. But her influence is indirect and subordinate, dependent on his whim, while his control is direct and forthright.

Islam incorporated into its faith the patrilineal kinship idiom and the images of male and female intrinsic to it and made those images sacred by embedding them in its founding myths and practices. Those myths and practices then along with more popular myths and practices, like the tales of Shahrazad and their retelling in time and place, continually reinforced the worth of these basic definitions in daily life. And so men in Islam came to be defined as in control of the economic, political, and durable domains, while women came to be defined as in control of the private, individual, and evanescent dimensions—the home and the night. The ideal mother, wife, and daughter came to be understood as the one who constrains—and allows the men around her to constrain—her potentially dangerous sexuality, her tendency to sedition as well as seduction.

Women disappear from view in my next chapters. The tendency for women to be excluded from public life, to drop out of historical consciousness, becomes apparent in the telling of my tale. I switch my focus from the cultural foundations of Islam to a historical overview of major political and economic institutions of Morocco during the first seven centuries after the coming of Islam. These are domains inhabited by men; hence, in summarizing them, I temporarily set aside my consideration of the relationship between political culture and sexual culture. Yet when I subsequently turn to Morocco's age of reconstruction, the link between political definition and sexual definition will again be prominent and will remain so through the rest of the book.

HISTORICAL SUCCESS
AND CRISIS

Islam and potent glory
bubonic plague

5

Islam and potent glory

Within only forty years of Muhammad's death, Islamic conquest forces already had reached Morocco, the far northwest corner of Africa, 3,000 miles to Makka's west. The story is told that the Muslim commander, ʿUqba ibn Nafiʿ, drove his stallion into the Atlantic's waves and when the steed would go no further, cried out that only this great body of water kept him from traveling on to spread the faith (Abun-Nasr 1987:28–32; Laroui 1977a:79–101; Levi-Provencal 1954:27–31). The western limit of the first age of Muslim expansion had been reached, and Morocco formed its outer boundary. In Arabic, the land was called *al-maghrib*, the far west, the land of the setting sun. The Muslim prayer of sunset takes its name from that location.

land and people

Al-maghrib, Morocco, is a spectacularly beautiful land set off by dramatic geographical boundaries. A 900-mile stretch of churning Atlantic forms its western border while a 240-mile stretch of blue Mediterranean is its northernmost boundary. The north is made even more dramatic because there the Rif Mountains loom over the sea. The Greeks thought that the gods inhabited this awesome land. There Atlas stood and Hercules walked. Snow-capped mountains, the Middle Atlas, form Morocco's eastern boundary and merge into the even higher High Atlas Mountains to the south. The Atlas is a rugged range that resembles the Swiss Alps, with omnipresent snow and no vegetation on the higher peaks. In spring, when the sun shines clean and strong, the snow begins to melt, water flows freely down the mountainsides, and blossoming almond trees cover the lower slopes.

Within these rugged natural barriers—seas to the west and north, mountains to the east and south—lies Morocco's heartland, its central plains through which rivers flow. When rains fall and the locusts do not strike, the plains produce wheat and barley in abundance. From Roman times, the plains have been Morocco's breadbasket as well as

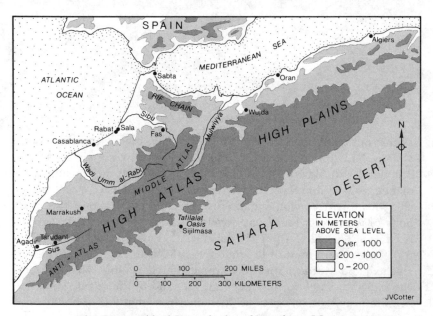

The Geographical Boundaries of Northern Morocco

the seat of its imperial dynasties. Yet much of the country's vitality has always lain in the deep south, the land beyond the High Atlas. There sprawls the Great Sahara, mostly dry and parched, yet streams of water trickling down from the snowcapped Atlas Mountains form long thin oases that divide the Saharan brown with ribbons of rich green.

From the beginning, diversity has been Morocco's earmark. Before the Arabs came, Northwest Africa was inhabited by Berber-speaking peoples. Theories about the origins of Berbers are diverse and contradictory. They were and are a composite people with diverse physical and cultural characteristics, the result of frequent in-migrations into the region. Most of the early migrations were apparently from western Asia, but contacts with southwestern Europe existed also. Berbers were not and are not a homogenous ethnic group; they did not develop an overarching consciousness of themselves as a distinctive entity; they do not refer to themselves as such (Abun-Nasr 1987:2). Collective identity, then and now, among peoples who happen to speak Berber, is based on other, more circumscribed ethnic and political criteria, having to do with distinctive sociocultural groups in which they participate (e.g. the Tuareg, the Moroccan nation) or with the distinctive dialects they speak, e.g. tashilhayt or tamizgart. In Morocco, three structurally similar but mutually unintelligible dialects of Berber are spoken. Hence, the only basis we have for lumping Berbers together is linguistic (Bousquet 1957: 8–13). Berber speakers were not and are not culturally, socially, nor genetically distinct at the level of the category as a whole. The label "Berber" itself comes from outside, from the Greek term *barbaros*, originally used to designate people who did not speak Greek.

Into these already diversified peoples came further waves of people, diverse migrations. Phoenicians, Greeks, Romans, Vandals, and Byzantines all came to Northwest Africa, interacted with the local people, and left their imprint. During the height of Roman power, what is now Morocco was first attached to Rome as an allied state, then later directly incorporated into the Empire. One of Morocco's indigenous rulers, Juba II, married the daughter of Mark Antony and Cleopatra. After the collapse of Rome, overarching political unity dissolved, but Morocco's population remained fairly prosperous. Compared to the rest of North Africa and the Middle East, Morocco's land is good and the water is abundant. After Rome and before Islam, the population lived in relatively dispersed agricultural units, made use of the Roman plow, planted barley, cultivated olives and almonds, and kept herds of sheep and goats (see Bulliet 1975:111–140 and 1981). Most were polytheists, although Christianity and Judaism had made some inroads.

Then came the Arabs and Islam, adding even greater diversity to an already enormously complex and diversified population. Multiple organizational models continued to be vital, especially on local levels, and portions of the Moroccan population continued to speak their particular dialect of Berber within their home and local community (Berber does not exist in written form, with the very rare exception of writing produced by a handful of Tuareg women). Approximately half of the Moroccan population speaks one of the three Berber dialects as their mother tongue, though most, especially the men, speak Arabic as well. Indigenous Moroccans come in all forms; they range from tall and elegant to short and stocky, from men and women with dark skin, brown eyes, and black hair, to those with fair skin, blue eyes, and blond hair. One can even find an occasional redhead.

Islam's beginnings

Morocco's natural boundaries are often given as reasons for the country's success in keeping western Europe at bay during the pivotal 1500-to-1900 era (A.H. 900–1300). Yet the geographical barriers did not keep out Islam, nor any of the earlier migrations. Quite the contrary, waves of other people descended upon Morocco's fair land. Other explanations must be given for Morocco's successful resistance to the West. Starting in the late 600s (the first century after the hijra), those waves of emigrants were Arabic and Islamic. They were proselytizers of the new faith who penetrated the Moroccan countryside and overcame initial resistance. In time, local peoples converted with depth and sincerity, and became themselves Islamic proselytizers. Morocco became a center of the Islamic faith. By the 1000s and 1100s (A.H. 400s and 500s), Morocco's peoples—long-term indigenous and more recently arrived—saw themselves as the upholders of Islam and founded a series of Islamic dynasties that came to dominate much of the western Mediterranean and claim the Islamic caliphate. The claim meant that they saw themselves as occupying the central political position of the faith, as being the true princes of all the Muslim faithful on earth. From early on, people in the far west, in the land we now call Morocco, have seen themselves as the pivot of the Muslim world (see Abun-Nasr 1987:26–118 and Laroui 1977a:90–129).

After the consolidation of its Islamic identity, Morocco closed its doors to conquest and kept the heart of its identity within the heart of Islam. Morocco's population is almost entirely Muslim (99 percent), and profoundly so. From the 700s (A.H. 100s), its peoples helped expand Islam at home and abroad.

economic revolution

Islam offered a persuasive personal faith and a flourishing economy —a combination that no doubt enhanced its popular appeal. There is much to be said for a faith that brings economic benefit on earth and promises paradise thereafter. Three prongs were central to Muslim ecomonic success: trans-Saharan trade, gold, and sugar.

trans-Saharan commerce and gold Islam's most dramatic revolution was its opening of the Sahara for large-scale commerce for the first time in human history, an innovation every bit as consequential for North Africa as the invention of agriculture or the forging of iron. Not even Rome in its heyday managed regular economic exchange across this formidable barrier (Bulliet 1975:138). Muslims accomplished this transformation by effectively harnassing the technological potential of the camel and combining it with the overarching unity and the network of connections provided by an expanding faith.

The spanning of the Sahara brought into systematic connection two dramatically different economic and ecological niches of the world, providing the financial base for economic and cultural explosion. Exchanges—cultural and commercial—between West Africa and Northwest Africa fueled civilizations on both sides of the sands. Fifty-two days by camel caravan separated the border oases of southern Morocco from those of the northern sub-Sahara. As many as five thousand camels often traveled together in a single caravan. Moroccan merchants sent caravans south carrying cloth, grain, manufactured goods, and Saharan salt. They returned carrying gold, truly phenomenal supplies of gold, which funded much of Morocco's Islamic civilization and its grandeur.[1]

As of the 800s (A.H. 200s), there were three main routes across the Sahara. The western one passing through Morocco by way of Sijilmasa (and then on to Fas and Sabta) was by far the most important. So great was the flow of gold along this route that between 912 and 951 (A.H. 299 and 340), ʿAbd al-Rahman of Cordoba collected 20 million gold dinars in taxes from it, over 500,000 gold dinars a year (Lewis 1951:169).

By the time of Morocco's Berber dynasties, the monetary supplies of the whole hemisphere were dependent on North African gold. According to Wolf, two-thirds of all the gold circulating there in the Middle Ages came from North African supplies, which Morocco dominated (1982:38–39; see also Hopkins 1973:82).

sugar cane and sugar cones Tall white cones of sugar were Islam's second great contribution to North Africa's economy.[2] The saying "sugar followed the Qur'an" is true. In spreading the faith, Muslims carried with them the small cane sugar plants, as well as the necessary knowledge and technology to cultivate this temperamental crop in the Mediterranean. Sugar cane requires a long growing season (from fourteen to eighteen months), abundant water, and steady warmth. If root temperatures fall below 70° Fahrenheit (21° centigrade), growth is severely retarded, and a single frost will kill the plant. Only the southern and eastern areas of the Mediterranean can grow sugar cane, and even in those regions considerable human intervention is required for success. Muslims developed the knowledge of how to intervene. They built irrigation systems and cultivated expertise concerning when watering should occur and in what amounts. Extant Egyptian records from the 800–1000 period (A.H. 200–400) indicate that the plants were irrigated twenty-eight times between sowing and harvest (Galloway 1977:183). Arabs developed similarly detailed knowledge concerning fertilization. Experimentation was an important part of the Arab approach to agriculture. As Galloway explains:

> Experimentation in sugar cultivation was part of the Arab agricultural revolution. The Arab cultivator . . . tried different methods of planting cane and made recommendations on the spacing of setts in the fields and the depth of the furrows. They knew that to improve the germination of setts, the setts should be covered with soil and stored in readiness for planting.
>
> (1977:183)

Muslims brought not only the sugar cane plants, but also the means of processing it into sugar. They built refineries and established complex distribution networks. Moroccan Muslims began to produce elegant white cones and to export them throughout the known world. From the 800s to the mid-1300s (A.H. 200s to the mid-700s), four areas dominated sugar production within the Mediterranean: Morocco, Egypt, Syria, and Palestine. But many thought that Morocco's sugar, expecially that produced in the Sus—a fertile coastal region to the south of the High Atlas—was the finest: "In the Sus they make a sugar that is known throughout the world; it is of the same quality as the sulaymani and tabarzid sugars, and it surpasses all others in taste and purity" (al-Idrisi 1836–1840 [1100]: 1:208).

Morocco flourished with the prosperity that Islam brought. The economic historian Archibald Lewis summarizes:

> But North Africa did more than become a prosperous commercial, industrial, and agricultural region in this period—far beyond anything it had been before. . . . It also exploited its African hinterland in a way no previous possessors of this area had ever done. . . . Routes were opened up across the Sahara to abundant gold supplies and slaves to be found in Senegal, Niger, and Sudan regions. Sijilmasa . . . was the most important caravan entry port for this commerce. . . . The flow of Sudan gold fertilized the Maghrib from the land side just as piracy, trade, and a middleman's position in Mediterranean commerce did from the seaside. It is understandable that North Africa should have been so rich, so industrial, and so powerful in this period. Nor should it be a matter of surprise that Maghribi dinars, coined from its rulers' rich stores of gold, were among the most important currency in the Mediterranean right down to the eleventh century.
>
> (1951:165–166)

Morocco became a center of commerce and production for the whole of the Mediterranean and was closely integrated with other Muslim centers. By the 900s (A.H. 300s), watchtowers were built all across North Africa's coastline so that messages could be transmitted across it in a single night, and Persian notes of credit were as acceptable in North Africa as they were in Isfahan (Ibn Hawqal 1845 [900s]:42, 70; Lewis 1951:171).

political revolution

Muslims brought new forms of rule as well as new forms of economy, and Morocco thrived on the combination. Each of the three main forms of Islamic political authority, Sunni, Shiʻi, and Khawarij, were realized in Morocco during the early years. From its beginnings, Morocco's constitutive repertoire included the full range of Islamic political diversity. In 789 (A.H. 173/74), Morocco's Islamic monarchy was established. It centered within Morocco's heartland plains but was built on universal Islamic supports. Regional political affiliation and universal Islamic identity were from the beginning interwoven.

blood descent: the Idrisi dynasty　In 788, Idris, a great-great-grandson of the Prophet Muhammad (through the bloodline of 'Ali's elder son, the politically compromising Hasan), arrived on Morocco's northern plains (Abun-Nasr 1987:50–53). Tradition says that Idris had participated in the unsuccessful 786 (A.H. 169) revolt against the 'Abbasi and tried to escape their reach by fleeing as far to the west as possible. He traveled 3,000 miles, and then, like proselytizer 'Uqba ibn Nafi', was stopped by the Atlantic ocean. Idris' manservant Rashid fled with him and became important in the history that followed. The two men found refuge among the Awraba Berbers of Morocco's western plains and established the foundations of a state. Six months after his arrival in Morocco, on Friday, the fourth of Ramadan 789 (A.H. 172), Idris was proclaimed Imam, the political head of a political-religious community of Muslims in the region (Eustache 1970–1971:25–27). He united the tribes of the area into a rudimentary polity and made Fas its capital. Yet his successful reign was cut short. In 791 (A.H. 175), after only three years of rule, Idris was poisoned, many Moroccans say by the 'Abbasi caliph, who did not want a competing blood-legitimated dynasty gaining power in Islam's far west (Eustache 1970–1971: 27–31).

Yet the Moroccan dynasty did not collapse. Idris' Berber concubine, Kanza, was seven months pregnant with his child. According to remembered history, the manservant Rashid convinced the people to wait for the birth and hope for a son so that Idrisi rule could continue. Two months later the son was born and proclaimed Idris II. Rashid governed the state while the child grew, but the faithful servant was assassinated when Idris II was only ten. In 803 (A.H. 187), at the age of eleven, Idris II was proclaimed Imam. He established the state, brought the dynasty glory, and ruled for twenty-six years. Trade, agriculture, the arts, education, and the city of Fas itself prospered (Abun-Nasr 1987:50–53; Laroui 1977a:109–112).

When Idris II died, the state was divided among his sons, each of whom governed a separate territory. The Idrisi state did not again achieve the ascendancy it had known under its two founders, yet it continued to provide an overarching political and cultural context within which the people of Morocco's central plains lived their lives for over a hundred years. Al-Qarawiyin, one of the three oldest universities in the world, was established during the Idrisi reign. The all-male institution was endowed through the generous gifts of two women. Al-Qarawiyin remained the center of Islamic scholarship for the millennium that followed; it remains that still.

The Idrisi state gave birth to Islamic political life in Morocco's central plains. But it did much more than that. In popular perception, the Idrisi not only initiated the Moroccan monarchy, but began Morocco's collective political identity that continues unbroken to the present. For Moroccans today, the Idrisi are the beginning of their political selves. The Idrisi based their political legitimacy in blood descent from Muhammad. They established within Morocco's political repertoire the sharifi claim as a possible criterion of rule. After the dynasty's collapse, the sharifi principle lay dormant, only to reemerge six hundred years later, during the great crisis of the 1500s (A.H. 900s), as the central criterion of rule.

achieved piety and earned leadership capacity: the Rustami During the same era, in the far south of Morocco, the land beyond the Atlas, a different kind of polity was established (Abun-Nasr 1987:42–29, Laroui 1977a:113–114). A group of Khawarij, the Rustami, also had fled from the Islamic center in the Middle East to North Africa where they created a political and economic community based on strict adherence to the Khawarij principles of egalitarianism, achieved piety, earned leadership capacity, and communal election. Driven by a "Protestant ethic," the Khawarij made excellent merchants and established the commercial city of Sijilmasa, which for almost a thousand years served as a key transfer point for trans-Saharan trade. The mystique that later became associated with Timbuktu then belonged to Sijilmasa. Through it flowed rivers of gold.

worldly success: the Banu Umayya in Spain When in 750 (A.H. 133/34) the Baghdad-based 'Abbasi dynasty overthrew the Damascus-based Banu Umayya dynasty, several prominent members of the Banu Umayya patrilineage managed to escape; they too fled to the far west of the Muslim world. The distance of the Islamic west from the Baghdad-centered caliphate made it appealing for all those trying to escape the 'Abbasi's reach—the Idrisi, the Rustami, and the Banu Umayya. While the Idrisi and the Rustami settled to the south of the Mediterranean, the Banu Umayya settled to the north, in what is now Spain (Abun-Nasr 1987:71–75). There they established a Muslim polity that by the 900s (A.H. 300s) was sufficiently strong to extend its authority into Morocco, expecially to the Sijilmasa/Fas/Sabta route of the trans-Saharan gold trade. Cordoba became a thriving city of half a million people where the arts, architecture, and economic life flourished—thanks in part to Moroccan gold.

culminating glory

In terms of the Moroccan monarchy itself, the Idrisi were followed by three Berber dynasties who ruled Morocco for over four hundred years and brought the country to its height of power: they gave Morocco its age of glory (Abun-Nasr 1987:76–118, Laroui 1977a:157–200). The Berber dynasties ruled from the central plains; Marrakush and Fas became the centers of the imperium. Trans-Saharan trade flourished, sugar production excelled, and Morocco basked in a wealth of gold. Political power echoed economic florescence. At the height of their authority, the Berber dynasties extended their rule north to Iberia, east to the Libyan desert, and south to the sub-Sahara and beyond. They became the dominant political force in the western Mediterranean, and the Moroccan heartland remained the center of this rule. People within that heartland became convinced of the distinctiveness of their own political-cultural identity, as well as their overarching importance to the whole of Islam.

The three Berber dynasties were the al-Murabitun, "Those Who Are Tied to God," 1069–1147 (A.H. 465–541); the al-Muwahhidun, "Those Who Believe in the Oneness of God," 1147–1269 (A.H. 541–

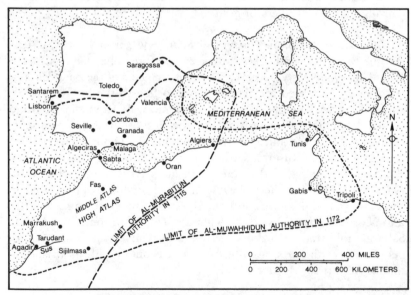

Morocco's Greatest Territorial Expansion

668); and the Banu Marin, the Sons of Marin, 1258–1420 (A.H. 656–823). Under the first two dynasties Morocco achieved its greatest territorial limits.

From the beginning, Morocco's distinctive monarchy relied on universal Islamic supports. Leaders of the first Berber dynasty took the title of "Prince of the Muslims," implying only slightly lesser stature than the caliphal title "Prince of the Faithful." Members of the second and third Berber dynasties claimed nothing less than the caliphal title itself.

There is much consistency in the three Berber dynasties. The original military strength of all three rested in Berber tribes of the deep south. All three burst out of the desert and onto Morocco's central plains. All three combined "strong-arm man politics" with "holy man piety" (Geertz 1968:8). All built flourishing political and economic systems in which arts, architecture, and scholarship excelled. All rested their legitimacy on this-world success and did not insulate their rule through more diffuse cultural formulations. In combination the three Berber dynasties gave Morocco a scintillating age of excellence where every dimension of life flourished: their navies were formidable, their armies victorious, their arts and architecture exquisite.

Morocco also excelled in learning. The Berber dynasties established a universal system of education that extended through the whole countryside. Students were provided with government scholarships that covered housing, food, clothing, and spending money for the duration of their studies, which could take as long as twenty-five years (Africanus 1896 [1526]). The study of the Qur'an, mathematics, astronomy, and medicine flourished. Scholars from all the known world, including Europe, came to study at Morocco's institutions of higher learning, where the core knowledge of the Islamic civilization was expanded, and the knowledge of ancient Greece and Rome was maintained. The most important institution of higher learning was the al-Qarawiyin mosque and university of Fas, established during Idrisi times. Its libraries held over thirty thousand volumes (Ibn Tasabet 1518). In Morocco's rich environment, some of the world's greatest thinkers flourished with the Berber monarchs as their patrons. They included Ibn Tufayl (1110–1185; A.H. 513–581), Ibn Rushd (1126–1198; 520–594), and Ibn Khaldun (1332–1406; A.H. 732–808). Ibn Tufayl (known to medieval Christian scholastics as Abbubacer) and Ibn Rushd (known to the West as Averroes) were men of medicine and philosophy, while Ibn Khaldun was the father of modern historiography and social science. Much of the material and thinking for Ibn Khaldun's famous social history of the world, the Muqadimmah (which literally translates "The Things that Went Before"), was gathered while he was in Morocco. Of Ibn Khaldun, Arnold Toynbee wrote, "he has conceived and formulated a philosophy of history which is undoubtedly the greatest work of its kind that has ever yet been created by any mind in any time" (1934:322).

The zenith of the last Berber dynasty, the Banu Marin, came with the reign of the "Black Sultan," Abu al-Hasan (1331–1351; A.H. 731–753), who brought the Sus, with its lucrative sugar industry and rich commerce in gold, into direct central government control (the Sus is the rich agricultural region that borders Morocco's coast, directly to the south of the High Atlas Mountains). With that wealth, the Black Sultan carried out his passion for Islamic scholarship and architecture. A number of the schools he built still stand as exquisite architectural monuments.

Together the first two Berber dynasties and the first half of the third represent the height of Islamic Morocco's economic and military power. It was an age of practical success, and that success was the monarchy's foundation.

Then catastrophe struck. The glittering age of Morocco's Islamic glory came undone. The crisis originated outside of Morocco's borders but struck Morocco to the core, bringing about not only the collapse of the ruling dynasty, but the collapse of the model of rule. Paradise was lost.

6

bubonic plague

Earthly power is fickle. In part, it must be seized. In part, it is bestowed by processes of history that lie beyond the ability of any given powerholder to control. In the 600s (the first century after the hijra), the cluster of variables that made for domination came to rest with the Muslim world, which then experienced seven hundred years of political, economic, and cultural hegemony. But by the 1400s (A.H. 800s), the foundations of world power were shifting, and the countries to the north of the Mediterranean were coming into their age of glory (Africanus 1896 [1526], Braudel 1973, Cornell 1986, al-Ifrani 1889 [1700s], al-Nasiri 1954–1956, Schneider 1977 and 1978, Wallerstein 1974, Wolf 1982). The shifts in power were particularly dramatic in the western Mediterranean, where Christian Iberia's gain was Islamic Morocco's loss. Two factors were crucial in the transformations: the differing impact of the bubonic plague upon the economies of the two regions, and the switch in international commerce from overland to oversea.

In the fourteenth century, after six hundred years of prosperity, Morocco's economy crashed. Previous declines had been short-term, but the 1350 (A.H. 750/51) plummet was systemic. One factor overrides all others: the bubonic plague, which first struck in 1347–1348 (A.H. 748–749). The initial wave of the "new" pestilence was devastating to the population, which had no resistance to it. Along trade and pilgrimage routes it traveled, leaving a gruesome path of death in its wake—dead people, dead camels, dead birds. As much as half of the Moroccan population perished.[1]

If the plague had not struck, the Berber model of rule might have endured for some time. After all, it had brought Morocco its age of brilliance. But it did strike, and the world changed. It brought the kind of turning point in history that Ibn Khaldun describes as "a general change of conditions . . . as if the entire creation had changed and the whole world been altered" (Ibn Khaldun 1969 [1381]:30).

contrast: Europe and North Africa

The plague hit Europe as well as North Africa and the Middle East, and the short-term effects were much the same throughout the Mediterranean—death of one-third to one-half of the population, the disruption of economic, social, and political life, and the questioning of world views. Yet the long-term effects were exactly the opposite in Europe as compared with North Africa and the Middle East. One can convincingly argue that the long-term effects of the plague on Europe were basically beneficial, that they spurred the transformations in agriculture, commerce, and social organization that enabled Europe to embark on its road to world domination; whereas for North Africa and the Middle East, the long-term effects of the plague were unequivocally negative, destroying the foundations of what had been a world dominating system (Dols 1977, Ziegler 1969).

The differing impacts were a function of the differing kinds of economic systems that operated in the two regions. Those of the Muslim world were highly developed, dynamic, and lucrative, and depended on a complex infrastructure that had taken centuries to build. The very prosperity and intricacy of the North African and Middle Eastern economic systems made them vulnerable to the plague's damage. There were more levels at which the plague's destruction could strike, more dimensions that could be ravaged, making it harder to rebuild.

In contrast, when the plague struck Christian Europe, its economic order was less developed and was in need of and already in the process of transformation, and the plague's destruction cleared the way for a new, more complicated economic reality. In North Africa and the Middle East, the plague undid world hegemony. In Europe, the plague helped set the context for hegemony's creation.

plague and Christian Europe

When the plague struck in 1350 (A.H. 750/51), Europe was still something of a backwater. The manor system of agriculture still dominated production, and the countryside was overpopulated. In Ziegler's estimation, the plague reduced the European population to more "reasonable proportions" and speeded up beneficial processes of change already in motion. "The moment . . . was one of great fluidity. . . . The Black Death did not initiate any major social or economic trend, but it accelerated and modified—sometimes drastically—those which already existed" (1969:239).

The plague pushed the disintegration of the manor system, freeing land and labor for new forms of economic and political life: "the Black Death introduced a situation in which land was plentiful and labor scarce. The scales were tipped against the landowner" (Ziegler 1969:239). The reduction in population left those who remained in an immeasurably stronger position to bargain with their employers and to acquire land. As agricultural production became a burden for large-scale landowners, manors broke up and peasants took over who with their own labor began to produce significant surpluses. European peasants here had an advantage over their North African and Middle Eastern counterparts in the relative ease with which land— taken out of production with the plague—could be put back in production in the plague's aftermath. Europe's rainfall was the critical factor. If peasants had land and seeds, they could begin production, whereas in North Africa and the Middle East, more complex support systems, such as irrigation, were needed.

In the plague's European aftermath, pay for urban workers rose and a new skilled class of workers came into being. The plague left the available capital and medium of exchanges intact, hastening the transition from a system of barter to a system of cash exchange, all necessary transformations if Europe was to experience its economic "takeoff" (see Ziegler 1969:233–255).

plague and Muslim North Africa

The long-term effects of the plague on the economies of North Africa and the Middle East were exactly the opposite (Dols 1977). Their infrastructural elaboration made them vulnerable. Sugar production and long-distance commerce are intricate systems with multiple interconnected links; the plague struck at each connection.

sugar production   The sugar production in which the Islamic world, particularly Morocco, excelled was a labor and capital intensive process. In the Mediterranean, a large body of skilled labor is needed to build and maintain irrigation systems, oversee the watering, carry out the fertilization, reap the crops, and manufacture and distribute the cones. The plague wreaked havoc with each aspect of production and made the overarching system almost impossible to rebuild. With the wave of death, expert knowledge was lost, skills vanished, irrigation systems fell apart, crops died, and land was left fallow. There was little sugar cane left to refine, and the manufacturing industry and the distribution networks collapsed.

The decline in population was a disaster for the sugar economy because sugar cane is a labor intensive crop. Labor became scarce and costly; this undercut the economic incentives for rebuilding the labor intensive system. Exacerbating the problem of overall population decline was the flight of the rural peoples to the urban areas. Sugar cane is a rural crop. In contrast to what occurred in Europe, when the plague hit North Africa and the Middle East, the population fled the cities in order to receive medical care. The Muslim world had a well-organized system of medicine which included hospitals, trained doctors, nurses, and medications. It was urban based. (European medical care was remedial in comparison.)

The bottom dropped out of sugar production in each of the four main Muslim centers—Morocco, Egypt, Palestine, and Syria. Some of the best statistics come from Egypt, where the most archaeological work has been done. In 1324 (A.H. 724/25), sixty-six sugar refineries operated full-scale in Old Cairo. A hundred years later, after the plague, only nineteen still existed, and none operated at previous capacities (Galloway 1977:191).

From the mid-1300s (A.H. 750s) to the mid-1400s (A.H. 850s), Morocco went from being the producer of vast quantities of what many considered the finest refined white sugar in the Mediterranean to producing only small quantities of the raw, dark product (Galloway 1977:188, Mintz 1985). In 1470 (A.H. 875), Morocco began, for the first time in its history, to export raw or only partially refined sugar to Europe for refinement there, first to Venice and Bologna, then to Antwerp and Holland. The move was significant because of the future it augured. North Africa was being transformed from a center of manufacturing into a center of raw materials production for a European-based manufacturing center. The change carried the familiar cluster of characteristics: "It transferred employment in the industry from producer to importer; it reduced the producer's interest in making fine quality sugar, and it made the producer subservient to the importer. The development of refining in Europe placed the producer in a dependent or 'colonial' relationship with the manufacturer" (Galloway 1977:188; see also Jacques-Meunié 1982:2:413). In the late 1400s (A.H. 800s), European economic imperialism had achieved its first foothold in North Africa.

By the mid to late 1400s (A.H. 800s), the Muslim world, the center of Mediterranean sugar production for five hundred years, had to import refined sugar to meet its needs. Trade deficits mounted. The sugar pillar of Muslim economic supremacy was lost.

agriculture The plague wreaked havoc on the whole of agricultural production in North Africa and the Middle East—not on sugar production alone. The disintegration of irrigation systems brought about general crop failure and famine. Famine led to yet more deaths and a higher cost of labor, and the downward cycle continued. The problems caused by the plague were exacerbated when an animal murrain hit North Africa's work animals at about the same time that the plague struck its human population, reducing the stock of plow and work animals, which further devastated agriculture (Dols 1977, Galloway 1977). In North Africa and the Middle East, the plague did not simply destroy crops and change the basis of land ownership: it destroyed the infrastructure upon which crop production depended. Many lands were transferred to less intensive forms of cultivation, while others fell out of the productive cycle.

long-distance trade The black plague also devastated the other pillar of Muslim economic prosperity, trans-Saharan commerce, especially in gold. That trade depended on an intricate banking, information, and transportation network that was built upon trust and personal connections that took years to develop. The plague collapsed these networks because so many of the merchants died simultaneously. When the plague finally subsided, newcomers could begin to buy and sell, but the elaborate network of relationships upon which sophisticated commercial exchange depended could not easily be rebuilt.

plague and dominion   When the plague struck, Morocco had known centuries of economic, political, and cultural domination. Its economic wealth lay in an intricate system of international commercial exchange in which prosperity depended upon the constancy of gold and silver prices, the steady production of manufacturing goods for export (e.g., refined sugar, paper products), the free flow of overland trade, and the availability of basic agricultural commodities. The plague struck at each of the mainstays and sent the system as a whole spiraling downward.

Christian military assault

The plague threw the Moroccan countryside into political and economic turmoil. When the last great Berber monarch died in 1358 (A.H. 759/60), numerous contenders for power arose. Former advisors, subdivisions of the dynasty, and subsections of the militia vied for power (Julien 1951–1952). The central administration disintegrated, education was damaged, and the legal system had difficulty functioning even at the lowest levels.

But the worst had not yet struck. It was soon to come: Christian military attack followed the plague's devastation. The first attack came in 1399 (A.H. 801/02) when Henry III of Castille crossed the Mediterranean and invaded the port of Tetouan, slaughtering half of the inhabitants and reducing the other half to slavery before abandoning the city and returning home. The second attack was no more lethal, but it was more ominous because the attacker did not leave: in 1415 (A.H. 818/19), the Portuguese invaded Sabta (Ceuta), the nothern terminus of the Moroccan gold route. They successfully captured the port and left a garrison of 2,500 men to secure it for posterity. The age of European colonialism had begun. The lines of south-north military invasion were reversing.

why the Iberians sailed

A Muslim state had lain to Iberia's south for seven hundred years, and boats capable of crossing the Mediterranean had existed for several thousand. Why the Iberian sailing and the Moroccan attack at this time? The convergence of three variables was responsible: economic need, Inquisition fervor, and technological advance.

economic need   Iberia was not only politically occupied by Muslims during much of the 700-to-1500 era (A.H. 100–900); like much of the rest of Europe in the Middle Ages, Iberia depended upon the hard currency and the luxury goods that the Muslim and Byzantine worlds provided (Schneider 1977). For Iberia, Morocco was the most important supplier. Iberia required Moroccan gold, silver, silk, sugar, dyes, and spices. As of the late 1300s (A.H. 700s), these goods were scarce because of the damage the plague had brought to North Africa's systems of production and exchange. Iberia was experiencing a "desperate shortage of hard currency, the demand for which had increased forty-fold during the previous four centuries" (Cornell 1986:4). In search of these goods, Spain and Portugal sailed south, and Sabta was a natural target. It was the northern terminus for Morocco's river of gold, the Sijilmasa trade route.

Inquisition fervor   Cultural factors also played a part in the southern sailing, for the plague had sent shock waves through Iberians' constructions of the world. The cosmic crisis appears to have been more severe for Christians, for whom a dominant interpretation was that God had intentionally wrought the plague's havoc upon them because of lack of faith. Self-blame and guilt dominated the Christian response.

The Muslim interpretation, on the other hand, was less inwardly focused and more circumspect. The plague caused self-searching, but Muslims were less ridden by self-doubt. They tended to interpret it not as a direct attack on themselves, but rather as one of those unexplicable crises that regularly strike humanity—like drought, famine, and locusts—the ultimate purpose of which only God knows.

The divergent Christian and Muslim interpretations created alternative perspectives on how to deal with the world in plague's aftermath. Many Muslims apparently went about trying to reconstruct the world in which they had formerly lived, while many Christians, especially those of Iberia, set about trying to change themselves and their world. They began by trying to prove themselves in God's eyes—and in their own eyes—by demolishing the Muslim and Jewish Other at home and abroad.

The Catholic Inquisition was officially instituted in Rome in 1184 (A.H. 580/81) and introduced into Iberia in 1237 (A.H. 635/36), yet it never really functioned until the plague's aftermath. Not until the

1400s (A.H. 800s) were the laws on the books regularly implemented in the day-to-day; not until then were they used to strike out against Jews and Muslims within the Iberian Peninsula and outside it (Moore 1976:117).

In Iberia, the plague's shaking of the cultural foundations resulted in an age of untold Inquisition fervor, a true holy war. Economic need and religious world view coalesced to fuel an unrestrained drive for inward purity and outward expansion, a drive that utilitarian goals alone could never have impelled, especially since utilitarian benefits were slow in coming. In the interim, holy rage filled the gap.

Inquisition within the Peninsula The Christian reconquest of the Iberian Peninsula proceeded with haste. The Inquisition provided the necessary tools: terrorism, confiscation of property, and propaganda. Remaining Muslim political strongholds within the Peninsula were overthrown. In 1492, a banner year for western Europe, Granada—the last seat of Muslim power in Iberia—fell. Seven centuries of Muslim rule were finished. Individual Jews and Muslims were pressured into converting, and even after they converted, their professions of faith were often held suspect. After 1480 (A.H. 885/86), Jewish and Muslim "converts" began to be burned at the stake, and the flight of Jews and Muslims from the Peninsula began in earnest.

In 1492, (A.H. 897/98), on the very day that Columbus sailed west in pursuit of economic riches, all remaining Jews in Spain "were given four months either to convert to Catholicism or leave the country. . . . In 1502 a royal decree gave all Muslims the same alternative . . . baptism or exile" (Moore 1976:118). After these rulings, the practice of any allegedly "non-Catholic" behavior was sufficient to bring a person before a tribunal that could lead to death. Evidence of continuing "alliance" with Judaism included the wearing of purportedly cleaner clothes on Saturday, the Jewish Sabbath, and the washing of a dead person's body in warm water (Moore 1976:118). Evidence of continuing Islamic affiliation included the practice of taking too many baths (Moore 1976:118, Crow 1963). In those days, Christians associated cleanliness with ungodliness.

beyond the Peninsula The Iberian quest beyond the Peninsula was spearheaded by Prince Henry the Navigator, of Portugal, a remarkable man—adventurer, pragmatist, and devout Catholic.[2] Prince Henry wanted to dominate the gold route that flowed through Morocco, an economic aim that was given impetus by his fervent desire to spread the true faith. "If we must choose a dominant theme in Prince Henry's plans, it was probably the destruction of Islam in Africa. The conquest of Ceuta [Sabta] seemed to open the way to a great enterprise which should reverse the Muslim invasion of the Peninsula in 711" (Livermore 1947:188).

Prince Henry had a twofold strategy of attack. The first was direct: to take hold of Morocco's commerce and destroy the Muslim state by seizing Morocco's ports, the northern termini of trans-Saharan trade. Hence the attack on and occupation of Sabta (the Mediterranean port for the Sijilmasa/Fas trade route). Yet the occupation did not accomplish what the Portuguese wanted; neither gold nor converts came their way. The Moroccan population viewed the invading Christians as the oppositional Other and remained avidly opposed to the occupation. Moroccan merchants instituted a trade embargo, taking their commerce elsewhere, when possible, rather than acceding to Portuguese control. Military assaults against the Portuguese were led by local authorities and waged by local populations. Raids were mounted from as far away as the Sus, 400 miles to Sabta's south (Cornell 1986:4).

The vigor of Moroccan resistance turned Prince Henry to his second line of attack—a long shot, but one that Henry thought worthy of attempt: to discover sea routes that would allow Portugal to bypass Morocco's middleman position and seize the sources of supply. The enterprise seemed unlikely to succeed. Most Europeans were persuaded that no ship could sail beyond Cape Bojador, a small promontory on Morocco's southern coastline. Many thought that dragons inhabited the distant waters and swallowed the ships that ventured therein; no one had ever returned from those waters to offer a different interpretation (Bovill 1968). Yet Prince Henry was not a man to be easily discouraged—especially since someone else would be doing the sailing—and searched for a man willing to attempt the feat. Prince Henry found him in Gomes Eanes, who in 1434 (A.H. 837/38) boldly set sail into the untraversed waters to the south of Morocco. Remarkedly, Eanes succeeded. He reached Cape Bojador and sailed beyond, docking on the African coast. To prove his triumph, he plucked a sprig of rosemary and sailed home.

Prince Henry was elated with Eanes' success. The first obstacle had been surmounted: ships could sail south around Morocco. But could they bring back gold? That was another issue. Henry continued to pursue both of his strategies—to try to control the flow of gold across Morocco's mainlands, and to try to discover alternative sea routes to the sources of gold that would allow him to bypass Morocco entirely.

In 1437 (A.H. 840/41), Prince Henry's land strategy was dealt a serious blow. Henry had persuaded his brother, King Duarte, to mount an attack on Tanja (Tangier). The Portuguese forces invaded the port and were soundly defeated by the Moroccans. The defeat was particularly painful for King Duarte and Prince Henry because their younger brother was captured in the fighting and died in captivity before they could manage to ransom him (Livermore 1947).

The defeat at Tanja turned Prince Henry's and Portugal's attention to the sea, and official state policy was altered so that the sea search became the primary goal (Cornell 1986:4–5, Eanes de Azurara 1936 [1450]). The altered focus paid off. Just three years later, in 1440 (A.H. 843/44), Portugal succeeded in producing a new type of vessel that could sail the seas in a new way, a form of sailing that would alter the course of world history.

technological advances, seafaring, and European dominance Technology was the third factor in the success of Portugal's outward expansion. Europe is a series of peninsulas. Its extensive coastline could be turned to its advantage only when the seas were opened for regular transport. That required the technology to sail the open seas and the ships to carry heavy loads across them (Wolf 1982:235). Those inventions did not occur until the 1400s and 1500s (A.H. 800s and 900s), when they became the technological foundations upon which Europe's outward expansion and economic takeoff were built. Before that, Europe's cold climate and its circuitous coastline had left it a relative backwater in an international commercial network whose central arteries passed through the warm and sandy lands of North Africa and the Middle East.

The new Portuguese ship was a crucial step in that direction:

> In 1440, a new type of vessel of Portuguese contrivance was put into use. The older ships, the *varinel,* combining oars and sails and therefore low and heavily manned, and the *barca,* slow and difficult to handle, were replaced by the *caravel,* light, long, and high. The necessity of coasting was now eliminated and full advantage of prevailing winds was gained by . . . [traveling] over the open sea.
>
> (Livermore 1947:189)

The caravel enabled sailors to leave the coast and take advantage of the open seas, unlocking a new era in world transportation. The swift caravel replaced the plodding camel as the carrier of trade, and Muslim dominance of international transport was undone.

Other technological advances followed. Europeans began to alter their riggings. They put their square rigging on the foremast and Arab lateen riggings on the main and mizzen masts, which gave the newly outfitted ships an advantage when sailing close-hauled as well as when running.

Another important innovation came in the early 1500s (A.H. 900s) when European shipbuilders began to install guns, not only on the caste and upper decks, but also on the main deck by cutting gun ports into the ship's hull. The result was the galleon—half-warship and half-merchantman—by which Europe came to rule the seas. Wolf summarizes the galleon's impact:

> The prizes in naval war no longer went to the captain who rammed or boarded his opponent, but to the naval artilleryman who knew how to maneuver his ship into position and to fire broadside. Thus at Diu, in 1509, Albuquerque destroyed the joint Egyptian Mamluk and Gujarati fleet [both Muslim] and opened the sea routes of the southern seas to Portuguese expansion.
>
> (1982:235–236)

Economic and cultural factors impelled Europe to take to the seas, but the technology to sail them in new ways and to build new ships to carry heavy cargo account for Europe's post-1500s (A.H. 800s) hegemony. Like the Arab traversing of the desert, the European traversing of the seas fundamentally altered human interactions and made possible new lines of communication, commerce, and exploitation. Those who controlled the pathways could, to a certain extent, control the world. Trans-Saharan trade belonged to Muslims and transoceanic trade belonged to Christians; those modes of transport partially account for their respective ages of domination.

success by sea and land With the invention of the caravel, Portugal began to penetrate West African waters and, in 1455 (A.H. 859/60), accomplished part of what it was after. It established maritime trade in gold with the people of West Africa, bypassing Morocco's overland routes (Cornell 1986:5).

The trade in gold whetted Prince Henry's appetite, as did the 1459 map by the Venetian Fra Mauro that came into Prince Henry's hands. According to this map, the Orient could be reached by sailing south to the tip of Africa, then east around it, and then due north. If such a route existed, it would allow Europeans to bypass the Muslim dominance of Asian trade as well as of African trade. Henry threw himself into the task. The first step was completed in 1487 (A.H. 892/93), when Bartholomeu Dias sailed around the Cape of Good Hope. Ten years later the Orient was reached (Wolf 1982:232).

In the meantime, Portugal had not entirely forgotten Morocco's ports and its wealth. In 1471 (A.H. 875/76), thirty-four years after its defeat at Tanja, Portugal launched a second attack on the city. This time Portugal won, and not only captured Tanja but took the nearby port of Asila as well. Portugal still sought to dominate Morocco's ports and products. Even for its transoceanic trade with West Africa—the purpose of which was to bypass Morocco—it needed Moroccan goods for exchange. Africans wanted Moroccan horses, grain, gold coins, and their brightly colored woolen cloths (Cornell 1986:5).

Iberia in the 1490s The 1490s (A.H. 896/905) were a momentous decade for Christian Iberians, the culmination of a century of conquest at home and abroad. In 1492 (A.H. 897/98), Granada fell, and thousands of Jews and Muslims fled to North Africa for safety. (Morocco, Algeria, Tunisia, and Egypt received major influxes of Muslim and Jewish Iberians during this era.) In that same year Christopher Columbus, flying a Spanish flag, thought he had discovered a water route to the Far East when in fact he had happened upon the Americas. Iberian Christians regained the Old World, and although they did not know it, discovered the New World, a discovery that in time would bring Iberia more hard currency, especially in silver, than its economies could handle (Wolf 1982).

Iberia's self-confidence soared, and in 1494 (A.H. 899/900), Portugal and Spain divided the world between them in the formal Treaty of Tordeiseillas; the Catholic Pope added his blessing. An imaginary line running from north to south was drawn 370 leagues west of Cape Verde Islands, located in the Atlantic Ocean off the western coast of Africa. Spain was "granted" dominion over all lands discovered to the west of the boundary, while Portugal was "granted" dominion over all land "discovered" to the east (Garraty and Gay 1972:623). This was the first of a series of European treaties that would divide the world, just as arbitrarily and just as audaciously.

Three years after signing the treaty, Portugal completed the last leg of the water route to the east. With an Arab navigator at the ship's helm, Vasco da Gama sailed around the Cape of Good Hope and continued all the way to Calcutta. The eastern water route to the Orient stood open. The seas were ready for war and commerce, and the world's hinterlands began to feel the weight of the sailing.

consequences of Iberia's outward expansion for Morocco

Iberia's outward expansion was disastrous for Morocco. It exacerbated problems already set in motion by the plague and created a host of new ones. The occupation of Moroccan ports did not bring Portugal its economic and cultural goals, but it kept Morocco from realizing its own. The 1415 capture of Sabta delivered the lethal blow to the last Berber dynasty, the Banu Marin, whose authority had been seriously undermined by the consequences of the plague. What power and credibility remained with them vanished with the Christian invasion. Not only had they failed to spread Islam abroad, they could no longer protect the faithful at home. In 1420 (A.H. 823/24), five years after the Portuguese took Sabta, the last Berber dynasty collapsed; the centralized organization of collective existence—the administrative, military, educational, judicial, and economic systems—came undone.

A cultural crisis was also at hand. The kind of crisis that Iberian Christians experienced with the plague now struck Moroccan Muslims as they tried to make sense of why Christians successfully occupied their ports. Questioning and introspection led to self-doubt: perhaps Moroccans had not been sufficiently faithful; perhaps they had taken the wrong path.

The central structures of collective existence collapsed; the logistics of daily life came to be handled on local and regional levels—for example, the selection of political authorities and the settlement of disputes. Others simply fell by the wayside—such as the upkeep of the irrigation systems, the manufacture of sugar, and the structural integration of the educational system. Others came to be addressed in a patchwork fashion—for instance, long-distance trade was accomplished as traveling merchants made personal alliances with local and regional powerholders.

Even military opposition to the Portuguese was locally and regionally organized. Fueled by long-established cultural perceptions, Moroccans avidly resisted the Portuguese occupation. Yet popular resistance lacked a central focus. Instead, a series of local and regional leaders mounted short-term assaults, after which they and their men returned home to their camels and their crops. These attacks were irritating to the Portuguese, but not sufficiently broad-based to pose a real threat. Portugal expanded its dominion, and Morocco spiraled downward.

INTERLUDE

The great crisis struck. Morocco's economic, military, and administrative foundations collapsed. World hegemony was passing into the hands of Western Europe. The question for Morocco was no longer one of dominance, but one of survival. It appeared that Morocco would cease to exist as an independent political entity, that it would succumb to the domination of another.

Yet, there was a way to remain a people. Moroccans reached back nine hundred years and 3,000 miles to the most basic foundations of their faith, to the fundamentals of the Prophet, male and female, and blood descent. From these cultural basics, Moroccans began to rebuild a flexible and potent central monarchy that served as the central pivot of Moroccan consciousness and collective identity in the centuries that followed. The reconstituted monarchy initially regained practical strength, but that strength was short lived. The world economy had altered in another's favor. But the cultural potency of Morocco's collective foundations allowed Morocco and its monarchy to survive—to stave off centuries of Western military assault and economic domination. Moroccans had not had a blood descendant of Muhammad on the Moroccan throne in six hundred years, but in the great crisis, they called for a glorious one to come forward. And he came, and life was renewed, and three great rituals continued to bolster collective life even when all else worked against it: the celebration of the Prophet's Birthday, first marriage, and the Great Sacrifice.

When the rivers of gold stopped flowing and the military power structures fell apart, the luminescence of Muhammad's bloodline shone forth. A new form of monarchy, a blood-descendant caliphate, was constructed, ritually renewed, and became that bright central light that allowed Moroccans to orient themselves and their form of rule even in the midst of military attack and economic failure. Superstructural strength compensated for infrastructural weakness, and Morocco endured, and endures still.

The historical question at stake is how this small country in northwest Africa, so close to Europe's shore, so coveted in Europe's eyes, and so weakened in its overarching supports, survived five centuries of tumult. The historical question demands a cultural resolution. In uncovering that resolution, the analysis moves away from a concentration on men, economic wealth, political power, and practical glory, and back to a focus on ritual, male-female definitions, and culturally created hope, back to a concentration on the way in which, when other means failed, political authority was secured through sexual definition and sacred longing.

CULTURAL SURVIVAL

sharifi resolution
Prophet's Birthday
the ʿAlawi blood descendants
first marriage
bride's blood
ram's blood
Ibrahim myth
metaphor
sexuality and sacrifice

7

sharifi resolution:
the Sa'di blood descendants

The century turned, Morocco's economic plummet continued, and the military threat from outside increased. As the 1500s (A.H. 900s) began, Portugal launched a new wave of assaults and in quick succession occupied seven Moroccan ports; it began colonial expansion into the countryside also. And there was a new threat: the Ottoman Turks attacked from the east.

Yet Moroccans remained firmly attached to their distinctive sense of self—political and cultural—and kept trying to renew themselves from within and protect themselves from without. They had long perceived the Christians of Iberia as the Other. They now came to see the Ottomans as the Other also. The Ottomans were Muslims, but they were not Arabs, not North Africans, not speakers of the holy tongue, and Moroccans did not see them in ennobled terms. The Iberians grew stronger in the north and the Ottomans grew stronger in the east, and Morocco's capitulation to one or the other seemed inevitable. But all was not what it seemed.

Faced with an ultimate crisis, Moroccans turned to the heart of their culture, to Islam, and from its essentials began to rebuild a plausible reality. They put forward the view that a blood descendant of Muhammad should come and reign. With all about them insecure, Moroccans sought a leader in whom Muhammad's blood still flowed—the most direct possible connection to the great Prophet—as if that blood could resuscitate Muslim life in the western Mediterranean. And it did.

the search for sharif

Throughout the land, the call for sharif to come forward and oust the Christians increased (the term *sharif* includes all those who consider themselves to be patrilineal descendants of the Prophet Muhammad; there are many).[1] In Fas, a sublineage of the last Berber dynasty came forward. They were called the Banu Wattas and, although they were Berber, they attempted to capitalize upon sharifi legitimacy and rebuild the central dynasty with themselves at the head (see Cour 1920). They miraculously "discovered" the intact body of Idris II—the great-great-great-grandson of Muhammad—who had ruled Morocco's central plains 600 years before, from 803 to 828 (A.H. 187–213). The discovery took place in 1437 (A.H. 840) in Fas. Would-be Berber monarchs found the body of Muhammad's blood descendant most directly associated with Moroccan soil still lying in it. After the discovery of this ancient sharif, the still living sharif of Fas began to play an increasingly important role in public political life (see Abun-Nasr 1987:115, Salmon 1905, and Sebti 1984 and 1986).

The political motivations behind the purported discovery are hardly obscure. The Banu Wattas hoped to capture the growing political credit associated with Muhammad's bloodline and link it to themselves in order to undergird their own caliphal claim. They built a mausoleum to the great sharif's body and paid it respectful homage. Yet their role as "the discoverers of the sharifi body" rather than "the people of the sharifi blood" was not sufficient to gain them popular support, and they fell. The Banu Wattas' attempt at central control failed, but Idris' "body" and the call for a sharifi ruler remained.

The "discovery" was itself an indication of the increasing potency of sharifi claims. As the historian Julien states, "The renewal of the Idrissid cult was not fortuitous. It was, so to speak, the consecration of the rebirth of sharifism" (1951–1952:211). All over the country-side, sharifs came forward, true or supposed descendants of the Prophet who claimed to have inherited part of his essence and therefore to be primary candidates for political rule. As military and economic in-dicators of legitimate political authority receded, the call for blood descent from Muhammad grew in strength, the long dead Idrisi were foregrounded, and Moroccan history was reformulated in a sharifi key.

analytical resolution

From an analytical viewpoint, the call for the political ruler to be "descended" from Muhammad is understandable. It tackled two fun-damental problems that Moroccans faced: it offered a way to make sense of the crisis, and it provided a program of action for emerging from it. From the sharifi perspective, the reason for Morocco's plum-met lay in the community's wrongful elevation of local tribesmen rather than the rightful members of the Prophet's family. God intended for blood descendants of the great Prophet to rule, but the community had strayed. Presumably, if Moroccans got back on track, Islam would again prosper in North Africa's far west.

The call for sharifi descent also provided a means of selecting a supreme political authority in the absence of military victory and eco-nomic florescence. Unlike the Berber model, sharifi legitimacy inhered, in theory at least, in the power of the ruler's blood, in his right to rule, not in the powerholder's real-world success. Presumably, God ordained that a given sharif rule, whether or not the world recognized him as a ruler. Given the reality of the 1400s and 1500s (A.H. 800s and 900s), the sharifi stress was felicitous indeed. By grounding po-litical authority in a designation that existed beyond this-world prag-matics, Moroccans could begin to rebuild a central political position based on timeworn cultural foundations. The true sharif was legiti-mate, no matter what his worldly fortunes. Sharifi rule offered a way to stabilize political loyalty around a given leader, even in the midst of on-the-ground failure; this stability then brought about the pos-sibility of on-the-ground success. As more and more people rallied to one sharif's side, the sharif began to win, and the reunification of the country and concerted opposition to the Portuguese became possible.

Yet it was by no means inevitable that this resolution would be translated into historical fact. History is littered with unrealized res-olutions and Morocco was littered with sharifs. The call for the ruler to be a sharif narrowed the field, but only relatively speaking, for there were, and are, in Morocco a multitude of people who claim direct descent from Muhammad's bloodline. For the sharifi resolution to work, sharifi loyalty had to be focused on one particular sublineage that for some reason excelled over all others, so that it could claim that in its members' bodies the Prophet's blood essence most clearly showed. That focusing came through a remarkable patriline—a man, his two sons, and his three grandsons—who managed the sharifi metamorphosis of Moroccan political life.[2]

Sa'di institution of the sharifi caliphate

Abu 'Abd Allah al-Qa'im, the founder

Abu 'Abd Allah Muhammad al-Zaydani was born in the mid-1400s (A.H. 800s), in the middle of the crisis. A member of the Bani Zaydan family, he was a sharif, descended from the Prophet through the bloodline of Muhammad's elder grandson, Hasan. The Banu Zaydan had come to Morocco from the Arabian Peninsula during the 1100s (A.H. 500s) and settled in a small southern oasis where they made a name for themselves as religious scholars and holy men, speakers of

---

FIGURE 7.1. Morocco's Islamic Monarchy: The Ruling Dynasties

1. *Idrisi*	789–959	(A.H. 172–348)	Arab sharif
2. *al-Murabitun*	1069–1147	(A.H. 465–541)	Berber tribesmen
3. *al-Muwahhidun*	1147–1269	(A.H. 541–668)	Berber tribesmen
4. *Banu Marin*	1258–1420	(A.H. 656–823)	Berber tribesmen
Banu Wattas	1420–1550	(A.H. 823–957)	Berber tribesmen
5. *Sa'di*	1548–1641	(A.H. 955–1051)	Arab sharif
6. *'Alawi*	1666–present	(A.H. 1077–present)	Arab sharif

NOTES:

The Banu Wattas are usually considered a regency rather than a full-blown dynasty. They ruled only a small part of the countryside. They were a patrilineal subsection of the Banu Marin.

All three of the Sharifi dynasties are related to Muhammad through his grandson Hasan, the child of Ali and Fatima. The specific genealogical links (all 39 generations) of the reigning 'Alawi dynasty are shown in Eustache 1984:7–16. This genealogy is known as *silsilat al-dahab*, "the chain of gold" or *silsilat al-ibriz*, "the chain of pure gold." The links of the Idrisi are equally noble and are shown in Eustache 1970–1971:3–24. The Idrisi and the 'Alawi share patrilineal ancestors in the first four generations after Muhammad.

---

the sacred tongue and descendants of the Prophet (Julien 1951–1952:222). They settled disputes, verified documents, taught in the Qur'anic schools, and oversaw the peaceful flow of trans-Saharan trade. Like other holy men, they sometimes traveled with the massive camel caravans to add their sacred stature to the more practical protection of the armed guards. The Banu Zaydan, like many holy lineages, were outraged by Portugal's occupation of Morocco's ports. They interpreted the attack as an assault on themselves and their faith and mounted a counterassault.

Abu 'Abd Allah's call to political leadership came in a time-honored Moroccan tradition, when he was in the holiest of places participating in the holiest of rites; it occurred while he was in Makka making the pilgrimage. In a dream, God told Abu 'Abd Allah that his two sons would spearhead the ouster of the Portuguese from Moroccan soil. Inspired, Abu 'Abd Allah returned to southern Morocco and moved from the relatively isolated oasis where he lived to the thriving commercial center of Tidsi (near present day Tarudant). There he showed what was to be his earmark, his ability to translate his patriline's sacred credit into lines of access to concrete military and economic supports.

Leo Africanus (al-Hasan al-Wazzan), an eyewitness to the times, describes the popular esteem with which Islamic holy men were regarded; and of all the holy men, the blood descendants of the Prophet were the most adored. People would bow upon seeing them, kiss the bottoms of their robes, and seek their touch in order to be healed (Africanus 1896 [1526]; see Gellner 1969 on how sainthood comes to be popularly recognized). Abu 'Abd Allah turned adoration into more concrete supports. He allied himself with powerful tribes in the area and made use of the fighting potential that inhered in their patrilineal organization. He began to collect funds from local people sympathetic to his cause, and with the money bought European firearms. Slowly, he began to build an important regional opposition movement (Brignon et al. 1967:205–234).

In 1510 (A.H. 916/17), the prominent Sufi mystic and brotherhood leader Sayyid Baraka greatly enhanced Abu 'Abd Allah's credit by publicly proclaiming him leader of all the Sus. In confirmation, local tribes from throughout the region came before Abu 'Abd Allah and swore formal oaths of allegiance (Cornell 1986:33). To commemorate the occasion, he took a new name, by which he was thenceforth called, and which indicated his political-religious aspirations: al-Qa'im bi 'Amr Allah, "One Who is Steadfast by the Command of God" (Cornell 1986:33).

In 1513 (A.H. 919/20), the One Who is Steadfast by the Command of God made a bid for national recognition. He traversed the High Atlas Mountains and entered the heartland plains, settling at Afughal. There, he expanded his sacred base of credit by allying himself with the most important political and religious leader of the previous age, al-Jazuli.

Many Muslims believe that each age produces a person who serves as a stellar guide for all others. He is the *qutb,* the pole, "a person who by his virtue and piety raises himself above his contemporaries and serves as their source of guidance" (al-Ifrani 1889:85). In the 1400s (A.H. 800s), al-Jazuli was considered to be the western pole of guidance. He himself acknowledged that role. He recounts how the Prophet Muhammad appeared to him in a dream and said, "Al-Jazuli, I am the most beautiful of God's messengers on earth, and you are the most beautiful of saints" (Drague 1951:52).

Al-Jazuli was the voice of Moroccan popular consciousness, the one who clearly argued that the political ruler needed to be a blood descendant of Muhammad. He wrote popular poems of praise for Muhammad and his bloodline and called upon the Moroccan population to follow the sharif. Al-Jazuli was key spokesman for opposition to the Portuguese. He was the voice of populist Islam, and most Moroccan brotherhoods trace their spiritual descent from him. (In Islam, spiritual affiliation, like patrilineal descent, is encoded in long lists of names. In the spiritual case, the names are of key teachers in each generation, and the long lists are known as the *silsila.*)

The person of al-Jazuli was so important that, when he died, the men who took up his cause carried his body with them as they traveled through the countryside trying to rally support for the sharif and opposition to the Portuguese (Abun-Nasr 1987:207). Finally, in 1484 (A.H. 889/90), they laid the great teacher to rest, burying him in a tomb at Afughal, and it was to Afughal that al-Qa'im went as he tried to expand his base of support. It was no accident that the man who was trying to distinguish himself as a sharif above all others traveled to the tomb of the man who was the most articulate spokesman for the rightfulness of sharifi descent. It was an age in which sacred credit was amassed in its most tangible form, and al-Qa'im came to al-Jazuli's tomb to wrap himself in al-Jazuli's shroud.

With al-Jazuli's sanctity supporting him, al-Qa'im set about consolidating the practical foundations of his position in the central plains. He allied himself with the two large tribal confederations in the region, the Haha and the Shiadma, known for their military strength and their long-time resistance to the Portuguese, and continued to buy

European firearms that entered Morocco at the nearby port Tarkuku (Cornell 1986:36). His political movement began to take on transregional dimensions.

Four years after his arrival at Afughal, al-Qa'im died. His followers buried him at al-Jazuli's side, and his sons, al-A'raj ("the Lame") and al-Shaykh ("the Leader") took control of the movement (see figure 7.2).

Al-A'raj headed the Sa'di cause to the north of the Atlas Mountains. In 1524 (A.H. 931/32), he conquered the great city of Marrakush and made it his capital. There, he addressed the practical tasks of government, including the reinforcement of his sacred position. Al-A'raj elaborated a formal administrative system, expanded his military forces, built a mosque, uttered prayers, and had the bodies of al-Jazuli and al-Qa'im brought to Marrakush for reburial in the exquisite tombs he built for them there. In death, the spokesman for the sharifi cause was laid next to the sharif who would be king. The tombs remain a center of pilgrimage to this day.

al-Shaykh, the leader

While al-A'raj, "the Lame," organized the Sa'di movement in the north, his younger brother al-Shaykh, "the Leader," consolidated power in

FIGURE 7.2. Patrilineal Connections of the First Sa'di Rulers

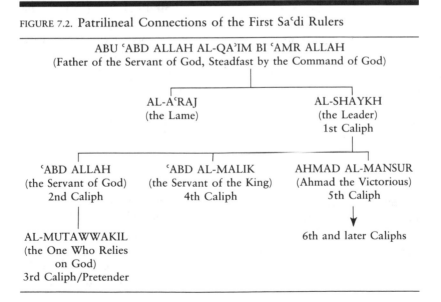

ABU 'ABD ALLAH AL-QA'IM BI 'AMR ALLAH
(Father of the Servant of God, Steadfast by the Command of God)

AL-A'RAJ
(the Lame)

AL-SHAYKH
(the Leader)
1st Caliph

'ABD ALLAH
(the Servant of God)
2nd Caliph

'ABD AL-MALIK
(the Servant of the King)
4th Caliph

AHMAD AL-MANSUR
(Ahmad the Victorious)
5th Caliph

AL-MUTAWWAKIL
(the One Who Relies on God)
3rd Caliph/Pretender

6th and later Caliphs

the south. Al-Shaykh took over the movement and brought it to fruition.

ritual consolidation of sharifi support   Al-Shaykh accomplished the momentous transition from large-scale transregional movement to overarching national dynasty by finding a means of channeling the diffuse but powerful popular legitimacy that now inhered in sharifi descent so that it consistently focused on his own bloodline. Ritual was the means. Because ritual has the ability to build reality beyond everyday constraints, it could be used to construct stability in an unstable world. It was the only resource in that age that could do so, since military, economic, and administrative supports could not, on their own, be stabilized.

Al-Shaykh was a ritual master. He had a keen sense of drama and timing, and used ritual to mark his family off as the blood descendants of the Great Prophet for whom the population searched, those kinsmen in whom the shining blood still flowed. He built an elaborate etiquette around himself. From the Ottomans, al-Shaykh borrowed a formal style of ceremonial hand-kissing that not only expressed the hierarchy of power, but created it. It organized experience to show that this sharifi was above all others, the dominant and powerful one.

From the Fatimi (an Egyptian dynasty whose legitimacy also inhered in blood descent from the Prophet), al-Shaykh borrowed the use of the imperial parasol. On Friday, communal mosque day, the Saʿdi leader, dressed in flowing white robes, rode from his palace to the main mosque, mounted on a fine Arab steed. One manservant held the imperial parasol high above his head while another fanned with him long white ostrich feathers. The onlookers saw him in his sanctity and experienced him in his glory. Surely this was the noble blood descendant for whom they searched!

From the Banu Marin (the last ruling Berber dynasty), the Saʿdi borrowed the practice of bringing scholars from all over the Muslim world to the capital city to discuss religious issues during the month of Ramadan. The practice continues to the present (Kably 1978).

To celebrate the Muslim feast day of ʿAshuraʾ, the Saʿdi provided for the circumcision ritual of several boys from the poorest families in the capital city (al-Ifrani 1889). Moroccans, like many Muslims, consider circumcision necessary for proper Muslim manhood, and they mark the occasion with a dramatic rite of passage. The ruler conferred this rite upon boys who otherwise would not have undergone it with proper ritual accent. The king gave them manhood in dramatic forms.

He sent them royal garments and royal gifts and had his horsemen fetch the boys on the ruler's horses. Decked out in shimmering finery, the boys were paraded through the streets and brought to the ruler's palace where he bestowed upon each his personal blessing. In demonstrating his concern for even the "least of these his subjects," al-Shaykh was trying to demonstrate his concern for the whole.

The ritual supports renewed the grandeur, authority, and legitimacy of the Saʿdi ruler, and systematically reinserted the sharifi image into popular consciousness by embedding it within popular experience. Al-Shaykh was greatly venerated by the population. Many regarded him as a mighty wizard who had the ability to perceive hidden realities. His presence was thought necessary for the victory of his troops; al-Shaykh personally led his men in battle and promised that he would "never break his word nor his lance" (*Chronique de Santa-Cruz* 1934 [1500s]:45–47). According to remembered history, he never did.

the practical base   With the sacred supports firm, al-Shaykh set out to construct a powerful economic and military system. The most striking characteristic of the Saʿdi was their ability to use ritual to stabilize diffuse popular support, and on that stability to rebuild extremely healthy economic and political systems. With wisdom and zeal, al-Shaykh revitalized them. As historian Vincent Cornell argues (1986), al-Shaykh was a man born before his time. In truth, he was a man unusual in any time, one who captured the forces of history and bent them to his own design.

military battles against the Portuguese   In 1511 (A.H. 917/18), the Saʿdi who had attempted to take the Portuguese fort at Agadir (Santa Cruz) were defeated because of Portugal's superior firepower, "their arquebuses and cannons, said by fleeing tribespeople to be 'mouths of the devil'" (*Chronique de Santa-Cruz* 1934 [1500]:35, quoted in Cornell 1986:34).

Once in power, al-Shaykh set out to rectify the matter. He exchanged raw materials with Genoese and Spanish merchants for European firearms (Cornell 1986:36). He had designs of firearms drawn and began manufacturing them in southern Morocco. By 1534 (A.H. 941/42), al-Shaykh was turning out cannons, rifles, and ammunition of Portuguese quality in the Moroccan city of Tarudant. He also expanded the size of the military and made it more efficient by organizing it along Ottoman principles. Additionally, he began rebuilding the Moroccan navy (see Cornell 1986:36–38 for a summary of al-Shaykh's military achievements).

In 1541 (A.H. 948/49), al-Shaykh launched a second attack on the Portuguese fort of Santa Cruz and this time won. Cornell summarizes the firearms used:

> In 1541 the final assault on Santa Cruz was undertaken with "forty to fifty" pieces of field artillery plus a great number of bombards, including six large "maymuna." . . . These great 420 mm guns were cast at the site of a siege and hurled stone projectiles 1.37 meters in circumference. The army supported by these guns included 20,000 spear-carrying infantry, 40,000 arquebusiers, 12,000 crossbow-men, and 50,000 porters and sappers. . . . The Captain of Santa Cruz, Don Gutierrez de Monary, requested 20,000 reinforcements from Portugal (about ten times the number of the actual garrison) to defend his position against the Moroccan assault [but they were not sent and he was unable to hold the fort].
>
> (Cornell 1986:37)

Al-Shaykh's victory began the dismantlement of the colonial system that the Portuguese had begun with the attack of Sabta one hundred and twenty-six years before. It set the Portuguese in flight from the port of Agadir and also from the more northerly port of Asfi (Safi). Soon they abandoned other ports also. By the mid-1500s (A.H. 900s) the Saʿdi had overturned the Portuguese land assault. The military occupation by the foreign Other was finished and the territorial integrity of Islamic Morocco was reestablished.

economic excellence: sugar and gold restored Al-Shaykh's economic achievements were equally impressive. He rebuilt the sugar industry by bringing it under central government control (Jacques-Meunié 1982:2:772–791). He constructed irrigation systems, put land back into sugar cane cultivation, and rebuilt refineries. Morocco once again manufactured elegant, tall white cones of sugar and exported them to the rest of the world. The Sus alone produced a million kilograms of sugar a year, most of which was sold to Europeans (Jacques-Meunié 1982:2:787). One-third of the nation's income during this era came from its commercial dealings in sugar (Brignon et al. 1967:187).

The accomplishment was particularly remarkable since sugar had already started to enter Europe from the New World colonies. Morocco was the only Muslim center of sugar production that managed to rebuild its sugar economy after the plague-induced collapse (see Galloway 1977:181). The rebuilding was a Saʿdi accomplishment.

Al-Shaykh also renewed trans-Saharan trade. He personally led military forces into the Sahara and reopened the ancient coastal route that had not been used for four hundred years. Furthermore, he established Moroccan domination over the Saharan salt mines at Ijil, giving Moroccan merchants a new source of supply for their West African exchange, in which Moroccan merchants traded salt for its equal weight in gold.

Al-Shaykh also secured the two other major trade routes that crossed the Sahara, built fortresses along them, and made the Sus the entrepot for all three. "A significant portion of the three to four tons of gold that annually flowed from Timbuktu" to North Africa was "now securely diverted towards the Sus" (Cornell 1986:39–40). Al-Shaykh, "the Leader," ranked as the country's largest importer of gold. Morocco again basked in the riches that white sugar and yellow gold brought.

With sugar, gold, and trans-Saharan trade revitalized, al-Shaykh turned to other dimensions of the economy. He opened copper mines, stabilized the monetary supply, and minted coins containing far more gold than comparable European coins. He also began to trade sugar and copper with European merchants in return for firearms and materials such as the tin that Morocco needed to produce its own weaponry.

taxes Al-Shaykh instituted a universal tax system, the first in centuries, and put forward a theological argument to justify it. According to Islamic law, Muslims are not to pay taxes in Muslim states unless exceptional circumstances hold. Al-Shaykh clarified why those circumstances held and collected the funds. Al-Shaykh's argument was twofold. In the past, peoples in mountainous areas had sometimes been excluded from taxation; that exclusion had legally been justified through the argument that the original people in those areas had spontaneously converted to Islam and hence their descendants should not be taxed. Al-Shaykh argued that the population of Morocco was far too mobile to distinguish the descendants of the spontaneous converts from the descendants of those who were not, and hence all should pay taxes, especially during times of external assault, times when the House of Islam itself was threatened.

The Sa'di were as practically sensible as they were theologically well versed. The story is told that when Al-Qaim's father first began to tax the people of the Sus, he demanded only a single chicken egg from each household. Given the smallness of the demand and the legitimacy of the authority making it, much of the population complied, only to find their names carefully inscribed on tax rolls. The next time, the taxes were not so slight (Abun-Nasr 1987:212).

monarchy restored　With sacred credit stabilized, and with economic and military supports firm, al-Shaykh made a bid for the national prize. In 1550 (A.H. 957/58), two hundred years after the plague first struck and over a hundred years after the interregnum had begun, Muhammad al-Shaykh marched into the city of Fas and from the great mosque was proclaimed caliph, the Prince of all the Faithful, Muhammad's political successor on earth. From the tops of minarets, callers sang out prayers to the Almighty God in the name of his Prophet Muhammad and his ruling descendant on the throne. Morocco once again had a shining Islamic center within its borders to which the population turned in homage and in self-definition. That center was based on the two most fundamental principles of political legitimacy in the House of Islam: that God meant to have a supreme political authority in this world, and that God especially blessed Muhammad and his bloodline.

During the 1500s (A.H. 900s), the Sa'di were the single claimants to the caliphate, the only major Muslim rulers to call their own the supreme political position in Islam. No one else claimed this, not even the mighty Ottomans, who militarily and administratively controlled most of North Africa and the Middle East. The Ottomans were Muslim, but they were not sharif, Quraysh, or even Arab, and did not then put forward the caliphal claim. In the midst of Christian assault only one effective claimant to the caliphate emerged, and it was established in Islam's far west, in al-Maghrib, the land of the setting sun.

To celebrate the reinstitution, al-Shaykh appended to his name the worthy title "al-Mahdi," "the Long-Awaited One." Many Muslims believe that at the end of the age a stellar figure will appear who will herald a new age of justice. Although al-Shaykh did not overtly claim the theological position of al-Mahdi, he took the title.

The power of al-Shaykh's person and the system he built were not lost on his opponents. Even the Portuguese saw him as a man of honor and inherent nobility. They describe him as "a valiant fighter, military genius, literateur, and an innovative administrator with a keen understanding of commerce and the politics of mercantilism" (*Chronique de Santa-Cruz* 1934 [1500s]:45, 77; cited in Cornell 1986: 35–36).

He was also feared. On June 7, 1549 (A.H. 956), Francis Yaxlee, an English merchant who traded in Morocco, wrote a letter to his friend William Cecil in which he describes the consternation with which Spain viewed al-Shaykh's growing strength:

> The Sherief, as the saieng goith here, hath lately usurped into his hands both the kingdome of Fez and sundrie other Estats of Barbery, and being thereby growne to great power, he is not a little feared in Spaine, speciallie because he hath in rediness a gret armie of both horsemen and footmen, and preparith sundre vessells, wherewith it is supposed he mindeth to passe into Spain.
>
> (*Les sources inédites* 1905–1960:1:11)

It looked as if the Mediterranean lines of conquest were shifting, and the south might sail north again a-conquering. The Spanish Hapsburgs were concerned.

murder   Yet al-Shaykh's brilliance was cut short. In 1557 (A.H. 964), the great caliph was assassinated by Ottoman soldiers while leading a campaign in the High Atlas Mountains, behind Imi-n-Tanut. The Ottomans had gained entry into the sultan's royal guard by posing as deserters from the janissarie forces in Algeria. In the deep of a High Atlas night, they entered the royal tent and slew the reigning Prince of the Faithful, severing his head from his body in a single blow. The assassins escaped, taking with them al-Shaykh's head, which they delivered to the Sublime Porte, the Ottoman ruler in Constantinople, 2,500 miles away by sea, 4,000 miles away by land (al-Ifrani 1889: 79–81).

The crime was especially heinous because it was committed during the month of the sacred pilgrimage, Dhu al-Hijja, a time when Muslims should commit no violence, shed no blood, especially not the blood of a descendant of the Prophet.

Al-Shaykh's headless body was taken to Marrakush and laid in the Sa'di tombs, near his father and al-Jazuli. His funerary slab sings the sorrow of his death:

> Salute to the mausoleum wrapped in mercy, the tomb which is
>   shaded by the skies!
> The breath of sainthood rises from it as perfume, and through it,
>   the breezes from heaven blow unto us.
> Because of your death, the sun of Faith has dimmed and the
>   seven earths have veiled themselves in darkness.
> O enraptured Soul that has been led to the tomb by a fateful
>   event, that has been stabbed by the arrows of death!
> The pillars of glory collapsed under the pain and the seven
>   heavens shook when they heard the news of your death.

Your coffin was transported to Eden escorted by the voices and
melodies of the angels.
The Pleiades took it with them in their celestial flight, but still
you lie under the ground that is covered with clouds.
O Divine Mercy, make him drink the nectar of your favors, and
let the cup always filled with ambrosia circulate endlessly in
front of him!
Destiny was accomplished on the date corresponding to these
words: *It is clear that the home of the Imam of faith, the
Mahdi, is Paradise.*

(al-Ifrani 1889:81–82)

The poem echoes the population's sadness. Moroccans wept at the
great caliph's death and the universe wept with them. The final line
is especially important. Whereas the rest of the inscription confirms
al-Shaykh's grandeur through poetic imagery, the last line confirms
it through "objective proof." It is a chronogram.

Chronograms are mathematical calculations made of verbal statements used to validate or refute the statement's truth. Each Arabic
letter has an assigned numerical value, and a linguist checks a statement by adding together the values of the letters within it. If the total
coincides with a year that is crucial to the statement's events, then it
is understood to be an objective "proof" of the statement's truth.
Chronograms were enormously popular in Sa'di times, a form of sci-
entific verification for that age.

When the numerical weights of the letters in the line "It is clear
that the home of the Imam of faith, the Mahdi, is Paradise" are added
together, one gets 964—the Muslim year in which al-Shaykh was
murdered. This was considered proof that al-Shaykh really was the
Mahdi, the Long-Awaited One, and that he was now in Paradise.

It is said that on the night of al-Shaykh's death a Fasi scholar who
was studying the night sky saw the caliph's star fall out of the heavens
and knew instantly that the great caliph was dead and ran to tell the
caliph's son the news. Whether this scholar truly saw the star fall or
learned of al-Shaykh's murder from other sources, the death of the
first Sa'di caliph was believed by the population to be of such cosmic
significance that the heavens themselves lamented his slaughter.

three sons

The Ottomans may have hoped to dismantle Morocco's new order
by assassinating its leader, but that did not occur. Al-Shaykh sired
three sons nearly as remarkable as himself, who ruled one after the

other and continued the caliphate's grandeur. Each had his own strength: 'Abd Allah was pious, 'Abd al-Malik was debonair, and Ahmad al-Mansur was victorious. Together, they brought peace and prosperity and gave Morocco a second golden age, reminiscent of the greatness the country had known during Berber times. The era was all too brief, but it was glorious. The last half of the 1500s (A.H. 900s) were as stable and secure as the first half had been tumultuous. Al-Shaykh and his three sons are described as "conceptually far ahead of their time in this still tribal and kin-based society . . . able to guide Morocco toward an all-too-brief era of technological innovation and social change unparalleled elsewhere in the Arabic-speaking world" (Cornell 1986:35). The Sa'di era was the turning point in Moroccan history and political culture, when the template of rule was consolidated that would allow Morocco to revitalize itself during the four hundred years of tumult that followed.

sacred supports   The three sons continued to secure the sacred foundations of the newly refounded caliphate. They invented new performances and added high drama and more intense color to others. They recited the Qur'an, built schools, gave scholarships, and gathered about them Islamic judges. Broad were the supports the Sa'di gathered under the sharifi parasol. They capitalized upon images of the popularly elected ruler, the divinely chosen one, pragmatic success, religious infallibility, genealogical descent, knowledge of the Qur'an, mystical perception, election by the faithful, righteous living, success in battle, and political sovereignty. The supports themselves were not new; all were a part of Islam's great constitutive repertoire. What was novel was their consolidation into a single political position, a blood-legitimated position of rightful political rule.

Of the three, 'Abd Allah the Pious is most remembered for his personal sanctity. The popular religious leader of the 1500s (A.H. 900s), Sayyid Ahmad ibn Mussa of Tazarwalt, was once asked,

> "Who is the *qutb* [the pole] of this age?"
> "Myself" Sayyid Ahmad u Moussa replied.
> "And after you?" asked the questioner.
> "A man such as that."
> "And after a man such as that?" persisted the interrogator.
> "*Mawlay* [My Lord] 'Abd Allah, and that is enough."
> (al-Ifrani 1889:85)

While 'Abd Allah was known for his piety, his younger brother, al-Mansur, was known for his religious high drama. Al-Mansur, more than the others, inherited his father's sense of sacred performance. He held audiences in which he spoke from behind a veil, accenting his mystery and his distance from all others.

Al-Mansur's consolidation of court and popular ritual was genuine wizardry. The utterance of the caliph's name was embellished with noble titles and benevolent phrases, speech acts that themselves brought power and prestige. His praises were daily sung in poetry; prayers for his well-being were daily chanted in song. The caliph's name and his bloodline were intertwined with that of Muhammad and became linked to goodness and hope. So elaborate were the rituals surrounding al-Mansur's court that one religious scholar (living in forced exile in Marrakush) accused al-Mansur of trying to play God (Abun-Nasr 1987:216). He was not; rather, he was manifesting God's immanence through himself, Muhammad's descendant, the rightful occupant of the caliphal throne.

economic foundation   Under al-Shaykh's three sons the economy flourished. Agriculture improved, the manufacturing base was expanded, and export trade soared. Ships flying the sharifi flag docked in Europe's major ports, including Amsterdam and London. Trade with England rapidly grew. In 1574–1575 (A.H. 982/83), Morocco's exports to London were valued at 28,639 pounds sterling, and included:

> 620,400 pounds of refined sugar
> 585 hogsheads of unrefined sugar
> 67,648 pounds of almonds
> 434,000 pounds of molasses
> 5,824 pounds of anise seed
> 190 ostrich feathers
> 13,440 pounds of dates
> 600 pounds of orange and apricot marmalade
> 3,200 goat skins
> (*Les sources inédites* 1905–1960:1:186,
>   quoted in Cornell 1986:43–44)

Long-distance trade continued to thrive. Salt flowed south, gold flowed north, and all traces of the plague and the Portuguese were erased.

the military   Al-Shaykh's three sons expanded the military. A professional army was organized and made more efficient by structuring it along Ottoman lines. Troops dressed in Ottoman style, Ottoman names designated individual units, and Ottoman strategies were used to wage conflicts. Schools for military instruction were instituted and ranks were earned on the basis of merit.

Yet the Sa'di continued to maintain alliances with the tribal forces of the countryside. These alliances were important in keeping tabs on the tribes and in providing the dynasty with an alternative fighting force should the professional army grow too strong and attempt to seize power, as it had done in Algeria.

administration   The central administration was organized on the basis of provinces, and it was efficiently run. The caliph personally read all reports from the provincial governors and answered letters promptly. Administrators were required to keep fixed hours of work so that correspondence would not be delayed. Each Wednesday, the caliph met with his cabinet—his ministers and other high government officials—to decide matters of state (Abun-Nasr 1987:216).

international relations   Morocco expanded its diplomatic relationships. Here, 'Abd al-Malik the Debonair shone. He spoke several European languages and his international correspondence was profuse. Equally important, he was suave, witty, and exceedingly bright. Others saw themselves reflected in 'Abd al-Malik's apparently quite striking eyes. Queen Elizabeth's advisors saw him as somehow basically Protestant at heart, while the Spanish saw him as somehow basically Catholic, and the Ottomans thought of him as one of their own. In point of fact, he was the servant of none but God, and came to rule from Morocco's central throne (Yahya 1981:46–85).

The Sa'di entered into a series of international treaties. As is often the case, the partners were strange bedfellows. The Sa'di aligned themselves with the Spanish against the Ottomans, as well as with the English against the Spanish—that is, with Catholics against Muslims as well as with Protestants against Catholics.

Spain was an unlikely ally. It was engaged in a holy war against all it saw as "heathen," and in its exuberance, it cast a wide net to cover wayward Catholics, Jews and Protestants, and all Muslims. The hostility of Spanish Christians towards Muslims—built on centuries of Muslim occupation—was particularly keen. Yet the Spaniards saw the value of an alliance with the newfound Muslim dynasty to the south, the Sa'di, in order to offset what they perceived as the more ominous threat of the Muslim rulers to the east, the Ottomans. "Wicked wizards" could apparently be distinguished by degrees.

For their part, the Sa'di were also involved in a holy war, but it was for another holiness, one that centered on Islam and the defense of their homeland against the Christian Iberians who wanted to destroy it. Yet, Moroccans too saw the value in an alliance with the "Evil Other" to the north to stave off the "Evil Other" to the east, the Ottomans. Moroccans too could distinguish the evil by degrees, and entered into alliance with the Spanish.

Yet Morocco also covered its bases against the fervent Spanish by entering into a pact with the British of mutual defense against Spain. Queen Elizabeth I instigated the accord, and the Sa'di al-Mansur agreed. Elizabeth was especially anxious to secure the alliance prior to 1588 (A.H. 996/97), the year of her victory over the Spanish Armada. Elizabeth and al-Mansur preferred to keep quiet about the treaty, which included the exchange of British firearms for Moroccan saltpeter, a substance necessary in the production of gunpowder. Elizabeth was having enough trouble with Catholics at home without incurring their anger, and the Pope's wrath, by openly sending firearms to the Muslims, trade officially interdicted by papal decree. Nor did al-Mansur want known his intention of sending saltpeter to England, for in his role as the Prince of the Faithful, he had officially banned its export to Christians. Still, bans aside, the Christian Defender of the Faith entered into a treaty with the Muslim Prince of the Faithful, titles that the monarchs of both countries hold to this day.[3]

culminating battle: three dead kings and the river of the storehouses
The culmination of the Sa'di military victories came in the battle of 1578 (A.H. 986) against the Portuguese at Wadi al-Makhazin (see Nekrouf 1984). Although the Portuguese had been driven from Morocco's ports, they retained the hope of regaining them. Portugal's wealth now traveled to it on ships that traversed the high seas, and ports along Morocco's extensive Atlantic coastline could help secure that trade. Portugal's King dom Sebastian thought his opportunity had come when al-Mutawwakil, a weak-willed grandson of al-Shaykh, came to him for help in regaining the Islamic throne (al-Mutawwakil—whose name means "the One Who Relies on God"— had briefly held the throne before being ousted by his uncle 'Abd al-Malik the Debonair). Al-Muttawakil's father ('Abd Allah the Pious), grandfather (al-Shaykh the Leader), and great-grandfather (al-Qa'im, the One Who is Steadfast by the Command of God) had fought long and hard to oust the Portuguese from Morocco's shores, but if the Portuguese Christians would set al-Mutawakkil back on the throne, he promised to hand them the Atlantic littoral, *por favor*.

In July of 1578 (A.H. 986), the Portuguese King dom Sebastian and

Morocco's deposed ruler al-Mutawwakil sailed south across the blue Mediterranean, docking on Morocco's northwest coast near the Lukkus river. The Iberian forces were massive; according to some estimates they exceeded 100,000 men. Al-Ifrani notes two figures given at the time of the battle itself, one of 125,000 and the other of 60,000 (1889:131, 132). Somewhere between 25,000 and 60,000 is probably more accurate. Whatever the precise numbers, the Portuguese forces were large, and in Moroccan understanding, far outnumbered the Moroccan troops.

Moroccans were outraged by al-Mutawakkil's alliance with the Portuguese, who had only recently been ousted from Morocco's soil. They saw the attack in symbolic terms as an ultimate contest between the forces of evil and the forces of good, an attempt by the Christian north to permanently extinguish the light of the Muslim south. The population rallied in opposition. The ancient battle of Badr became the orienting frame of reference through which they thought, and fought, the battle. Nearly a millennium before, the infidel forces had come marching to destroy the true faith, but Muhammad and his men stood firm, and in their steadfastness God had delivered them. Moroccans urged each other to fight like the men at Badr, that they too might be delivered. Holy men rode through the troops at the height of battle encouraging them to valor (al-Ifrani 1889:131–137).

The debonair 'Abd al-Malik was in Marrakush, his capital city, when the invasion occured, sixteen days' march to the south. His younger brother al-Mansur, the head of the armed forces, was in Fas. Needing time to devise a battle plan, 'Abd al-Malik dispatched a series of letters by which he maneuvered the Portuguese King into his own design. First he encouraged the king to stay put. He wrote to King dom Sebastian saying,

> You have already demonstrated your courage in leaving your country and traversing the sea to enter this land. If now you stay in place until I can bring myself to you, it is because you are a true Christian and brave; if not, it is because you are a dog, the son of a dog.
>
> (al-Ifrani 1889:132)

Once he had formulated his plans, 'Abd al-Malik sent another letter encouraging dom Sebastian to march but one day to meet him at Wadi al-Makhazin, a riverbed near the town of Qsar al-Kabir. He concluded the letter by saying, "I am marching sixteen days journey to meet you, will you not march a single day to meet me?" (al-Ifrani 1889:133).

The location of the battle was crucial. By bringing the enemy leaders, the ruling dom Sebastian and the deposed al-Mutawakkil, to this spot, ʿAbd al-Malik had checkmated them. The battle occurred on Monday, August 4, 1578 (A.H. 986) and lasted only seven hours. As ʿAbd al-Malik had planned, the Portuguese forces set themselves on the low ground on the far side of the riverbed. During the night, ʿAbd al-Malik had his men destroy the only bridge leading from that low ground to the other side of the river (al-Ifrani 1889:133). When morning came, the Moroccans were gathered on the high ground, the white sharifi banner flying above them, its gold-embossed Qur'anic verses reflecting the sun. The battle was begun.

At the height of the fighting, as ʿAbd al Malik had foreseen, Atlantic tidal waters flooded the riverbed, and since he had destroyed the only bridge, the Portuguese troops had no place to flee. Thousands were drowned, including dom Sebastian and al-Mutawakkil. The Moroccans had literally pushed the Portuguese back into the sea. Victory was theirs.

Yet, in the fighting, the Moroccans lost their caliph. ʿAbd al-Malik died in circumstances that have never been clarified—possibly by Ottoman poisoning, possibly from wounds he received in battle (al-Ifrani 1889:77, Abun-Nasr 1987:214). In the Western world, the battle takes its name from the three rulers who came to fight and died; it is called "the Battle of the Three Kings." In the Muslim world, it is known by the river that saved Morocco's system of rule, Wadi al-Makhazin, "the River of the Storehouses."

At the end of the fighting, ʿAbd al-Malik's younger brother, al-Mansur, was the only royalty still standing. Victory and the caliphate were his, in the most dramatic of forms. It was then that he was dubbed al-Mansur, "the Victorious," one of the ninety-nine names of God. The title was well earned, for Ahmad had helped his brother devise the battle plan and had personally led the troops to victory.

The battle dramatically undergirded the sharifi template of rule. If a sign was needed to convince Moroccans that God intended for this family of blood descendants to rule, this was it. Morocco's sharifi caliphate won a momentous victory at a crucial juncture in Mediterranean history, adding military verification to their already considerable repertoire of legitimizing supports. The battle was yet another reinforcement of the sharifi model within Moroccan experience and consciousness.

The battle brought about the death of one of Europe's most powerful kings, which in turn brought about the Portuguese loss of autonomy for a time (dom Sebastian left no sons, and the Spanish Hapsburgs took over Portuguese rule for sixty years). The battle renewed the Iberian fear of Muslim military strength, a fear that had somewhat abated after the Lepanto victory. Now a new Muslim power was on the rise, and the decisiveness of the victory worried the Europeans. The Spanish Hapsburgs were especially troubled.

The sharifi caliphate had to be taken seriously. That much was certain. Mediterranean rulers set about trying to secure alliances with al-Mansur, who came to be known in Europe simply as "the Golden One." (Shakespeare modeled the Prince of Morocco in *The Merchant of Venice* upon al-Mansur and also used him in creating his Othello, the dark and passionate Moor, honest and loyal, "who comes from a land of deserts, rocks and hills whose heads touch heaven.")

Embassies were dispatched from major capitals all over the Old World with rich gifts for this newfound king. Portugal sent ornate chariots piled high with conciliatory gifts. Included were 300,000 ducats of silver and "an innumerable quantity of vases and precious objects" (al-Ifrani 1889:146). So impressive were the gifts that the people of Fas poured into the streets and gazed in astonishment as the horse-drawn chariots clattered by.

The gifts of the Prince of Castille were next to arrive and equalled those of Portugal in their beauty and their worth. They included a magnificent string of pearls and, most dramatic of all, huge sapphires that the Castillian prince had taken out of the crown of his father to send to the victorious Muslim king (al-Ifrani 1889:146).

The Hapsburg embassy created quite a stir. Its size was unprecedented and set in motion much speculation in Europe and North Africa. It was composed of no less than forty persons. The Spaniards came carrying gifts and congratulations for Morocco's king (Yahya 1981:102–103). When they docked their boats and unloaded their baggage, Moroccans marveled at the number of people and the quantity of goods. The size of the Spanish embassy was itself an indication of the extent of the Hapsburg concern.

The Ottoman embassy followed. Included in its offerings was a finely carved sword and scabbard. What impressed the Moroccans most was the steel of which the blade was made. Never had they seen steel so strong and so pure (al-Ifrani 1889:146).

Powerholders in France, England, and the Netherlands also sent embassies laden with gifts. No ruler who wanted connections with "the Victorious One" failed to dispatch men and presents to the great caliph's court. Al-Mansur and Morocco basked in victory. Paradise lost had seemingly been regained.

outward expansion—the caliphate manifested   In celebration of his victory over the north, al-Mansur undertook a massive military expedition to the sub-Sahara, and in 1591 (A.H. 1000/01) conquered Timbuktu and the Great Songhay Empire (territory covered by present day Mali, Niger, and Nigeria). With this victory, prayers again on both sides of the Sahara and within it were sung out in the name of the Muslim caliph who reigned from Morocco's central throne.

In scholarly circles, the interpretation of the expedition, like the documentation itself, is confused. For our purposes, what is important is that the military drive into sub-Saharan Africa was meant to verify al-Mansur's claim to be the true caliph of Islam. The true Prince of the Faithful would not be limited to one small corner of the Muslim empire, but would spread across it (Yahya 1981:145–167). Al-Mansur sincerely believed that he was God's chosen ruler and that it was his duty to reunite the community of Muslims under his blood-legitimated authority. "He issued a *fatwa* (legal opinion) in which he enumerated his justifications for the invasion. . . . First on the list was the need to bring about the unity of Islam under his Qurayshite leadership" (Yahya 1981:157). The unity was possible because the "Sun of Prophetic, Imamic, Hashimite, and ʿAlid Caliphate had risen"—al-Mansur (al-Fishtali, quoted in Yahya 1981:157).

The millenarian aspects of the conquest cannot be overlooked; al-Mansur undertook the expedition one thousand years after the beginning of the Muslim calendar. A.H. 1000 was a date of enormous eschatological significance; many Muslims believed that the Mahdi would then appear. Al-Mansur even gave some hint that he might be the Mahdi, and his conquest of the Songhay was a move toward laying that claim (Yahya 1981:157–162).

That gold could also be obtained was all to the good. The Saʿdi was not a world divided; sanctity and economy went hand in hand. To portray the expansion as "really" economic at base is simply false (see Yahya 1981:156). Morocco already had considerable stores of gold, had the means of acquiring more, and, in fact, the takeover was in the long term economically counterproductive. Utilitarian gain was not the only issue involved. The expansion into the Great Songhay was the first step in al-Mansur's plan to reunite the Muslim world, to bring the dispersed Household of Faith back into one. As his court poet sang to him (al-Fishtali 1973:117–126), he was the "caliph of caliphs," the one in whom Muhammad's blood most clearly shone, and he would "reconquer the land of the Pyramids." "And if his sword draws him, he will take the Ottoman throne also."

8

Prophet's Birthday: light's truth

After the Battle of Wadi al-Makhazin, Morocco reached a new level of stability and influence. In confirmation, al-Mansur developed a ritual to celebrate the glory of the Prophet and the glory of his descendants on the throne. Begun more than a thousand years after Muhammad's birth and three thousand miles away, the ritual communicated the new model and offered ultimate validation by associating it with the honor of the Prophet and the truth of God's light.

The ritual was an innovation; it is not a part of the canon of Islam. For the first centuries after Muhammad's death, there were not elaborate official celebrations of it. Those began in the Muslim east in the 1100s (A.H. 500s) and spread west, first entering Morocco through the port of Sabta in 1291 (A.H. 690), seven hundred years after Muhammad's birth. The Muslim governor of that city claimed that ritual celebrations for the Prophet's Birthday were needed in order to counter the population's growing fascination with Christmas (al-Maqqari 1949 [1600s]:389). From Sabta, celebrations spread to the rest of the Moroccan countryside, mostly as local-level ceremonies. The Banu Marin briefly articulated them on the national level, but their ritual did not last.

The Saʿdi made the celebrations a dramatic and durable national institution that survives to the present. Their articulation moved rite from the peripheries to the center of collective life. ʿId al-Mawlid, the Prophet's Birthday, quickly took hold and became one of the three most popular ritual celebrations in Morocco, a position it holds to this day (Paquignon 1911, Salmi 1956, Shinar 1977, Westermarck 1926).[1]

The Saʿdi were attracted to the ritual because it accented the importance of Muhammad's birth and the power of his bloodline and at the same time validated Morocco's existence as a distinctive political entity. It was a true national ritual celebration (Paquignon 1911, Shinar 1977). In it, the Moroccan nation expressed its unity and had that unity read back to it as enduring truth. The performance took place in the nation's capital; the great king invited representatives of every part of the countryside to gather inside the great palace walls to celebrate the great Prophet's birth. There the life of Muhammad was feted, as was the life of the nation and the life of Muhammad's descendant on the throne.

The Saʿdi caliphs expressed their dynastic power in numerous dimensions: economic revitalization, military might, administrative efficiency. Yet it was in the great sacred performance of Muhammad's birthday that they created their most durable legacy, the sustaining foundation that renewed sharifi legitimacy and power when all else faltered. The Prophet's Birthday reflected sharifi glory while its practical foundations were firm, and then compensated for them once they had weakened. In sacred performances, the Moroccan monarchy was continually reborn.

incomparable palace: al-Badiᶜ

Pierre Bourdieu pinpoints the way in which the physical construction of space—for example, the layouts of houses, streets, and cities—channels popular experience and shapes popular consciousness, setting the physical dimensions in which people construct their lives, physical dimensions that shape conceptual imagination (Bourdieu 1977, Comaroff 1985).

Al-Mansur's ritual elaboration of the Prophet's Birthday took place in a space worthy of it, in a great palace that he built in Marrakush. Building was begun in 1578 (A.H. 986), five months after al-Mansur took the throne. It took fifteen years to complete. The palace was officially opened two years after the Muslim millennium, in *anno Hijrae* 1002 (A.D. 1593) Al-Mansur dubbed it al-Badiʿ, "the Incomparable," one of the ninety-nine names of God. It was magnificent.

Marrakush itself is a place of incomparable beauty—a cameo set in the dry brown Haouz plains. Adobe walls enclose the city, keeping the beauty within and the desert without. The city is a vast oasis through which rivers flow and breezes blow. Graceful palms adorn its streets. The entire city has a soft, dusty rose hue that comes from the high iron content of the adobe from which the buildings are made. At its center lies the Kutubia, a great mosque built in the 1100s (A.H. 500s) whose adobe minaret reaches so high into the sky that the distant snowcapped peaks of the Atlas Mountains are its backdrop.

Near the walls of that mosque al-Mansur built the palace, sparing no expense. Craftsmen were hired from all over the Mediterranean, black and white marble was imported from Italy, crystal from Austria, and tiles from Andalusia. When the palace was completed, the grounds covered several square miles of the city. Streams and lakes were dispersed throughout. Orange groves and herb gardens graced its central courtyards. Its pools were raised in order to hide a labyrinth of underground passageways that allowed servants to carry out their tasks without intruding upon the visual calm. Sweet fragrances, the sounds of flowing water, and soft breezes mingled within the palace's high walls (see Deverdun 1959:392–401 and al-Ifrani 1889:179–195, 237–256).

Europeans who saw the palace were dazzled by its beauty. The marble, they said, gleamed as if it were always wet, and whole rooftops glittered with gold. Quotations from the Qur'an were chiseled into the stucco and glazed into the tiles. Strong cedar beams supported high, elaborately painted ceilings. Water flowed into the palace's water basins through silver castings of pythons, leopards, and lions. The central throne room was so stunning that one diplomat described it as celestial: "The signs of the sky were represented with so much splendor, that one could believe one saw the sunrise when looking at it" (al-Ifrani 1889:179–195).

The palace was opened with a great feast. Guests included foreign diplomats, Moroccan dignitaries, and representatives of the local population. They ate from golden plates and drank from crystal glasses; at the end of the meal, the caliph personally presented each with a lavish gift (Deverdun 1959:392–401). Al-Badi' was the center of the most dramatic peacock throne of the time, a court reminiscent of Baghdad's at the height of 'Abbasi power. Al-Mansur, the "Golden One," and his court were the talk of Africa and the Middle East as well as all of Europe.

ritual of the Prophet's Birthday

Like the organization of space, the clarified channeling of human behavior in the ritual setting creates and reinforces particular representations of reality. The ritual moment builds distinctive experience and understanding, which the regularity of the performance systematically reinserts into lived history.

When most effective, rituals fuse particular cultural representations—such as the new model of political authority—with taken-for-granted conceptions of the universe and individual drives and emotions. In the Prophet's Birthday celebrations, the sharifi caliphate was made a link to the basic Muslim understandings of the truth of the universe as well as to the evanescent drives of earth—food, sexuality, and wordly wealth. Up to God and down to pleasure: the ritual of the Prophet's Birthday transformed the sharifi monarchy into a pathway for both.

Precise descriptions of al-Mansur's celebrations come to us from an eyewitness, al-Fishtali, who was a scribe and historian in the Sa'di court. (Al-Fishtali's descriptions are included in al-Ifrani's broader account. Unless otherwise attributed, throughout the following, I draw upon al-Fishtali, as quoted in the 1889 edition of al-Ifrani's work, pp. 237–256.)

Preparations began months in advance. Al-Mansur commissioned the wax merchants of Marrakush to make hundreds of candles. Many were cast the size of human beings. Most were white and resembled marble statues, but some were deep red. The colors themselves, white and red, carried the main themes of the ritual: the white light of the truth and the powerful red blood of Muhammad's descendants.

Twilight of the evening before the Prophet's Birthday set the festivities in motion. The candles were brought next to the old wall where the porters who carried brides through the streets on the way to marriage stood ready to place the candles on the same litters. Once the candles were in place, they lifted the litters to their shoulders and the great procession began.

The city was spectacular when lit by candlelight. The adobe walls caught the moving patterns of dark and light. Distinctions between object and silhouette blurred and the whole world became a shadow play. The candles were carried swiftly through the narrow streets while drums beat, ghaitas played, and the crowds applauded. Most people on the streets were men—as in most public festivities—but a few women were gathered there also, while other women watched from nearby rooftops. When the candles passed, the women let out their shrill ululations of joy.

candles, virgins, and arousal

Al-Fishtali describes the candles as from a distance resembling a moving forest of palm trees; the natural world itself seemed alive with motion in praise of the Prophet. Yet, as the candles came closer, they took on human form, and looked like young virgins on their way to marriage. That al-Fishtali should think of brides as he viewed the candles approaching is not surprising. The candles were about the size of women; they were swathed in the brocade cloths that brides wear, and were carried through the streets on bridal litters; the gold and silver threads of their wrappings caught the light and shimmered.

By evoking the image of virgins on their way to marriage, the candles evoked a visceral response in the waiting crowds. They rallied human passion and intensified the emotional pitch of the performance. The singing and clapping grew stronger and the ululations increased. Communication took place from body to body, and the crowd was physically drawn into the festivities.[2]

This ritual reached down to individuals by arousing the passion associated with the bride on the night of first marriage, the quintessential moment for Muslim manhood and womanhood. For men that moment is defined as the height of temporal pleasure and personal power. It is then that a man changes a girl into a woman by piercing her previously untouched hymen and spilling her blood, opening the womb for possible birth. For the girl, it is also a high moment, but of a very different sort, for she is the passive participant, adorned and adored, who lies in wait for the man to perform on her own body the action that will make her a woman. He is the initiator; she is the responder, dependent upon him for the most basic definition of her being.

The ritual of the Prophet's Birthday plays upon the sensual and the sacred, weaving one through the other, and making the sharifi caliphate crucial to both. Those not immediately aroused by Islamic fervor might be drawn to the ritual by passion of the more earthly sort.

In either case—or, better yet, in both—the same purposes were served. All was to the glory of God, Muhammad, and the sharifi caliph.

Sensuality was evoked but not allowed long to rest on virginal females, for as the candles neared, one was reminded that they were candles, not brides, and their purpose was to celebrate Muhammad's great light. It was to that purpose that they were being carried to the palace of the reigning prince, Muhammad's own blood descendant, who occupied the Moroccan throne. The porters left their burdens at the palace gates and the festivities ended for the night. All became dark and quiet.

dawn: the caliph's bringing of light

While the earth was still covered in darkness the sharifi caliph, dressed in shimmering robes of pure white, left his palace. The great gates opened and he emerged to lead the waiting crowd in prayer. While darkness still hung, the many-times-removed grandson of Muhammad called out the words "God is Great. There are no others like him. And Muhammad is His Prophet." The crowd followed—bowing, kneeling, and touching their foreheads to the ground, performing the motions that are a part of Muslim prayer. And then the light began to come; the dawn began to break; Muhammad's Birthday was begun.

The iconic image could not have been clearer. Muhammad's luminous descendant stood before the faithful and led them in the prayer that ended the night and brought in the Prophet's Birthday, bringing back the Prophet's light that could pull humankind out of the earth's shadows into God's truth.

The king blessed the crowd and invited them to pass through the great gates and into his palace for a celebration of the light-giving lamp of Muhammad, the truth of this universe, and a celebration of the pleasures of this world. In the largest of the al-Badiʿ courtyards, al-Mansur seated himself on a magnificent central throne. The brocade-swathed candles shone before him, while torches—arranged in giant candelabras—blazed behind him.

The image of the caliph bathed in light greeted the crowds as they entered, "each according to his rank." First came prominent religious judges, followed by esteemed Qurʾanic scholars. Then came "the pious persons," a rank that included heads of religious brotherhoods and other holy men. They were followed by wazirs, the king's key advisors. Next came other invited guests, including foreign diplomats and local and regional leaders from the Moroccan countryside. Then came the soldiers, and finally people from the streets. Al-Fishtali states that everyone who desired admittance was given entry.

Once inside, the crowd sat down on the brightly woven carpets and leaned against cushions that had been scattered about. The seating, like the entering, was in ranked order, an important visual reproduction of the proper order of social hierarchy. Here in this spectacular palace, where the truth of the universe was celebrated, the population was physically reminded that if all would enter and sit in proper rank around the reigning blood-descendant caliph, all would receive God's truth and earthly pleasure.

Once the crowd was seated and quiet, Arabic recitations began. A man gifted in the art of formal speech would tell the life of the Prophet "from beginning to end," in the holy tongue of Arabic, "the very sounds of which move men to tears and ecstasy" (Arberry 1955:21). The Prophet's virtues were sung. How noble and good this son of the lineage of Ma'ad, who stood sturdy in war and steadfast in truth! His miracles were called forward, as when he spoke to a rock and it burst into flowers—as when thirsty in the desert one night he reached for the moon, took it from the sky, opened it, and drank the water that spilled onto his hands. The honor and nobility of the Prophet was then compared to the honor and nobility of his descendant who now sat on the caliphal throne. Their likenesses were underlined, the glory of the two revealed, and the power of the Prophet's bloodline affirmed. Then followed poets and dramatists who sang out the same themes.

Next a lavish feast was served, a gift of the caliph. The order of serving echoed the order of seating. Touch and taste as well as vision reminded the population that if the proper order were followed, all would be fed. Whole roasted rams were served on great platters, followed by tagines of chicken, lemons, and olives, then couscous and pigeon and almond pastry. Poets sung, music played, and the smell of myrtle twigs and rose water filled the air. Hour after hour of pleasure passed.

Finally the day concluded with al-Mansur's presentation of gifts to the day's best performers—the most convincing dramatists, the most moving poets. The gifts included gold plates, crown jewels, and royal swords.

qasidas: poetry of praise

Rituals do not always include poetry, but the Moroccan celebrations of the Prophet's Birthday do (see Salmi 1956). The most important works are formal poems, *qasidas,* here composed in honor of the reigning monarch. I will summarize and quote a long qasida sung to al-Mansur (al-Ifrani 1889:249–256). Like other qasidas written for the Prophet's Birthday, it is composed of three parts: erotic passion, prophetic honor, ruler loyalty.

part 1   The poem opens with the pain caused by an unnamed Other who has cruelly separated the poet from his beloved. In spite of the separation, the poet's passion flourishes, and in his mind's eye he sees her being carried away on a litter, one of several litters carrying women that are part of a huge camel caravan winding its way east across the desert and away from him. The lover ponders the scene, trying to figure out the caravan's ultimate destination. At the end of North Africa's long desert, will they turn north to Lebanon or south to the Hijaz? Will they go to the land of the Prophet, to the hills near Tayma or to the plains where the "the white gazelles frolic"?

In his mind, the poet begs the camels to stop, but they travel on, and his "heart contents itself with following with ardor the traces of the litters." He sees them by day and night, watching them "when darkness obscures the horizons" and when "dawn breaks forth." The lover is moved by the beauty of the litters: "the distinctiveness of their form, their varying colors," and "the white cupola that arches above each of them." (The similarity between the visual image of the litters in the poetry and the visual experience of the litters in the candle procession is clear). When morning comes and the heavenly stars have faded from view, he says that now the female litters are the stars on the desert landscape. The day progresses, and he finally learns their destination: they are bound for a sacred enclosure. In thought, he travels there also, and the scents of its fine herbs renew by night and day the lover's ardor for his beloved.

part 2   Suddenly, the poet halts and turns away from the woman of his desire: "A pious duty draws him." Now it is he who is camelback-riding towards Makka, the center of pilgrimage. At first, the poet states that he hopes that the journey will help him "forget his love and find consolation," but as he approaches the spot "where the faith saw its first fruits," his perception changes. He now realizes that his love for the woman was only secondary and temporal, a covering of his true and enduring passion for the faith of Islam and the life of the final Prophet.

As he reaches the top of a sand dune, he comes upon a huge procession, "so massive it looks like a sea," and is startled to see that at the center is the Prophet, Muhammad himself. Overjoyed at the sight of the founder of the faith, the poet sings the Prophet's praises. His first praises are for Muhammad's political accomplishments on earth, his ability "to crush the powerholders of his day," "to bring about the downfall of Caesars." The poet then affirms that this political superiority comes from Muhammad's bloodline. Muhammad's forefathers are mentioned by name: "the family of Nizar, issue of Maʿad, son of ʿAdnan." Through the bloodline flow the qualities that Muhammad exhibited in stellar form. Muhammad is "the best of the creatures of the universe . . . whose mission was announced long in advance." The poet thinks of Muhammad's miracles and reminds the listener that the greatest of them all was the conveyance of the Qurʾan. The Prophet "is a great sun whose blazing light blots out falsehood, delusion, and error." God and truth shine through him.

The poet then turns to the Prophet with a personal plea. The intimate link is made. Will the Prophet please stand up for the poet when his sins are weighed on the day of judgment?

Then, returning to a focus on the greatness of Muhammad as a worldly ruler, the poet greets by name his four successors, that is, Abu Bakr, ʿUmar, ʿUthman, and ʿAli. The last, ʿAli, is particularly acknowledged, for he was of "the greatest saintly family" and he transmitted "to his descendants a great part of divine favor."

Suddenly, Muhammad and the procession disappear. The poet's passion, first aroused by the woman, but now with nobler focus, quickens. He is nearly overwhelmed by his desire to reach Makka, the center of Islamic pilgrimage, and drives his camel ever faster. The listener now learns that the poet is on a mahari, a great desert camel bred for speed and racing. The beast pounds across the desert with its neck outstretched, itself enflamed by the desire to reach the holy center.

part 3   Yet again, abruptly, the poet halts. Speaking directly to the Prophet (though the Prophet is no longer physically present), he states: "But what, perhaps I should turn my bridle, because I occupy a certain rank around one of your descendants, the illustrious head of my country?" The poet realizes that having been renewed by the sight of the Prophet, his duty is *not* to ride on to Makka, the place of pilgrimage, for he has already received pilgrimage's goal—the visceral experience of the sacred. Sanctified places are for renewal, not for remaining. His duty now is to return to the service of Muhammad's descendant who occupies the caliphal throne. Realizing this, the poet turns around and spurs his camel to the west, away from Makka, toward Morocco.

The poet then focuses upon Morocco's reigning king and never wavers from him. Al-Mansur's greatness is sung. The poet says that it is al-Mansur who decides who will occupy the thrones of the day. It is he who gives "the crowns to the Kings of the century." When compared with other powerholders, the sharifi Prince of the Faithful is the lion who sends the others fleeing into the scrub brush where they cower and try to hide.

The poet recalls al-Mansur's victory over dom Sebastian and praises his military forces. So powerful is the luminescence that the blood-descendant ruler has inherited from Muhammad that it passes to his troops also. When they fight at night, "their lances give forth light to guide them." "They have conquered numerous countries and have imposed an enormous tribute on the princes of the Sudan." Through them, the caliph will reunite the Muslim world. He will come to possess the lands all the way from Morocco to Baghdad and the Yemen. "And if his sword draws him, he will take the Ottoman throne also."

Of al-Mansur, the poet says that he is "the Imam of men," Islam's true political leader, the protector of the spiritual community of faith. His right to rule comes from his noble origin, his bloodline. His dynasty is "of the branch that most closely resembles the father trunk." "On him converge the virtues that are transmitted only by blood." He is from the noble family "that rules the world of the race of Zidan." "These princes are the pillars of faith, the supports of royal authority," rulers "whose great designs reach above Saturn . . . members of a family that God has glorified . . . by giving them His law and His verses of Verbs and Distinction," the Qur'an, and by making them rulers over all.

The poet then expresses his hope that the sharifi prince may always "possess the universe and protect the religion in the kingdom of Sulayman" and that for him, "victory will always break forth." With that benediction, the poem ends.

echoes

The verbal progression of the poem reproduces the visual progression of the candle procession. It begins with passion for the female, then turns to the nobler passion of adoration of the Prophet, which in turn leads to a concentration on the Muslim ruler in the present, Muhammad's descendant. The three foci, like the three sections, are intrinsic to this qasida form of poetry. The poems are a political attempt to institutionalize eros—to turn sexual passion into religious fervor and political loyalty.

The three sections—female passion, Prophet praise, ruler allegiance—remain basically distinct, with interconnections under-developed. There is some carry-over from one section to the next be-cause all three occur in a single poem. Some of the passion initially aroused for the female transfers onto the second part that concerns the Prophet Muhammad, and some of the passion for the female and some of the adoration of Muhammad extend to the current ruler, the focus of part 3. But there is not the degree of carry-over, not the forceful metaphorical intermingling, that one sees in many kinds of poetry and many forms of ritual performance.

The three sections remain basically distinct for good reason. The question of the degree of closeness between erotic passion, adoration of Muhammad, and devotion to current rulers is a delicate issue of Sunni faith. To meld them too closely would be blasphemy. So the links are there but *sub rosa,* present but understated. Occasionally, in the presentation of legitimate political authority, vagueness is the better part of valor.

power of icons

An icon is an enduring physical representation of truth in which the specifics of physical form are crucial to the meaning constructed. Of the importance of icons to the human species, the biologist Stephen Jay Gould states: "Scholars are trained to analyze words. But pri-mates [humans included] are visual animals, and the key concepts and their history often lie in iconography. . . . [Icons are] not frills or summaries; they are foci for modes of thought" (1987:16–25).

The ritual of the Prophet's Birthday builds powerful, multifaceted icons—living icons in flesh and blood—in which sound, sight, smell, touch, and taste carry the same messages, present the same forceful arguments.

An argument is a convincing association of the unknown with the known, an attachment of possibilities to unshakeable truths. The ef-fectiveness of the argument depends on the strength with which the bond between possibility and truth is made.

The iconography of the Prophet's Birthday presents the argument that legitimate political authority flows through Muhammad's blood-line and results in the ruler one sees on the throne. This is a plausible, though not inevitable, inference in Islam, an inference which the ritual reinforces through iconic presentation. Blazing light, Muhammad, the Qur'an, and Morocco's sharifi Prince of the Faithful are brought together in a moment of heightened physical arousal and heightened learning receptivity. Input from every perceptual domain leads to the conclusion that the light of truth indeed shines through the reigning descendant on the throne.

The Prophet's Birthday begins in darkness which is pushed away by the king, the reigning Prince of the Faithful, whose garments catch the moonlight and shimmer. He leads his people in prayer. By following him even in darkness, the faithful participate in bringing light to the world. Dawn comes. The night is finished, and men, in ranked order, follow the caliph into a palace of incomparable beauty where earthly pleasures and the light of Islamic truth abound.

The ritual creates a cosmic argument that links the sharifi caliph with truth, then undergirds it with a more temporal argument concerning the relationship of the sharifi prince with the pleasures of this world. The ritual demonstrates that Morocco's Prince of the Faithful brings both truth and pleasure. The prince bestows upon Muslim men the words of the Qur'an, God's light, connection to Muhammad's bloodline, virgins on litters, sumptuous food, lovely sounds, sweet smells, and poetry.

formation of basic level category of ruler

The ritual of the Prophet's Birthday establishes the basic level category of "ruler." The ritual consolidates a persuasive mental image (the icon) and a convincing motor action (submitting oneself to him) that in combination build the category. A "ruler" is shown to be a blood descendant of Muhammad seated on a great throne surrounded by white light, and the action due him is submission.

From the basic level category, superordinate and subordinate categories are then formed. Above the ruler is Muhammad, the higher level political figure whose authority comes from an even more distant and abstract God. Muhammad can no longer be seen and God has never been available for view, but glimpses of both can be gained by focusing on the ruler and using analogous imaging and analogous actions. As the ruler's own ancestor, Muhammad is something like him, only much grander. The deity is much grander still, not at all like the ruler in person, but bearing some resemblance to the great light that surrounds him, yet much more intense. The action due each is submission, with the greatest submission belonging to God. "Islam" means "submission." Political authorities on the regional and local level also come to be viewed through this same definition. They are smaller in scale and less influential, and what is due them is a lesser degree of submission.

Islamics

The ritual of the Prophet's Birthday grounded the sharifi model of rule in Islamic truths, as the words of the Qur'an—the unalterable truth—illustrate:

> In the Name of God, the Merciful, the Compassionate . . .
> The Prophet is nearer to the believers than their selves . . .
> Those who are bound by blood are nearer to one another
> in the Book of God than the believers and the emigrants . . .
>
> You have a good example in God's Messenger
> for whosoever hopes for God and the Last Day. . . .
> O believers, remember God oft,
> and give Him glory at the dawn and in the evening.
> It is He who blesses you, and His angels,
> to bring you forth from the shadow into the light. . . .
>
> . . . O Prophet, We have sent thee as a
> witness, and good tidings to bear and warning,
> calling unto God by His leave, and as a light-giving lamp.
> Give good tidings to the believers
> that there awaits them with God great bounty . . .
> (Sura 33, The Confederates, 1, 7, 22, 42–44, 46–47)

The ritual of the Prophet's Birthday experientially embedded the sharifi caliphate in these foundations. It affirmed the existence of a single God outside of nature who created everything in it, a God whose truth is appropriately represented through the metaphor of light, a convincing representation for a metaphysical God since light is both tangible and intangible, focused and diffuse, a connection between the realm of this earth and the realm beyond. Al-Nur, "Light," is one of God's ninety-nine names.

According to the Qur'anic text, God sent his truth to earth, conveying it through the human prophets—all of whom were male. That truth is the "light of the Revelation" that brings humans "forth from the shadows into the light" (Sura 33:44). Yet, it will only bring humans forth if they remain steadfast. Unfortunately, humans have trouble with this, and God laments: "If they had been asked to apostatize they would have done so. . . . Yet they had made convenant with

God before that . . . and covenants with God shall be questioned of" (Sura 33:16).

In order to show humans how to remain sturdy in truth, God sent the revelation one last time, in complete form—the Qur'an; and he sent Muhammad as an example. Humans must now learn to abide by God's truth, for God will send no other book and no other prophet. Muhammad is God's seal on prophecy, the light-giving lamp whom God adores. God demands that others adore Muhammad also.

The Qur'anic passage confirms the power of blood descent: "Those who are/bound by blood are nearer to one another/in the Book of God than the believers and the/emigrants" (Sura 33:7). The power of blood is only briefly mentioned in the Qur'an, but the Sa'di gave it full ritual elaboration, thereby accenting the aspect of the scriptural text that most bolstered their worldly claims.

universals

Yet the sharifi form of rule does not rest on Islamic fundamentals alone. It ritually embeds itself in the essential dilemmas of human existence, in the plight of mortals everywhere. What is the nature of the universe and its truth, and how can humans connect with it? How are our connections with one another related to that truth? Particularly, how is the most intense of human connections—sexual intercourse—related to the universe's construction? These are questions asked by all of humanity.

The ritual uses the culture's imagination to develop plausible answers to these questions, answers that are constructed in a particular time and place but made broadly convincing by articulation through powerful physical experiences (candles, poetry, the glimmering prince) and convincing imaginative abstractions (a supranatural God, men who can connect with him, women who are more earthbound).

The ritual of the Prophet's Birthday uses sexual passion to attract people, but then clarifies a proper hierarchy of passion. Through verb and icon, it argues that sexual passion is temporal and fleeting, while more enduring passion is associated with God, the Prophet Muhammad, and the Muslim ruler in the present. Noble passion is all male.

Islam does not deny the pleasures of this world, but they must be put in their proper place. Sexual passion and pleasure are to be aroused and satisfied. But a more enduring and noble passion must be the central focus for mankind, a passion focused on God's truth, imagined as light—passion which is made accessible through God's light-giving lamp Muhammad and through Muhammad's descendant who occupies the caliphal throne and who also sheds great light.

The ritual establishes a hierarchy of connection to universal truth which is at the same time a hierarchy of power in the world, and it excludes the male-female sexual connection from that hierarchy. Islam (like Christianity) minimizes the heterosexual bond by building a supranatural dimension and excluding female sexuality from it. The ritual brings into being a universe of meaning that supports Mernissi's and Bouhdiba's contention that the dominant sexual culture associated with Islam includes a strong opposition to the heterosexual bond: "the male-female connection [is posed] as a threat to man's connection to the Divine . . . [so that] men do not psychologically invest in the heterosexual relationship" (Mernissi 1987a).

This is not an inevitable construction in culture. Some cultures use sexual intercourse and the heterosexual bond as a template for connection with the divine (e.g., the Tamiar of the Malay Peninsula). Yet Islam and Christianity in their dominant forms do not. The Moroccan construction, like the Catholic, stresses the "purely" physical aspects of the sexual act and underplays possible metaphysical dimensions. Sexual intercourse tends to be interpreted in Islam as a physical release for tension (an intrinsically transitory act) or as a brief physical act whose purpose is more durable, that is, the reproduction of children; but in neither case is the sexual act itself considered to be something of lasting importance, itself an embodiment of divine truth. As culturally defined, sexual intercourse and the heterosexual bond are undervalued in relation to more enduring things—truth, God, ultimate connection—envisioned in male terms. Male power and male connection is valorized over heterosexual love.

The Qur'anic text excludes women from the hierarchy of authority. God sent his truth to earth through the male archangel Jibril, who conveyed it to the prophets, all of whom were male, including the last prophet, Muhammad, who is the recipient of the complete words of truth and light. Muhammad's male blood descendants carry on his essence. They share in his ability to shed light on the pathway to truth, and hence are the proper holders of Muslim political authority in the present.

The Moroccan practice of the Prophet's Birthday excludes women from the ultimate hierarchy of authority as well. When al-Mansur initiated the celebrations for the Prophet's Birthday in the 1580s, all those present within the great palace walls were male, as were all those gathered four hundred years later when Morocco's current king and descendant of the Prophet celebrated the Prophet's Birthday during the 1980s. Authority passes from God to Muhammad to the political ruler in the present. Legitimate political authority is grounded in the basic understandings of the nature of the universe and the nature of the sexes. The validity of this model of rule is built on the back of the cosmos and on the fronts of women.

intermingling of levels

Not everyone could attend the national ritual, but the sharifi caliphs ensured the attendance of representatives of the entire population. To the great ritual in the great palace, the rulers summoned the political, economic, and religious leaders of the countryside. Local leaders experienced the national ritual thanks to the caliph's beneficence, and then returned to local areas to tell of what they had seen to construct local festivities that echoed the national occasion. The local celebrations took on local color, and exhibited—then and now—some diversity. Yet the underlying themes of the light of God's truth that shines through Muhammad and his bloodline remain the same, as do the central symbolic elements through which they are substantiated: candles, Qur'anic recitations, and poetry that sings of the power of blood. Through participating in the local festivities held throughout the countryside, the population was linked into a single whole. The multiple festivities led to the center. The many pathways led to the caliphal throne.

The ritual quickly became widely practiced and deeply felt, a part of the constitutive repertoire of Moroccan experience, a cultural fundamental of deep local and national meaning that drew upon and reinforced the central foundations of Islam at the same time that it was linked to the universal dilemmas of human existence. In the centuries that followed, the ritual continued to be practiced. Some caliphs developed it more, some less, but it became a part of the Moroccan cultural repertoire, a part of Moroccan existence, one of those holy days that marks the passage of seasons, years, and the lives of individuals. It is practiced every year at the national center and throughout the countryside. In 1987, four hundred years after the Sa'di innovation, Morocco's king and blood descendant Hasan II performed the ritual in the twelve-hundred-year-old mosque-university of al-Qarawiyin in Fas. He was dressed in shimmering white robes and seated on a carpet in the center of a glistening room. A glorious Qur'an was set before him and throughout the evening he periodically turned the pages and recited the holy words to himself in inaudible tones. Blazing candles surrounded him, as did Qur'anic scholars who sang out verses from the holy book and poets who sang out praises for the Prophet and his reigning prince, a member of the Prophet's own bloodline, thirty-nine generations removed. The all-male ritual was broadcast on national television throughout the evening and into the early part of the night. Then later in the night, throughout the countryside, Moroccans left their homes and went to holy places near them and lit candles to God, the Prophet, and the shining prince.

of wolves and wool

The Prophet's Birthday is a straightforward political ritual that legitimates the Moroccan monarchy. Given that dimension, there are those who would depict the ritual as simply dressing the sharifi wolf in sheep's clothing, as covering the real-world powerholder in the sacred garments in which this wolfly caste is wrapped. But this is an oversimplification that not only obscures how the ritual works, but why it works so well. The ritual is a potent political support because it is not a political support only. Its multiple dimensions account for its power.

We *are* talking about wolves, about practical political powerholders who could manifest themselves mightily and ruthlessly, and occasionally trampled through the countryside, leaving ravage in their wake. But we are also talking about wool, about warmth and comfort, about religious and political protection and economic success.

The barely disguised wolf is only one form that political power could take. To think of the sharifi caliph as always harmful and usurping is as naive as to think of him as always benevolent and good. He could be either, and usually was both. Powerful central rule meant increased taxation and physical coercion, but it also meant a level of commercial, manufacturing, and agricultural prosperity that was simply unknown at other times. There was real-world utilitarian benefit to monarchical rule.

But more than utilitarian benefit is at stake. The ritual of the Prophet's Birthday speaks to issues of ultimate meaning and individual worth. After all, it is a pathway to truth. It is a means of asking, and to a degree resolving, the question of what is the truth of the universe and how humans can connect with it. The experience with truth comes through the sharifi prince who brings the celebration to the population. Morocco's reconstituted monarchy, the sharifi caliphate, is both a means to an ultimately valuable end and an end in itself, the connection to the truth of the universe as well as the legitimate form of rule on earth.

The interwoven dimensions of the ritual make for a complicated reception. The practical exercise of political power is embedded in cosmic truth, so that even if a straightforward political wolf were to appear on the Moroccan political scene, to destroy the wolf might also mean to destroy the wool, a fact of which Moroccans have been, and are, keenly aware. The most forceful undergirdings for political rule, I suspect, often do not rest on the population's simple-minded blindness, but rather on their deep-seated understanding—conscious or unconscious—of the complexity of issues at stake, their comprehension that essential meaning and political coercion are often inextricably bound; and to destroy the one may be to destroy the other.

9

the ʿAlawi blood descendants

The glittering age of the Saʿdi and the glittering life of their victorious ruler abruptly ended. In the early 1600s (A.H. 1000s) another wave of plague hit Morocco, killing one-third to one-half of the population, including the great caliph himself. As in the earlier outbreak, the plague ravaged the economic foundations of collective existence. Administrative, military, and social structures came undone. And, this time, a healthy economy could not be rebuilt, for the world had shifted in Europe's favor.

economic crash: colonial world economy

After the 1347 (A.H. 748/49) onslaught, the plague periodically struck Morocco. In 1603 (A.H. 1012/13) a particularly lethal wave hit, similar in potency to the first. Animals and people died, irrigation systems fell apart, refineries closed, commercial networks collapsed, and land was left fallow. As in the earlier outbreak, sugar production and long-distance commerce were the hardest hit. And, once again, the plague was followed by a second crisis, international in origin, that sealed its destruction. Indirect economic assault followed the 1600s (A.H. 1000s) outbreak, and in the long term its effects were more damaging than had been the post-plague military assault of the 1300s (A.H. 700s). While the military assault could be countered, the economic assault could not be, and full economic recovery became impossible.

By the seventeenth century (A.H. 1000s), Europe's maritime expansion had reached fruition and the colonial world economy was in place. Europe had become the center of a vast trading and manufacturing network that channeled the world's surpluses to its benefit (see Wallerstein 1974 and 1979). Key goods which Morocco had formerly supplied now entered Europe cheaply and in greater abundance from Europe's overseas colonies. The 1603 outbreak of the plague pulled the rug out from under the Moroccan economy at a critical juncture in history, circumventing the potential for economic comeback. Formerly central, Morocco was pushed to the periphery of the new world economic order.

The main channels of Morocco's economic prosperity were lost: sugar, gold, and domination of international transport. Sugar cane was now grown in abundance in Europe's colonial plantations in the Canary Islands and Latin America—regions that had environmental advantages over Morocco, including sufficient heat and rainfall, so that plants could be grown without the extensive capital and labor input required in North Africa. Elaborate irrigation systems were unnecessary, fertilization did not have to be extensive, and the consistent warm weather prevented the regular reduction of sugar content brought by waves of cool weather in Morocco. Sugar cane was cheaper to produce in Europe's colonies, and sugar cones were cheaper to refine at home. Europe built an extensive manufacturing industry to handle its sugar needs.

By the beginning of the 1600s (A.H. 1000s), the New World colonial production of sugar was so extensive that it entirely undercut Moroccan production. Moroccan sugar became an overpriced commodity in a saturated world market. The bottom fell out of Morocco's sugar economy, this time permanently. Morocco ceased to produce its elegant white cones of sugar and would not produce them again for four hundred years, not until the late 1900s (A.H. 1300s).

Morocco's trade in gold and silver was equally undone. By the early seventeenth century hard currency, especially silver, was entering Iberia from Latin America in such quantities that Iberia's economy had difficulty handling the inflationary onslaught (Wolf 1982). Morocco was now a superfluous high-priced source of supply.

Subchannels of Moroccan economic prosperity were also destroyed. New World dyes, particularly cochineal, a bright red, were discovered and exported to Europe, reducing the importance of Moroccan commerce in hinna' and other natural tinctures. In the 1700s (A.H. 1100s), England invented a new means of setting dyes that obviated the need for alum, which it had depended upon Morocco to supply. In the 1800s (A.H. 1200s), South Africa's colonists established ostrich plantations and sent the elegant black and white plumes to Europe by ship, thereby undercutting Morocco's overland trade in them.

Furthermore, Morocco lost its privileged position in international transportation as great circumglobal water routes replaced desert passageways as the dominant lines of international exchange. Boats replaced camels. By the mid-1500s (A.H. 900s), Europe was connected to the Americas and to the western coast of Africa by regular lines of shipping. In the latter part of the century, Europe became connected to Asia by water routes also. In 1570 (A.H. 978/79), the first Manila galleon traveled east across the Pacific, establishing a new water route to Iberia. Loaded with Asian spices, dyes, and silks, the ship was docked at the New World port of Acapulco where the goods were unloaded—unopened—and carried across the short Central American isthmus, then reloaded on Iberian ships waiting on the Atlantic side. The Iberian ships then set sail east to the Spanish motherland where the goods were opened and sorted, and some sent back to Latin America. It was a long route, but boats are exceedingly fast and cheap when compared to camels; what is more, they were Europe's own means of transportation, and kept European money at home rather than dispersing it on Muslim transporters.

The new world political economy was so disastrous for Morocco that by the time the Moroccan population recovered from the plague of 1603 (A.H. 1012/13) and turned its attention to the shattered economic system, there was little left to rebuild. The issue was no longer one of sharifi legitimacy—or of any other cultural variable—stabilizing the sociopolitical environment so that the economic foundations could be rebuilt. The foundations of economic prosperity had themselves been lost, and Morocco could not reestablish a lucrative economic base no matter how perspicacious the ruler, no matter how persuasive the form of rule. The structure of the world economy had changed.

By sailing away from Morocco's shores, Iberia had accomplished what it could not by occupying them. Moroccans countered Prince Henry's land strategy, but in the end, his other line of assault, his long shot of ocean routes, brought about Morocco's economic demise. Formerly at the front stage center of the world economic order, Moroccans emerged from the plague in the 1600s to find that the stage had moved—first to Iberia, and then on to the rest of western Europe.

political culture resolution: ʿAlawi renewal

Yet political and cultural collapse did not follow the economic plummet. Moroccans and Morocco survived. Moroccans continued to have a profound sense of political and cultural self prismed through their country's central monarchy and Islamic performances. Moroccans used this sense of self to reconstitute collective consciousness and collective life within Morocco's boundaries, and to repel would-be colonizers from without. Morocco could not surmount the economic difficulties the new world economy imposed upon it, but it could strike a bargain with them, and did, through the orienting power of its sharifi caliphate and the regenerative foundation of sacred performances. Essential, too, was the remarkable determination that characterized the Moroccan population in the centuries of turmoil and compromise, the 1600s–1900s (A.H. 1000s–1300s).

The bubonic plague and the bottomed-out economy took the ruling dynasty down with it, but not its form of rule; the Saʿdi dynasty fell, but not the model it had established, the sharifi caliphate. A new line of blood descendants of the Prophet Muhammad came forward to fill it.[1]

The ʿAlawi dynasty took over the caliphal throne in such a way that it captured the full power of sharifi legitimacy while casting aspersions on the right of the previous dynasty to rule. The ʿAlawi continued to support the argument that the blood descendants of Muhammad were the rightful occupants of the Moroccan throne, but they argued that the Saʿdi were not true blood descendants—they were not members of Muhammad's patriline. They were members instead of the patriline that had produced Muhammad's wet nurse. This innovative interpretation preserved the legitimacy of the sharifi model of rule while explicating the decline of a particular dynasty. The Sa'di were not true descendants; they were not the rightful rulers. Yet they were not totally devalued either. After all, their ancestors had provided Muhammad with milk, an important issue in Islamic law that affects legal relationships, for instance, whom one can marry.

The resources the 'Alawi utilized in their climb to power were strikingly similar to those used by the Sa'di. Like the Sa'di, the 'Alawis were a family of religious scholars who had emigrated to Morocco from the Arabian Peninsula in the 1100s (A.H. 500s). They too had settled in a southern Moroccan oasis where they became important to its organizational life. (The 'Alawi settled in the long thin oasis of Tafilalt, located to the southeast of the Atlas Mountains, from which the oasis receives its water. The oasis includes the great commercial emporium of Sijilmasa, the ruins of which lie next to the present-day city of Rissani.) The 'Alawi, like the Sa'di, were native speakers of Arabic, the holy tongue of God, and members of the Quraysh, the broad-reaching descent category from which Muhammad came (as did all the early caliphs in the first centuries of Islam). Most importantly, the 'Alawi were direct descendants of Muhammad, and from a popular perspective their descent is unquestioned.

Like the Sa'di, the 'Alawi began their ascent to dynastic power by transforming diffuse popular credit for Muhammad's blood descendants into more concrete military and economic supports, with which they then waged local and regional battle, increasing their cultural credit and furthering their economic and military supports. Like the Sa'di, the 'Alawi too secured their political movement on the luminescence of Muhammad's bloodline. Region by region, Morocco came into their political control.

Yet while some of the basic resources overlap, the two dynasties markedly differ. The first Sa'di exuded a certain subtlety and holiness, while the first 'Alawi were a scrappy lot who pulled the country together with wheeling and dealing, just what the times demanded if a new sharifi dynasty was to be born and to restore to Morocco some of its former glory. Even their flags reflect these differences. The Sa'di banner was pure white, the 'Alawi scarlet red.[2]

Mawlay al-Sharif, "My Lord, the Descendant of the Prophet," is credited with having fathered the dynasty; his son Muhammad I is recognized by the 'Alawi as being the first monarch, but it was another son, Mawlay al-Rashid, who brought the dynasty to power (see appendix b). Al-Rashid combined the well-established sharifi template with more practical supports and set the 'Alawi on the throne. Moroccans already expected a bloodline of Muhammad's descendants to come and rule; Mawlay al-Rashid demonstrated that the 'Alawi were it.

In his climb to power, al-Rashid mobilized numerous resources. He fought and defeated his brother in an in-house bid for power. He used his patriline's sacred credit to align himself with military tribes. He expanded his base of sacred credit and military power in the north of Morocco by allying himself with a mystical brotherhood there, and also established trading connections with Europeans for their firearms.

In addition, he used his family's broad-reaching patrilineal and commercial connections to spread information, recruit military forces, collect funds, and transport weapons. Their home, Tafilalat, was an important trade emporium, the logical stopover on the great trans-Saharan trade route that connected the Mediterranean with the Sahara by way of Fas, the Tafilalat/Fas/Sabta route. Tafilalat has plentiful supplies of water and dates. It lies on the northern border of the vast Sahara. The people of Tafilalat, the Filali, were (and are) dispersed in a broad-reaching commercial network all along that route, and it was this sociocommercial network that Mawlay al-Rashid reoriented for political purposes.

In 1666 (A.H. 1077), al-Rashid entered Fas and was proclaimed the caliph, the reigning Prince of the Faithful. The Moroccan monarchy was renewed and a new family of blood descendants sat on the throne. The 'Alawi made the millennium-old city their capital, and once again men called out from the tops of its minarets prayers in the name of the Prophet Muhammad and his ruling blood descendant on the throne.

Mawlay Isma'il

Mawlay al-Rashid put the 'Alawi dynasty on the central throne, but his brother, Mawlay Isma'il, ground it into the countryside, embedding it into local institutions and inscribing it on the individual's subconscious. Mawlay Isma'il is perhaps the most forceful dynast that Morocco has ever known. A small and powerful man with penetrating eyes, he ruled Morocco for fifty-five years, 1672–1727 (A.H. 1082–1139), and brought the whole of the vast territory into central administrative control.[3] He was admired and he was feared. It is still said (by officials in the capital city, as well as by farmers in the outback) that during his reign a woman could walk alone from the Sahara to the Mediterranean, decked out in her finest gold, and never be molested.

Mawlay Isma'il amassed considerable wealth and used it to rebuild the country's military, economic, and administrative infrastructures. He established a powerful military centered on a standing professional army of black slaves. He rebuilt long-distance trade routes and established fortresses along them to preserve the peace. He expanded the administration and made local-level appointments in the nooks and crannies of the countryside.

Given his success, it might appear that Mawlay Ismaʿil reversed the economic and organizational tide. But he did not. His wealth was built on predatory expansion, not on a renewed manufacturing and agricultural base. There was capital, but it was not infrastructural or regenerative. It was capital skimmed off the edge of a new world economic order, and eventually Europe became powerful enough to stop the skimming.

Privateering—piracy—was an important source of Mawlay Ismaʿil's income. Like a number of European monarchs, he brought privateering under central government control, making it a state monopoly. Income from privateering was to the ʿAlawi what the sugar monopoly had been to the Saʿdi. His seizure of goods carried by European ships was an innovative adaptation to a changed world economy in which Morocco no longer produced or transported significant amounts of wealth.

Morocco's geographical location, like that of southern England, gave it an advantage in seizure of ocean trade. The direction of the Atlantic's winds and currents meant that ships bound for the Iberian peninsula as well as for other locations in the Mediterranean tended to sail close to Morocco's shores, and Moroccan-based privateers took full advantage of the situation (see Brown 1976). The pirates of Sala (Salé), Morocco, like the pirates of Cornwall, England, had a reputation for effectiveness that spread over the high seas.

Since the goods carried by these ships typically had been either seized or in some other way colonially extracted from indigenous peoples, the pirates were not in moral terms fundamentally different from those who carried out the trade. It was all part of a colonial world economy, and for a while, Morocco extracted a share of the booty seized by Europe.

Piracy provided two main sources of income, the first from the goods themselves and the second from the people who were captured. The goods were either sold back to the companies from which they had been taken or sold on the open market. Captives, on the other hand, were typically sold into servitude or military service, where they remained unless ransomed by people in their homeland. The number of seizures during Mawlay Ismaʿil's rule was great. Ports like Sala burgeoned with seized goods, foreign captives, and an occasional priest who came as go-between for those to be ransomed. Mawlay Isma'il ensured that a large part of the income from goods and captives came to him in the form of a piracy tax.

internal economy: Mawlay Isma'il and overland trade

Although Morocco had lost its position of dominance in world trade, regional trade still operated and vitally connected Morocco with the rest of West Africa, North Africa, and the Middle East (Cigar 1981). Mawlay Isma'il secured long-distance trade so that goods flowed freely, but he also extracted from that trade, taxing it along key emporiums all along the routes. Some scholars argue that Mawlay Isma'il was so vigorous in his taxation that by the end of his reign the great overland trade routes had shifted east, away from Morocco, in order to escape his formidable demands. In any event, the central coffers were filled in Mawlay Isma'il's day through predatory taxation on international and regional trade. That income provided him with the funds that he used to rebuild Morocco's infrastructures, but the central government's effectiveness in reaping those surpluses and constructing those systems depended upon the great predator himself. When Mawlay Isma'il died, the income and the underlying structures collapsed. Yet once again the sharifi caliphate, and Morocco's sense of national self, did not.

strong nation, weak apparatus

After Mawlay Isma'il's death many of the practical institutions of central political existence came apart. Declining income from production and exchange meant that the central dynasty lacked funds to pay for military and administrative personnel. Those systems came undone and with them the ability to collect taxes, which further reduced central funds and further undermined the organizational foundations of the state.

From 1727 until 1912 (A.H. 1139 until 1330), Morocco's state apparatus was weakly developed, yet the sense of nationhood remained strong, thanks to the unifying focus of the central monarchy and its ritual means of renewal. Morocco was a central polity, but one that falls outside of common Western paradigms, for there was no central bureaucratic structure that united the country as a whole, no rigid territorial boundaries to which one could invariably point. The nation was rich in political identity and weak in bureaucratic forms: it consisted of those peoples who looked to the sharifi caliph as their central ruler and acknowledged that allegiance through ritualized political acts—oaths of loyalty, the utterance of the ruler's name in Friday prayers, the reading of one's future in the ram sacrificed by the ruler in the nation's capital. Ritual was the means of integration.

lands of governance and lands of dissidence

Ritual bound the population into a single entity around its monarch. In terms of other connections, the links between the central monarch and his people varied, yet can be summarized by two dominant forms of integration. In the first, the link was administratively direct, and the regions involved were known as *bilad al-makhzan,* "the lands of formal government." In the second, the link was administratively indirect; it rested more on political influence than political control, political loyalty rather than political apparatus. The regions involved were known as *bilad al-siba,* "the lands of dissidence." Any given region could switch from one form of political integration to the other, and many alternated between the two (see Burke 1972). The critical distinction between them was whether or not people in the particular regions freely paid taxes and sent military conscripts to the central ruler. In bilad al-makhzan lands, "lands of formal government," they did. In bilad al-siba lands, "lands of dissidence," they did not.

Many scholars argue that the people in bilad al-makhzan territory accepted the sharifi caliphate's political and religious authority while the people in the bilad al-siba territories accepted his religious authority only, refusing his political claim. This is wrong. Such a dichotomy between political and religious allegiance was important in postrevolutionary French political culture (it is a variation of the church-state dichotomy), but was not crucial to Moroccan political culture at the time. The interpretation is largely a colonial creation that many scholars unquestioningly adopted thereafter.

In truth, the connection was everywhere political. The majority of people in Morocco's bilad al-siba as well as bilad al-makhzan lands looked to the sharifi caliph as the central political ruler, the rightful political successor to Muhammad. They dissented about the right of the legitimate political ruler to collect taxes and demand political conscripts during times of peace. There is support for this dissenting position within the political repertoire of Islam.

Numerous historical documents illustrate that Moroccans in bilad al-siba as well as bilad al-makhzan territories accepted the central ruler's political authority while debating the range of behaviors that proper political authority included. Throughout history statements from chieftains in the outlying areas have been recorded to the effect that they will not send taxes or conscripts to the rightful caliph, but let anyone attack him and they will defend him to the death. Illustrative also are the cases where the central ruler's troops were defeated by local militia who had no hesitation about killing the ruler's soldiers, but when it came to the ruler himself, they made certain that he did not die, and in fact carefully escorted him back to his capital city and set him back on the caliphal throne.

One of the most informative documents on the political conception of central government rule in the bilad al-siba areas is the remarkable book of al-Zarhuni, a young man of the High Atlas Mountains who in the 1700s (A.H. 1100s) recorded the caliph's destruction of his father's religious lodge and associated community. Al-Zarhuni's father was a local holy man and political authority in a "land of dissidence" region. He accepted the sharifi caliph's position as supreme political authority but refused to comply with what he considered illegitimate demands—for instance, when the caliph sent him notice that that he was to report to the imperial courts bringing with him the famous sword he possessed. The elder al-Zarhuni did not openly refuse the ruler's demands. In classic Moroccan style, he did not say no—he just did not go.

After some months of verbal jousting through letters sent back and forth, the sharifi monarch finally decided to force al-Zarhuni into compliance. What was at stake was not the literal sword, but rather whether or not al-Zarhuni would bow to the ruler's definition of political authority that was far more expansive than his own. Al-Zarhuni would not, and the caliph sent troops to force him to comply with the ruler's definition of reality. Still al-Zarhuni would not, and the monarch's forces set in flight the local community and destroyed its means of subsistence; they tore down dwellings, demolished the irrigation system, and—most destructive—burned the olive groves, searing in long-term economic waste.

The pious al-Zarhuni held out hope for God's deliverance until the very last moment, refusing to believe that it would not come until the troops of ravage were within his sight. Then he fled with his son deep into the craggy mountains and lived as a hunted refugee. What is most remarkable about the document is that the younger al-Zarhuni and his father never wavered in their conviction that the ruler's assault was wrong, nor in their equally firm conviction that the man who wrought the destruction was the true political ruler on earth, the reigning caliph, the rightful Prince of the Faithful. Al-Zarhuni begins the book with a lament about the caliphate—a song of sadness that God established such a flawed political institution to oversee the world. But he never questions that the caliphate is the proper form of rule, nor in the end that the current occupant, Mawlay Isma'il, is the proper man on the throne. The deeds are wrong but the system of rule is seen as intrinsically legitimate. This indigenous document, written by the son of a political authority in a bilad al-siba region during the age of dissidence, is far more informative on the nature of the political bond linking central ruler and outlying areas than are most Western comments on that bond that try to gloss over its political content, insisting that the bond is somehow religious only and therefore not of great political consequence.

The bilad al-siba areas were not integrated into the center through direct lines of administrative control, yet they were a part of that central polity. People in them looked to the ruler as caliph, as overarching political authority, and the sharifi ruler was a key political actor in those regions, as Ross Dunn clearly illustrates (1977). Local power-holders there sought the sharifi ruler's formal acknowledgment of their local authority. They sent letters and gifts and dispatched emissaries to call on the great ruler in the capital. They attempted to obtain the monarch's formal investiture in the form of a document on which was placed the ruler's imperial seal, a parchment from the center that helped stabilize local political authorities in the dissenting peripheries. Local powerholders also sought the ruler's mediation in major disputes, his representation in major conflicts, and his military aid when threatened from outside. They typically treated his representatives with lavish displays of honor. Requests from the central monarch were taken seriously, even if not complied with to the letter. Morocco's sharifi monarch was the nation's political ruler, the key actor in the political life of the entire countryside, center and periphery.

orienting center

The post-Isma'il period is characterized by the power of political culture and the weakness of political apparatus. To borrow Marxist terms (but not Marxist interpretation), it was an age of superstructural strength and infrastructural weakness. Yet, the infrastructural weakness did not bring the country's collapse; its superstructural strength bolstered it. Political culture sustained the population and the polity when more practical supports faltered. Through its forcefulness, Morocco remained a distinctive polity through centuries of assault.

A horse decked out for gun play. The trappings bring to mind the
dress of unmarried females.

Unmarried females. They, along with older women, stand somewhat removed from the main religious festivities.

Cow Sacrifice performed on the Prophet's Birthday in the High Atlas Mountains.

The bride is carried into the groom's father's compound. Her feet are not to touch the ground from the moment she leaves the interior of her own household until she is in the interior of the groom's household.

Gun play. Horsemen race at full speed toward the tent where the honored men are sitting.

and political prosperity, he sometimes actively destroyed it—burning crops, slashing trees, and killing people. The population was not blind to his actions. What renewed the cultural foundations when so many events of daily life spoke against them?

Great sacred performances sustained the monarchy in this age. They were the unifying apparatus that brought the nation into one. In the constancy of ritual performances, the necessity of the caliphate and the benevolence of the sharifi form of rule were affirmed in popular experience and consciousness. In the age of tumult, rituals gave the population access to the experience of their nation as unified, their ruler as powerful and legitimate, and their faith as unrivaled and victorious. The Prophet's Birthday continued to be performed; the rites of marriage and sacrifice were added to it. Together, they sustained the monarchy and allowed it to serve as the light-shedding prism that drove the darkness of the threatening Other away.

10

first marriage

Swiftly the glittering bride is carried through the dark streets. As she enters the groom's household, the ghaitas play, the drums beat, and the crowd bursts into applause. Singing intensifies and women let out their shrill cries of joy. Held high on porters' shoulders, she is paraded around and around the central courtyard. Her beauty is lauded. Her adornment is admired. Finally, she is taken to the nuptial chamber. Her glittering garments are removed, revealing a pure white gown. Laid on the bed—passive and white, her eyes thickly rimmed in black—she brings to mind the ram of the Great Sacrifice. In silence, she awaits the ruler-bridegroom. Finally he enters, and in an act of some violence, he forces his way into her, causing the lifeblood to flow. By shedding blood he is transformed into a man and can now shed the identity he borrowed from the ruler, the identity that enabled the boy to engage in this power-laden act. To become a man, the bridegroom took on the ruler's being; he girded his loins with the ruler's power. Now, through bloodspilling, he is a man—a community decision maker, the head of the household, the one who initiates earthly birth. The ruler has given that definition, while the bridegroom has given the ruler entry into the most intimate domains of his being.

ruler and rite

During the 'Alawi era, local marriage ceremonies renewed the monarchy. They made it seem ineffable, part of the very structure of being, linking the population to it through passionate longings, sexual identity, and procreative hopes. In local rites, the sharifi monarch gave young men—and by extension young women—their coming of age. The groom was metaphorically transformed into the ruler at the beginning of the ceremonies and remained the ruler until the bride's blood was spilled. Through the transformation, the ruler's role as archetypal man, reproductive exemplar, was affirmed. The precise year in which these practices were begun is not known, nor is the information crucial to the argument made here. What is important is that during the era of institutional weakness and foreign assault, popular marriage practices revitalized the monarchy, making it seem intimate, powerful, and holy. In many places, they accomplish that transformation still.

Westermarck's *Marriage Ceremonies in Morocco* (1914) is still the most extensive source of documentation on first marriage practices. The work is descriptive rather than analytical and is exceedingly thorough. It is an invaluable source of documentation on Moroccan marriage ceremonies before the advent of the colonial era. The template of marriage ceremonies discussed below is drawn from an analysis of Westermarck's descriptions, my observations, and those of others.[1] While any single ceremony may not have all of the elements described below, the greater number of ceremonies have most of them.

The Moroccan ritual is a classic rite of passage, a formal mechanism by which a community gives its boys and girls passage into adulthood, demonstrating for them who they are and what they are to become. It is an exercise in definition and control exerted through straightforward communal supervision of the act of sexual intercourse and the bond of marriage.

Like many rites of passage, the Moroccan ceremonies begin by placing those undergoing the rite in an in-between state; a state classically described by Victor Turner (1977a) in his analysis of circumcision ceremonies among the Ndembu of sub-Saharan Africa. Turner characterizes it as a time of "liminality," when the world is turned upside down, rules are suspended, and nonstructure reigns. In his view, the liminal state releases the individual from the constraints of the past, wipes the slate clean, and allows for creative expansion which psychologically readies the initiate to take on new roles in the future.

Moroccan first marriage ceremonies are true rites of passage, but they fit Turner's typology only in part: they are liminal, but they are *not* nonstructural. Here, the liminal state is one of increased structural constraint, not release from it. The initiates are directly practiced in the behaviors they must adopt if they are to become successful adults. The Moroccan rite presents adult structure to the initiates in intense and clarified form, directly embedding it within their bodies.

For males, the in-between state is accomplished by the boy's transformation into the monarch. To become an adult male, the boy first becomes the quintessential male, the Moroccan king, the blood descendant of Muhammad who reigns from Morocco's throne. The transformation is dramatic. The young man takes on the ruler's persona, embodies his postures, affects his attitudes, adopts his authority, and becomes central and pivotal to all that transpires. The transformation physically moves the boy out of his father's house and onto the streets, and publicly lauds him as a man capable of participating in the community.

For the female the liminal state is an equally dramatic one, but of a completely opposite sort. While the boy is practiced in becoming active, central, and public, the bride is practiced in becoming passive, demure, and private. The ceremonies physically take her off the streets and into the house; a common place of preparation is the bed.

Through the ritual practices, new definitions are cultivated in the young man and the young woman; they are written on their bodies, inscribed in their minds, embedded in their psyches.

birth of a senior male

The transformation of the young male into a man is a dramatic task. In the pragmatics of daily life as well as in the underlying definitions of the culture, young males occupy an ambiguous place between adult men and females. To become "a man," the neophyte male must be taught to embody new behaviors and operate in new domains, to unequivocally move out of the female world that he has inhabited so that he can dominate it.

From birth, the young man has spent much of his time as a highly dependent member of his father's household, where he often carries out tasks appropriate to women and children but not to respectable senior men. When a father entertains guests, unmarried sons often take the place of female servants; they serve food to the senior men and in so doing embody the extremely subservient gestures that females then exhibit—eyes downcast, body slightly bend forward, no sign of active engagement on the face; all physical cues—except the actual presence of their bodies—saying that they are *not* there.

The rite of passage must transform the junior male, who has been trained in subservience, into a senior male capable of operating in the world of real men, capable of being a central actor who will head his own household, make public decisions, beget children, and sacrifice a ram each year on their behalf. The ritual must inculcate within the young man the model of adulthood he must embody. Later marriages do not involve the same intense preparations because the groom already is a man. The first marriage has to make him one.

The rite accomplishes the metamorphosis by cultivating within the young man's body the new definitions he is to hold, so that his body brings him the understanding of what he is to do and who he is to be. Or more precisely, it is the king's body that brings him that understanding, that shapes his imagination. The metamorphosis into "ruler" pushes metaphor to its limits—for a time the young man seems to truly become the ruler and behaves as such. Others treat him as king: he walks the streets as the most honored of men. Through the transformation, the boy learns the demeanors he must adopt to be a successful adult; he maintains many of them throughout his life, especially within the privacy of his own household, where he remains the king.

Morocco shares many aspects of its marriage ritual with other places in the Islamic world, but the groom's transformation into the Prophet's blood-descendant king is unique. This specific articulation of the ritual may have occurred during the reign of the Mawlay Isma'il, whose reproductive prowess was unparalleled and might have inspired the population to more closely identify their young men with him. Mawlay Isma'il is reputed to have sired over seven hundred sons. Although that number is no doubt an exaggeration, documents in Tafilalat indicate that he did produce and support at least a hundred offspring. Mawlay Isma'il was not a man given to mediocrity in any domain. It would make sense if the innovations in popular marriage practices occurred when Mawlay Isma'il was king, for they accent the monarch's role as quintessential creator; the ritual definition is one that

Mawlay Isma'il approached in fact. But precisely when this innovation took hold is not as important for the purposes of this book as the fact that it occurred and became an important ritual support for the Moroccan monarchy.

night of the bridegroom

Ceremonies for the groom often begin with the "night of the bridegroom," when a group of friends of the young man gather outside his father's household and call him to come out—to come out of his father's house, out of his state of dependency, so that the celebrations and the transformation can begin. Finally, the young man emerges and formally greets those gathered, who reply, "Be blessed and lucky." The groom then invites the young men into the house for bachelor festivities that last through the night.

day of the sultan

The next morning the more serious preparations begin. While darkness still abides, the groom's bachelor friends again gather outside his house and again call him out. When he emerges, his friends cover him completely in a finely woven white wool cloth, a *ha'ik,* which physically places the groom in an in-between state. He can neither see nor be seen. He is transformed—a white-cloaked, faceless figure walking the streets in goodness. His individual identity is gone; he is about to acquire a new one. Thus covered, the groom's friends lead him to the public square, the *musalla,* that serves as the gathering place of senior men for the communal enactment of the Great Sacrifice. At the holy place, where earthly death occurs in order to build the hope of transcendent life, the young man is transformed into the nation's ruler. The transformation takes place at the same time that the cosmos itself is in process of transformation, when night is changing into day, the time when, in the rite of the Prophet's Birthday, the shimmering king emerges from the great gate and leads the waiting population in the prayers that bring the dawn.

In his transformed state, the young groom becomes the object of deference, honor, and obedience. He is called either Mawlay Sultan ("My Lord, the Powerful One") or Mawlay al-Sharif ("My Lord, the Noble Descendant of the Prophet"). "Mawlay" is an honorific title used in Morocco for important sharif. During the 'Alawi era, it became closely associated with the reigning monarch and with other prominent members of the royal family. The term carries respect. When combined with the title "al-Sharif," "the blood descendant of Mu-hammad," it is an even more honorific title and is also the name by which the founder of the 'Alawi dynasty is known to history.

"Sultan" means "the Powerful One." It is one of several titles by which Morocco's kings are known. It is derived from the Arabic verb *salata*, "to be powerful." It has been in use as a common title for the rulers in the Muslim world since the 900s (A.H. 300s). The worldly title "sultan" is especially appropriate for a coming-of-age ceremony in which the young man's socialization into a worldly adult and his initiation of the biological process of birth are the central concerns, for "sultan" is the most worldly of titles that the Moroccan ruler holds. Whereas the caliphal title of "amir al-mu'minin," "Prince of the Faithful," refers to the legitimate political authority, whatever his actual range of power, the title of "sultan" refers to the actual holder of political power in a given region. Moroccan rulers typically append both titles to their names—for instance, Sultan Mawlay Isma'il, amir al-mu'minin. During the colonial era, the French substituted the title of "king" to cover the authority that the word "sultan" previously had held. "King" is commonly combined with "Prince of the Faith-ful" just as sultan used to be, so that the current monarch is typically referred to as King Hasan II, amir al-mu'minin. Yet many Moroccans continue to refer to him as Sultan Hasan II, and it is the preferred title in wedding ceremonies.

In the ceremony at the *musalla,* the holy grounds, the groom's friends are also transformed. They become the ruler's advisors. The "best man" becomes the chief advisor, the grand wazir of the Moroccan government. The advisor-friends physically guide the sultan through the stages of transition.

A public procession is organized. The reigning monarch is at center and his advisors surround him. The four closest to him carry imperial flags to demonstrate to the population that the reigning monarch is in their midst. As the ruler and his court process through town, the musicians play and the advisors sing:

O Great Majesty O God, O God;
the one who is girded with a sword,
Good luck to him for ever, O dear one, O God.
            (Westermarck 1914:95–97)

Many Moroccans sing this song, or some close variation of it. The song invokes God's presence, and then focuses upon "good luck" and the "sultan-bridegroom's" sword. Although in a few places the young sultan-bridegroom may wear an actual sword at this point, the reference is for the most part metaphorical. "Sword" is the same double entendre in Arabic as in English, meaning both sword and phallus. The wazir-friends wish their leader good luck and hope that he is girded with a sufficiently powerful "sword" so that creation can begin.

hinna' rehearsals in blood

Next come the *hinna'* ceremonies, experiments with the blood-red hinna' dye that prepare the sultan-bridegroom for the actual blood-spilling that later occurs. Often two hinna' ceremonies are a part of the groom's preparation, the Little Hinna' and the Great Hinna'. In the Little Hinna', the groom takes the "hinna'-blood clot" from his mother, the woman who bore him. In the Great Hinna', he begins to use the hinna'-blood clot for his own procreative purposes.

Little Hinna': taking the clot from the mother   The Little Hinna' often concludes the sultan-bridegroom's first procession through town. He returns to his father's household but does not enter. He formally sits down in front of his house, surrounded by his entourage, and calls his mother to come out. She emerges carrying four items: candles, water, hinna', and an egg, all highly charged symbolic substances. The candles represent the light of God and bring to mind the Prophet's Birthday. Water is the literal lifeblood in these dry lands, and is also, as for all people, the substance in which children are born. The hinna' stands for blood, the blood the mother spills giving birth to the child. The egg stands for reproduction. In combination, these four items help build the experience of the sultan-bridegroom's regenerative powers. Water and egg also serve more practical purposes, for they will be mixed with the hinna' to make a paste of the powdered dye.

The mother acknowledges the sultan-son's presence with the formal invocation, "May God be gracious unto you," and hands the four items to the sultan's grand wazir, who lights the four candles and gives them to the four "scribes" who kneel around the sultan-bridegroom. The wazir breaks the egg, mixes it with hinna' and water, and while stirring it with the little finger of his right hand, he and the other wazirs sing:

> In the name of God the Merciful and Compassionate, O God
> I take refuge with God from the devil, the stoned one, O God
> We have made our lord Bilal our leader and O God
> We have made our lord 'Uthman our leader and O God

We have made our lord 'Isa our leader, O God
We have made our lord 'Ali our leader and O God
His face is like the moon and O God
Stretch out your hand we shall paint you with hinna',
O my lord descendant of the Prophet
Stretch out your hand from your sleeve,
O my lord descendant of the Prophet
Today your luck has stood up,
O my lord descendant of the Prophet.

(Westermarck 1914:98)

The song begins with the formal invocation of God's name, "In the name of God the Merciful and Compassionate," a powerful speech act in Moroccan life, used before all important occasions, including the Great Sacrifice. The singers then seek refuge in God from the devil, "the stoned one," who stalks the goodness of the world, like the goodness of the sultan-bridegroom who sits before them. (In many places, actual stones are later thrown at the devil during the groom's preparations.)

The singers then compare their leader to the great leaders of Islam in the past, including Bilal, Muhammad's slave-servant who was an early convert to the faith and became the first *mu'adhdhin*, the first man to call Muslims to prayer. The sultan-bridegroom is then compared to 'Uthman, the third caliph of Islam, a close companion of the Prophet who came from the powerful Makkan family that established the first imperial dynasty in Islam. Those gathered then compare their leader to 'Isa—Jesus—a pure prophet in Islam, who, according to the Hadith, will preside over the day of judgment. Finally, the sultan-bridegroom is compared to 'Ali, the fourth caliph, the Prophet's cousin and son-in-law. The words of the song repeatedly remind the sultan-bridegroom that he is the holy blood descendant of the Prophet Muhammad, and conclude with telling him to reach out his hands. When he does, the grand wazir smears the hinna', the "blood," on them.

The sultan-bridegroom's advisors then dance, one after another, with the bowl of hinna'-blood on their heads. The last wazir-dancer lets it drop and break. This, too, is a rehearsal of what is to come. Violence is a necessary part of the bloodspilling.

Great Hinna': channeling the blood clot into creation The Great Hinna' is an even more direct rehearsal of the bloodspilling. It typically concludes another procession through town for which the sultan-bridegroom is again dressed in white. An imperial parasol is held high above his head, and the advisors sing:

> Glory to God,
> Glory to the Creator,
> Glory to the Eternal,
> The Creation has begun.
>   (Jamous 1981:271)

The song proclaims the sultan-bridegroom to be the one who initiates earthly creation, a role which directly links him to God, the creator, the eternal. One of God's ninety-nine names is "al-Khaliq," "the Creator."

Whereas the Little Hinna' takes place in a mundane setting, outside the sultan-bridegroom's house, the Great Hinna', the great blood rehearsal, takes place at the musalla, the sanctified public grounds where the groom was previously transformed into sultan. Here, where each year the community of faithful sacrifices to God to recovenant its relationships and insure the possibility of eternal regeneration, the sultan-bridegroom is prepared to participate in earthly procreation.

The sultan-bridegroom sits in a chair. His wazirs flank him on the left and right, and everyone else sits or stands near him. He is presented with gifts, and honor and praise are heaped on him. Then follows a ceremony of mockery.

The mockery is squarely aimed at the sultan-bridegroom, who is to remain composed and dignified throughout it, thereby demonstrating his ability to control himself, to rise above the verbal banter of everyday life, an important quality of honorable men. The mockery itself directly connects the bridegroom to the real sultan and the ritual of the Great Sacrifice. Until ceremonies of ruler mockery were banned by the French during the colonial era, they were a part of the Great Sacrifice, organized by religious scholars at the universities of Fas and Marrakush. One of the scholars would become "sultan for a day," and a ceremony of raucous fun-making would follow. In those days, the actual sultan typically attended either the ceremony in Fas or in Marrakush and laughed in good-natured amusement at the fun poked at himself. The ceremonies concluded with the mock-sultan making a formal request of the real sultan, who was obliged to grant any request within his power. The ceremony of ruler mockery was, in Gluckman's sense, a classic ritual of rebellion (1963:18). The world was turned upside down, the ruler became ruled, and rulership itself was mocked. Yet the ceremonies ended with the formal reaffirmation of the structure of power, the system of rule, and the ruler again took his rightful place and bestowed goodness on the ruled, especially on those who had mocked him.

After the sultan-bridegroom has withstood his trial by mockery, the great rehearsal of bloodspilling begins, the Great Hinna'. Two or three young girls, sisters or cousins of the sultan-bridegroom, mix the hinna' in a bowl and then present it to him. The mixing by females is important, for it reaffirms that females possess the clots of blood, but they need to give the clots to males if creation is to occur. The sultan-bridegroom puts his right hand into the bowl of thick blood-hinna' and keeps it there while two of his wazirs lead him to the door of the still-empty nuptial chamber (the bride will be brought later that night). The sultan-bridegroom, now in the lead, opens the door and enters. He takes his hinna'-laden right hand and forcibly presses it against the wall, leaving bold imprints for all to see. The number of imprints is taken to represent the number of children the sultan-bridegroom wants. Once he finishes the ceremony of handprints, those with him recite in unison, "Now they are married. Now they are married."

As to what the act of handprinting and the final statement mean, there are various interpretations. The French anthropologist Raymond Jamous states, "What this means exactly is that the marriage is consummated sexually, which is not yet true physiologically" (Jamous 1981:272). Jamous assumes that hinna' ceremony represents sexual intercourse and that sexual intercourse consummates the first marriage ceremonies.

My interpretation of the hinna'-blood display and the final statement, "Now they are married," is different. I contend that blood-spilling rather than sexual intercourse consummates these first marriage ceremonies, and the handprints are a direct and obvious play on that bloodspilling. The difference in stress is slight but crucial. Blood, rather than intercourse, I argue, consummates these ceremonies. In point of fact sexual intercourse may or may not have happened before that night and may or may not happen on that night. Yet as long as the male spills blood and it is publicly exhibited, the rite of passage takes place and the young man becomes a man and the young woman a woman, each acquiring the rights and duties associated with the new status. Ideally intercourse occurs, but it may not (a cock may be killed and its blood used). The bride may not be virgin, and the blood that the groom publicly exhibits need not be from the phallus' breaking of the bride's hymen.

With this in mind, it becomes clear that the sultan-bridegroom's handprints on the wall are direct representations of the blood he will sacredly spill that night (by whatever means), and the statement "Now they are married" celebrates the bloodspilling that will take place, bloodspilling that itself is seen as initiating creation. The Qur'an clearly states that God created man of a "blood-clot" (Sura 96, 1–2). By placing his handprint on the wall, the sultan-bridegroom demonstrates his pivotal role in biological creation. He is its center. He taps God's creative power and channels it to earth. He takes the female's blood clot and guides it into children. Through metaphorical participation in the creative act, the sultan-bridegroom is empowered, and he allows others to partake in that power by dipping their little fingers into the hinna'-blood.

purification at the spring: battling between senior and junior males

Next, the sultan-bridegroom and entourage proceed to a village spring for a ritual of cleansing. Again the sultan-bridegroom's body is entirely covered with a white woven cloth so that he cannot see or be seen. He is still in an in-between state. Again he is flanked by advisors who wave the imperial flags, again he is accompanied by the imperial court. While they proceed, they sing:

> We have made him our leader with our steps,
> O good people pray for the sake of the Prophet
> till it becomes morning.
> (Westermarck 1914:126)

In singing, the entourage acknowledges the rightfulness of the sultan-bridegroom's leadership by noting that they have followed in his footsteps. They then link the action of bloodspilling in which the sultan-bridegroom will engage that evening with the Prophet Muhammad; after all, properly supervised procreation is the Prophet's concern. God commissioned Muhammad to establish a community of Muslims in the world, and Muslim men, by renewing earthly creation, reestablish that community. In engaging in this momentous act, upon which the fate of the community as a whole turns, the sultan-bridegroom is in need of prayers, for his responsibility is great. By morning, the act will be finished.

On the way to the spring, the procession is "attacked" by the married men of the region. Here the ritual gives play to the conflict that exists between senior and junior males, those who head the community and those who will replace them. In some ways, the senior men want to admit the young man to their ranks, since the regeneration of the community of Muslims depends on their doing so. In other ways, they resent the young man for his entry, for it augurs their own death. The ritual allows the senior men to give both aspects of the relationship overt expression, yet it then brings the conflict into resolution. It forces the elder generation to accept the young man into their midst by temporarily making him their superior, the reigning Prince of the Faithful. The young man gains entry to the category of senior men through the palace door.

Yet the ritual also allows the senior men to save face. It gives them the appearance of choice-making in the mock battle on the way to the spring. The senior men try to steal the flags and, if strong enough, will capture the sultan-bridegroom himself and "imprison" him, releasing him only when his advisors promise to give a grand feast in honor of the married men.

Food—the substance of consumption—is crucial in the construction of reality in North Africa and the Middle East and is central to each of the rituals I describe. In the rite of passage of first marriage, the food carries the message that the senior men will admit the young man to their ranks only if the juniors appropriately honor them. That honor must be shown in concrete acts and physical substances. Here again, palpable substance both creates and demonstrates human abstractions. When the young men promise them food, allegiance, and remembrance, the senior men release the sultan-bridegroom and allow him and his entourage to proceed to the spring.

At the spring, the married men "attack" for a second time, and a free-for-all ensues in which each man tries to push the others into the water. The married men focus their efforts on the sultan-bridegroom. If they succeed, his *baraka,* his grace and goodness, will be imparted to the spring, and the whole community can partake of it. Again, the good of the whole is shown to depend on the reigning sultan.

At the end of the free-for-all, the sultan-bridegroom washes himself. Then all proceed back to the village. For the first time the married men join the procession, signaling their acceptance of the young man. This time the senior men follow the others, but they soon will lead them. The procession is bound for the mosque.

sanctification at holy places

As the sultan-bridegroom gets closer to the time of bloodspilling, he must be increasingly sanctified. He and his closest advisors enter the mosque and proceed to the private quarters of the religious teacher. There the chief advisor, the grand wazir, removes the sultan-bridegroom's old clothes and sprinkles his head with water. The religious teacher shaves the sultan-bridegroom's head and clips his nails, acts of purification that are often done before men undertake the religious pilgrimage to Makka. The shaved-off hair and cut fingernails are put inside the sultan-bridegroom's old clothes, and these are taken to his mother, who carries the bundle on her back as if it were a baby. The child of the mother is finished; the father of children is emerging. Again tactile substance carries and creates the conceptual abstraction.

Now purified, the sultan-bridegroom is dressed in fine clothes sent as presents by his bride—a long white robe, a white turban, a silken cord, and a newly-woven white blanket. The robe is the kind that men wear on all major religious occasions, particularly the Great Sacrifice. The turban is a sign of manhood; only married men don it. The silken cord is used to hold the turban in place. The blanket is used to cover the groom in his final journey through the streets. Often the fringe of the blanket has been carefully tied in a formal ceremony attended by women and girls only; there the blanket is laid over the bride and its fringe is carefully tied into hundreds of tiny knots while she remains perfectly quiet and still. The purpose of the tying is to bind the sultan-bridegroom to her. The choice of tier is important: she must be the first and only wife of her husband and must have borne him several male children. Again, what is most fervently desired in the abstract—the husband's devotion to the wife and her success in bearing his children—is reproduced through concrete actions and real persons of this world.

Once the sultan-bridegroom is dressed, the blanket is laid over him, covering his entire body from head to foot. He is still in the midst of transition. He enters the mosque a bachelor and exits it dressed as an adult male, a member of the class of men he is in the process of joining. Yet he and his dress of manhood must still be covered, for he is not yet fully a man.

The blanket covers his head so that he cannot see. His grand wazir leads him out of the mosque and lifts him onto a saddled mule. With that act, the bachelor grand wazir gives up his role of leadership to a married man. Another procession, by far the grandest, is begun. Riflemen lead it and periodically fire their long thin muskets into the air, announcing to all that the sultan-bridegroom is present and creation is about to begin. Next comes the sultan-bridegroom surrounded by a cluster of white-cloaked men, all of whom are called "sharif." At this important stage of transition, the "ruling" blood descendant is upheld by the other blood descendants of the Prophet, who encircle him with the strength that comes from Muhammad's blood. One man ceremoniously waves a white cloth in front of the sultan-bridegroom (as is done for the real sultan), and another holds the imperial parasol over his head. The other men follow. The musicians, as usual, are last. As they proceed, the men sing:

O Muhammad
O he who is shaded by the veil,
On you be the peace of God;
And O beauty of the turban,
On you be the peace of God.
    (Westermarck 1914:129)

Muhammad is invoked by name and through the visual representation of the veil and the turban, through which the sultan-bridegroom is metaphorically linked to him. Muhammad is sometimes called "the veiled one," and any Muslim depiction of him should show his face covered with a veil (as in Nizamis Khamsa's famous painting *The Night Journey of Muhammad*, 1540, British Museum). Muhammad is the beauty of manhood, the beauty of the turban, and the young sultan-bridegroom in his turban and veil is drawn close to Muhammad, the best of all men.

In mountainous areas, the procession then climbs up to a high place that is considered to be sanctified, often a saint's tomb, where interaction with God is thought to more easily occur. Among the Anjira of northern Morocco, the procession climbs to the mountaintop shrine of the saint Mawlay ʿAbd al-Salam, whose name literally means "My Lord, Descendant of the Prophet, the Servant of Peace." (Saints' tombs and shrines are located throughout the Moroccan countryside, and grooms are often taken to them as a part of the marriage ceremonies.) Each member of the procession throws stones at the pile of rocks there to drive away Iblis, the devil, who may have accompanied the procession because he wishes to destroy the sultan-bridegroom's goodness. The stone-throwing echoes the stone-throwing that occurs every year on the plain of Mina on the day of sacrifice and thereafter, when each pilgrim throws stones at three pillars, also for the purpose of driving away the evil of the world.

The sultan-bridegroom then turns his mule in the direction of Makka, the holy of holies, and, with his hands in a prayerful position, whispers, "I am under the protection of God and the Prophet Muhammad." He then faces the mountain and whispers, "I am under the protection of God and under your protection, O Mawlay ʿAbd al-Salam, give me health." The ceremonies on the mountaintop conclude with a formal prayer led by a local religious teacher. All the men present bless the sultan-bridegroom.

Once the peak of holiness has been achieved, the faithful leave the mountaintop and journey back to the plains where the blood sacrifice will be made. The physical movements echo those of Ibrahim's sacrifice (chapter 13). The men go to the mountain for communion with God, and once that connection has been made, journey back to daily life where the faith must be carried, first making the covenant that they will remain steadfast in blood.

The groom's preparation, including this final procession, invokes the same themes as the candle procession of the Prophet's Birthday —passion for the woman, praise for the Prophet Muhammad, and honor for the reigning prince. Yet the marriage rite presents them in reverse order. First comes honor for the reigning sharifi prince (with whom the young man is fused). Then comes praise for the Prophet, who is made present in word, deed, and iconic image; and finally, the ritual concludes with the focus on the passion for the young woman. The thematic reversal is necessary, since the marriage ceremonies must end with passion realized. While the ritual of the Prophet's Birthday leads men away from the female, transferring erotic passion onto more noble foci (Muhammad and the sharifi prince), the ritual of first marriage must lead young men to that passion. It must take them away from things of heaven to things of earth—for the rite of marriage is an earth-bound ritual centered on blood, intercourse, and reproduction. Yet to properly take place, these earth-bound things must be guided by the nobler focus on God, Muhammad, and the sharifi prince, not severed from them.

gun play—manhood rehearsed

The procession winds its way down the holy mountain to the wide open plain, where more earthly pleasures abound. The sultan-bridegroom now enjoys an evening of festivities that presents manhood to him in entertaining and passionate form.

The arrival of the sultan-bridegroom is greeted with jubilation. A carpet is rolled out for him, just as for the real sultan. The groom walks down the carpet and seats himself on a thick Moroccan rug piled high with pillows for the evening's festivities.

"Gun play" is often the center of the evening's entertainment. It is called *la'b al-barud,* the "play of the guns" or, more literally, the "play of the gunpowder." The muskets used in this competition are loaded with gunpowder only; they have no shot. When fired, they emit a thick white cloud of smoke. "The play of the guns" is a form of gaming that reminds men—in sight and sound—of what they are about.

Gun play pits different troops of men against one another. The competition is collective rather than individual, appropriate to a society where collectivities of men are the fundamental building blocks, and especially appropriate to a ritual that initiates a young man into the class of adult men. Each troop consists of nine to fifteen men who are linked by some kind of common bond, such as patrilineal kinship, place of residence, or friendship.

The troops perform one by one, and their performance is measured against an ideal. In a matter of seconds, horsemen must take their animals from a dead stop to breakneck speed, then abruptly bring them to a halt at the end of the racing field while simultaneously firing their long thin guns into the air. The actions must be performed in unison, which demands that the men have absolute control over their horses. The final sound should erupt as a single outburst rather than a series of volleys.

The horsemen are the picture of manhood. They are dressed in white robes and white turbans and wear conspicuously pointed knives. They hold their long thin muskets high in their right hands. They are the male, mounted on the animal, the female, which they will control. The horses are decked out in glittering trappings that bring to mind the clothing that women wear on the night of marriage. The harnesses and saddles are rich pink and purple brocades; their gold and silver threads shimmer and shine in the sun, like the embroidered cloths in which the candle-virgins are swathed in the Prophet's Birthday's procession and those in which brides are draped as they are carried to be wed. Tassels hang from the horses' harnesses, closely rimming the horses' eyes, just as dangling tassels or coins rim the eyes of virgins as they dance. The horses represent nature, nature which men have to bring under control. More directly, the horses represent women, especially brides.

The horsemen gather in a straight line about 150 meters away from the men they are to entertain. At a signal from the head of the group, the men spur their horses to full speed in an amazing burst of energy, pounding across the plain directly towards the group of seated men, evoking the pleasure of high passion. Gun play is a Moroccan variation on the game of "chicken." It appears that the horsemen will stampede into the seated crowd, but at the very last second the men pull their horses to a skidding halt, simultaneously firing their long muskets into the air. Without much subtlety, the sequence mimics the sexual act—the men mount their horses, release their animal energy in a burst of passion, then jerk that passion to a final halt for their own pleasure and fulfillment with a single outburst of sound and white smoke from their pointed guns.

At all times, the men are in control—of themselves, their horses, and their guns. Dignified and calm, they show little emotion, despite the drama of the feat, which hovers near violence and disaster.

The seated men must also be brave. They are to remain still while the horses barrel down on them, moving away only at the very last second if a horse should stampede too far. A man who moves away too soon will be the subject of good-natured derision. (I have seen horses go into the crowd, and people are occasionally hurt. In fact the great Mawlay Isma'il acceded to the throne because of a gun play accident that killed his brother.)

A troop that has performed well will be called back from the racing field and served tea in crystal glasses presented to them on silver trays held high by formally dressed, white-robed men. The men remain on their horses for the tea ceremony. They sit in calm dignity sipping the hot tea until they have finished, a public exhibition of absolute control—control over self and over the animal-female that they have just taken to stampeding wildness and then brought back again, forcing both self and animal-female into absolute submission.

Women and children, if present, are bystanders only. They line the sides of the racing field while the men face each other. The distinction between male and female is shown in the disparate cries of approval. If the seated men approve of the performance, they acknowledge it in a single outburst of sound that echoes the single outburst of their guns. Female pleasure in contrast is signaled by long, ululating cries, waves of varying high-pitched sound that only females emit and that bring to mind the female as opposed to the male response to sexual intercourse. The most basic of kinesthetic experiences, including the physical act of intercourse and the male and female responses to it, are directly used in building the reality that the ritual of first marriage systematically constructs.

Gun play is a public exhibition of who males are and how they are to behave. In it, ejaculation becomes a male group experience. As metaphor, it operates on a pseudodefinitional rather than a true definitional basis. The horse calls to mind aspects of the female, the rifle evokes qualities of the phallus, and the gunshot shares a resemblance with ejaculation. Through the metaphorical equivalence and definitional intermingling that thereby occur, the gun play communicates and reinforces basic understandings and experiences of how the world is ordered and what kinds of postures, attitudes, and actions a man must adopt. It also underlines the dominant cultural perspective on sexual intercourse, that is, that sex is a natural, exhilarating, and pleasurable drive, but one that must be controlled by men of faith in order to keep it from evolving into violence and disaster. When men of faith control sex, they can channel it to the good of the whole, for entertainment as well as for its ultimate aim, the continuance of the earthly community of Muslims through the regeneration of men's patrilines on earth. That continuance is what the communally supervised intercourse of first marriage ceremonies is about. Communally authorized intercourse and procreation are to the glory of God. Muslim men are to utter the name of God, "Bi'smi'llah," not only before racing the horse, sacrificing the ram, and spilling the blood of the bride, but also before every act of intercourse, and ideally, at the moment of ejaculation. (Earthly intercourse itself is not taken to be a holy event, but the child that emerges from it is. Islam sees intercourse as polluting and hence men must wash after it, especially before performing their prayers, and must not engage in intercourse when involved in sacred rites like the pilgrimage and the fasting of Ramadan. When engaging in the sexual act, men should take care that the woman's head does not face Makka, but rather be oriented away from that holy place; her orientation is the opposite of that of the ram of sacrifice.)

bloodspilling

The preparations have brought the groom to the moment in which he must pierce the bride. They have taken him out of the household and onto the streets and put him in a place of honor. They have transformed him into the archetypal male, and established a degree of separation between himself and his mother. They have practiced him in bloodspilling, affirmed his dominant role in creation, and have washed, cleansed, and purified him. Finally, the preparations have reminded him of how to control his "gun," how to control his own nature and the nature of the female who will be presented to him that night. The groom leaves the gun play to go to his bride, who, like the horse, shimmers and shines in her sparkling clothes and glittering jewels when presented to him.

11

bride's blood

The glittering bride is exhibited to those gathered in the groom's courtyard and then taken to the nuptial chamber where her outer garments are removed, revealing pure white gowns; in white she must meet the sultan-bridegroom. She is often laid directly on the bed, where she is to lie passive, in striking resemblance to the great ram of sacrifice slain by Muhammad and by Muslims ever since. Even her eyes suggest the similarity, for they are boldly rimmed with black kohl. Some groups explicitly voice the link between the bride and the sacrificial ram. Among one group, when the women of the groom's household see the bride approaching, they sing out to her, "Bring a ram with black rings round its eyes, let us sit down with this excellent woman" (Westermarck 1914:201 and 1911:141). For others the link remains simply a visual metaphor.

The groom, dressed in the white robes that senior men wear for sacred occasions, enters the room, utters the holy words "In the Name of God the Compassionate, the Merciful," and prepares to spill the bride's blood. In some places, he smashes the bride's headdress before beginning intercourse. In other places, he forcefully lets down her hair or tears her gown. In still others, he "kicks her lightly, so as to become her ruler, and puts his sword on the bed" (Westermarck 1914:242). Whatever the preliminary actions, violence is to mark the culminating act. The violence is interpreted as leading to communal good, to the proper birth of Muslim children; it legitimates the male's dominance of violence elsewhere.

Local custom varies as to whether the woman is to actively resist or passively submit to intercourse, but the certainty is that she is not to actively participate in it, for this ritualized intercourse between the man and the potential mother of his children is to be dominated by the man and submitted to by the woman. It is something to be done *to* her, not by her, and a "proper" bride does not show pleasure in it, for she is seeking entry into the kingdom of mothers. Active resistance and passive submission are two facets of the same cultural paradigm, built from the themes of rightful male control and rightful female abnegation of her supposedly overwhelming desire for erotic passion. Some local groups so highly cultivate the pattern of female resistance that occasionally the groom cannot subdue the bride and calls in his grand wazir to hold her for the bloodspilling (Westermarck 1914:265), much as the ram of the Great Sacrifice is held.

Whether or not the bride actively resists, ideally her hymen will be so resistant to penetration that brute force is required to break it, which causes the bride's blood to flow onto her white trousers. The groom then hands the bloodied trousers to the women who are waiting outside the door of the nuptial chamber. The women ululate with joy upon seeing the blood and either parade the bride's trousers through the crowd or hand them over to the men, who, in some parts of Morocco, then use them for target practice (sexual subtlety is not a characteristic of these rituals).

The focus of the whole event is the spilled blood, for it is the blood that consummates the rite of passage, confirms proper male and female roles in creation, and initiates both bride and groom into adulthood. Ideally, the blood should come from the phallus-broken hymen, but there are variations.

broken hymens

Should the bride's hymen be ruptured before the wedding night, there are several ways to still accomplish the proper order of things. (A broken hymen does not necessarily indicate lack of virginity, though that is how it is commonly interpreted; for instance, the hymen can break spontaneously while a girl is riding horseback or muleback.) The most dramatic and thankfully least practiced way is that the bride is slain. Having failed to shed her blood in response to the sultan-bridegroom's penetration, she is made to shed her blood by her death, becoming the literal rather than the figurative sacrifice. Her blood on the ground compensates for the lack of blood on the bed and restores honor to the young man who so carefully was prepared to cause her to bleed.

The groom himself does not kill her, for she is not his blood, not his responsibility, but rather hands the sullied bride over to a man whose blood she shares, her father or her brother, one of whom kills her on that very night. Westermarck describes this practice, at the turn of the twentieth century, among one group in Morocco. The bridegroom leaves the room, and the women come to look for the blood.

> If they find blood on the bride's . . . *sarwal,* drawers, they make a quivering noise and dance in the room, the bride's sister dances in the room with the trousers on her head. It is then hung up in the yard so that all the people should see the marks of virginity. Should there be no such marks, the bridegroom's family would exclaim, *Ddi kalbtak ʿaliya* [*khudh kalbtak ʿalayy*], "Take away from me your bitch"; and the bride's father or, in his absence, her brother would shoot her dead in the room or in the yard, besides which all the money and presents given would be returned.
>
> (Westermarck 1914:236)

No one I know ever witnessed a girl sacrificed, though many told tales of some girl somewhere distant who was in that manner slain. Past and present, the actual slaying of a bride whose hymen did not bleed has been rare. Yet, the voicing of the possibility takes its toll on females, for it boldly inserts that possibility into lived existence. The practice exists as a speech act even if not as a physical act.

That people verbally entertain the thought of slaying a bride demonstrates how much the ritual is constructed from the male perspective and oriented toward male ennoblement. The groom is not expected to spill any of his blood. Even his sperm is not at stake; it is neither inspected nor publicly exhibited, and in fact may not even be spilled on the wedding night. Even if he fails in his ritual duties, his life is not put in jeopardy, while his bride's is. Basic cultural interpretations of male and female inform these practices and heap honor for marriage's successful consummation upon grooms, and impute serious, even potentially fatal, blame for its failure upon brides.

A second way to address the problem of a hymen broken before marriage is to have it replaced by a sheep membrane in a rather painful operation that has long been a part of folk tradition in North Africa and the Middle East. Here, knowledge of the problem must exist in advance, and the replacement must be carried out in absolute secrecy. Typically, only women extremely close to the bride are privy to what has been done.

Another option demands both foreknowledge and cooperation from the groom and is the most common means of compensating for the lack of hymenal blood. The groom hides a pigeon or cock in his robes when he enters the nuptial chambers, and, after the door is shut, takes it out and formally sacrifices it. He places its head on the girl's trousers, utters the name of God, and slits its throat. In order to become a proper Muslim man and prove to himself and others his determinative role in human birth, the groom must spill sacrificial blood, but this can be accomplished through substitute sacrifice.

physical affirmation of male dominance of birth: sultan and everyman

The Moroccan marriage ritual demands that the sultan-bridegroom dramatically spill blood in order to confirm his dominance of creation. I suspect that anthropologists have been off the mark in single-mindedly concentrating on females and virginity in Mediterranean marriage practices, as opposed to males and their act of bloodspilling; it is striking how male-focused is the ritual, at least as practiced in Morocco, and how female-focused have been the anthropological interpretations of it.

I submit that virginity, like the death of the animal in sacrifice, is a secondary rather than a primary factor in these rites—frequently present, but not absolutely necessary for the marriage to be properly consummated. What is important is that the men spill blood in an act of some violence, so that they demonstrate for themselves and others their procreative role.[1]

The stress on the unbroken hymen—on virginity—is one way to ensure that the physical world conforms to the assumption of male dominance. The action itself creates a vivid icon of the groom forcibly opening the bride's womb, preparing and consecrating it for proper creation; the womb submits to his dominance through bloodspilling.

Of course, an unbroken hymen has the additional advantage of indicting that the bride's birth canal has not been touched by another man, which adds to the drama and empowerment that the groom feels, further aggrandizing him in this male-dominated marriage ritual. But virginity is *not* always demanded, whereas bloodspilling is, a clear indication of what is culturally primary and what is secondary.

According to Westermarck, there were in the early twentieth century whole groups of Moroccans who neither demanded nor expected the bride's virginity and yet continued to demand the male's spilling of blood on the night of marriage. Among these groups, the substitution of the blood of the fowl for the blood of the bride had reached the level of customary practice, rather than individual strategy:

> There is always blood on it [the bride's trousers], because, if the bridegroom suspects his bride of not being a virgin, or from his own experience knows that she is not so, he has a cock ready to kill, then, if necessary, smears her chemise with its blood; I was told that it never happens that a bride is sent away on account of lost virginity.
>
> (Westermarck 1914:240)

The practice of the substitution of animal blood for hymenal blood is old in Morocco. Mouette describes it during the early 1700s (A.H. 1100s), when the great Mawlay Isma'il was still on the throne:

> If he finds her not a Maid, he takes off the Cloaths he has given her, and without seeing her Face, restores her to the Kindred, who conduct her back to the Father, and it is in his Power to Kill her, if he will go to the Rigour. When Matches are among Relations, those Ceremonies are seldom practis'd, for Fear of disgracing the Family; but for saving the Formalities, the Husband kills a pigeon upon a pair of Drawers, which he throws out [to the women] and then unveils his Wife's Face.
>
> (Mouette 1710:43)

I submit that the violent spilling of blood is a culturally instituted, self-reflexive act that physically builds the notion that males dominate earthly creation, despite the fact that so much of daily life speaks of the female's prominence in reproduction; she spontaneously bleeds, she carries the child inside her, she gives it birth. The high drama of the ritual's actions, the blood and violence, is necessary to block physical perceptions built in the day-to-day. The ritual establishes a reality in which the male usurps the female's "natural" domination of birth-giving and ties everyone, male and female, to that articulation, for this is the way that Muslim children are properly conceived.

The ritual gives physical embodiment to the culture's insistence that males dominate earthly birth by structuring a tangible experience of it. Most Moroccans, male and female, understand reproduction to take place in this way, and fervently hope for the male's successful penetration. Not only the male's status but the female's status depends on it. The most reliable way for a woman to secure a place of honor in this world is by giving birth to a man's male heirs. The female is not thought capable of initiating birth, but she is thought capable of interfering with it, of frustrating her husband's desires for male children though bad *niya,* evil intentions, of which she may be unconscious. Hence the proper Muslim female must relinquish control of sexuality, even control over her own body, to the man.

passivity and seclusion

The young man is prepared for adulthood by becoming public and active, sacred and potent, controlled and responsible. The female is prepared in precisely the opposite manner. The young man's identity is collapsed with that of the most powerful public figure in the land, the nation's ruler. The young woman's identity is merged with no public figure. She does not even become the "king's wife." (In Morocco the king's wife is not a public figure, but rather a silent and secluded spouse; her face is not commonly seen; her name is not generally known.) The bride's individuality, not her communal importance, is stressed. She is often quite young; thirteen, until recently, has been a common age for the bride at first marriage (the groom has been older, often in his late twenties). The bride is simply herself, a member of her patriline, and her personal qualities, especially her beauty, are accented.

The groom is compared with what is durable and sacred; the bride is associated with what is temporal and transitory—for instance, with goods for consumption, such as honey and dates. The groom acts; the bride submits. Her sequence of preparation demands and inculcates submission. Things are done to her, not by her. She is groomed, exhibited, beautified. She is made to dance by other women who physically move her shoulders back and forth while others sing of her beauty and speak of her forthcoming marriage as barter. Others wash, dress, and console her while she lies passive, often weeping.

The custom of applying hinna' is a crystalline presentation of the whole of her preparations. The hinna' is applied to the bride's hands and feet in a painstakingly slow process which others perform on her body while she remains completely still; it can take from two to eight hours. She typically sits or lies on the floor or a couch while women skilled in the art of hinna' application carefully etch her hands and feet with patterns of dye. Small thread-like cylinders of the thick hinna' paste dangle from the tip of the pointed object the applier holds in her right hand. The small cylinders are laid on the bride's hands, wrists, ankles, and feet in delicate filigree patterns of abstract design and exquisite beauty.

After the hinna' has been applied, the bride's hands and feet are heated over hot coals. Then those around her wrap her hands and feet with cotton and gauze; when they are finished the bride looks like a burn victim. The bindings should remain in place for at least twelve hours. The bindings, like the heating, help set the dye. When bound, the bride cannot eat or drink or use the bathroom by herself. She is completely dependent on others even for the most basic processes. All this is done for the sake of beauty and adornment, all in hope of gaining her husband's favor. Ideally, the hinna' is reapplied by the same slow procedure the next day, feet and hands again heated and again bound. The result of the dyeing is an etching of deep-red lace gloves and anklets, embedded in the skin itself, that lasts for almost a month. The hinna' represents the bride's blood (a girl's first hinna' application comes with the onset of menstruation), while the application conveys marriage's aim. It suggests that if the bride will be silent and passive while others guide her blood, that blood can be turned into things of beauty—sensual appeal at the first level, and the production of sons at a deeper level. These things will make her valuable to a man.

The sharply differing roles cultivated in the groom and bride are dramatized in their respective hinna' ceremonies. The sultan-bride-groom is the center of his ceremonies, the pivotal actor in them. He puts his own hand into the bowl of hinna' and presses his handprint—the sign of his distinctive self—on the wall to indicate how many children he plans to create. The bride, in contrast, is the passive recipient. Others use her blood, or its metaphorical equivalent, hinna', to adorn her, while she lies quietly submitting.

The overarching sequences of the two ceremonies convey radically different messages. The groom's illustrates his position as the center of active power; he is the creator, the decision maker, the public communal figure upon whom the good of the whole depends. The bride's illustrates her proper role as sublimated respondent, a temporal thing of beauty whose sensuality will be found pleasing, it is hoped, by the man she marries. His pathway to adulthood is to become public and pivotal. Her pathway is to become quiescent, private, and adorned. His preparations involve expanding his physical range of maneuver, taking him out of the house and onto the streets. The bride's preparations involve the reverse. Her spatial range is constrained, made more circumscribed, more restrictive (Mernissi 1987a, Naamane-Ghessous 1987). The ritual cultivates these primary understandings through the body; it verifies culture's imagined assumptions by presenting them in palpable form. The rite gives groom and bride physical practice in behaving as adults, but they are very different kinds of adults. Those differences are summarized in figure 11.1.

The ritual also guides the emotional displays of the marriage rites, as well as the interpretations of them. The sultan-bridegroom is to be stalwart, controlled, not to exhibit any feelings, while the bride is to be overwrought. She is to weep through much of the ceremony, and her tears are collectively interpreted as illustrating her inability to control her emotions.

In point of fact there is real grief involved in the bride's transition that is absent from the groom's. She is being severed from the household in which she is an inalienable member and entering a household in which she has no inalienable rights. The groom, in contrast, remains in his own patriline's household, but gains a position of in-

---

FIGURE 11.1. Male and Female as Defined in the First Marriage Ritual

Bridegroom	Bride
identified with the national ruler	identified with herself and her sex
central, collective, and durable	beautiful, temporal, evanescent
sacred, comparable to the prophets	worldly, comparable to dates and honey
public, active, in control	private, passive, controlled by others
emotionally restrained	emotionally overwrought
holder of beneficent power	holder of both good and evil power
biological reproducer	the conduit for male reproduction
erect, straightforward	shy, turning away
controlled eruptions of sound	long ululating cries
white/solid color	multicolored/shimmering
the initiator of action	the responder to action
the one who touches	the one who is touched
the one who spills blood	the one from whom blood falls
the sacrificer	the sacrificed

creased importance within it. Yet, it is not the legitimate reasons for her expression of grief and the legitimate reasons for his lack of grief that are publicly emphasized. Rather, the culture both cultivates and uses the patterns of emotional display to undergird basic cultural assumptions about male and female, and interprets the groom's lack of display as illustrating the male's emotional strength, and the bride's emotional exhibit as demonstrating the female's emotional frailty.

The ritual of first marriage also reinforces the notion that males at their best are unequivocally good, while females, even at their best, are both good and evil, through no fault of their own but rather through their female nature. The different reasons for the veiling of the groom and the bride revolve around this. The sultan-bridegroom is veiled because he is so good that he needs protection from the evil that pursues what is truly good in the world. In contrast, the bride is veiled because she is of mixed valence, both good and evil, and others must be protected from the harm that she might inadvertently cause. In some places, stones are thrown at the bride as she is taken away from her father's household to "shoo away" the evil she might unknowingly leave behind (see Westermarck 1914:165–192).

Physical substances, physical actions, and spatial organization are used to carry and cultivate basic understandings. In rural areas, the bride often rides to the groom's household on muleback. Sometimes the groom's mother holds the mule's tail, guarding its anus, on the supposition that if any one should touch it, the bride would be bewitched. Not only does this practice suggest a merging of bride and animal, but it begins the mother-in-law's control over the bride's body.

In some places in Morocco, a young boy is placed behind the bride on the mule. This helps to steady the heavily veiled young woman and also serves as a graphic reminder of her ultimate aim on the way to her groom's household—to produce male heirs. The bride may also carry a lamb in her arms while en route to her future father-in-law's compound, a sign that she will cause no harm to his herds.

The ritual of first marriage is structured to give the female practice in the restraint necessary for her to succeed in her new role. The whole thrust of the bride's preparation is to reduce her range of maneuver, to center her in the household and on the bed. This training is crucial if the bride is to succeed in her new role. The bride's movements are heavily restricted, especially in the early years of marriage. She is often limited to her husband's household. Westermarck notes that, at the turn of the century, some local groups would not allow the bride to go back to her father's home for a year after the marriage. Elsewhere, she had to await the birth of the first child. The ritual of first marriage gives her intense practice in containment and offers her ways of finding meaning in limited places.

body of the Muslim house

The spatial organization of traditional houses helps reinforce the definitions that the ritual of first marriage builds. The lay of the house in North Africa and the Middle East has been a constant reminder of what the culture understands a woman to be. The traditional house is modeled on the female body, and entry into it mimics male entry into the female in the sexual act.

The streets leading to the houses are typically small, narrow, and convoluted; they are dead ends, which helps keep strangers away. The walls of the houses are high and windowless. There is but a single mode of entry, a small, low doorway that is somewhat difficult to pass through (one often has to bend down to get inside). Even after gaining access to the initial opening, one is not yet within the main part of the household, but rather one must first follow a dark, circuitous hallway that finally breaks forth in the central courtyard—a place of great pleasure. The image is clear. Entry into the female is difficult, but if one gains access, then pleasures abound. There are flowing fountains, orange trees in blossom, and hibiscus in bloom. The women, shimmering and shining, sit there, rightfully secluded, shielded from public view, guarding their pleasures for the men who have rightful access to them.

The ritual practices of first marriage ceremonies, like the physical layout of traditional houses and streets, play upon universals of the female body and universals of sexual intercourse, and then embed very particular cultural definitions in them, definitions that in fact are relevant only to a given time and place. The fusion of the two—of undeniable givens and imagined cultural assumptions—makes it difficult for the female to distance herself from the cultural definitions because they are written on and through her own body. To discard the definitions would be in some real way to damage her essential self; she cannot easily break loose of her own being. The embedding of cultural particulars in universal truths is one of the most powerful and durable means of reproduction that culture has available to it.

heightened anxiety

The marriage rite of passage is a time of high anxiety. To show that he is a man, the boy must initiate actions, be central to all that goes on, and bring the ceremonies to conclusion. The groom's anxiety focuses on impotence, impotence that has to do with bloodspilling as well as sexuality. Will he be able to pierce the hymen and spill the blood? Will he effectively provide a sacrificial substitute if not? The problem of impotence is exacerbated because the groom often has not slept for two or three nights before he goes to his bride. When a young man brings a fowl to the nuptial chamber, it may well be to cover the risk of his own sexual impotence as well as the possibility of a previously broken hymen.

Writing in 1721, Windus speaks of the problem of impotence and the pressure put on the bridegroom to perform:

> He is to make what haste he can, that he may deliver her Drawers to the two black Women, who keep the Door, and are to carry them to the rest of the good Women; and if such Signs appear on them as are expected, the Musick plays; but if he doth not send out the Drawers, the Musick must not play: and it behoves him to bestir himself about this Matter; for, besides the hazard of his Reputation, the company will meet every Day 'till the Drawers come.
>
> (Windus 1725:36)

If a male does not spill blood (either by piercing the bride's hymen or through a substitute), he is shamed. The groom's inability to spill blood is sufficiently common that prescribed practices exist to protect the bride from being wrongly accused of being at fault. For instance, in Fas, if a groom says that he has not been able to spill blood because the bride's hymen was already broken, her family can dispute his claim by calling in two midwives and a religious judge who will form their own opinion on the matter. If they find the groom in the wrong, he will be publicly denounced. Yet there is no thought of killing him, which shows how differently the collectivity treats male and female "failure." Hers can bring death, at least in common parlance. His can bring only temporary dishonor.

The bride's anxiety also centers on whether or not the groom will spill blood. Hers is exacerbated because she cannot accomplish that bloodspilling. She must depend upon him. Her fate, in a very real sense, rests in his hands.

The bride's anxiety also stems from her severance from her family. She is given away, sacrificed by her patriline in order to bear the patriline of another. Her patriline is sorry to lose her, but it must give her up in order to gain its own vessels for reproduction. The songs sung to the bride before she leaves her father's household often speak of her upcoming marriage as "barter." There is much truth in the phrasing. She, the evanescent part of the patriline, is bartered so that the permanent part—the male dimension—can be secured through the reproduction of male heirs, an earthly process for which "outside" women are needed. The patriline's women must leave the households of their birthright and enter households of others where they have no inalienable position. They must earn their right to stay in those households, and the earning depends upon the reaction of the groom and the groom's mother, people over whom the bride has little or no control, especially at first. Abject submission is usually the best strategy.

heightened learning

Up to a certain point heightened anxiety increases learning potential, especially for information with which people are already familiar but in which they need repetition and practice. We codify things more speedily and more thoroughly during times of emotional charge. The emotional pitch of the Moroccan first wedding ceremonies combines with the clarity with which male and female definitions are presented to create an intense socialization process, a true rite of passage that transforms young men and young women into adults. The young males and females are already familiar with their culture's definitions, but the ritual gives them intense practice in them and undergirds them with emotional strength.

The ritual places incredible pressure upon the groom to be central, stalwart, and performing, and upon the bride to be passive, emotional, and dependent. These are not necessarily qualities that the groom and bride previously exhibited in daily life and will not be the qualities that they will always exhibit in the future. Young men are often tender and gentle. Young women are often forceful and assertive. Yet both must learn to systematically channel their individual personalities into culturally acceptable patterns if they are to be successful adults. For most, there are no other options available. Certain qualities must be exhibited if the young men and young women are to recognize themselves, and have others recognize them, as adults. Much of the rite of passage not only gives the bride and groom physical practice in these qualities, but also gives them a supportive audience which reads back to them their worth.

emotions in bounds

While it is true that the ritual plays in part on increased anxiety, the ritual also serves to keep the anxiety within bounds. It does not leave the young men and women alone—without guidance—to deal with the trauma of transformation. Quite the contrary, it gives them a precise script and a concerned community that helps ensure its proper performance. The part of the young bride centers on beauty, passivity, and sensuality, qualities that lead to successful wifehood and motherhood. The part of the groom centers on his elevation to nothing less than central ruler, the most potent and powerful man of the time. On a deep subconscious level, the initiates become powerfully tied to the scripts that culture presents to them, for the scripts help them through one of life's most momentous times.

The link between the groom and the sharifi Prince of the Faithful is particularly intense. It is the sharifi king who gives the young man his coming of age, who turns him into a potent public figure. The prince is a man of power who is considered to be capable of linking with the creative processes of the universe and channeling them to earth. He is the guide for all others. In order to undergo the rite, the young man submerges his identity into the ruler's. Even after the ceremony's completion, the identification between ruler and ruled often continues to be intense, and the groom uses the ruler's persona as the measure of the man he wishes to be.

In the ceremony of initial marriage the central ruler enters the bedroom and becomes associated with the most intimate physical act and the most intimate definitions of self. So close is the identification between ruler and ruled that to do away with the sharifi caliphate becomes a question of virtual suicide, and is not, by most Moroccans, seriously contemplated.

Islamic and universal essentials

The Moroccan ritual of first marriage grounds itself in Islamic and universal essentials. The sexual drive is one of the most forceful with which mortals are endowed and the desire to leave progeny one of the most complicated. The ritual seizes upon the universals of sexual drive and longing for progeny and constructs a cultural resolution of them by creating a universe in which the power of reproduction rests with a God beyond nature and men who can bring it to earth. The Qur'an is clear on God's dominance of creation:

> That We may make clear to you,
> And We establish in the wombs what we will, till a stated term,
> then We deliver you as infants.
>
> (Sura 22, The Pilgrimage, 6)

We created you . . .
Have you considered the seed you spill?
Do you yourselves create it, or are We the Creators?

(Sura 56, The Terror, 58—60)

No female bears or brings forth, save with His knowledge;
and none is given long life [but] who is given long life
neither is any diminished in his life, but it is in a Book.
Surely that is easy for God.

(Sura 35, The Angels, 12)

Do not associate others with God; to associate
others with God is a mighty wrong.
And We have charged man concerning his
parents—his mother bore him in weakness
upon weakness, and his weaning was in
two years—'Be thankful to Me, and to
thy parents; to Me is the homecoming.'

(Sura 31, Luqman, 13—15)

The Qur'an is equally clear on the elements that God uses in human creation. There are two, blood clot and sperm drop:

'Recite;' In the Name of they Lord who created, created Man of
   a blood-clot.

(Sura 96, The Blood Clot, 2—3)

Of what did He create him?
Of a sperm-drop
He created him, and determined him.

(Sura 80, He Frowned, 19—20)

It is He who created you of dust
Then of sperm-drop
Then of blood-clot
Then He delivers you as infants,
Then that you may come of age,
Then that you may be old men—
Though some of you there are who die before it—
and that you may reach a stated term;
haply you will understand.
It is He who gives life, and makes to die.

(Sura 40, The Believers, 68—69)

usurpation

God is the force, men are the links, and male *par excellence*—the exemplary creator—is the blood-descendant king. The ritual constructs the experience—it builds the reality—that males dominate creation's blood, counteracting everyday perceptions by violently creating emboldened ones in which that dominance is demonstrated to be true. Sperm already belongs to the man; the ritual gives him control of the blood also. The ritual's violence is necessary to override the normal perceptions—to give the cultural construction dominance over the natural ones, to push the man towards the heavens, and leave the woman behind, even in the natural birth process.

The Moroccan ritual of first marriage "demonstrates" that while it is accurate that the female spontaneously bleeds, it is the man who systematically guides the bleeding into life. The rite makes the male the cultural usurper of the female's biological role. It gives males power over earthly birth and relegates the female to physical vessel for male-initiated creation.

The ritual accomplishes this usurpation by metaphorically collapsing every man's identity into that of the blood-descendant king—the powerful, potent, and renewing Central One. On this level, man's dominance of creation's blood as well as its sperm seems plausible and man's participation in the cosmic processes seems possible. The ritual of first marriage makes men the conduit between God's power of reproduction and life on earth, and of all men makes the Moroccan ruler the most worthy link.

12

ram's blood: Great Sacrifice

The sun shines clean—almost white—with light. The king emerges from a mosque, white robes gleaming. Robed men close in around him, encircling him in a great body of white. Briefly the circle breaks open to give entry to a ram; its fleece is pure white, its horns are mighty, its dark eyes are boldly encircled in black. Often the ram tosses its head grandly as it is led to the center. Two men seize the ram, force it on its back, turn its head toward Makka, and hold it fast. The king takes a knife in his right hand, utters God's name, and plunges the knife deeply into the ram's throat. The blood spurts, the ram struggles, then in a surge of life manages to stand up, only to collapse on its side in a pool of blood, heart still pounding. The whole of the nation watches this bleeding ram, for in its dying lies their hope.

innovation

Early in their reign, the ʿAlawi dynasty began the practice of having the blood-descendant king sacrifice a ram on behalf of the community of believers as a whole. It was a dramatic innovation, a performance which the ʿAlawi modeled on that of their noble ascendant Muhammad in his enactment of the ram sacrifice in Madina in 624 (A.H. 2). Through the innovation, the ʿAlawi monarchs became the sacrificial link between God and nation, the means by which God could see the collectivity's faith and grant his favor. Through the performance, the Moroccan monarchs inserted themselves into the single most powerful canonical ritual in Islam and into the mythic foundations upon which it rests.

Muslims throughout the world participate in the Great Sacrifice. Each year Muslims on pilgrimage in the Arabian Peninsula and Muslim heads of household throughout the lands take a knife in their hands and slay an animal on behalf of their families. But the ʿAlawi monarchs instituted a new level of sacrifice, a national level, which they personally performed. Morocco's sharifi caliph became the only head of any major Muslim state to himself slit a ram's throat on behalf of the political community he leads. It was an audacious act made by a self-assured young dynasty.

Records indicating the year in which the ʿAlawi practice was begun are not yet uncovered. The dynasty came to power in 1666. In 1671 Addison observed the Great Sacrifice in Morocco and does not mention the ruler's performance of a sacrifice on behalf of the nation. He speaks only of household sacrifices. Yet, Saint Olon (1695) witnessed Mawlay Ismaʿil's enactment of a great national sacrifice just a few years later. His description makes it clear that the practice had been firmly instituted by this time. It was repeated in the years that followed (see, for example, Chenier 1788:2:197).

It seems likely that Mawlay Ismaʿil began the practice, though it is plausible that he reinstituted a practice that earlier Moroccan monarchs had performed, a practice for which documentation is obscure or nonexistent. What is important is that Mawlay Ismaʿil performed the Great Sacrifice on the nation's behalf in basically the same way that his many times removed great-grandson King Hasan II performs it today. Mawlay Ismaʿil had the force of character necessary to think of, implement, and make popularly convincing such an act. His own name may have been a partial inspiration. He is the only Moroccan king in the twelve hundred years of the monarchy to carry the name Isma'il, the name of the child that the Prophet Ibrahim nearly slew.

Whatever the year and for whatever reasons the performance was begun, what is crucial here is that it became an important part of collective experience and has remained a part of that experience ever since, for nearly three hundred years. It is, I submit, the most powerful ritual support of the Moroccan monarchy. It bolsters the king's legitimacy by having him perform the most dramatic action in which humans can engage for the most noble of purposes, the causing of earthly death in order to overcome the limits of earthly life, in order to connect with the divine.

Each year the sharifi monarch stands before the political community he serves and slays a great beast of this world, causing its natural blood to flow, so that the great God may see the depth of the people's faith and grant them his favor. In taking the title of "amir al mu'minin," "the Prince of the Faithful," the Moroccan king lays verbal claim to the supreme political position in Islam; in performing the act of communal sacrifice, he demonstrates its truth. He is the community's representative to God, the collectivity's sacrificial link to transcendence.

anticipation and preparation

Moroccans keep the sacrifice to an unparalleled extent. Nearly every head of household, rich or poor, slays a ram, and many families spend as much as 20 percent of their annual income on the Great Sacrifice. French statistics indicate that more overseas workers return home for this festivity than for any others. Buses, boats, planes, and cars are filled with Moroccans coming back to the land of their birth to celebrate the sacrifice with their families.

The Great Sacrifice is known by a variety of names in the Muslim world, but in Morocco it is called simply 'Id al-Kabir, which literally means "the Great Ritual." It lives up to its name. Nearly everyone participates in the sacrifice. Even people who verbally distance themselves from the faith tend to join in. They are physically drawn into the world view and reality that the ritual builds; their actions take them to places where their words may not.

The Great Sacrifice is a time of exhilaration. Preparations for it commence weeks in advance, as men begin to frequent markets to purchase their rams. Large white rams with long horns and deep black markings about the eyes are the most highly prized, for that is the kind the Prophet Muhammad is believed to have sacrificed.

Animal markets burgeon. Men who come on donkeys and men who come in Mercedes bargain side by side. They draw out the decision-making process. There is much banter, merrymaking, and laughter. Mutual advice and sincere help is given in the purchase of the sacrificial animals that are the source of familial pleasure as well as a gift to God and a donation to the poor.

The excitement in houses and streets reaches a communal pitch experienced at no other time. People evaluate the purchased rams, particularly comparing overall size and the length of their horns. Many leave their rams conspicuously tethered in the streets or in their courtyards for others to see. Frank admiration extends to those who have purchased a magnificent beast for divine sacrifice.

Women on rooftops and in neighborhood streets compare the size of household rams, for the size indicates the manliness of the husband as well as how much he values his wife, the conduit of his children. A man who brings home a ram that is seen as too small will be met with his wife's wrath and derision: "Are you not a man?" "Can you not provide for your family?" Not only the ram's overall size, but the size of his horns, testicles, and phallus are the subject of commentary. People straightforwardly acknowledge the sexual connotations of this virile representative of the natural world; it is a measure of a man's reproductive capacity on earth at the same time that it is a measure of his faith in God. It is also the man's own sacrificial substitute, the being that allows him to keep his manhood intact, to go on living.

The day preceding the ritual centers on preparations for the momentous event, on putting one's body and soul in order before the act of sacrifice. Men are the focus of the most intense preparations, though women may participate in them also. Many Moroccans fast during the preceding day. Many increase the number and length of their prayers. An 'arafa, a vigil, should be held on the evening before the sacrifice. Everyone—men, women, and children—must be freshly bathed and clothed before dawn, before the time of transformation begins.

day of sacrifice

The Great Sacrifice begins early. Women typically put on everyday clothes and go to the kitchen where they begin preparing breads and sweets. Men in contrast awaken and undergo the intense preparations necessary to distance themselves from the natural world and make the connection with the divine. They partake of neither food nor drink until the sacrifice is over. They abstain from sexual intercourse, which is seen as polluting. They bathe and cloak themselves in garments of pure white. They leave the domestic sphere, the horizontal domain of women and children, in order to contact God, journeying beyond the temporal dimension of food and females to a public communal place sanctified by the gathering of Muslim men. Together the men recite holy verses, pray, and participate in communal sacrifice, creating a vertical link to God, and thereby creating hope for the human whole at the same time that they reaffirm their own role as the carriers of faith. Women stay at home, dispersed in individual households, waiting for their men to return and bring them hope.

king's sacrifice

The most important of the communal sacrifices, the one that unifies all others, takes place in the capital city and centers on the reigning king. He gathers with key men at the mosque near his Ribat palace. No females are present.

First, a prominent religious scholar preaches a sermon beseeching the 'Alawi ruler to take care of the faithful, to serve goodness, to work for justice, to embody the best of Islamic ideals. The Prince of the Faithful, kneeling on the floor like all of the other faithful present, listens quietly to the sermon. No visible signs mark his status. He is dressed in a white robe with a pointed hood, like the other men. There is no gold, no crown, no marked spatial separation from the others. He sits in their midst, towards the right of the crowd on one of the front rows, flanked by brothers and sons. Here in the mosque, in this holy place, all men are equal.

The sermon concludes with prayer. The king participates with all the others. There is striking beauty to the common prayer. In one great white body, hundreds of men bow, stand, kneel, and touch their foreheads to the ground in ritual motion. United in common action, individual distinctions blur as those gathered become a graceful whole, one body preparing for sacrifice.

Here in the presence of God, the ritual underlines the commonality of all men of faith. The Qur'an is clear on the equality of men when compared to the Godhead. Even Muhammad, the final Prophet, was only a man—a flawed man—but an enormously important one. "He was only a Messenger, and Messengers have gone before." He was not divine, nor are his political successors, who do not even hold his prophetic status. In the mosque, the king is but another of the faithful striving for connection, and that truth is given physical affirmation and visual play.

After the prayer's conclusion, the men leave the mosque and enter an outer courtyard—a physical movement that recalls the pilgrims' journey from 'Arafat to Mina, from the mountain to the plain, from the more sacred domain, where all men are equal, to the domain of everyday life, where an overarching ruler is needed. In the transition from mosque to courtyard, the king passes from being simply one of the faithful to being the first among equals, the living man upon whom collective responsibility most clearly rests, the man who must embody in stellar form the qualities that all men seek. He is the archetypal male, the man who is at one and the same time the overseer of the political community of Muslims in the world and the community's collective representative before God—the symbolic embodiment of the political whole.

In the courtyard, the blood-descendant monarch stands at the center of the crowd of white-robed men, who gather closely about him in a circular body of white that iconically recalls the pilgrims' encircling of the Ka'ba in Makka. The Moroccan sun shines clean for these communal sacrifices, which take place in the open air of early morning. The sky is almost white with light, its rays reflecting off the knife that the king holds in his right hand. A large ram with long horns and white fleece is brought in. Two men seize the great beast, turn it over on its back, point its head towards Makka, and hold it fast. The ruler utters "Bi'smi'llah al-Rahman, al-Rahim," "In the name of God, the Merciful, the Compassionate," and plunges the knife deeply into the ram's throat. The knife thrust must be forceful enough to cut the ram's major arteries, but not so forceful as to take off the head in a single blow. The ram struggles, and then, in a surge of life, may stand back up, the rich red blood flowing from its neck. The nation intently watches the ram's actions, for therein lies its destiny.

There is a profound calm to these motions that enact the drama of death and life, obliteration and transcendence, before the believing community. All that is extraneous is set aside and life's essence is revealed. The culmination is, after all, the causing of death so that God may, in his wisdom, turn death back into life.

Once the ram has finally fallen, one of the men present quickly lifts it and places it in the back of a waiting jeep that speeds it to the king's palace. (In the past it was carried through the streets by a slave who ran on foot or galloped on horseback with his heavy burden. See Saint Olon 1695 and Chenier 1788:2:197). If the ram arrives still alive—with heart still beating—this is taken to mean that the coming year will be prosperous for Morocco. To still exude life after such a violent blow has been struck is a sign of the presence of God, for while humans can change life to death, only God can turn death to life. A ram that continues to live after the neck has been nearly severed indicates that God acknowledges the worthiness of the sacrifice, and will bestow his blessing on the nation in the year to come.[1]

The king's sacrifice is shown on television throughout the day and discussed on radio and summarized in newspapers. In households, streets, and shops, people talk about the sacrifice—how impressive the beast was and whether it tried to stand back up once the death cut had been made.

local community sacrifices

Ideally, all the senior men of the umma would gather around the reigning prince for his performance of the sacrifice, but the vastness of the countryside and the size of the population prevent it. Nonetheless, the convergence is metaphorically achieved through the simultaneous enactment of communal sacrifices throughout the land. While the king performs the national sacrifice in the capital city, the senior men of local communities all over Morocco gather and sacrifice, typically in wide open spaces, *musalla,* consecrated as sacred for the occasion. (The musalla is where the groom is transformed into the sultan during the popular rituals of first marriage.)

The king is figuratively brought to these local festivities. The delegated head of the king's government is central to them. Men cluster around him in much the same way they cluster around the king in the capital city. He is dressed in gleaming white robes, participates in the common prayers, and sets the sacrifice in motion. The ritual performance depends on his presence and his initiative.

A local religious leader, a teacher or a religious judge, stands by the government official and preaches a sermon in the name of the king, the reigning Prince of the Faithful, the victorious one of God, and then leads the men in prayer. Next, the sacrifice takes place. The words and actions of the king's sacrifice are repeated in the local area, but here the religious and political dimensions of the sacrifice are often pulled apart. The delegate of the king's government is at the center of the sacrifice, but, most often, it is a religious leader who actually slays the ram. The meat of the slain animal is given to the region's poor. Almost everywhere in Morocco, only men attend. In the rare instances (in certain large cities) where women are present, they stand in the rear, visually and spatially separate—behind and apart.

In the combination of the central orienting sacrifice of the nation's ruler and the sum total of local community sacrifices, the nation is vertically expressed. Moroccans believe that the communal sacrifices must precede the local household sacrifices. If an individual sacrifice were to be performed before the community-wide event, it would be invalid: it would not be a sacrifice made to the Almighty God as a covenant of the Great Sacrifice. For it is the literal gathering of senior Muslim men—their actual physical proximity—that figuratively establishes the holy peak so that communion with the God beyond nature can take place.

The communal sacrifice is a concrete realization of the umma, the community of the faithful, and that realization empowers individual men to participate in individual sacrifices in their own households. Often men take the knife they will use in the family sacrifice to the community event, thus directly connecting the two through the instrument of animal death and spiritual rebirth, sanctifying their own knife through the holy gathering of males. The sacrifice performed by the senior male *par excellence,* the king, and by other senior men throughout the countryside sets the individual sacrifices in motion. It also lifts them out of the local setting, tying the household sacrifices to the nation as a whole and to the community of Muslims past and present.

household sacrifices

Men return home from the communal sacrifices to perform their household sacrifices. The Hadith prescribes that they go home by a different route than that by which they come. Some say that the return home by another way marks the transformation that has occurred in the individual men because they have participated in the sacrifice performed by the living umma.

Others say that, by taking a different route, the participants protect themselves from wanton beings, the *jinn,* that may have seen them traveling to the sacrifice and may be lying in wait for them on their return. Jinn are believed to be capricious spirits, shadow beings, who may work along with Iblis, the fallen angel, in the service of evil. In rallying together, men of the umma can protect themselves from these evil spirits, and by taking another route home, individuals can confound their evil designs. As the final sura of the Qur'an states:

In the Name of God, the Merciful, the Compassionate
Say: "I take refuge with the Lord of men,

the King of men,
the God of men,
from the evil of the slinking whisperer
who whispers in the breasts of men
of jinn and men."
                    (Sura 114, Men, 1–7)

The sacrifice in the household is made on behalf of the sacrificer and his family. It is a reenactment of Muhammad's slaying of a second ram, when he said, "This is for Muhammad and the family of Muhammad." All married men—heads of Muslim households or potential heads of households—must perform a sacrifice, even if they live in their father's home. They must sacrifice to consolidate their own convenant with the divine and thereby bring benefit to themselves and their progeny or their hoped-for progeny.

Men are central to the household sacrifices. In some families women are not present at all but remain in the house while the men perform the sacrifices outside. Yet in most families women attend the household performance. The men stand in front, while women and children sit or squat in a closely knit group somewhat removed from the locus of action. Among the women and children there is much patting of hands, touching of shoulders. Often the women's bodies are turned slightly away from the sacrifice, so that they must slightly turn their heads to see it.

The men, in sharp contrast, stand erect in front, single, upright figures dressed in white, with space separating each man from the others. The visual impression of the sacrifice, the physical icon that embeds itself deeply in the body conscious, is one of men standing individually and boldly, ready to enact earthly death to bring about transcendent life, while the women and children huddle beneath them, dependent on the men for whatever fate they bring (Combs-Schilling, fieldnotes, 1976, 1977, 1978, 1985, 1987, 1988).

The message imprinted through multiple sensory channels is that men of faith bring hope to their families and, by extension, to all of humankind. There is uncertainty as to whether any given man will achieve divine connection; they must be prepared and they must be faithful because they are mere humans trafficking with the divine. Yet, there is certainty that men are the links. If life is to be regenerated, males must do it. The Great Sacrifice sustains an experiential reality in which the weight of responsibility falls heavily on men, while the weight of dependency falls, equally heavily, on women.

The ram, proud and regal, is brought in, led by a tether, until it stands in front of the dominant male. Once there, just as in the earlier communal sacrifice, the ram quickly is seized, turned over, faced towards Makka, and held fast. The male head of the household takes the knife in his right hand, calls out the name of God, and plunges it deep into the ram's throat. The blood begins to spurt, the ram collapses, and then may manage to stand up again on all four legs.

The family watches intensely to see what the sacrificed ram will do, for the family's future, like that of the nation, is read in the ram sacrificed on its behalf. A ram that manages to stand on all fours after its throat has been slit is an auspicious sign, an acknowledgement that God recognizes the worth of the sacrifice and is likely to shed good fortune on the family during the coming year. In standing back up, the ram reenters the vertical dimension, the dimension of God, transcendence, and men. When it falls back down, it succumbs to the horizontal plane of nature and women, and death is sure to follow. If the sacrificed animal does not manage to stand, or if the blood flows darkly and slowly, family misfortune probably lies ahead.

After the hoped-for lifesurge, the ram falls for a final time, and lies dying before the believers, its trembling white body resting in a huge pool of blood. It is a sobering moment, a moment of suspension. The life forces fight hard within the beast. The ram alternates between motionlessness and violent movement. It will be quiet and still, then suddenly begin to kick its legs and heave its sides. It takes what seems a remarkably long time for the ram to die. The ram will appear to be gone, only to show a renewed spurt of life; then quiet again settles, and some men conclude that the animal is dead and start to take it, but others, older and wiser, will say, "It is not finished. Leave it alone." They are right; the ram again struggles, kicking its legs and vainly attempting to stand, but the head does not move and the neck is still except for the blood spurting.

Finally death comes and is sobering. Emotions ranging from sadness to joy are often felt and expressed, often in combination. People speak of the future, of the children that are gathered around, of the children that are still to come, "In Sha' Allah," "God willing." Women often lift small children into their arms and smear a bit of the blood of sacrifice on their faces, while humbly requesting that God watch over these little ones, so that like Isma'il, they may grow to adulthood. Child mortality is a problem in Morocco, and Moroccan mothers, like good mothers everywhere, do all in their power to prevent it; the dabbing of sacrificial blood gives them some hope that they can weight the universe in their child's favor. The rite of sacrifice focuses on children and the future, on the hope that a man's progeny will number like the stars and may like them be durable in the heavens.

Women may also dot some of the blood on themselves and their older children; foreheads, cheeks, and chins are favored spots. Through physical contact with the blood that the men have spilled, females and children can share in the power of sacrifice.

After a few moments of serious silence, there are sighs of relief, a bit of laughter, usually brought by the children, and people begin to turn to the tasks at hand. One of the men makes a small slit in the ram's hide, next to one hoof, and blows air into the slit, thereby inflating the hide like a balloon. The inflation separates the hide from the layer of fat that covers the ram's muscles and skeleton. The hide is then cut down the middle and easily removed in a single piece. The whole process takes only a matter of minutes. Next a bone is severed in each of the ram's hind ankles, which allows it to be hung by its hind feet; the remaining blood falls onto the ground.

As the ritual turns from the sacred to the everyday, women take over. The internal organs (the stomach, the intestines) are given to the women to clean, as is the hide to be made into a rug, and the meat for feasting. The liver, believed by many to be the center of passion, is the first part of the ram to be eaten. The women cut the liver into pieces, skewer it on rods, and cook it over hot coals, giving it first to the men to eat, taking what is left over for themselves and the children. The feasting begins and lasts several days. Part of the ram of sacrifice must be given to the poor. That is a Muslim duty. The amount given usually varies from one-quarter to one-half of the animal.

The ritual of the Great Sacrifice presents the full sequence of life and death and reminds those gathered of the fragility of earthly things and of the power of a beyond-earthly God. That death actually occurs in full view of the participants demands emphasis. A great ram is brought in—vital and living—then is slain. To watch death, to see life flow out of a living creature, is a sobering experience. Yet this earthly death builds a reality of a beyond-earthly life. On one level, the participants see the life forces surge in the dying animal; these life forces are collectively understood to be signs of God's presence, signs of God's ability to restore life where death has struck. On a deeper level, the ritual physically confirms that it is beings of this world— like the ram—that die, while the community of faithful stands living, a dramatic icon that offers the assurance that by connection to God, humans can escape death's grasp. The Great Sacrifice is a performance of hope. That hope is male. It constructs a cosmos within which everlasting life is possible and demonstrates the means by which it can be achieved—by men of faith sacrificing on behalf of the communities they serve, the head of household on behalf of his family, the head of state on behalf of his nation.

13

Ibrahim myth

The sacrifice ritual gives physical embodiment to Islam's great sacrifice myth. It dramatically recalls, palpably presents, the awesome
trial of the Prophet Ibrahim, a drama that addresses humanity's fundamental dilemma—that of life and death, and the hope for existence
beyond death's bond. The myth acknowledges the fragility of human
ties, the transitoriness of even the most valuable of human bonds, and
our human impotence to save ourselves and those we love from death.
For Muslims, the dilemma is expressed through the telling of the poignant tale of Ibrahim, whom God calls upon to sacrifice his son as a
sign of faith.

Ibrahim's story is piercing because he is so faithful a servant of the
one God. In many ways, Ibrahim is the most endearing prophet that
the Qur'an presents; he is discussed more than any other prophet except Muhammad, and Ibrahim's relationship with God is a tender

one. Almighty God calls Ibrahim his "friend," and Ibrahim turns to God not only as creator, but as companion. To Ibrahim's name, the Qur'an regularly appends the words, "the pure of faith; he was no hypocrite."

During Ibrahim's time humanity had turned away from God, but Ibrahim steadfastly turned towards him. At first Ibrahim was drawn to the great celestial bodies, thinking one after another of these—the stars, the moon, the sun—must surely be the Godhead, so great was their beauty as they arched their way across the sky. Yet, in the end, Ibrahim understood that they were not divine and forsook them, swearing that he would not believe in cosmological things that rose, then set. Ibrahim found the one God and never wavered from him.

Ibrahim's faith had important consequences for all of humanity. In the Qur'an, God makes clear that of all of his creations, human beings are his favorite. Yet, by Ibrahim's time, God had grown weary of them—humans were so faithless—and considered turning away. Yet the straightforward sincerity of Ibrahim's loyalty endears humans once again to their creator, and God decides to continue interacting with them.

In earth's terms, Ibrahim's belief in God cost him dearly. His family and friends rejected him. The rejection by his father was painful. Ibrahim tried to convince his father of the true faith, but his father refused it and ended up renouncing not only the faith but his son as well. Ibrahim was forced to walk away. The limits of his filial piety were reached only when to continue to express it would have damaged his relationship with the one God.

Ibrahim was renounced by the local community. People hated and reviled him and desired to "cast him into the furnace" (Sura 37, 98). Yet Ibrahim remained steadfast, and year after year, decade after decade, he continued to prophesy, the lonely servant crying out in the human wilderness. Finally, when Ibrahim was an old man, he grew weary. Long rejected by the family of his birth, he had no sons to give him hope for the future, to bring him the only kind of hope that earthly life can offer—that as long as the son, and the son's son, lives, some of the father lives also. Ibrahim turned to God for refuge, saying, "I am going to my Lord; He will guide me"; and in God's presence, he humbly requested, "My Lord, give me one of the righteous" (Sura 37, 100–101).

And God granted Ibrahim's request and gave him the child Isma'il, a "righteous" son born of the concubine Hajar. The birth of the child healed the pain of the years, and father and son drew close. Tenderness and affection filled the old man's spirit, and there was much cause for rejoicing. Yet, when the son reached "the age of running with him," God made the dreadful demand, and the agony began (Sura 37, 103).

The following account is taken from the *Encyclopedia of Islam*. It combines statements from the Qur'an (Sura 37, 100–110) and from the Hadith. For the reader's clarity, I have put the Qur'anic quotations in italics.

> Ibrahim then received in a dream the order to make a sacrifice to God. In the morning, he sacrificed a bullock and divided its flesh among the poor. In the night the voice again said to him: "God demands a more valuable offering." He killed a camel. In the following night, the voice said, "God demands thy son as an offering." Ibrahim awoke in horror and cried: *"O my son, I saw in a dream that I shall sacrifice thee; consider what thinkest thou?"*
>
> *He said, "My father, do as thou art bidden: thou shalt find me, God willing, one of the steadfast."*
>
> Taking a knife and a rope they went together to the mount. . . . Ibrahim directed the knife against the throat of his son but three times it slipped and glanced aside. Then a voice called to him, *"Ibrahim, thou hast confirmed the vision; even so We recompense the good-doers. This is indeed the manifest trial."* Then a ram appeared which . . . had hitherto been in Paradise; it was offered as a sacrifice.
>
> [God said] *"And We ransomed him with a mighty sacrifice, and left for him among the later folk, 'Peace be upon Ibrahim.' "*
>
> (*Encyclopedia of Islam* 1927:2:532)[1]

The Ibrahim myth makes the dilemma of life and death painfully accessible. There is no general way to envision death, but the picture of Ibrahim about to kill his son is excruciatingly vivid and draws humanity to it, as Kierkegaard says, by "the shudder of the idea" (1983[1843]:9). God demands death in its starkest form, murder of one's beloved, suicide of self. Ibrahim must kill his son. The son must participate in his own murder. The myth turns human impotence on itself. Since the father cannot insure the child's life on earth, God demands that the father slay the child. Through the slaying God makes humans active agents of death rather than passive recipients who sit and wait for death to strike.

God demands the blood slaughter of the most sacred relationship of this world as a sign of man's ability to submit to a God who exists beyond the world. Man must submit no matter what the cost, no matter how great the demand, for only God, not man, is in control of ultimate things.

The story is pedagogical. It teaches humans the proper ordering of power and authority in the universe. The God outside of this world is omnipotent, all powerful, all demanding. Life in this world is inherently limited. If humans would forge connection with that which is everlasting in the cosmos, they must be willing to sacrifice everything of this world, even the most precious earthly thing, which in this patriarchal society is defined, by the reality created in the myth itself as well as by realities created elsewhere, as the bond between father and son. Even the most valuable thing of this world must be slain in order to forge divine connection.

And Ibrahim submits. Islam means submission. Three times, he takes the knife to the son's throat. Then comes the great irony and the ultimate resolution. Because Ibrahim is willing to slay the child at divine command, God provides a substitute—a ram—and restores the child to the father, for long life on earth and eternal life thereafter. What is more, by withstanding the trial, Ibrahim creates for all of humanity a means of divine connection. Through males of faith sacrificing, humanity can connect with transcendence forever.

mechanisms for embedding male domination in collective hope

The myth and the ritual use multiple means to make convincing this cultural construction of invented truth. Binary oppositions, visceral practices, palpable embodiments, psychological underpinnings, sexual definitions, economic divisions, and ideological cloakings all play a part. I address only a few.

The potency of the myth and ritual draw upon the human tendency to express our existential dilemmas as great binary oppositions which our cultures then resolve (Lévi-Strauss skillfully developed an analytical framework for analyzing these oppositions; it remains useful as long as it is not enshrined as singular truth). The Islamic myth of Ibrahim poses the dilemma of life and death as a battle between God and nature—a battle between a single, omnipotent God who exists outside of the world and earthly life which is inherently transitory. The myth elicits the opposition by demanding that the natural father slay the natural son at divine command.

The myth then offers the means by which the ultimate conflict between eternal God and transient earth can be resolved, by males of faith sacrificing. Males are established as the worthy link precisely because they can distance themselves from earthly concerns. The cry of nature would be to spare the son; the call of God is to slay him. To draw close to God implies distancing from earth; the Arabic term for wisdom, 'aql, includes the notion of control of natural inclinations. It is 'aql that woman are most often said to lack because they are more identified with nature, less able to reach beyond it.

The myth verifies that males are the intervening link, the stairstep to transcendence, by associating God and men with geographical locations that physically confirm the truth of this invented assumption. The myth depicts men as leaving the world of women, nature, and the plains in order to connect with God on the mountaintops. The myth embeds its cultural assumptions in the topography of the land. It associates women with the temporal realm of nature, with the dry flat plains that in North Africa and the Middle East are dependent upon the high points—the mountains—for water.

In North Africa, the earth's pinnacles actually cause the rain-laden clouds blown in from the ocean to give of their waters to the land; the mountains pierce them and make the waters flow. The mountains then store that water on high peaks as snow and ice that melt throughout the year and send trickling streams of life out into the desert, forming long thin strips of green oases that divide the desert's brown. In North Africa, the mountains are the source of life, and people know it. Islam's monotheism convincingly associates mountains—the vertical dimension—with males, and the plains—the horizontal dimension—with females (figure 13.1). That humans are most obviously alive when vertical and less alive, or even dead, when horizontal adds potency to the created assocations.

The link between males and mountains might be thought of as "natural," given the mountain's high peaks. Yet it is not universal.[2] It is, however, profoundly developed in Islam through the great tale of Ibrahim's sacrifice that leaves females behind on the plains, puts men on mountaintops, and places God beyond them in invisible dimensions humans can neither see nor understand but with which erect men on high pointed pinnacles can connect.

The myth elevates the father and son to the position of worthy sacrificers. They travel to the mountaintop where connection with God will take place. On that mountain, the dominance of the father is affirmed. He is the male most able to connect with the divine; in demonstration of it, he stands up while the son lies down. Submission of both father and son is required, but the greatest submission is required of the son. The father is to actively kill the son, while the son is to lie passive and let himself be killed. In this high place, the son (the junior male) represents the horizontal plains, the feminine, and his posturing hints of sexual intercourse and the role of the female (see figure 13.2). The hint becomes more explicit as the father takes the knife—a common representation for the phallus throughout the world—and tries to spill the son's blood from his closed white neck—here a representation for the vagina.

Then comes the paradox and the resolution: in being willing to sacrifice, the son is saved, not only for life on earth but for life everlasting. By taking the knife to the son's throat, the father successfully engages in "intercourse" with the divine that gives the son spiritual birth, that causes the son to stand up after his bout with death and bestows upon him long life on earth and life everlasting. This cosmic connection, this ultimate intercourse, results in a new, more profound kind of birth than earth and females can offer, the birth into eternal life. The father secures that birth for the son and for himself. He makes the enduring transformation, the connection to the forces that are neverceasing in the universe.

But a bloodspilling is still required, and God now provides the sacrifice. God, who first demanded that the father totally deny all things of nature, including his son, now gives nature back to the father, but in domesticated form. God sends a ram as worthy substitute. The ram takes Isma'il's place as the representative of all the dependents of senior men: women, junior males, and other children included. The man turns the ram over on its back so that its white underside shows,

---

FIGURE 13.1. The Sexual Topography of Transcendence

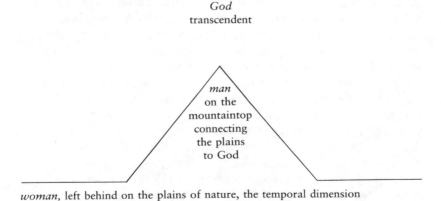

God
transcendent

man
on the
mountaintop
connecting
the plains
to God

woman, left behind on the plains of nature, the temporal dimension including its sexual organs. The man then thrusts the knife into the ram's neck and from that profound act emerges the eternal hope for humanity.

The ram is of course male—important to the building of the myth's implicit assumption of male dominance of communal, cosmic, and transcendent things. The culture constructs a sacrificial intercourse and birth that overcomes the limitations of male-female intercourse and female birth and makes it an all-male event—even in terms of the animal substitute. The ram is not simply male; he is quintessentially male. With his weighty phallus and testicles and his remarkable reproductive capacities, the ram is the epitome of natural maleness.

Hence the lesson: pure maleness of earth must be slain by pure males in order to make connection to the divine and achieve transcendent hope on behalf of the whole. By taking the knife first to the son's throat, and then (by God's grace) to the ram's throat, the father secures eternal hope for the human whole, including his own son, and father and son walk down from the mountaintop together. The father's children come to number like stars and his son becomes a prophet like him. What is striking about this cultural creation of everlasting hope—of a cosmic form of intercourse superior to that of males and females, of birth superior to that offered by females—is that it is entirely masculine.

FIGURE 13.2. Posturing on the Mountaintop

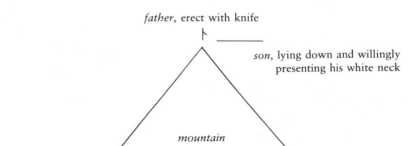

God, present as an invisible voice

father, erect with knife

son, lying down and willingly presenting his white neck

mountain

women, left behind on the plains

transcendent birth—the mother absent

Hajar, the natural mother, is absent from Islamic cosmic trial, so absent that she does not even appear in the Qur'anic text. The Qur'an's tale of ultimate sacrifice is a purely male story, involving a male-imaged God, a father, a son, and a male domesticated animal. The Qur'an mentions the mother in connection with Isma'il's natural birth, but not in connection with the transcendent birth which the father, together with God, gives. The mother plays no part, has no say. Apparently, the mother has no idea that the son she bore is about to be slain by his father, severed from her for all time (such knowledge is not given textual voice, not codified into collective remembrance). So distant is the mother in awareness, understanding, and space that she cannot possibly participate in the play with death that brings about eternal life. Hajar is down on the plains—probably baking bread or washing clothes—while the fate of her son and the fate of the cosmos are being decided.

In truth, we do not know precisely where Hajar is, since the holy text does not give her note. When I asked individual Moroccans where Hajar might have been and why, there was agreement that the mother was on the plains, entirely unaware of what was happening, and rightfully so, for she might have tried to intervene in the attempted slaying and thereby have inadvertently prevented humanity's convenant with the divine. If she had known, they agreed, she would have tried to prevent the father from taking the life of the child. As a good mother, she would not, and could not, have understood that the father's willful agreement to slay the child—in this cosmic construction—was right.

Moroccans agreed that the mother's natural tie to her child would have prevented her from fulfilling God's command. If God had asked Hajar to sacrifice the child, without exception the people with whom I spoke said that Hajar would have said "No." And Hajar is not faulted for this. They explained that the mother's natural tie to her children makes her a good mother, one whose energies are focused on reproduction and nurturance of individual human beings. Her closeness to nature demands that she give birth to individuals and transform the wild things of nature to human use—animal skins for clothing, roots and grains for human food.

In popular Moroccan understanding, the mother's association with nature is her greatest asset and her greatest limitation. It is the reason she must be excluded from the crucial events that require a distancing from individual and temporal concerns and connection to enduring and transcendent things. Moroccans say that the mother could not have performed what was required of humans in order to forge an enduring connection with the divine. By not slaying her son, the mother would have tried to save her son's life on earth, but ironically she would have lost him for all of time. Popular understanding of the textually absent Hajar is that she would have missed the point, would not have been willing to sacrifice her son, and hence would have lost for all of humanity the hope for divine connection. This is the nature of women as codified in basic cultural understandings, understandings upon which the founding myth depends, understandings that the ritual powerfully reproduces through time.

Hence the Islamic construction—this cultural invention of reality—reinforces Ornter's argument (1974) on the propensity for human communities to associate males with what is enduring, what exists beyond nature and transcends it, and to associate females with what exists within nature and is inherently limited. It is biological truth that females give natural birth; it is a cultural invention that the female's natural birthgiving capacity rightfully excludes her from enduring things, from transcendent questing and cosmic decision making. The framing of the female as natural and by consequence inherently limited in terms of cosmic and collective things has not always been the case, but it is well-developed in the Mediterranean monotheisms—Islam, Judaism, and Christianity. When so developed, the resulting construction—part invented myth, part enduring truth—becomes extremely durable.

Islam's sacrifice myth and its ritual enactment profoundly reinforce the cultural notion that knowing men must handle great collective and cosmic events on behalf of unknowing women and try to shield them from cosmic truths too hard for women to bear because they are more nature-bound creatures; hence Isma'il's words in the Hadith, "Give my mother my shirt that it may comfort her and do not tell her how thou didst sacrifice me" (*Encyclopedia of Islam* 1927:2:532). In this invention, knowing men are culturally defined as those who must handle collective decision making and transcendent questing precisely because they can distance themselves from nature, while women are culturally defined as incapable of that decision making precisely because they are the vessels for natural birth, hence not distanced from nature.

The sacrifice myth and practice build a reality in which males give birth to that which is eternal and enduring, in contrast to females who give birth to that which is temporal and limiting. The Ibrahim sacrifice myth and practice make males the spiritual usurpers of the female's biological role by creating a cultural form of male birth that is superior to it. Sacrifice gives to those who have a less obvious role in natural birth the dominant role in transcendent birth, as if in compensation. The culture then ties everyone to this imagined construction, for therein lie their own hopes.

In truth there is not much subtlety to the culture's insistence on the maleness of the divine link. Everything gathered on the holy mountain is male, not only all the actors, but also the referents. There is an abundance, a plethora, of pointed objects: the mountain, the knives, the erect men.

modeling on sexual intercourse and human birth

In seeking to construct a plausible experience of divine connection and transcendent birth, Islamic culture explicity draws upon the most basic kinesthetic experience of existence, the most forceful connection of this earth—human sexual intercourse—and the roles of males and females in it. Yet Islam then makes the cosmic intercourse an all-male event: the erect father standing on the mountaintop in response to the command of a male-imaged God thrusting the knife towards the reclining son's throat in order for divine connection to be made, and then actually plunging the knife into the ram's throat. The plunging of the knife into the animal's white neck bears stark similarity to the plunging of phallus into vagina. And it serves an analogous but higher purpose—birth into transcendence, as opposed to birth into this world.

The similarities between the male's sacrificial intercourse with the divine and his ritualized intercourse with the woman is especially prominent in the intercourse that is a part of Moroccan first marriage ceremonies. The spilling of the bride's blood at the marriage ceremonies verifies the male's dominance of biological birth, while the spilling of the ram's blood in the Great Sacrifice verifies the male's dominance of transcendent birth. They are graphically similar. The thrust of pointed object into the women's vagina opens the womb of earthly birth. The thrust of pointed objects into the ram's throat opens the womb of the universe for the possibility of everlasting rebirth. The former involves a female, but the ritual is constructed in such a way that it confirms that the male is dominant. The latter is an all-male event. Both are cultural means of overcoming the female's physical dominance of birth.

Anthropologists have often characterized sacrifice as a gift, as in Hubert and Mauss' classic *Sacrifice: Its Nature and Function* (1898).[3] It is not. Sacrifice is much more physically active than is gift giving and, consciously or unconsciously, sacrifice is structured to draw to itself the power of the most basic biological templates of action—intercourse and human birth. Sacrifice is, I suggest, an active attempt at intercourse with the sacred, the purpose of which is to secure enduring connection to that dimension and if possible to secure birth into it. Sacrifice not only mimics male-female intercourse, it also mimics female birthgiving, the dramatic and forceful action involving high drama and pain in which new life emerges. The resultant beings themselves are similar. The bleeding ram and the newborn infant are both covered in white—white tufts of wool on the ram, curdlike white vernix on the infant. Both lie in fetal positions and quiver in pools of blood. Both represent hope, the ram representing hope beyond the limits of this world, the infant representing hope within it. In both cases the most lasting kind of hope is male—the male ram, the male child.

Death, especially death at knife point, is a momentous event, as anyone who has witnessed it can testify; but death in a form that mimics the basic processes of life is riveting. It pulls people to it by the deep-seated familiarity it taps—basic biological givens, universal human hopes. The sacrificial construction embeds cultural particularities (that men must handle corporate decision making and are the collective links to transcendence) deep within universal truths (the very real physical differences that distinguish male and female and their differing roles in intercourse and childbirth). The embedding makes the cultural inventions seem inherent in the universe, thus ruling out cultural alternatives—for example, that females could make the divine connection on behalf of the whole and that their ability to give natural birth specifically prepares them for doing so.

consequences

hope   The consequences of the Moroccan construction of sacrifice are multiple. Sacrifice builds a reality of profound hope, as Moroccans convincingly explain. As mentioned, Moroccans look with sincere intensity to the ram in the throes of death, for therein resides their own hope. If the bleeding ram manages to reenter the vertical dimension, it is taken as an enormously auspicious sign. Verticality itself—erect maleness—is associated with vitality, and in sacrifice made the link to eternal life. In contrast, the ram's fall back to the ground is the collapse back into the passive horizontal dimension of the female, an indication of natural death.

What is more, the yearly rite of sacrifice not only serves to recreate the hope for divine connection, but it serves to recreate the divine: for in the Great Sacrifice, God is shown to be present and fully capable of bestowing transcendent life if he so wills.

patrilineality Islam's great sacrifice myth also glorifies patrilineality, for it depicts the most valuable of human ties as that which links father and son. It is the threatened severance of *that* tie that is the ultimate test of humanity's loyalty, rather than one of the plausible alternatives—the father's sacrifice of the daughter, the mother's sacrifice of the son—alternatives which would make for a very different construction of society and the sacred. It is father and son who in combination achieve God's favor and bring eternal hope to human life.

patriarchy Myth and ritual also profoundly reinforce patriarchy— the presumed rightness of senior male domination of public decision making, political prowess, and sacred prestige—by embedding collective hope in it. The Ibrahim myth and the ritual of sacrifice build a male-paved pathway to transcendence. Muhammad inserted himself into this male construct by ritually repeating the sacrifice. He then insured that all Muslim male heads of households also would be inserted by demanding their yearly performance of the sacrifice. The power of ritual insertion—of entering the meaning of the myth by entering the practices through which it is expressed—rests on ritual's ability to structure the human imagination through metaphor.

14

metaphor

The myth of Ibrahim creates a male hierarchy of power; the ritual of the Great Sacrifice inserts living actors into that hierarchy and makes their placement convincing by establishing metaphorical equivalence. At its most basic, a metaphor is a figure of speech that carries the definition of one thing to another. Metaphor creates a relationship between two compared subjects, demanding that their definitions be mingled in order to understand what each is; for instance, "the Prince of the Faithful is a lion." Metaphor builds the intermingling through form, not through verbal markers such as "like" or "as." The simplest metaphor is one in which the subject of a phrase is stated to be the same as the predicate. Metaphor places no restrictions on the equivalence it asserts. It boldly states that one is the same as the other without specifying what the equivalence involves, thereby demanding that the reader/observer actively use his or her imagination to resolve wherein the likeness lies, what qualities the two subjects hold in common. The reader/observer must, so to speak, fill in the blanks.

Much of the power of metaphor lies in the fact that it is suggestive rather than explicit, condensed rather than expansive. "The Prince of the Faithful is a lion" is a far more compelling and memorable statement than "the Prince of the Faithful is similar to a lion in that both of them are bold, grand creatures with great physical strength." Metaphor elicits the reader/observer's involvement, sets in motion imaginative play, and unlocks memory. Metaphor in fact goes far beyond simply inspiring the reader/observer to consider how the two things are comparable by suggesting that there is a level on which the two are identifiable; that suggestion fundamentally alters the meaning of both. In metaphorically comparing prince and lion, the definition of each is irrevocably altered.

metaphor in poetry and oratory

Much more complex types of metaphorical equivalence can be established in poetry and oratory. The form of the linguistic communication is itself more complicated, and hence there are other options available for establishing equivalence beyond the basic one of stating "A is B." Michael Silverstein highlights the metaphorical capacity of form in poetry and political oratory, and refers to it as poetic structure:

> . . . By *poetic structure* we do not mean just stress-group measures, or syllable-length measures, or anything limited to what the natives want to call "poetry." The poetic structure of an utterance is not limited to some patterns of sounds. I invoke here the modern linguistic understanding of what we call *poetic structure*, or the *poetic function* of language, which is, simply put, this: construct utterances with unit lengths measured out, in as many layers as you want, so that units in relatively similar (or regularly computable) positions in some higher structural layer have some special metaphorical pseudodefinitional (or antidefinitional) relationship, which in effect suggests categorical identity (or oppositeness).
>
> (Silverstein 1981:5)

In poetry and oratory, complex metaphorical equivalence can be built through form, through the placement of words or word phrases in similar structural positions within the linguistic statement, so that to understand the meaning of any one of the structurally equivalent terms demands the imaginative comparison with and synthesis of the

other terms that occupy the same position. A simple example of metaphorical equivalence built through form is the following:

> God sent his revelation to Ibrahim.
> God sent his revelation to Muhammad.
> God sent his revelation to the Muslim community of the faithful.
>
> (Islamic proverb)

Ibrahim, Muhammad, and the community of the faithful are metaphorical equivalents; each is the indirect object of the transitive verb
"sent." The person who would understand the utterance must understand the syntactical content built within each phrase, the semantic
load of each word, and must also imaginatively compare and syn-
thesize the definitional links between Ibrahim, Muhammad, and the
Muslim community of the faithful. The referents cannot be fully
understood without viewing them in relation to one another, without
giving thought to qualities they share, qualities that are highlighted
through the comparison. Through this metaphorical intermingling, the
hearer not only learns important things about Ibrahim, Muhammad,
and the Muslim community of the faithful, but also about God and
his revelation.

Metaphorical equivalence established through form demands an
understanding of the subtleties of the configuration through which it
is presented, for only then can one know what is being metaphorically
compared. Cultures vary in the forms through which they structure
metaphorical equivalence; yet the forms are so embedded in the native
speaker's subconscious that they need not reach the level of verbal
recognition for the structuring of equivalence to take place and the
intermingling of meanings to occur (Silverstein 1981:6–9). The outsider, by contrast, must consciously uncover the common meanings
of words, the consistencies of syntax, and the systematics of form
before the positionally established metaphorical equivalence can be
understood.

poetic and ritual structure compared

Ritual too makes extensive use of metaphorical equivalence built
through form. Rituals are to human enactments as a whole what poetry is to language. Each is a finished piece, complete and meaningful
in itself, that partakes of and affects the larger reservoir of meanings
of which it is a part. Each turns the larger meanings in particular
ways, systematically restructuring them by presenting them in condensed, suggestive, and yet complete form—a single poem, a single

ritual. Rituals and poems are at one and the same time slices of life and yet particularly full expressions of living, holistic creations that circumscribe the referents and comparisons through which meaning can be built. For understanding to occur, a poem or a ritual must be viewed not only in terms of its parts and the relationship of those parts to meanings that exist outside, but also in terms of the relationship of those parts to each other and to the meaning built from their internal interplay within the circumscribed whole.

Neither poetry nor ritual rely solely on the systematics of form to create meaning, but they have an unusual capacity to elaborate meaning through form, to evoke and systematically channel the imagination by creating metaphorical associations that call for the intermingling of particular definitions. Poetry and ritual can structure meaning through the placement of words, people, and actions in similar positions so that the meaning of any one cannot be understood without examining the meaning of the others that occupy the same position.

structural creation of metaphorical equivalence in ritual

Silverstein's definition of the metaphorical potential of poetic form applies to rituals; that is, in ritual one constructs discernible actions in as many layers as one wants, so that actors or actions in relatively similar (or regularly computable) positions in any given structural layer bear some special metaphorical relationship to those in other layers, which, in effect, suggests categorical identity and demands definitional intermingling.

The use of metaphor in ritual evokes imaginative elaborations upon the meanings that positionally equivalent actions or actors hold in everyday life. Ritual opens those meanings to alterations through the demanded comparison with other actors or actions that hold the same position. Only by creatively combining the definitions that structurally equivalent actors and actions hold, and searching for their points of likeness and opposition, will the ritually constructed meaning be understood. Metaphor demands imagination and creativity and yet at the same time is highly constraining in the kinds of understandings it allows to be built, for it defines the parameters of comparison (e.g., the Great Sacrifice offers no female metaphors).

For Muslims, the myth of Ibrahim is humanity's archetypal interaction with God, an awesome act involving awesome players. By ritually repeating Ibrahim's sacrifice, Muhammad metaphorically inserted himself into the mythic event and demanded that the popular understanding of himself be built through the merger of his definition with that of Ibrahim. The population responded as he wished, and the definitions of both Muhammad and Ibrahim were enhanced through the association. What is more, Muhammad created the mechanism by which current heads of household would be compared with Ibrahim and with himself forevermore by demanding their yearly repetition of the sacrifice. Metaphorical equivalence was ritually established, and the definitions of each—Ibrahim, Muhammad, and all Muslim sacrificers—enhanced the other; each became more than the sum of the parts. In its age of great crisis, the Moroccan monarchy creatively inserted itself into the Ibrahim myth and Muhammad's performance by reenacting the communal sacrifice as did their forefather Muhammad, making itself the intervening link. Morocco's monarchs performed a sacrifice on behalf of the believing whole, not simply on behalf of the families they served. Through this innovation, the monarchs created their metaphorical equivalence with all the previous actors and entered the foundations of the Muslim faith by becoming closely allied with Islam's most noble prophets; at the same time they became allied with individual heads of households throughout the land. Up to the prophets and down into the households—this is the kind of connection the monarchy's performance of Ibrahim's sacrifice allowed.

The metaphorical intermingling is profound. At the center of the Great Sacrifice is the metaphorically established equivalence of Ibrahim (the father of believers), Muhammad (the final prophet, the conveyor of the complete revelations), the sharifi caliph (the present guardian of the Muslim political community on earth), local communal authorities, and the heads of individual households. All hold the same position within the ritual performance. All stand before God sacrificing a ram on behalf of the communities they head. Their metaphorical equivalence is established through numerous dimensions:

- in their *preparations*—the demand for bathing and prayer
- in their *dress*—the white garments
- in the *words they utter*—they speak precisely the same words before the sacrifice is made, the Bi'smi'llah: "In the name of God, the Merciful, the Compassionate"
- in their *posture*—they stand on the right side of the ram, turn it towards Makka, and take the knives in their right hands
- in the act of *sacrifice*—all perform the same action with the same animal; they insert the knife deeply into the ram's throat so that the main artery is severed
- in the *consequence of the action*—if successful, the sacrifice will

bring God's blessing on them and on the communities they represent through the sacrifice.

It is striking how effective the metaphorical equivalence is. In their long white robes, with their hoods drawn closely around their faces, the distinctiveness of the sacrificers blurs; they all become the archetypal man standing before the believers. Current actors and their present definitions enter the myth, and mythic actors and definitions enter the world. The Moroccan king and current heads of household stand alongside Ibrahim and Muhammad in sacrificing a ram on behalf of the Muslim communities they serve. Each takes the knife in his right hand, repeats the holy words, and plunges the knife deeply into the ram's throat; each time the blood falls, the animal struggles, then swoons, then may stand back up, then falls a final time in a replica of what people believe Ibrahim and Muhammad to have done and what faithful followers of Islam have done ever since.

intermingling of definitions

Because they occupy the same structural positions in the action of sacrifice—in the way they prepare, dress, speak, posture, perform, and interpret the event—definitional intermingling and enhancement occur. Ibrahim, Muhammad, and sharifi Prince of the Faithful, local authorities, and the heads of individual households come to be seen and understood in relationship to one another. The Prince of the Faithful and the heads of individual households can no longer be understood simply through everyday definitions, for they are now inextricably linked to the great prophets of old; and Muhammad and Ibrahim can no longer be understood simply through distant and sacred definitions, for they are brought to the everyday. Each must be viewed through the axis of ritual combination. In metaphorical transformation, the accessible becomes distant and the distant become accessible.

Lived reality and emotional forcefulness travel up the hierarchy of metaphorically equivalent actors (from the heads of individual households to local community sacrificers, to the sharifi Prince of the Faithful, to Muhammad and Ibrahim), while sanctity and profundity travel down. Ibrahim and Muhammad take on the vividness of the here and now. They are brought to the local setting and associated with the trees, the people gathered, the ground upon which the blood falls, as well as the emotional potency with which the sacrifice is experienced. They are made more palpable, more convincing, less remote in time.

Current sacrificers become more sacred. They are distanced from their local settings, raised out of mundane constraints, and made larger than they otherwise seem. They are endowed with religiosity, made more transcendent and more authoritative. Through metaphorical re-definition they are empowered to perform the weighty action upon which the community's future hinges, the taking of earthly life for the most formidable of purposes—to gain God's pleasure. That perfor-mance in turn underlines the more general moral rightness of their power in household, community, and nation.

prophets and prince

Metaphorical intermingling creates a definitional synthesis between Ibrahim, Muhammad, and all living sacrificers; the definition of each enhances the other. Yet it creates the strongest definitional intermin-gling between the prophets and the living Prince of the Faithful. Only the current king performs an overarching communal sacrifice, as did Muhammad and Ibrahim. Only he stands before God as the collective embodiment of the believing whole and attempts a sufficiently worthy slaying on the collectivity's behalf. The title "Prince of the Faithful" asserts the monarch's role as political representative of the Muslim community. The act of sacrifice confirms it. Ibrahim stood before God representing all the faithful of earth for all time. Muhammad stood before God representing all Muslims. The Prince of the Faithful stands before God representing all living Muslims—especially those who re-gard him as political ruler. The metaphorical intermingling is intense; the reigning prince is understood to be like Ibrahim and Muham-mad—sacred, powerful, and collective, the rightful communal deci-sion maker, the dominator of word and violence, the communal care-taker of the whole.

prince and patriarchs

The definitional intermingling between the prince and the heads of households is also intense. The prince stands in between the prophets and the present. The resemblance between the prince and the current sacrificers is almost uncanny and results in a true blurring of defini-tions. Who stands before one? Is it the Moroccan king—the reigning Prince of the Faithful? Or is it the head of an individual household? In metaphorical truth it is both, which makes for a profound inter-mingling not only of the definitions that each holds but of the power that each wields. Metaphor gives the sharifi Prince of the Faithful entry into individual households throughout his land at the same time that it gives the heads of individual households entry into the central palace and the central mosque. Through the intermingling, the prince has his authority secured by being anchored in the persuasive immediacy of the household setting, while the heads of households have their authority elevated, made more general and more noble, by their association with the living prince.

So firmly is the identity of the king intermingled with that of the household heads that the king's power is daily renewed in the power plays that take place in the households throughout the land—the firmest, most direct kind of support a national ruler can have. For individual heads of households to undercut the authority of the overarching ruler would be to undercut their own power base and vice versa. For the sharifi prince to undercut the authority of individual males in the households would be to undercut his national credit. Hence, most Moroccans neither participate in, nor even contemplate, such an action, for it would be a kind of political suicide. Prince and patriarch continue to reinforce each other.

subtle persuasion

There is a subtlety to the metaphorical associations built through the regularity of ritual form that does not exist in boldfaced verbal assertions. To state straightforwardly, "the Prince of the Faithful and the heads of households are Ibrahim and Muhammad" would be considered blasphemous as well as foolhardy. But to structure a ritual so that their equivalence is built through form is acceptable. The dignity, formality, and subtlety with which metaphorical equivalence is ritually structured, much like the formalism of poetic structure, allows for the presentation. In the controlled setting of the ritual performance, Ibrahim, Muhammad, the sharifi prince, and the heads of individual households imaginatively converge, and that convergence is experienced as real.

ritual definitions and the everyday

Ritual builds definitions. It selects key actors, casts them in bold relief, and systematically shapes the meanings by which they are perceived. The ritual of the Great Sacrifice demands that the sharifi Prince of the Faithful and individual heads of Muslim households be viewed in terms of Ibrahim, the father of faith, and Muhammad, God's last prophet. The emergent ritual definitions are both independent of and related to other definitions that emerge in everyday life. Ritual is a part of the flow of on-the-ground historical experience as well as a circumscribed clarification of it. Ritual's fullness, independence, and capacity to orchestrate experience enables it to build definitions in pure and clarified form, definitions that impact upon all others, for they are experienced as pristine.

The sharifi caliph and heads of households are not always experienced as sustaining, as links to blessing on earth and the hope for transcendence thereafter. Women are not always silent and peripheral. Other definitions and experiences exist, definitions that can be quite oppositional to the ones that are ritually built, as when the sharifi caliph comes to the countryside burning and destroying, as when heads of households fail in earthly duties and spiritual obligations, as when women are forceful and dynamic and seek to directly influence public life. Yet, when effective, the ritual definitions come to dominate, for they are experienced as essential definitions—definitions in purest form. Their cultural worth enables them to overshadow all others.

sustaining hope

The Great Sacrifice helps create the dependence of the family unit on the male heads of households and the dependence of the nation on the reigning prince. People could move away from the sacrifice; they could stop performing it. But if they did, they would lose what has from birth been a familiar and comforting means of bringing hope, of invoking divine blessing on themselves and their households, an issue about which most people—male and female, old and young—are fervently concerned. The Moroccan nation could move away from their prince and his sacrifice, but in so doing, they would lose what has for hundreds of years been a dramatic means not only of drawing God's favor on the nation, but of clarifying who the nation is and what it is about. They would lose self-definition as well as hope.

Most Muslims have no ruler who sacrifices on their behalf, and by consequence they do not have a sacrificial means of collectively representing themselves before God. Morocco has a collective representation—the king in sacrifice—and for most of the population that representation remains powerfully persuasive. Morocco's Prince of the Faithful continues to sacrifice, to call God's attention away from the great crush of humanity onto the members of the Moroccan nation, and to give God reason for bestowing blessing upon them. In this ritual, where the Prince of the Faithful is a means to an end rather than an end in himself, a channel to divine grace rather than the source of it, the king finds his strongest support, for, whatever else he may be, he remains a divine connection.

15

sexuality and sacrifice

Sacrifice builds a form of death that is convincing as a pathway to eternal life by modeling itself on the actions that bring about life in this world. In mimicking the processes that set life in motion, the knife sacrifice evokes the potency of sexual intercourse and childbirth and engenders a profound physical response in the ritual's participants, a subliminal recognition of the momentousness of the actions involved: the death that is actually occurring, the sexual intercourse that is being iconically elicited, and the birth that is hoped will result. The combination—death, intercourse, and birth—loads the ritual with physically grounded as well as imaginatively abstract understandings and insures that communication takes place from body to body, from body to mind, and from mind to body.

Because sacrifice is a cultural rather than a biological phenomenon, it can operate outside of biological constraint—and does. Most notably it eliminates the female from the spiritual birth process. The myth of Ibrahim and the ritual practice of the Great Sacrifice give the culture's imagination full play in physical "proof" that men do not need women for ultimate things (compare Di Piero's "I do not want to need their blood"). Myth and ritual "verify" that men give birth to what is durable without the presence or aid of women.

Sacred performances are experiential realizations of culture's imagination—imagination given flesh and made to live among us. The knife slaying of the Great Sacrifice viscerally constructs, on an annual basis, the cosmology upon which it depends, a cosmology that it continually recreates. That cosmology consists of a male-imaged God beyond nature, men on earth who are able to conquer their human nature and connect with him, and women who are spirtually marginalized because they cannot. The ritual confirms the reality of these inventions by soldering them onto biological truths: differences in male and female physical form and basic biological templates of sexual intercourse, birth, and death. The foundations are biologically real. Culture's constructions are not. They vary from society to society.

Islam shares its emphasis on a single God outside of nature, men as the sacred links, and women as more nature-bound with the two other Mediterranean monotheisms, Judaism and Christianity. The common features of the three and their distinctiveness when compared to other theisms emerge in a comparison of sacrifice myths and practices.

sacrifice compared

The perception of the male as able to control his nature and consequently to be the rightful dominator of public power and sacred gain is built on its opposition, that is, the female as unable to control these things. The perception of the female as more subject to her animal nature is widespread within human communities. Ortner (1974) cogently summarizes the human tendency to associate the female with nature and the male with that which lies beyond—culture and civilization. The association appears to derive from the fact that women involuntarily bleed each month and are the ones who give physical birth to children in an involuntary act of nature.

The close association of females with nature may be panhuman, but that association need not exclude women from ultimate sanctity *unless* one locates ultimate sanctity outside of nature. Many polytheisms do not. The Mediterranean monotheisms do; they elevate God beyond this world, and with that elevation women take a mythic fall. (Here it is underlying cosmological givens, basic cultural assumptions, that I wish to examine, not the practical exercise of power, an issue I will turn to later.)

God stepped out of nature, and women fell from the holiest of places. The ascent of a male-imaged God beyond nature is matched by the cosmic descent of women. No longer are females central to quests for transcendence. No longer are they active participants to sacrifice myths and practices. No longer are females able to envision and achieve transcendence through their own bodies, through their own female forms, but only through men who forge the link. Gone are the goddesses, the priestesses, and the female lines of access to eternal life.

The cosmic fall of the female in Mediterranean monotheism is both built by and illustrated in the sacrifice myths of these traditions. Sacrifice myths the world over are ways in which humanity addresses its most poignant dilemma—the inevitability of human death and the inherent transitoriness of human bonds, even the bonds humans hold most dear. But such myths are constructed in radically different ways.

polytheisms

Polytheistic myths typically allocate some ultimate sanctity—some ultimate powers of communal good and transcendence—to wild things of nature and, by consequence, to women, whom humanity most often associates with it (see Bloch 1986, Comaroff 1985, Lan 1985, Sahlins 1985, and Valeri 1985). In polytheistic traditions, the dramas of cosmic creation and human-cosmic intercourse typically involve both male and female elements. Male-female sexual intercourse and the female's dominance of human birth figure more centrally in their mythic constructions. They imagine the creation of earth as resulting from the interplay of male and female forms, not as the single-handed work of a male-imaged God (monotheism's construction). They typically imagine human-cosmic intercourse as involving earth's women as well as its men, not as an all-male interaction.

Dande For example, the polytheistic Dande conceive of fundamental life force as resting in the dark, damp plains where the tall grasses grow—a cosmic reference modeled on the beauty of female pubic hair and the vagina. According to their traditions, it was male interaction with these life forces that gave birth to human communities (see Lan 1985:89–90).

Hawaiian The ancient Hawaiians considered life's beginnings to rest in the interaction of sky and earth, male and female. First the heavens warmed the earth by rubbing against it. The warmed earth produced a generative substance, Po, which in turn exhibited itself in male and female forms; from their commingling the most basic species of life were born (Valeri 1985:4–5).

Merinan According to the sacrifice myth of the Merina of Madagascar, in the beginning the ultimate powers of regenerative life rested with the wild of nature, with the Vazimba—vital, dynamic, chaotic beings full of life's basic regenerative substance (Bloch 1986). In the myth the Vazimba come to be represented by a primordial mother. In order for their vitality to be channeled by humans for collective use (so that stable human communities can be formed and reproduced through time), these primordial Vazimba must be brought under control. The human son of the primordial Vazimba mother accomplishes this; he drives them beyond the inhabited world. And yet to do so, he must make use of their power. The primordial mother herself allows this to happen. She sacrifices herself so that her son and all humans can have potent but ordered life. She drowns herself in a great lake in order to bestow upon those broad waters her regenerative powers. These powers forever rest there and can be drawn upon by her son and by the other humans that follow. Yet, at first, her son is unfamiliar with these powers, which are so great that he inadvertently kills his own son in a ritual of circumcision when he draws upon the waters. Yet, in time, the son—the founder of the kingly lineage of the Merina—learns how to tame, control, and utilize wild and violent female power, to tap it without being engulfed by it, as do other senior men in the ages that follow. The Merina myth, like Merina social organization, culminates with male dominance, but it is dominance that acknowledges ultimate dependence upon female potency.

That dependence is actively demonstrated in the Merina ritual of circumcision, a sacrificial rite that brings the creation myth to the lived present (Bloch 1986). Most of the ritual is meant to conquer the female, to take the male child away from his mother in order to make him a man, but female elements are used in taking the child away (fertile plants and herbs, wild and powerful waters), and the ritual concludes with handing the child back through an open window—a play on intercourse as well as the womb—to the mother and the household, formally affirming in cosmological and performative terms her power in the process, her domains of ascendancy. Men dominate ordered life, but it is domination born of a different kind of cosmology, one in which there is overt conflict between the sexes on the cosmic level.

Polytheistic myths and practices typically conclude with male supremacy, but it is supremacy won through active battle with the female, not achieved through female absence, omission, and silence, through *a priori* exclusion of the female from the major cosmological plays, as is the case in the creation and sacrifice myths of the Mediterranean monotheisms. Active battle makes the female a worthy, even if defeated, opponent. Absence is, on the cosmological level, totally marginalizing.

Greek The Ancient Greek myth of Agamemnon's sacrifice offers a fruitful comparison to the sacrifice myths of the three monotheisms. It is a product of the same geographical region, the overarching structure of the myth is much the same, but it includes radically different images of female and child.

The Greeks basked in a wealth of gods and goddesses. The ultimate deity, a kind of male super-god, was the sky-god Zeus, but a plethora of other gods and goddesses inhabited the sacred universe, including Aphrodite, the goddess of tender love and erotic passion who was herself endowed with ultimate sanctity and transcendent powers (Friedrich 1978). Of the religious worship that surrounded Aphrodite, Clark states, "Perhaps no religion ever again incorporated physical passion so . . . naturally that all who saw her felt that the instincts they shared with the beasts they also shared with the gods" (1956:83).[1]

The Greek cosmos celebrated variety, male and female, good and evil. They told and retold their myths in many versions. The combination of multiple, often unreliable, deities and multiple tellings resulted in a complex and dynamic picture of the universe. Cosmic reality for the Greeks was not chiseled in stone.

There are many Greek sacrifice myths—Oedipus killing his father, Clytemnestra killing her husband. I will focus upon one involving Agamemnon, the mighty warrior who does battle at Troy. My retelling comes mostly from Euripides' *Iphigeneia in Aulis* and *Iphigeneia in Tauris,* though parts of Aeschylus' are also utilised.[2] The three main characters are Agamemnon, his daughter Iphigenia, and Artemis, Zeus' daughter, herself a deity, the goddess of the hunt, the protector of wild animals and other wild things, pregnant humans included. The call to sacrifice, it is told, happened in the following way:

Before sailing to Troy, Agamemnon sought a sign to ensure his victory over the Trojans. To this purpose, he tossed a pregnant rabbit high into the air and released his mighty eagles in pursuit of her. The eagles seized the rabbit, pierced the mother and offspring with their long talons, then tore the lifeless beings into pieces which fell down upon the troops; this was interpreted as auspicious.

The army received their sign, but also aroused the fury of Artemis, the protector of wild things, especially pregnant females. Incensed by what men will do to innocent, natural things to guarantee military victory, Artemis flew to Agamemnon in outrage and demanded that he pay for his wrongdoing by sacrificing the one pure thing of nature with which he was associated, his daughter Iphigenia. Agamemnon was required to slay not his eldest son but his youngest daughter, the one innocent creature in Agamemnon's much plagued household.

Agamemnon agrees, but his compliance is never steady. He tells Artemis that he will slay his daughter, but uncertainty and cowardice continue to overtake him. He cannot decide whether his motives to slay are noble or base, and he cannot figure out how to accomplish the sacrifice. Finally he gets Iphigenia to the place of her dying through a trick. Agamemnon tells his daughter that he has arranged to marry her to the great Achilles before the Troy sailing, and bids her to travel to the place whence the boats will depart—the place where she is to be sacrificed—by telling her that it will be the place of her marriage. (The father as trickster is one of many negative images of the dominant male in this myth. On the whole, he comes off poorly; Euripides' chorus does not like him and makes its dislike known.)

Achilles for his part learns of the lie and goes to Iphigenia. So impressed is he by her wisdom, goodness, and bravery that he offers to stand by her against her father at the place of sacrifice, even though he knows it will mean his own death. (There are too many troops even for his swift sword.)

Iphigenia refuses. The hero of this sacrifice myth is a heroine—wise, sturdy, and steadfast, viewing with calm understanding, and some sympathy, men and their violent fury, but knowing in her heart of hearts that they are wrong. Achilles' offer is not the way to set things right; she, the young female, knows. Once Iphigenia learns the truth—what her father did, what the goddess bids, and what she, the daughter, must do—Iphigenia agrees to it, and bolsters her weak-willed patriarch in what must be done.

Iphigenia is willing to insert herself into her father's wrong in order to set the world right and save Greece. She is a Christ-like figure, innocent and yet so full of understanding that she comprehends the necessity of her own slaying, the rightfulness of Artemis' demand because of what men have done. She is a worthy sacrifice.

Iphigenia does not accept death, as is common in Western and Eastern tales of mother sacrifice, in order to save the life of her child—a "nature-bound" maternal response. She consciously decides to be sacrificed because she understands the structure of the cosmos and is willing to take her place in it, so that the communal whole might go on living.

In a noble soliloquy, Iphigenia tells her mother not to weep for her, for she, Iphigenia, will be the savior, dying on behalf of all of Greece; she will be going to the temple of Artemis and no tears are allowed there.

> Now mother, listen to the conclusion
> that I have reached. I have made up my mind to die.
> I want to come to it
> with glory, I want to have thrown off
> all weak and base thought. Mother,
> look at it with my eyes,
> and see how right I am.
> All the people, all the strength of Greece
> have turned to me. All those ships,
> whether they sail, whether Troy falls,
> depend on me. I will be the one
> to protect our women, in the future,
> if ever the barbarians dare to come near. . . .
> All these good things I can win by dying.
> Because of me, Greece
> will be free, and my name will be blessed there.
> I must not cling to life too dearly.
> You brought me into the world for the sake
> of everyone in my country,
> and not just for your own.
>   (Euripedes, tr. Merwin and Dimock, 1978:85)

Iphigenia walks to the battlefield to be slain. The troops are gathered and the sea of men momentarily parts to issue her into the center. Before her stands the high priest and her father Agamemnon. Iphigenia's only request is that they not bind her. She wishes to go to death unfettered by male constraint, and she does. Unbound she lies down on the cold altar and awaits the knife thrust from the high priest's hands, her father standing beside him. The priest lifts the long knife high into the air—pauses—then plunges it down towards Iphigenia's white neck. The troops, humbled by Iphigenia's bravery and innocence, cast down their eyes. After all, she is dying to set right the wrong they committed, and they cannot bear to watch her die, but they hear the knife strike the hard stone. Tentatively and ashamed, they glance up. To their astonishment, Iphigenia has vanished, and in her place lies a hind, a female red deer, the blood flowing freely from her white neck.

The goddess Artemis has provided the substitute. At the very last moment, she is so moved by Iphigenia's bravery and wisdom that she snatches Iphigenia away from the place of dying, transports her to a place worthy of her, the goddess' temple in Taurus, and makes Iphigenia a high priestess. Artemis places on the altar a worthy substitute, a wild female of nature, whose death can still set right the world.

Later, at the temple in Taurus, Iphigenia saves her own brother from sacrifice—she is her brother's keeper—and puts a halt to all child sacrifices there. In the end, Iphigenia becomes a semidivine, transcendent being.

Where religious visions of reality allocate at least some sanctity and durability to the natural world, what is striking is the plethora of females and female elements in their sacrifice myths. Where religious visions deny ultimate sanctity and durability to the natural world, as in Christianity, Judaism, and Islam, women fall out of the communal quests for ultimate connection, the mythic searches for communal good that establish not only who is capable of reaching for the heavens but who is capable of ruling on earth.

Mediterranean monotheisms

In Islam's central myth, a male-imaged God outside of nature demands of the human father, Ibrahim, the sacrifice of his human son Isma'il and then, because of the father and son's faith, substitutes a male domesticated animal, a ram. The Judaic myth of Abraham tells much the same story. A male-imaged God beyond nature demands of Abraham the sacrifice of his son, Isaac, and again, because of Abraham's compliance, at the last moment God substitutes a ram for the child.

Christians incorporate the Abraham myth into their Old Testament tradition, and it informs how Christians think of life, death, decision making, and being male and female in this world. Kierkegaard's extensive exploration of the story (1983 [1843]) is but one of a multitude of examples. The Abraham myth is the logical counterpoint of the Oedipus myth—a second great myth that informs Western society, especially in the post-Freudian age, a myth borrowed from the ancient Greeks. Oedipus inadvertently kills his father. Abraham intentionally plans to kill his son. Together these stories provide a great range of possibilities for elder and younger generations in their competitions for power and ultimate worth, but they provide no female possibilities.

Christianity also includes a second sacrifice myth which serves as the paradigm myth of its distinctive religious tradition. Again, it is a male-imaged God outside of nature who demands a son in sacrifice, but this time it is the God, as God the Father, who sacrifices God the Son, Jesus. No substitute is provided; no animal replaces the child, although Jesus is often called the Lamb of God. In this great reckoning, Jesus the Son of God must die to set the balance right, to bring eternal hope to the human whole. Jesus is crucified on the cross, his head pointing to heaven, his blood spilling on the ground. This sacrifice myth presents the ultimate conquest over nature. It is the most vertical of all the monotheistic myths; the horizontal dimension of earthly life and death is truly overcome, for Jesus as the Son of God arises on the third day and lives forevermore and promises believers the same eternal existence.

The Christian myth, like other sacrifice myths, structures a universe in which humanity's children can be saved, which brings humanity comfort. The Christian myth is particularly comforting to human fathers, since, for them, the Son of God is a true substitute for their own sons. No son of a human father dies on the cross.

Yet Christianity does not offer the same comfort to humanity's mothers. For while Jesus has a God as a father, he has a human mother, and as a human son he dies painfully on the cross to his mother's great sorrow, and the collective weeping lasts for centuries. The Son of God arises, but the mother's son is slain, and Michelangelo's *Pietà* pierces the heart of us all.

Worse, Jesus on the cross distances his mother from himself. In the first three gospel tales of crucifixion, Matthew, Mark, and Luke, the mother of Jesus is not mentioned. Women are noted as "watching from a distance," but Mary is not said to be among them. Only in the gospel tale of John does Mary appear, and there in a troublesome scene (John 19:25–27). Jesus looks down from his place of sacrifice and informs his mother that the disciple John is now her son, signifying that, for her, sons should be interchangeable—as if a mother with a son dying on a cross could be convinced of that untruth. With

Jesus' statement, Mary has no claim to her son, or to her feelings. The scripture goes on to say, "From that moment, John took [Mary] into his household" (John 19:25–27). The scripture implies that Mary was taken away from the place of sacrifice before the great cataclysmic event. In the only gospel that includes Mary's presence, she is removed before the crucial moment. Like her comatriarchs Hajar and Sarah, the mother of Isaac, she is absent from that sacrificial event where the universe is made right. Mary gave Jesus natural birth; Jesus gave humanity transcendent birth, without his mother's aid or presence.

The maleness of the monotheistic sacrifice myths is complete. In the Islamic, Judaic, and Christian tales, everything gathered at the sacred place is male: a male-imaged God, a father, and a son. There is no important female in sight. She has been moved off the sacred stage, beyond the sacred door, into individual households where she bides by hearth and home, tending to what is private, personal, and evanescent. We are all individuals and value the birth and nurturing that earthly mothers give. Yet, in the monotheistic construction, the mother's domination over individual birth and child care fades in significance with the great cosmic birth and transcendent care that men in connection to the great male God are envisioned to give. It is a question of relative worth of things, and the Mediterranean monotheisms take ultimate worth away from women and out of the households and put it onto male-dominated streets and mountaintops.

How different is the myth of Iphigenia, where females, youth, and nature are lauded. Female elements abound—the deity who calls for the sacrifice, the child to be slain, and the animal that substitutes for her (see figure 15.1). The young daughter's decisions and actions are pivotal; she is the one who understands the universe and mediates between it and humanity. Iphigenia is the worthy sacrifice who can set right the cosmos because she understands and is willing to be slain. She brings hope to the community as a whole, and at the same time saves herself from slaughter, spares her mother grief, rights the wrongs against nature committed by her father, and then saves her brother —and all children—from sacrifice at the goddess' temple. Iphigenia is a savior, communal and individual, not through her ability to give birth to natural things, but rather through her ability to represent humanity to itself and to the cosmos, and solve the structural conflict of things. And she is replaced in sacrifice by a female deer, not a male sheep—a wild animal, not a domesticated creature. Iphigenia's sacrifice is a myth of nature, youth, and the female cosmically ennobled, not of nature, youth, and the female cosmically put aside.

public power

Yet, Euripides' rendering of Iphigenia's sacrifice did not come to dominate all sacrifice myths in ancient Greece. Other, more constraining images won out (Case 1985). It is also accurate that the diversity of male and female deities in the Greek cosmos did not make Greek women joint participants in the practical exercise of public political life. Even in sexually diverse polytheisms, males have tended to monopolize the pragmatic structures of power. Yet, the lack of complete male monopoly of the cosmic dimension is important, for at least in that domain male dependence on the female was expressed, which meant that the female could think of herself and her body in transcendent ways. Much more marginalizing is the monotheistic construction.

While the male dominance of public political life is widespread, the forms of that dominance are differentially expressed—on earth

FIGURE 15.1. Mediterranean Sacrifice Myths Compared

	Ibrahim and Isma'il (Islamic)	Abraham and Isaac (Judaic)	God and Christ (Christian)	Agamemnon and Iphigenia (Greek)
Who Demands the Sacrifice	god (male, beyond nature)	god (male, beyond nature)	god (male, beyond nature)	goddess (female, in nature
Who Performs the Sacrifice	human father (elder male)	human father (elder male)	divine father(male-imaged, elder)	human father (elder male)
Who is to be Sacrificed	human son (young male)	human son (young male)	divine/ human son (young male)	human daughter (young female)
What Substitutes	domesticated male animal	domesticated male animal	human aspect of divine/ human male	wild female animal

265

and in the heavens. The practical repercussions of those differences on the level of practical power and individual psyche deserve exploration. Here, the important point is the cultural specificity of the cosmic constructions, notably the differences between the polytheistic expression of active conflict between things of the heavens and things of this world, between male and female, and the Mediterranean monotheistic construction of a transcendent, male-imaged God who conquers nature and in so doing excludes females from transcendent questing.

Monotheism's particular construction of male domination establishes its rightfulness on an *a priori* level of abiding cultural assumptions. Women are marginalized not through active conquest but rather because of a powerful construction of the "intrinsic" nature of things that excludes them from momentous decision making and transcendent questings. The Mediterranean monotheisms engender male domination at the level of basic definitions, basic habitats, male and female, sacred and profane. They embed the definitions in the basic parameters of the cosmos and parameters of the self, defining who can operate in which domains with what kind of effectiveness.

The crucial difference is one of presence versus absence, active versus passive conquest. In many polytheistic myths, the female is powerfully present and actively, explicitly, and dramatically conquered. In the Mediterranean monotheisms, she is absent and conquered through ultimate passivity wrought by nonpresence. Monotheism smooths out cosmic conflict and sexual conflict by making the great cosmic intercourse an all-male event. Collective good is hence more clearly and straightforwardly achieved with less overt battling. This may be a part of the appeal of monotheisms; Islam is now the fastest-growing religion in the world, a position previously held by Christianity. In combination, Christianity and Islam account for more than half of all humanity. In the smoothing out, male dominance becomes intrinsic to the cosmic order, to everyone's hopes for ultimate good, and to everyone's definition of sexual self.

One must not underestimate how much these myths inform basic understandings and basic postures in the world. They are founding myths undergirded by humanity's most poignant dilemma, its most heartfelt hope. They shape how people think, frame their experience, and act in the world. So culturally embedded is the female exclusion from ultimate good, communal questing, and the dominant structures of public power that women's public powerlessness need not be implemented in law, because it is so firmly written within the self. Only in the last century has it come under serious challenge; it is far from being overturned. That is true in Morocco; that is true in the United States. There are no laws to prevent women from becoming members of Morocco's national parliament; there are no laws to prevent women from becoming president of the United States, but they are excluded by cultural fact, by a great collective unconscious that informs us all.

Through silence and omission of the sexual Other, the Mediterranean monotheisms create a formidable patriarchy that offers no readily accessible ways for the female to think of collective good, collective decision making, and ultimate transcendence through herself and her female body. They do not even allow her the role of worthy though defeated cosmic adversary. They pull the female out of the cosmic dramas, push her away from the momentous settings, and relegate the female instead to the role of nature-bound individual. All this is done through intrinsic givens that make it easy to associate hard-nosed decision making, collective quests, the use of violence, and the ability to forge sacred trusts with males, and difficult to associate them with females.

Rituals are concrete realizations of culture's imagination. The Islamic rite of the Great Sacrifice, the Jewish celebration of Rosh Hashanah, the Christian practice of communion all bring myths of sacrifice to the present.[3] All three provide convincing experiences of the universe that compensate for the male's inability to give natural birth by allocating to him the role of birthgiver to things beyond nature. Through icon and action, they present the argument that men are able to give birth to what is transcendent precisely because they do not give birth to what is natural. Man's distance from natural birth thus puts him a giant step closer to God and legitimates his dominance of women and children. And there they are—monotheism's prophets—on earth's peaks—Mount Arafat, Mount Moriah, the hill of Golgotha—communing with the great male-imaged, abstract God who lies above and beyond them. On the plains far below, carrying the shame of their closeness to nature, are the unnamed, anonymous, undifferentiated women.

Sacrifice uses the most profound of physical actions—intercourse, birth, and death—in producing the most profound of abstractions—an abstract God, an abstract heaven, an abstract life everlasting—and then solidifies both in undergirding its invented truth that men are the intervening links between the limited and the limitless. It is a construction of power that draws upon the whole of the cosmos, the whole of the world, and the whole of male and female definitions in producing a male hierarchy of hope and domination.

private intimacy—the female blighted

Not only does the monotheistic construction exclude females from the dominant structures of public power, it interferes with the private intimacy men and women might be capable of. In building transcendent hope, it undermines the more palpable kind of earthly hope, intercourse, and exchange that could be achieved through the male-female bond, through the merger of sacred and sexual connection.

The monotheistic traditions with their beyond-nature God and male links to transcendence correctly see themselves in competition with the male-female link; ergo the common depiction of the garden of Eden in which humanity fell because of the woman, because she listened and responded to her natural desires and caused man to respond with her, enticing him to her and to earth's pleasures when he should have been focusing on God. "By the tale of Yusuf be admonished, and guard against their stratagems. Does thou not consider that Iblis ejected Adam by means of woman? (*The Thousand and One Nights* 1889:9).

Not only is the female fallen but she is feared, for she can, consciously or unconsciously, tempt man into mortality and make him fall with her. The female's ability to lure the male away from what is enduring into the temporal pleasures of this world can interfere with his ability to forge connection with the divine. These are reasons why the man must be on his guard around her and keep her at arm's length. Man must keep the relationship with the temporal creature temporal. He must not let her into his essence, for she might undo him. In the final analysis, when it comes to the really important dimensions of man's being, man is to keep his eyes on the prize—on the God who exists beyond this world—and not turn back to gaze at this world's woman. The fear of the female is prominent in Moroccan society (Mernissi 1987a); it is not foreign to Western societies either.

consequences

One can have great sympathy with the human hope for life beyond the bonds of this world, a hope that may have given rise to the construction of a deity who exists beyond nature. But the sacrificial exclusion of the female from this construction has had devastating consequences. It has limited how the female can think of herself and circumscribed how the male can connect with her. Monotheism's sacrifice is the ultimate reinforcement of the image of the proper female as quiescent virgin mother, and the ultimate denial of her role as sexually dynamic sacred companion. Rituals of sacrifice institutionalize the victory—in imagination and practice—of Fatima and Mary over 'A'isha and Mary Magdalene.

According to medieval tradition, Saint Augustine said that females, at the moment of death, become male so that they can enter heaven. There are those who contend that females must become malelike in order to enter the top echelons of what we currently define as important and enduring in this world. Bouhdiba's summary of Islam applies to the dominant traditions in all three monotheisms; they are "nothing less than the sacralization of the masculine and the trivialization of the feminine" (1985:213).

The profound consequences for women who grow up in the context of these monotheistic cultures of not being able to think of collective good and ultimate communal hope through their own bodies and selves have yet to be fully explored, but the ravages we see.[4] They exist in secular as well as religious forms, public and private dimensions, in the dearth of women heads of state, in the relative scarcity of women in the top levels of business, science, technology, and religion, in the female questioning of her own ultimate worth, and in the violence done to women and children by males they know. Thirty percent of all female homicides in the United States are committed by husbands or lovers.

There are of course prominent subthemes in each of the monotheistic traditions that lie outside those I have depicted. One can however argue that the subthemes (such as the cults that surround the Virgin Mary in Catholicism and female saints in Islam) actually help support the dominant themes by giving individuals personal release from them without posing a threat to their structural domination, expanding the individual's universe of meaning while enabling the structures of power to continue to operate in the same patriarchal way. There is diversity in and among the three Mediterranean monotheisms, yet there is formidable commonality in their male construction of earthly authority and everlasting life. Changes are rumbling in each. But for now, the male pathway to ultimate transcendence and communal good endures. Morocco is simply a paradigm for all three.

coherency in sacrifice

Morocco's paradigm is powerfully coherent. In Islam, biological, household, community, and cosmic sacrifices—in physical and metaphysical dimensions—precisely reinforce, clarify, and validate one another. The father determines the sociobiological identity of the child and sacrifices on the child's behalf. Senior males determine the political life of the community and sacrifice on its behalf. The prophets of old illuminated the human pathway to the divine and sacrificed on behalf of all of humanity. A profound coherency of spilled blood, male links, and cosmic design exists in Islam. Into this universe of meaning, the Moroccan monarch steps when he takes the great knife in his right hand and slays the great beast on the nation's behalf. All of Islam shows coherence, but the Moroccan tradition is the most coherent. In a world in the throes of wild fluctuation, coherency has considerable appeal.

stable authorities and sacrifice

Stable, popularly legitimate male authoritarian regimes dominate the Muslim world. They include military dictatorships, monarchies, and presidencies. Durable patriarchy dominates all; even the elected presidents tend to wield autocratic authority and rule for life. The regimes range from the so-called revolutionary to the reactionary. They are notable not only for their relative stability (the Latin American cycle of coups is not present here), but also for their widescale popular appeal. Autocratic regimes do not merely survive; they thrive. I suggest that there is a relationship between their popular appeal and the basic underlying cultural assumptions that are created in Islam's myth and practice of sacrifice. Sacrifice is after all the most powerful cultural reinforcement possible for senior male domination.

Given the potency of its sacrificial paradigm, it is not surprising that the Muslim world includes within its boundaries the majority of the world's ruling monarchies (for instance, monarchs reign in Morocco, Jordan, Saudia Arabia, Oman, the Arab Emirates). Monarchy is a system of authority that combines the adoration of senior men, patrilineal links, and the forcefulness of inheritance through bloodline—characteristics powerfully undergirded by Islam's Great Sacrifice. Nor is it surprising that the Muslim world's most stable monarchy is the Moroccan one—the regime in which the monarch not only claims blood descent from the Prophet, but each year takes a knife in his hands and slays a great ram on behalf of the whole— the ultimate support for the power of stellar men and of blood.

reconstructing the cosmos in the mundane

This universe of meaning—of a God beyond nature and of males distanced from it, reaching to God on behalf of the whole—is each year reconstructed in the Great Sacrifice. Yet many have overlooked its importance because of the speed with which the ritual takes place and the lack of elaborate formality with which it is celebrated, especially in the households.

The central part of the household sacrifice takes about four minutes. The household members gather, absolute quiet settles, the head of the household stands central and erect, the white ram is brought in, admired, and slain. The blood falls, the ram struggles and may or may not stand back up, and death takes place. Deeper quiet briefly ensues and then it is finished.

I submit that there is little formality because it is not needed. The purpose of formality—of elaborate prescriptions for ritual entry and exit and extensive repetition within the ritual core—is to evoke the cosmic dimension, to elicit the perception that one is in an important place at an important time, dealing with important matters in serious ways. The Great Sacrifice does not need those techniques. The myth lies so firmly in people's minds, the dilemma it addresses is so deep in people's souls, the actions so profound in people's perceptions, the repetitions so extensive in human history (every year for over 1,350 years) that the internal elaboration that marks so many ritual occasions would here be superfluous. Hence, in this ritual that takes place outside of all kinds of dwellings, with minimally marked beginnings and endings and rapid unfolding, the heart of humanity is pierced.

The popular celebrations of first marriage take days; the ritual of the Prophet's Birthday takes hours; the ritual of the Great Sacrifice takes only minutes. Yet in the final analysis it is the Great Sacrifice that is the most profound. In those brief moments, the cornerstones of humanity are uncovered and on them the unshakable pillars of Muslim and Moroccan existence are secured—the male domination of violence, communal life, and the hope for transcendence. Atop the central pillar stands the white-cloaked sharifi prince.

TWENTIETH-CENTURY SUCCESS

colonial dichotomy
body and soul

16

colonial dichotomy

The Prophet's Birthday, the popular rituals of first marriage, and the Great Sacrifice gave the Moroccan monarchy a durable and uncompromised base of legitimacy with which it renewed itself and national life during the centuries of turmoil. The substratum of cultural groundings made popular and persuasive the patriarchal model of rule. The substratum was essential to Morocco's successful resistance to the West. Despite four hundred years of assault, Morocco entered the 1800s (A.H. 1200s) with its political and cultural identity intact, and with a still favorable balance of trade. Then things worsened; the slide to colonial domination began, but even then Morocco's culture remained secure, and in time became the means through which Moroccans ousted the colonialists from the land.

The French took Algiers in 1830 (A.H. 1246/47) and from their Algerian base launched attacks against Morocco. In 1844 (A.H. 1260), the French forces defeated Moroccan troops at the battle of Isly, the first major Moroccan defeat in almost three hundred years. Yet Moroccans maintained their independence.[1] In 1859–1860 (A.H. 1276/77), Morocco suffered a more damaging defeat at the hands of Spanish forces in northern Morocco. Moroccans were charged a war indemnity of 20 million douros, which they could not pay. In consequence, Spain seized Moroccan customs receipts for a twenty-four-year period. In this era of weak state apparatus, customs receipts were the most reliable source of income for Morocco's central government. With the seizure, much of this income went to Spain, a debilitating economic blow (Brignon et al. 1967:285, 290–291).

Yet even in this bound position, with a crucial economic pillar gone, Morocco continued to fight off European occupation, and more than ever the population expressed their oppositional identity through the institution of the sharifi caliphate, their blood descendant monarchy, their collective representation of self. The French stepped up attacks on Morocco's eastern border and the Spanish increased their attacks on the north, but Moroccans fought off the European forces in the sharifi caliph's name. The vigor of popular resistance demonstrated to the Europeans that the cost of a Moroccan takeover would be great. The continued potency of Moroccans' collective representation of self and the availability of the patrilineal model of military organization enabled them to mount a keen resistance to outsiders, especially in short-term skirmishes (Dunn 1977). Morocco's polity might have been ailing but it was far from dead, and Western powerholders, like Moroccans themselves, scurried over each other trying to make direct connections to the sharifi ruler. Their very real deference to the monarch shows how much potency remained. France, Spain, England, Germany, and the United States all staked a foothold in Moroccan territory during the 1800s, but none were able to seize the whole.

There are scholars who portray the success of Morocco's resistance as purely a function of intra-European competition, an overly Eurocentric view. The same European countries vied in other parts of the world and yet one or another definitively won. The strength of Morocco's political identity as well as the sharifi monarchy's ability to actively maneuver one powerholder against the others were contributing factors in Morocco's continued independence, in its ability to remain outside the French camp for eighty-one years after Algeria became a colony and thirty-one years after Tunisia fell.

capitulation

When the capitulation finally came, it was economic and military at base, not cultural or civilizational. Practical variables dominated. The number of Europeans in the country had soared. In 1832 (A.H. 1248/ 49), there were two hundred and fifty. By 1894 (A.H. 1312/13), there were nine thousand. French and Spanish military attacks increased. Most debilitating, Morocco's indebtedness to European banks had skyrocketed. By 1906 (A.H. 1324/25), Morocco owed European banks 206 million francs and, what is more, had mortgaged away the means of settling the debt. France had by then acquired the right to 60 percent of Morocco's daily customs receipts (Brignon et al. 1967:326). Making matters worse, Morocco's monarch, ʿAbd al-ʿAziz, was psychologically captivated by the foreigners and their gifts, and the Moroccan population resented his lack of leadership against the outsiders.

In 1906, the caliph's brother, Mawlay Hafiz, rallied Moroccans in a wave of anti-European fervor and ousted the weak-willed ʿAbd al-ʿAziz from the throne. Mawlay Hafiz had full intentions of reestablishing Morocco's independence from Europe. Yet, once in power, he discovered that the dependence on Europe ran far deeper than his brother's personality. The structure of the world economy had shifted in Europe's favor, and at this point in history Morocco could not extricate itself from the West's economic grasp. In the end Mawlay Hafiz, the great Islamic warrior, was forced into signing the capitulation papers (Julien 1978:89). In 1912 (A.H. 1330/31), Morocco became an official part of colonial France. Moroccan independence was lost, but not the sharifi sense of high drama. Mawlay Hafiz showed the colonialists what he thought:

> Before he left, the sovereign, whose lucidity and sharifian dignity had been without a single failing, wanted to show that, for an indefinite time, it was the end of free Morocco. As a symbolic act he destroyed the sacred emblems of the ʿAlawi sultans: he burned the scarlet canopy that was held over his head during official ceremonies. His sedan-chair was broken into pieces and thrown into the fire. Only the holy books were spared.
>
> (Julien 1978:90)

international and national power

A dialectic governed Morocco's relationship to the dominant world powers in the 1800s and 1900s (A.H. 1200s and 1300s). The West possessed superior military and economic might, but that did not give it absolute domination—far from it. The cultural legitimacy of the sharifi monarchy, its unifying expression in ritual performances, and its ability to catalyze the population into opposition continued to play an important role. The local-international dynamics are similar to those that Rashid Khalidi (1985) describes for Lebanon in the 1980s (A.H. 1400s). The outside powers played an important part in conflict and turmoil that developed in the local settings, but they could not control it. They affected history, but not as they pleased.

Moroccans continued to actively construct history even after the French colonial "victory." France colonized Morocco, but it realized neither its hopes of economic windfall nor a permanently enlarged "greater" France (Pascon 1977). The French occupation cost Morocco dearly—but it cost France as well.

French protectorate

The formal capitulation papers were signed in 1912 (A.H. 1330/31), yet two major limitations shaped Morocco's French colonial era. First, the whole of the Moroccan countryside was not brought under French military control until much later, until 1933 (A.H. 1352/53), by which time the independence movement had begun. No sooner had the French consolidated the Moroccan colony than it began breaking away. Second, Morocco was legally established as a French "protectorate" rather than a full-blown colony. By the edicts of international law, the officially recognized purpose of setting up a protectorate was to revitalize (hence "to protect") the political system in place, not to insert a new one. In Morocco, France could not put forward the argument that it made elsewhere, that no previous polity existed. The fact of an eleven-hundred-year-old monarchy could not be wished away.[2]

Nonetheless, some scholars argue that a protectorate is simply a colony by another name and point to the fact that, while the colonizers left the weakened shell of an indigenous polity in place, they divested it of all practical power, concentrating that power instead in the hands of the colonial shadow government that effectively ruled. This interpretation of the placement of practical power is correct, but its evaluation of overall political power is not. Political power never rests solely on economic, administrative, and military might. Morocco's indigenous polity was not an empty shell; it became crucial to the independence movement.

One has only to compare Morocco with Algeria to see the startling differences between a protectorate and a legal colony. Algeria was ravaged by the length and extent of its colonial era (from 1830 to 1962—A.H. 1246/47 to 1382/83). Its economic, military, and administrative institutions were destroyed, its population was decimated, and its cultural foundations were battered. In the end, France did not get what it wanted out of Algeria either, but it destroyed the integration that Algeria had known and left the country and its people searching for an authentic identity. The protectorate occupation of Morocco, though momentous, was limited by comparison.

What is more, the length of time the two countries were under French rule and the differing extents of the colonizations were themselves in part a function of their differing precolonial political orders. Once again, one must not interpret a single historical fact—for example, the length of the respective colonial eras—as simply derivative of European intentions and actions. The North African side of the equation was critical as well. Morocco's precolonial polity was more resistant to Western assault than was that of either Algeria or Tunisia for reasons that had to do with its own internal constitution (Combs-Schilling 1984).

Yet, despite these stark comparisons, some scholars continue to argue that the indigenous political system that remained in place in Morocco—the sharifi caliphate—was a figurative system lacking real power. They are wrong. Figurative and symbolic systems always play a role in practical politics, and in Morocco their role was determinant. The maintenance of even a depleted form of their indigenous monarchy enabled Moroccans to maintain the continuity of their political and cultural identity, their symbolic representation of self, and their national integration in great sacred performances. National identity is no trifling matter; the nation is an imagined community that depends upon the spontaneous support of large sectors of the population to endure through time (Anderson 1983). Moroccans had centuries of experience in constructing a viable political entity from the cultural nugget of the sharifi caliphate, and they did so once again to end France's colonial reign.

Muhammad V and the battle for independence

The French dominated the practical structures of power, but they never captured the heart of the nation, which remained sustained and renewed in the position of the sharifi caliphate and in the performances of Islam. The French thought that they were in control, that they had left Morocco an empty shell of religious authority only. They were unaware that the "shell" would be their undoing.

Yet, even if France had known what would happen, it is doubtful that it could have done anything about it. Morocco's sharifi caliphate, unlike the Tunisian beylicate, was too legitimate a popular institution to be eliminated by colonial fiat. France had enough trouble bringing Morocco into its colonial camp without trying to eradicate the monarchy, symbol of self for over a thousand years. It would have been an enormously unpopular move, a catalyst for popular rebellion. Hence the survival of the sharifi caliphate into the Protectorate era was itself far from simply a function of French decision making. The historical and cultural wealth of Morocco's monarchy was the driving factor behind its colonial durability.

Yet France was confident of its colonial power, especially after hand-selecting the new sultan in 1927 (A.H. 1346/47). The French chose the youngest son of the previous ruler, the eighteen-year-old Si Muhammad, instead of one of his older brothers, because the French believed him to be docile and obedient. They were wrong. Try as they might—surrounding him with French advisers, friends, and ideology—they could not control the bright young man. In time he came to occupy legitimately the position the French had set upon him; he became the true Prince of the Faithful and led his people to independence.

Berber dahir

The Berber *dahir* (legal ruling) of 1930 (A.H. 1349/50) began Muhammad V's coming of age, and the coming of age of Moroccan resistance. By the laws of the Protectorate, the Moroccan monarch had to sign any legal ruling that was issued by the central government. At first, France formulated the rulings, and the young king signed. One of those rulings was the Berber dahir.

The Arab-Berber division in Morocco is linguistic rather than social and cultural. As mentioned in chapter 5, there are native Arabic speakers and native Berber speakers, but the linguistic division is not translated into distinctive clusters of sociocultural traits by which one category of speakers can be divided from the other. For over a thousand years Berber speakers and Arabic speakers have intermingled and intermarried, obfuscating any clear-cut division. Many Moroccans are bilingual, and it is not uncommon to have a family in which one parent speaks mostly one language and one parent mostly the other, and the children move easily through both. Some local groups who mark themselves as socially and culturally distinctive, for example the Mzuda of the Haouz plain, include as a part of their subgroup both native Berber and native Arabic speakers. There are people who claim Berber descent and speak only Arabic, and there are people who claim Arabic descent (even prophetic descent) but speak only Berber.

Berber-Arab is thus not a definitive sociocultural divide, yet the French tried to make it one by passing the Berber dahir. The dahir elevated local customary practices in predominantly Berber-speaking areas to the level of state law, substituting it for Qur'anic law, and simultaneously moved the appeal system for criminal cases out of the sharifi high court to the French high court.

Local peoples everywhere have customary practices attuned to local legal needs. For people who are part of broad-reaching, codified legal systems, such as those that existed in precolonial Islamic Morocco, the local practices add flexibility and nuance to the centralized systems. In many parts of Morocco, native Berber speakers as well as native Arabic speakers had, and still have, such customary practices. What the French tried to do was make it appear that since Berber speakers had these local practices—practices that like those of many of the neighboring Arabic speakers were sometimes in conflict with Qur'anic law—the Berbers were not really Muslim and should not be subjected to the law of the Qur'an nor to the sharifi high court. They were mistaken.

The dahir was a straightforward attempt by France to divide and rule, to separate "Berbers" off from "Arabs" and take them out of the Islamic and the sharifi legal system. Underlying the dahir was the French belief that "Berbers" were somehow more intrinsically Western and potentially Christian than "Arabs" and could be brought to the side of France if they could first be separated from the Qur'an and sharifi rule. It was absurd.

rituals of dissent

Instead of dividing the population, the dahir worked to further solidify an already well-consolidated national identity. It pulled together nearly the whole of Morocco's Islamic population, Berber-speaking and Arabic-speaking, in opposition to the outsider. The dahir fused in common concern traditionally trained Islamic scholars, the "old turbans," and the young Western-trained intelligentsia, both of whom saw the Berber dahir as an attack on Morocco's selfhood and on Islam (K. Brown 1976:198–201).

Appropriately for Morocco's political culture, popular opposition to the dahir was first expressed in the ritual domain, in the recitation of formal prayers of disaster, Ya Latifs. The Ya Latif is a form of

Islamic prayer recited only in a great crisis, such as famine, plague, earthquake, and locusts. In popular perception, the Berber dahir called for their recitation, and men began entering mosques and uttering the Ya Latifs. Everyone knew who and what the disaster was—the French, the colonial era, and the Berber dahir—but no one straightforwardly called them by name. More ambiguously and more powerfully, men entered holy places, turned their faces to Makka, and began praying for God to deliver them from peril. A common prayer went, "Oh Savior, deliver us from ill treatment by fate and do not separate us from our brothers the Berbers." The Ya Latifs were begun by an octogenarian prayer leader in Sala (Salé) and spread throughout the country, even to the great al-Qarawiyin itself, the thousand-year-old mosque-university, the bastion of Islam in Morocco (Brown 1976:198–201; Julien 1978:160).

The French reaction to the prayers was brutal and focused upon the young intellectuals. Embodying the worst of colonial mentality, the French characterized the young participants as:

> . . . the group of a few hooligans with some certificate of study or another who take themselves for Gandhis and Zaghlouls without doubting for one minute that the latter represent a threat to England because they are a collective consciousness, whereas the primary school renegades are merely its digestive tubes.
>
> (Julien 1978:160)

Young intellectuals were arrested, beaten, and jailed, and a number were publicly humiliated. The bright young Hassan al-Wazzani, who had completed his exams at the French School of Oriental Languages and was close to obtaining his diploma from the School of Advanced Studies in Political Science in Paris, was arrested and flogged with leather straps in the streets of Fas. The official French reaction was to applaud this treatment of him (Julien 1978:160). It was not a high moment for French civilization.

Moroccans for their part did not simply pray. As with rituals in the past, collective performances consolidated popular experience and consciousness, which was then expressed through diverse channels, many of them quite pragmatic. Throughout the countryside organizing meetings took place to consider what was to be done about the dahir. The young intellectuals contacted the new journal *La Nation Arabe* (printed in France) and convinced them to do a feature article on the dahir. By means of the article, the whole of the Islamic world learned of the peril to Islam that the French Berber policy posed in Morocco, and opposition to the Berber dahir became an international cause célèbre for Muslims and Arabs in defense of themselves, their cultural identity, and their faith (Julien 1978:160, 163).

The young intellectuals greatly affected the twenty-one-year-old king, as did the popular reaction to the dahir. Although Muhammad V originally had signed the dahir, as he came to understand its contents and its repercussions, he sided with the Moroccan population against the French, and argued not only that the dahir was wrong, but that it had been deceitfully presented to him.

Despite the widescale Moroccan opposition and the advice of a number of junior officers on the colonial staff, the senior French officials did not withdraw the dahir but rather let it stand, further alienating an already alienated population. Not until 1934 (A.H. 1352/53), with the appointment of a "more enlightened" French resident-general, was the dahir altered. A new dahir was issued that, although it maintained the customary tribunals in Berber areas, put them back under the jurisdiction of the sharifi high court. It was a victory of sorts for the Moroccan nationalists (Julien 1978:163).

French officials thought that the revised dahir had settled matters, and in a moment of brazen self-confidence decided to show their "support" for the sharifi caliphate and for Islam by having Muhammad V journey to Fas and lead prayers at al-Qarawiyin. Without much sublety, the French were trying to heal the wounds the dahir had created, and were attempting to use ritual to do so. From their perspective, they would reconsolidate popular support for the Protectorate by having the reigning blood descendant of Muhammad lead prayers in al-Qarawiyin, bastion not only of Islam but of resistance to the French-instigated Berber dahir. Prayers would again be recited in that thousand-year-old mosque, but this time under French auspices.

monarchical symbol

So Muhammad V went to Fas surrounded by his French entourage, and thousands of Moroccans poured into the streets to greet him. They shouted "Long live the King. Long live Morocco." The French were shaken by the outpouring of popular sentiment for the young king and the Moroccan nation, and, in a kneejerk reaction, whisked Muhammad V back to Ribat, not allowing him to perform the promised prayers. It was a remarkably shortsighted move. By not allowing the monarch to carry out the sacred duties that were rightfully his— and that the French had just publicly acknowledged as rightfully his by organizing the whole event—the French underlined the fact that they had no intention of allowing Morocco's popularly recognized ruler to rule, belying the verbiage in which they couched the Protectorate. French practice demonstrated what their clouds of words did not: the colony was meant for the colonizer. In reaction, the people of Fas took to the streets, and hundreds were arrested and jailed.

The Fas visit and resultant arrests were a second dramatic rite of passage that framed the way Muhammad V came to understand himself, his role in the world, and his position vis-à-vis the colonial power. The visit provided him with a potent visceral experience of the popular expectation that he lead. In consequence, he began actively seeking redress for the indigenous population and alternative sources of information about what was happening, thereby coming into contact with the writings of young nationalist 'Alal al-Fasi (1948), whom he invited to the palace. The meeting of the men was a meeting of minds, and the two became a forceful combination for Moroccan independence, the bright young rightful ruler and the perceptive young ideologue.

political elites

The position of al-Fasi and the other young intellectuals in Moroccan independence needs clarification. They consolidated the ideological foundations of resistance and built an international catchment of support. They also affected Muhammad V, who was sincerely inspired by their ideology. But they did not directly mobilize the masses of the population, who were instead inspired to colonial resistance by the young ruler who motivated the majority of them on the basis of the age-old legitimacy that the blood-descendant monarchy already held. Most Moroccans saw the sharifi king as their legitimate ruler—a symbol of themselves, their collective identity, and their faith—and wanted him back in power. They did not need an intellectualist ideology to tell them that; the understanding was already a part of their bodies and their minds. Nowhere else in the Muslim world did the drive for colonial independence so center on the return of the precolonial ruler to power, and the strength of its cultural foundations enabled the Moroccan monarchy to play that role.

The consolidation of nationalist identity and anticolonial resistance on the position of caliph makes much sense in terms of Morocco's precolonial past. The monarchy had long served as the crucible of self and nation. When the new ideological articulations came from the young intelligentsia, they too were fit into this previous social and cultural construction, and they fit well. The young ideologues handled crucial organizational tasks (communication between cities, mobilization for specific events) and inspired important sectors of the national population and the international community that otherwise might not have been drawn toward the monarchy-centered drive for independence. But they did not directly pull the Moroccan population into opposition (Combs-Schilling 1984).

The comparison with Tunisia helps highlight the distinctive role played by Morocco's intellectuals. Tunisia also had a precolonial monarchy, but that monarchy lacked the depth of cultural support and the popular legitimacy of the Moroccan institution, and it collapsed with the French takeover. Consequently, Tunisia's road to independence was different. The Tunisian population was directly mobilized for independence by their young ideologues, led by the fiery young Habib Bourguiba with his blue eyes and French wife, and by their political party, the Neo-Dastur.[3] In Morocco, in contrast, the sharifi caliphate catalyzed the population and brought together in common concern the various sectors of the population. As core symbol of the political community and individual identity, the sharifi caliphate did not need an elaborate organizational infrastructure to orchestrate the population's response of resistance, for the population spontaneously rallied around their ruler.

For years, Western analysts—operating from a monolithic model of nation-statehood—tended to overplay the role of political elites and political parties in postcolonial states, no matter what the actualities of the situation. They tended to suggest that the marginalization of Morocco's ideologues and their political parties was a strategic coup on the part of a politically shrewd Muhammad V, achieved by playing key actors and groups off each other. But that is only a partial truth. Muhammad V was able to "marginalize" the elites because in popular terms they *were* marginal. Their postcolonial position was in a very real sense a reflection of their place in the anticolonial drive to independence.

The blood-descendant monarchy was the center of popular aspirations. The other players were channels to it. A Western-style ideological construction articulated through words and disseminated through written books and pamphlets was, like the notion of political parties, unnecessary for most Moroccans. They wanted independence for themselves and for their established form of rule, the sharifi caliphate, not for some new ideology or some new party. This is not to deny that political maneuvering played a part, as did the assasination of Bin Baraka,[4] but only within the larger context of Moroccan political reality, where the sharifi caliphate was the center. In Morocco, all power, all pathways led to the blood-descendant king; that was not new. And the newfound ideology and the newfound political party became but one more pathway leading one important part of the population to the throne of its prince.

three high dramas

Moroccans and their monarchs had long been adept at turning ritual into history. During the colonial era they turned history into ritual with equal panache. Three events stand out in the Moroccan drive for independence: the king's meeting with Roosevelt, his Tanja speech, and the Great Sacrifice of 1953 (A.H. 1372).

World War II and the meeting with Roosevelt In the short term, World War II slowed Morocco's drive for independence as tens of thousands of Moroccan men left their homeland to give their lives to "Free France." Yet there was one crucial moment when Muhammad V met with President Franklin Roosevelt in Dar al-Bayda'. The meeting brought together the legitimate ruler of the United States, a young country that had managed in less than two centuries to become one of the most powerful nations in the world, and the legitimate ruler of the millennium-old Morocco, which in its heyday had held world glory. In age-old strength Morocco had been the first nation to officially recognize the independence of the United States, in 1789 (A.H. 1203/4; Muhammad V's great-great-great-great-grandfather, Muhammad III, conveyed Morocco's recognition to the United States in a formal letter). Now the tables had turned: Morocco was colonized and seeking recognition for its right to independence. Given the values upon which American culture rested and given Morocco's ready recognition of U.S. independence from Great Britain, many Moroccans were confident that the United States would support Morocco's drive for independence from France. They saw President Roosevelt's visit as an indication of support and a promise that direct recognition would soon come. It did not. After the war, the United States stood by its ally France. Still, the Roosevelt-Muhammad V meeting had its impact upon Morocco's collective consciousness.

From a long-term perspective, World War II helped ensure Moroccan independence. Morocco's sons who managed to survive the great war returned home, expecting an end to colonialism. They had fought and died as equals with the French, in order to keep France from being colonized by Germany, and they expected France to now release them from the colonial bond. But the French did not. On the contrary, after the war, France tried to pull Morocco ever more firmly into its grasp.

Tanja speech Another important occasion in the drive for independence came in a formal speech that Muhammad V delivered in a
scheduled visit to Tanja in 1947 (A.H. 1366), the first time that the
sharifi monarch had set foot on Tanja soil in over fifty years. The
speech had been written and reviewed by French advisors and was
scheduled to be given on April 10.

But on April 7, Senegalese troops, who were a part of the official
French military in Morocco, opened fire on the Moroccan population
in the streets of Dar al-Bayda'. Apparently, a Senegalese soldier had
molested an Arab woman in the streets. Those around her had reacted
in her defense, at which point the Senegalese opened fire and mas-
sacred hundreds of innocent people without any intervention by French
officials, policemen, or other French military forces that were in the
area (Julien 1978:229–300).

The Moroccan population was shocked and outraged by the massacre. It was the unthinkable horror that could result from the structure of the colonial system, in which French troops held the weapons
and Moroccans were left defenseless in their own country, even in the
case of entirely unwarranted attack. Muhammad V visited the site of
the massacre, then boarded the night train for Tanja, his son Mawlay
Hasan and his daughter Lala 'A'isha beside him. Through the long
night, the ruler decided upon his course of action.

In Tanja he delivered the speech, but omitted the final phrase of
French homage that the colonial writers had inserted and that praised
"the French in particular, whose love for liberty leads the country
towards prosperity and progress" (Julien 1978:200). Muhammad V
concluded instead with a phrase of homage not for the French, but
for the Arab League that had been established a year before. He reaffirmed Morocco's distinctive political and cultural identity that rested
with Islam and affirmed Morocco's intrinsic unity with the rest of the
Arab world.

The substitution might have gone largely unnoticed, except that
the French had already distributed copies of the speech to the press,
with particular emphasis upon the last pro-French line. Hence the
quiet omission became a public act of defiance accomplished with
dignity in the presence of numerous foreign correspondents, in attendance because of the international status of Tanja.

The speech had its impact. The French were incensed and the battle
was begun between the legitimate ruler and the French holders of
pragmatic power. Unlike the organizationally intense Bourguiba, who
crisscrossed the Tunisian countryside physically mobilizing the population to opposition, Muhammad V, dignified and already central,

ground the Protectorate to a halt by withdrawing from action—refusing to sign all rulings that the French put before him, rulings that legally demanded his signature in order to be put into effect, because of Morocco's legal status as a Protectorate. The French cajoled, pleaded, and threatened. At one point, Muhammad V briefly capitulated, but then readopted his stance of noncompliance and thereafter never wavered from it. He turned routine political life into a ritual drama of opposition, and the facade of the French Protectorate came crumbling down. While claiming to be in Morocco to support Morocco's political institutions, including its sharifi caliphate, the French had steadily pursued their own aims, a policy masked by the sharifi ruler's signing of the French-instituted dahirs. When the sharifi monarch refused to sign, the Protectorate, with its shadow government that held power but not legitimacy, was shown for what it was.

France found itself faced with an enormous dilemma. By the internationally recognized laws of the Protectorate, France could not implement actions without the sharifi ruler's signature. Yet he would not sign. Senior French officials pursued a variety of ill-fated strategies, then finally, in a secret meeting, decided to replace the sharifi ruler. As they saw it, they had put Muhammad V on the throne and now they would replace him (see Julien 1978:200 and Auriol 1971:7:372–383).

Great Sacrifice On the afternoon of August 20, 1953 (A.H. 1372), French soldiers burst into the king's palace, seized the reigning Prince of the Faithful and his two sons, and whisked them into waiting vehicles without even allowing the dignified monarch to change out of his pajamas (he had been resting when they came) or to say goodbye to his daughters. They violently pushed the son who was to be the future king, Mawlay Hasan, into the waiting car, which then sped to a plane that carried the king and sons into forced exile, first to Corsica and then to Madagascar. The French had seized and exiled Muhammad V, but in a final touch of independence, he refused to make it legal. He would not sign the abdication papers the French put before him.

In the place of the enormously legitimate Muhammad V, the French put on the throne an elderly and incompetent patrilineal uncle, Mawlay 'Arafa, who signed everything the French put before him, including, at one point, a menu.

Deposing Muhammad V was a serious miscalculation. The French finally understood the power of the caliphal position but mistakenly thought they could bring that power under control by replacing the occupant, not realizing that by this point in history, Muhammad V and the sharifi caliphate had fused and the Moroccan population would accept no other.

While the exile itself was a serious miscalculation, the French choice of timing makes it one of the most inept in colonial history. The French cast out Muhammad's blood descendant who ruled the Moroccan throne on the eve of the Great Sacrifice, preventing the legitimate Prince of the Faithful from sacrificing a ram on the nation's behalf. They exiled the king when, more than at any other time, Morocco's collective fate rested in his hands.

Through the choice of timing, the French handed to a population already adept at turning history into drama the stage and script for immediate and irreversible anticolonial revolt. They made inevitable the Moroccan interpretation that the French were trying to sacrifice the legitimate Muhammad V despite God's call that he be spared. The French were taking the knife to this Isma'il's throat, and they were not Muslim, and they were not listening to God's command. The Moroccan population—and in their understanding, God himself—would have nothing to do with it. The French cardinal de Retz summarized the impact: "The exile of the sultan was one of those capital mistakes after which one can do nothing that is wise" (Julien 1978:317).

France expected a strong organizational response to the move, and had a quarter of a million French troops on Moroccan soil, ready for action. Again France miscalculated. Instead of a violent military response, the population systematically withdrew into inaction. On the night of the exile, many Moroccans spilled into the streets with quiet dignity, gazed at the moon in silence, and saw there the face of Muhammad V. I have heard men tell of the event with tears in their eyes. For them, the interpretation became reality. The French were attempting to sacrifice Muhammad V and the cosmos itself echoed the sorrow. On the next day, on the morning when the whole of the Muslim world was performing the sacrifice, Moroccans throughout the countryside refused to slay a ram until the rightful Prince of the Faithful was returned to the land.

Given the lack of violent military response, the French thought they had things under control, but as Julien notes in an astute aside, "the silence of the people was a lesson to the resident [general], but he did not understand it" (Julien 1978:317).

As the days and months passed, there were scattered acts of Moroccan violence aimed at the French, but for the most part, the Moroccan reaction was to withdraw from action, to refuse to live life normally until the rightful ruler was returned. (In contrast to Algeria, in Morocco most of the indigenous violence that took place was aimed at Moroccans who failed to comply with the collective withdrawal.) Moroccans boycotted life. They closed their shops. They stopped smoking, reducing the Protectorate income from the tobacco concession by 80 percent. They stopped praying—that is, they refused to enter their mosques and recite their prayers until they could be uttered in the name of the rightful caliph, Muhammad V. Everyday life itself became a ritual drama of resistance. Moroccans would not resume life as normal until the true caliph was returned.

With the exile, the French ensured a quick end to the colonial era. Compromise was no longer possible. The population had turned against them, and Morocco's boycott style of resistance proved effective. The French found themselves in the implausible position of imprisoning people for not opening their shops, for not smoking, for not saying their Muslim prayers.

Beleagured by its colonies—France had lost Vietnam in 1954 and was fighting for its colonial life in Tunisia and Algeria—France gave up. On November 17, 1955 (A.H. 1376), amid great jubilation, Muhammad V returned to his homeland: his first words called upon God to bless Morocco and its people. Legal preparations for severance began, and, on March 2, 1956 (A.H. 1376), Morocco became the first Maghribi country to win formal independence from France. The first country to be attacked when Europe came into its age of domination (in 1415, A.H. 817/18), Morocco had been the last Maghribi country colonized (in 1912, A.H. 1330/31), and now was the first freed from the colonial bond. Muhammad V, the Prince of the Faithful, stepped back onto the Moroccan throne.

17

body and soul

It gave us three other treasures: memory, recognition, and victory over the annihilation of the past. No success is sweeter than this!

—*A tale of Baghdad*

For centuries, Europe dominated the world. Yet Morocco's spirit and definition remained intact through the prism of its monarchy and its sacred performances. Western scholars have tended to privilege Europe's domination—and interpretation—of history in a flagrant denial of other people's participation, past and present. A reexamination of the Moroccan material calls the Western-centered approach into account. For hundreds of years Europe controlled the practical structures of world power, yet Morocco maintained its historical vision in other dimensions, particularly in Islamic rituals in which Moroccans reminded themselves of the truth of the universe, the truth of male and female definitions, and the truth of their own political order. The ritual prism has so focused the imagination of most Moroccans that they have never long averted their eyes.

historical conclusion: cultural wealth

When Muhammad V stepped back onto the throne, the soul and body of the Moroccan nation was reunited. Back at the center of the political apparatus was the male upon whom earth's potent processes converged—sexual passion, sexual intercourse, birth and death. Back at political center was the conduit through which the universe's power was conveyed—truth's light, creation's blood, and eternal hope. Returned was the blood-descendant prince, the enduring representation of self, the circumscriber of Islam, the nation, and the intimate dimensions of personhood. Back on the throne was the blood-descendant king who during the colonial siege became the body politic—the crystallization of national self who reminded the population of itself, of its distinctive identity, of its ability to change the world, and, in the end, of its ability to transcend the world's limitations. With independence, the Prince of the Faithful with his burgeoning wealth of cultural credit took charge of the pragmatic structure, the ruling apparatus of the nation-state.[1]

Muhammad V and the Moroccan population set about the task of nation building, and did it well. Much practical good resulted from the unification of the age-old system of legitimate political authority with a new-found apparatus of political rule. For centuries, the monarchy had been replete with meaning but weak in apparatus; the French colonial government had been replete with apparatus but weak in meaning. Postcolonial Morocco combined them. Most postcolonial nations have one or the other, meaning or apparatus. Morocco had both, and greatly benefited from their union.

Morocco does not have the feel of (and in many ways is not) a Third World nation. The national structure does not always work at the speed one might like, but it works—no small accomplishment. Roads are paved, mail delivered, a full range of the world's products sold. Starvation is no more present than in the United States, and perhaps less.

Morocco not only survives, it thrives. The arts flourish, the intellect soars, commerce expands. Painters, poets, novelists, and commercialists are in abundance and produce remarkable combinations of old and new, past and future, of what is particularly Moroccan and what is quintessentially human. Together the Moroccan monarchy and its performances endowed postcolonial Morocco with deep and abiding good.

national identity

Moroccans possess a profound conviction of their own national identity and purpose. Many twentieth-century states are arbitrary colonial creations; Morocco is not. Hence it has not had to devote time and energy to the task of forging a national identity among people who have no intrinsic reason to see themselves as one, as has occurred elsewhere, often at considerable cost—as in Biafran resistance to Nigeria, Sikh resistance to India, Tamil opposition to Sri Lanka, and the Kurdish rebellion against Iran, Iraq, and Turkey.

stable political order

The combination of monarchical focus and ritual forum has endowed Morocco with stability unusual outside the First World. Morocco has had no major turnovers of power. Whatever merits and deficits the political system possesses, it has been stable, and many of its postcolonial achievements have been impressive: in education, transportation, mass communication, housing, land reforms, and agricultural renewal. Some observers argue that Morocco shows the greatest popular strength and the least government suppression in the development of trade unions and political parties of any North African state. Some economists argue that, among debtor nations, Morocco is one of the few making decisive moves to resolution.

strength of past, national ego, and openness to others

The sharifi monarchy and the sacred performances provide Moroccans with a rich awareness of their formidable past. For over a thousand years, Africa, the Middle East, and Europe have met in Morocco. Nations are like individuals in that a strong sense of ego can result in a relative openness to change and renewal—to creative conflations of past, present, and future. In Morocco this has been the case. The central position and the central performances secure Morocco's distinctive sense of self. With its foundation firm, Morocco freely borrows what it finds useful from elsewhere, without ever calling its own identity into doubt.

ruler's symbolic production

The wealth of Morocco's political culture—its monarchical center and its ritual expression—helps keep xenophobia at bay. Xenophobia is not much prevalent in Morocco, though it is alive and well in other North African and the Middle Eastern countries, especially in those that indiscriminately adopted Western models at the expense of their own selfhood during the 1960s and 1970s (A.H. 1380s and 1390s). The leadership of these countries experienced widescale popular disenchantment when the First World models did not bring First World economic and political power, as the cases of Iran, Egypt, and Tunisia demonstrate.

In the countries where Western enchantment so reigned that the elite denied the essence of their national self, the embrace of the West typically created a cultural chasm. The elite opted for the Western models and benefitted from them. The masses—both for reasons of exclusion and reasons of choice—tended to remain loyal to systems of meaning built in the past, meaning that transformed the flow of days from simply flow and days into rites of passage. In that situation, opposition leaders had at their disposal a profound system of meaning that mobilized the masses in union with each other and in opposition to those in power. An elite that consistently separates itself from what is meaningful at the local and individual level is engaging in suicide unless it can consistently deliver on utilitarian fronts. Iran has already had its revolution of this sort, and popular political opposition based on this kind of division is widespread in Tunisia and Egypt.

Morocco did not make that mistake. It took from others, but never at the expense of the great stores of meaning that had been built in the past. Many Moroccan men wear Western suits but they still don the white robes of the Great Sacrifice. They drink wine but they do not forget how to say God's name. The king appears in French-tailored clothes and talks of computers, parliamentary elections, and women's rights while resting his fundamental legitimacy in Islam, his descent from the Prophet Muhammad and his occupancy of the position established upon Muhammad's death—the Islamic caliphate. The depth of Morocco's Islamic legacy and the breadth of diversity it can encompass while essentials remain the same—*mutatis mutandis*—allow new practices and new forms of meaning to be incorporated without severance from the richness of the old. Having denied neither Islam nor its past, Morocco and its central ruler do not have to scurry to "refind" them in an age in which Islam has been renewed as a center of political identity.

In Morocco what one sees with the international shift to cultural "roots" is a slight shift in emphasis. The king makes more public appearances in white robes and fewer in Western suits. He quotes the Qur'an more and the *Magna Carta* less. He talks of Muhammad and

Ibrahim more than of Shakespeare or Kant, yet Morocco still rests its national identity in cultural breadth, not narrowness—in an expansive Islam rather than in rigid dogmas.

The continuity in Islamic symbols and ritual practices and the extent to which the central ruler dominates them are reasons why in Morocco politically oppositional "fundamentalist" Islam has not caught fire.[2] Islamic extremists in Morocco are few. They do not have readily available a set of potent popular practices and symbols that ally them with the masses and separate them from the ruler, because the ruler never made the mistake of making that divide. One can effectively argue that the shah of Iran handed popular Islam to the opposition, and that that was stupid. In Morocco, in contrast, the king not only remains linked to Islam but he is a means of Islam's popular reproduction, a regenerator of Muslim symbols and practices. The king gathers Islamic legitimacy around himself; he does not sever himself from it.

international dialogue

There is real strength in the national ego of Moroccans. In part it comes from Morocco's great past continually brought to the present; in part it comes from the international role that the monarch plays in the here and now. Much of political discourse in the twentieth century takes place in an arena where international powerholders are the parties of dialogue. Whether or not individuals feel that they are a part of that dialogue depends in part on whether or not they identify with their political representative, and whether or not that political representative is perceived as playing an important international role. In Morocco, the identification with the political ruler is intense, and his international role is perceived to be crucial, a perception aided by Moroccan press, television, and radio. Hence the pride that many Moroccans experienced when the king traveled to England to greet and be greeted with honor by Queen Elizabeth; when he invited the Catholic pope to Morocco and received him, a novel historical event in which the Islamic Prince of the Faithful embraced the head of the Catholic Church; when Morocco's king called the Arab Conference of Fas II and made important headway on the question of Palestine; when he asked Israel's Peres to fly to Morocco, and Peres did, and discussions took place; and when the monarch called an emergency meeting of all the heads of state of the Islamic world after an outbreak of Shi'i-incited violence during the Makkan pilgrimage of 1987 (A.H. 1407). The monarch's international role helps revitalize his connections to his people, for in addition to everything else, the blood-descendant monarch provides Moroccans with a link to world power, enabling them to feel a part of the give-and-take of world exchange, an important perception for individual psychological health in the late twentieth century.

The international role the king plays depends in part on the position's historic credibility. It lies far beyond that warranted by present-day practical logistics. Morocco has 25 million people and no dramatic wealth in an Islamic world of 900 million people where oil wealth has accrued to some Muslim nations in trillions of dollars. Yet the cultural resources add up: Morocco's monarchy lays effective claim to the last Islamic caliphate the world knows, it has been in power for twelve hundred years, the current dynasty has reigned for over three hundred years, and the Prophet's blood flows in its veins. These foundations bring the Moroccan monarchy a degree of cultural legitimacy abroad as well as at home. No other ruler of a major nation in the Islamic world possesses the same store of credit. Other forms of ruler and ruled are new, not extending back beyond this century. That includes Jordan's Hashimi Kingdom and Saudia Arabia's House of Sa'ud, both twentieth-century creations in which Great Britain played a major role. Although people in other Muslim countries typically do not recognize Morocco's king as *the* legitimate Prince of the Faithful, many recognize him as *a* legitimate Prince of the Faithful, and bestow on him a degree of honor for the position he holds.

increased legitimacy

The monarchy's legitimacy has increased during the 1980s (A.H. 1400s). Several factors are at base. Internationally the decade has been a time of disenchantment with the superpowers, an overarching shift towards moderate rulers, local alternatives, and indigenous styles of rule. The Moroccan monarchy was well placed to take advantage of these shifts. It is a middle-of-the-road system that adopts templates and practices from the West, but not at the expense of its own heritage. It never severed itself from indigenous meaning. The monarchy's link to the past and to the heart of Islam—continually reaffirmed in ritual—shields the ruler from much critique. The Saharan war also has contributed to monarchical support.[3] Moroccans see themselves in a righteous struggle for the return of their land. That war has been especially effective in rallying former leftist critics to the monarch's side.

In addition, the 1980s have been a time of visible development of the symbols of popular democratic institutions. The national parliament is now housed in magnificent chambers in the capital city. Pomp and circumstance open each session. Front stage center is the sharifi king in shimmering white robes speaking wise Arabic words. All the parliamentarians are gathered. All are male. All are in robes of the Great Sacrifice. The tasks the parliament handles are not yet extensive, but the apparatus is in place and extends throughout the countryside. Popular democracy is being dramatically performed at the capital city, even though the domain over which parliament exercises power is not yet large. In classic Moroccan style, first comes the ritual form; what should follow is substantive practice. In its democracy as well as its monarchy, sacred performance comes first.

bureaucratic woe

Yet, all is not well. The postcolonial unification of the indigenous sources of political legitimacy—monarchy and ritual—with the colonial apparatus of power has its underside. The apparatus itself was built by the French to compensate for lack of legitimacy. It is an overbearing, overcentralized, gargantuan structure instituted to deflect, absorb, and obfuscate local initiative, which the colonialist could not trust since he, the occupier, was not legitimate. The apparatus includes a highly trained professional army, an extensive information-gathering network, an administration that brings the whole of the countryside into its grasp, and a highly centralized structure of economic decision making, communication, and transportation. With independence, a top-heavy apparatus that had been built to operate in the absence of political legitimacy came into the hands of a top-heavy center of legitimacy that had been built to compensate for its lack of apparatus.

The fusion was powerful. The legitimate monarch now had at his disposal a burgeoning practical arsenal that allowed him to match the white-robed arm of legitimate rule with the military-clad arm of coercive reach. With lightning-like speed the institutions of the central government penetrated the countryside. Within a few years, every nook and cranny of Morocco was brought into the central apparatus' hold; penetration was wide and deep.

The good engendered cannot be denied. Nation-states need unifying organizational structures, lines of communication and implementation along which policy, information, and power flow. A unified administrative hierarchy is a prerequisite of the nation-state functioning in the late twentieth century. The administrative hierarchy brought Morocco not only political communication, implementation and control, but also doctors, phones, schools, electricity, and television. It also took from throughout the countryside the nation's brightest youth and gave them scholarships that allowed them to be educated in the finest universities in the world.

Yet, the conjuncture has a potentially lethal side also: the legitimacy of the monarchy has insulated the organizational structure from the consequences of the apparatus' dysfunctioning. The problem is a familiar one, endemic to large-scale bureaucracies in the twentieth century (Merton 1940). Meant to be an organizational form for speedily accomplishing goal-oriented tasks, bureaucracies often end up reproducing their own internal structure rather than getting things done—producing more offices, more paperwork, more links. This is too often the case in Morocco and is the consequence of passing the governance of the body politic from the hands of rulers and ruled to the hands of those who man small offices in dimly lit corridors in a myriad of office buildings in a plethora of small streets throughout the land.

The problem of bureaucratic quagmire is everywhere with us—in the First World as well as in all the other worlds. Yet the problems of bureaucratic bog are particularly damaging in former colonies, where bureaucracy was often developed with a degree of elaboration and red tape far beyond the norm in order to circumvent the possibilities of vitality, innovation, and creativity at the local levels. It is not happenstance that in Morocco, as in so many former colonies, every task has to be done in ten different offices with ten different signatures and ten different stamps. Bureaucratic gauntlet-running with its associated organizational exhaustion was, and is, a form of control that has reached frightening proportions. It not only slows the accomplishment of crucial tasks, it actively blocks their way. The French-instituted bureaucracy may well be the colonial era's most damning legacy.

The problems with which Morocco must deal are momentous, and overpopulation lies at the center. Morocco has reaped the "benefits" of First World medical care without the benefit of global wealth. Like much of the world, Morocco produces many more people than its economy can possibly absorb.

While it is true that the monarchy's legitimacy has increased during the 1980s (A.H. 1400s), at a deeper level a crisis brews, embedded in overpopulation and an archaic bureaucracy that bars solutions. The debilitatingly involuted bureaucracy is run by senior men bent on soliciting submission from junior males and marginalizing females. The flashpoint at present lies in the highly educated and unemployed youth who haunt Morocco's streets and coffee shops and have nothing—absolutely nothing—to do. Statistics for the most part are ungathered and unreliable. Yet some who are placed to know use the figure of at least 40 percent overall male unemployment in the 18-to-35-year-old range. It may be significantly more. They also estimate—with more precision—that now, each year, only 25 percent of the educated youth that come on the job market obtain employment that uses the skills for which they were trained, leaving the other 75 percent unemployed or underemployed.

The problem of youth unemployment is exacerbated in that it is not simply the children of the lower and middle classes who find themselves without jobs, but also the children of the elite, many of whom have attended the world's best universities, have enormous drive, talent, and high aims, and are accustomed to power. Most were educated overseas and have come back to invest in their country's future. Many have found no place in it. They sit and think and talk to each other about possible solutions. They—the educated unemployed—are the potential Achilles' heel in the Moroccan body politic that could bring an otherwise highly legitimate system crashing down. The overarching importance of the unemployment crisis is a fact that some at the center, including the monarch himself, seem to grasp, but it is one that will take remarkable ingenuity and decisive action to address.

At present, Morocco has a highly legitimate overarching political system centered on the monarchy that includes a bureaucratic morass that no longer serves either monarch or populace, and is manned by senior males who have inappropriately applied patriarchial and patrilineal culture to new domains of activity, with damaging consequences for everyone.

Legitimacy provides insulation from short-term accountability, not isolation from it, and one wonders how long the population will continue to blame the practical problems that face Morocco upon those who surround the king, and not upon the king himself. Thus far, this displaced critique continues, even when it comes from the unemployed educated youth. The sharifi parasol continues to shield the king from most of the negative exposure, and yet the negative exposure grows. The remarkable survival of the Moroccan monarchy has rested upon its ability to change when the situation demanded. The situation demands. Reality must be pragmatically constructed as well as ritually performed. That is the task at hand. If addressed, Morocco's monarchy may well be around to celebrate its thirteen hundredth anniversary in 2089—but neither you nor I will be there to see it.

ritual conclusion: prism in the present

The demands of intellectual distillation are such that anthropologists often take a single-focused approach to collective phenomena and have often treated ritual as symbolic communication only—conflating ritual with symbols and culture with "ideology" to the exclusion of practice. But ritual and culture are more than that, and the overemphasis on abstract symboling has drawn our attention too quickly away from the palpable substances and physical actions that are essential to the symboling itself. An experience-oriented perspective needs to be adopted, for ritual is lived experience, not simply abstract commentary on experience.

inscription on body and mind

Ritual's power to create reality rests on its ability to fuse physical substance, palpable action, and imaginative abstraction. Great performances unite body and mind in holistic experiences of beauty and thematic integrity. Every dimension reconstitutes every other. In undergirding the sharifi caliphate, Moroccan rituals combine basic human dilemmas, physical substances, and palpable actions with abstract conceptual symbols. Blood, black circles, burning candles, and knives are fused with intercourse, childbirth, and death to build a stunningly powerful conceptual framework that is kinesthetically and imaginatively secure—a foundation that reinforces the sharifi monarchy by having the physical world read back the veracity of the cultural abstractions, and the cultural abstractions renew the veracity of the physical world.

basic issues: truth, individuals, and durability

The issues that underlie the three Moroccan rituals are humanity's most poignant. The Prophet's Birthday concerns the truth of the universe. Where does truth lie? How can humans connect with it? First marriage addresses the lives of individuals on earth. What are human beings? What are the two sexes? Is the universe's truth mindful of them? What is the male-female connection to be? How should it be organized so that humans beneficently reproduce themselves on earth? The Great Sacrifice explores the connections between the two dilemmas. Is there a way that individuals can step outside the limitations of their earthly existence and connect with what is durable in the universe and achieve birth into transcendence, thereby forever breaking death's bonds and connecting with everlasting truth?

No matter what the culture, no matter what the creed, all human beings know these yearnings: for a cosmos driven by truth and light, one with which humans can connect; for affirmation of one's life on earth; for connection with another, connection that is psychological as well as sexual, connection of soul as well as substance; for the reproduction of oneself through the physical processes of this world, through progeny; and finally, the ultimate longing—the deep-seated desire to leap into transcendence.

The Prophet's Birthday, the rite of marriage, and the Great Sacrifice affirm that the dilemmas can be solved in humanity's favor. Truth can be brought to earth. Men of faith, by participating in sacrifice, can forge the ultimate connection through which individuals merge into everlasting truth and have eternal life.

Of all men, the blood-descendant king is central. On the Prophet's Birthday, he refracts truth's light and sheds it all around. In the rite of marriage he serves as guide to proper earthly creation and proper sexual relationships, and finally, in the Great Sacrifice, he serves as conduit to the uncreated, eternal divine, facilitating the passage of individuals on earth and the community as a whole toward transcendence. All these things are bound to the sharifi prince. That binding makes it a hard spell to break, and from many perspectives, who would want to?

basic substance: blood

The legitimacy of the blood-linked monarchy is written in the most basic substance of existence, in red blood flowing on ground and bed—the blood of the sacrificial ram and the blood of the deflowered bride. The establishment of a blood-legitimated monarchy stimulated the development of multiple blood-centered rituals. Some are canonical, like Ibrahim's sacrifice, and some hover at the edge of or spill over into heresy, like the practices of the Hamadsha, who cut their heads to make themselves sane, and of the women of Sala (Salé), who soak up blood spilled in car accidents to use in magical potions to bond their husbands to them. But *all* such rituals physically reinforce the power of blood in the world, a reinforcement crucial to the substratum of the monarchy's legitimacy.

basic colors: black, white and red

Basic color categories further renew Morocco's sharifi caliphate. As noted in chapter 2, Berlin and Kay (1969) have found that when languages linguistically recognize only three basic color categories, they are the three categories represented by focal white, black, and red. It is easy to see why they are most basic. In color terms, nothing is more central to human experience than the dark of night and the white of light. When the multicolored day ends, it passes into life's basics, earth's black shadows and the moon's white light that sheds its luminescence on earth's pure substances—on water, snow, mountaintops, minarets, and human eyes. Muslims revere the moon. The Islamic calendar is reckoned by it; the sighting of the new moon ends Ramadan's fasting and begins each of the year's months. The Prophet drank from the moon, and Muhammad V's face appeared—to many of his grieving people—in it. Many North Africans look forward to night with its soft and gentle shades of black that rest the eyes from the glare of the day. The sun shines hard on the Sahara and can bring death. The night brings respite and is kind. To the basics of black and white, humanity adds the color that most represents itself, the red of lifeblood, the red in which we all are born.

These three colors, black, white, and red, underlie sharifi rituals. These basic colors are used to encode the validity of the monarchy on the perceptual fabric of human existence. In ritual, the population experiences the white-robed monarch shimmering with white light, leading his population from darkness to light; the white-robed monarch spilling red blood from a pure white ram with thick black rings around its eyes; the white-robed monarch spilling red blood from the pure bride clothed in white with thick black kohl around her eyes.

Power comes from being part of the basic structures of the cosmos, and ritual colors lie at the basic level. Despite the opinion of some anthropologists, colors matter beyond their contribution to ritual formality. They are not always arbitrary. I suggest that the use of the most basic color categories brings with it the popular experience of basics, and the great orienting rituals of Morocco make striking use of that characteristic. An unconscious physical response is involved so that the body—by means of brain processes that code physical perceptions—recognizes the three colors *as* basic. To the degree that rituals effectively wed central cultural assumptions to the basic colors of existence, they inscribe those cultural assumptions on the perceptual structure of the human brain. Moroccan rituals successfully insert the sharifi caliphate into the three basic color categories, so that in a subtle but powerful way its validity is substantiated and renewed through the presentation of black, white, and red—painted on the environment, embedded in the body, written in the mind.

basic kinesthetic experiences: sexual intercourse

The three rituals draw to them the basic actions, the basic kinesthetic experiences of mortal existence. They especially utilize the basic template of sexual intercourse.

Sexual intercourse is not simply a physical drive. It is a deep psychological need for complete and worthy connection, and for understanding the truth that that connection brings. Sexual intercourse goes far beyond the exchange of substance and physiological release. It concerns the exchange of souls. It can be a meeting of minds and hearts as well as bodies, one that reaffirms the self in connecting with another. Intercourse can bring immediate sexual gratification which is pleasurable, but that is the least permanent of its boons. It is also a moment of wholeness, completion, and connection in a much-torn life—a stay against the world's madness and random sorrow.

Sexuality, that powerful drive that lies at the base of so much of human existence, lies at the base of all three Moroccan rituals. The Prophet's Birthday metaphorically calls to body and mind the sexual act and establishes a hierarchy of proper connections of mortal to mortal, and mortal to God. Marriage physically encodes people's understandings of the sexual act, how it is to be properly done, and what it is for. Sacrifice metaphorically and metaphysically enacts sexual intercourse and uses its connective power to fuse man to God, so immortality is gained. Each of the sacred performances brings the power of sexual intercourse to it and uses that potency to undergird the culture's vision of the world.

The Great Sacrifice also draws to it childbirth and death. Childbirth is metaphorically made present. Death actually occurs. In sacrifice, the male heads of households dress in white robes, take a knife, and break open the thin white skin of the still ram's neck so that the lifeblood can flow and the hope of transcendent life can be gained. The action vividly recalls the male head of household dressed in the same white robes using his phallus to break open the thin white membrane of the still bride's vagina, so that the lifeblood can flow and the hope of life on earth be gained. Through metaphorical similarity, the actions fuse into one. The results are markedly similar. As previously noted, the white ram as it lies dying vividly evokes the image of the newborn. Both are covered with white—the white coat of the ram, the white vernix of the newborn child. Both are in the fetal position. Both are quivering beings lying in pools of blood. Both are hopes for life—especially, for Muslims, the male ram and the male child.

Knife sacrifice augments its power by pulling the actions of intercourse and childbirth to it. Sacrifice constructs a form of death that is convincing as a pathway to eternal life by utilizing the basic action schemata that bring about life on earth. On the level of basic kinesthetic experiences, knife sacrifice is forceful because it evokes such deeply stored templates of human being.

Moroccan rituals not only play upon the most basic experiences of life—birth, intercourse, and death—but systematically combine them with the physical attributes of the male form—a single, erect figure in white—to create a powerful basic level experience that physically confirms the male's dominance of these processes. Verticality is made male. At the level of felt bodily experience as well as at the level of creative imagination, the ritual confirms that males engage in the decisive actions upon which the fate of the whole depends. Their actions cause pain and spill blood, but they also bring life, thereby verifying the male's legitimate dominance of coercive power, public decision making, and the human quest for transcendence. The rituals embed that legitimation in physical postures, basic actions, and the symboling process. The Moroccan rituals culminate in demonstrating that of all males, it is the sharifi Prince of the Faithful who matters most. For it is he who takes the pointed object (knife or phallus) and breaks open the white tissue (neck or hymen) so that the lifeblood can flow and life can occur: life on earth and life in the everafter.

basic level categories: ruler and man

In combination, basic level substance, basic colors, and basic kinesthetic experiences produce the basic level category upon which the sharifi caliphate depends—the category of "ruler," which is a conduit to the universal faith and a link to the definition of self.

The ceremony of the Prophet's Birthday develops the religious undergirdings of the category of ruler by surrounding the king with candles and torches, establishing the sharifi caliphate in the mind's eye as the source of truth's light. Ibrahim's sacrifice and the ritual of first marriage show the Prince of the Faithful to be the archetypal man who stands before the population in pure white robes spilling the blood of ram and bride so that regeneration may occur. The image is riveting. He is the "white one" who, through guided pain and violence, brings hope. What is due him is honor and obedience, and the modeling of one's own behavior on his in daily life.

Morocco's category of ruler is directly linked to the central foundations of Islam (the caliphate) as well as to the essential foundations of self, a fusion that powerfully undergirds the ruler's legitimacy. So intertwined are the two definitions—Muslim ruler and Muslim man—that it becomes hard for a man to think himself, define himself, and gauge his achievement of manliness except in reference to the sharifi king. The legitimacy of Morocco's monarchy does not rest on an abstract cluster of criteria that categorically distinguishes the ruler from all other men (such as divine right, leadership in battle, eldest son of previous ruler, elected leader of an administrative body), but rather depends on the ruler being like every other man only more exemplary, the best-of-category representative. The linchpin of the Moroccan system is that the position of king is written on every man's definition of self—but no woman's—so that every man carries it with him as a part of his identity (for some more, some less, but for every man a part), and to lose the form of rule would be in part to lose himself. Few people intentionally destroy the foundations upon which their own identity rests.

This is a powerful definition of ruler because its net of legitimacy spreads so wide and deep—extending to the structures of the cosmos, the basic foundations of individual identity, the basic processes of human life. The ruler can have visible faults and yet still be perceived as the collective link to Islam and the best of men overall. The definitional intermingling of ruler and Islam and ruler and man gives the ruler an enormous store of credit that he can use to rally the population to great sacrifice if he so wills. That sacrifice can be made for the common good: to resist the West, to innoculate children, to build canals. It can also cover enormous errors, for accountability is so diffuse. As currently constructed, the sharifi parasol displaces most criticism away from the king; it falls on those standing near him, not on the king himself. Morocco is a stellar example of a political system that can ride out short-term failures, rising high above them since more basic understandings and loyalties are at its base. For many Moroccans, the definition of rulership is so closely tied to the popular experience of Islamic faith, nation, and self that to move away from the position would not simply be an act of political opposition; it would be a form of apostasy, an act of self-destruction—and the position endures.

King Hasan II continues to express the monarchy's legitimacy in ritual, reenacting ancient performances, inventing new ones. Like the Sa'di al-Mansur, he has a keen sense of timing, aesthetics, and overarching purpose. The Prophet's Birthday, the rite of first marriage, and the Great Sacrifice are still performed and remain compelling. For the Prophet's Birthday, the king often travels to the millennium-old mosque-university of al-Qarawiyin. He sits in a great room, surrounded by holy men and light. He is dressed in white robes, holds prayer beads in his right hand, and turns the pages of the holy Qur'an and sings softly its words. The men around him also sing. They chant of faith and glory and of honor for the reigning prince, Muhammad's descendant still on the throne. The men come from far and wide to give him laud.

Marriage ceremonies continue to be performed and to intimately link monarch and populace. The king continues to give the nation's children their coming of age and to bring them hope for their own reproduction on earth.

Most important, each year at the Great Sacrifice, the king stands before the nation and sacrifices a ram on their behalf. Through the fallen ram, God sees the people's faith and grants his favor. The ceremony is repeatedly shown on television throughout the day and on the days that follow. The performance simultaneously affirms the equality of all Muslim men before God and the superiority of the reigning prince on the throne. It combines people's deepest longings with simple good times with family and friends.

■　　■　　■

king and attempted coups

These fragments I have shored against my ruin.
—T. S. Eliot,
The Waste Land

The late 1960s and early 1970s (A.H. 1380s and 1390s) witnessed popular critiques of central governments the world over, Morocco included. The expressions and results of the critique are important, for they illustrate the strength of the Moroccan monarchy even when criticism is rife. Ideological critique came mostly from the left, from university-trained intellectuals, whose constructions of reality were informed by leftist socialist models. Yet that critique was never connected to a sufficiently large sector of the Moroccan population to pose a physical threat to the dynasty. For much of this era, the parliament was suspended by royal order. (There have been no suspensions since 1976, A.H. 1396.)

The practical threat to the monarchy came from the right, from military generals, who had the organizational structure to back up ideas of opposition. Top military leaders staged two attempted coups against King Hasan II, one in 1971 (A.H. 1391) and one in 1972 (A.H. 1392). Neither was successful.[4] In combination they rank among the most remarkable events in the history of coups. In both cases, the rebellion leaders actually had the king in their hands, at gunpoint, but in neither case could the military men bring themselves to deliver the lethal blow, and in their uncertainty the king regained his footing and overturned the coups from within. I suggest that the inability of the coup leaders to aim squarely and shoot firmly when the king was in their grasp has to do with the enormous legitimacy that the position holds, legitimacy that the ritual prism constantly refracts. Their inability to slay the prince illustrates the power of the human body to encode cultural perceptions and for those perceptions to affect history.

The 1971 coup attempt took place on the king's birthday at his Sukhayrat (Skhirat) palace, where Western diplomats, women, and alcohol were in abundance. (This was in the days before Hasan II's playboy image was modified.) While the coup was organized by top army generals, large numbers of the rank and file troops apparently did not know precisely what was happening. They had been involved in a "routine maneuver" on the Ribat–Dar al-Bayda' road. When the troops passed by the king's palace, the military leaders turned them into the royal grounds, staged a revolt, and captured the king and his guests. While some of the troops were truly oppositional, others were simply following the orders of the higher ups, in the acceptable style of junior males' absolute submission to senior authority.

There was considerable violence. Several diplomats and high-level officials were killed, but the king himself went unharmed. Though we will never know exactly what happened, since those involved were killed immediately after the coup failed, it appears that the king was protected in the early hours of the most intense violence by being hidden away in a more distant part of the palace by one of the top organizers of the coup, one of the top military generals himself.

The generals were less than clear about what they wanted and how they planned to get it. In a style reminiscent of French colonial authorities, they apparently hoped that the king would hand them the practical reigns of power and keep for himself the "symbols." They tried to force Hasan II to sign papers to that effect, but he would not sign, not even under duress, and, as the hours wore on, the generals were not sure what to do.

After the violence had subsided and while the coup leaders tried to reformulate their plans, the king was taken to the large ballroom where most of the birthday guests were being held. After a short while, a rifle-wielding young soldier marched into the room, came over to the king, and sharply demanded that he follow. The king—certain that the time for his death had come—had no choice and followed the young man down one of the long palace corridors.

Upon turning the far corner, Hasan II was shocked to see the young man fall suddenly to his knees and beg for forgiveness, saying that he had not known what the generals were doing. The king, a remarkably cool man in crisis, asked the young man how many others there were like him, and in that back corridor of the palace with a young soldier before him on his knees, Hasan II organized a countercoup from within, mustering sufficient loyalty from the rank and file troops so that he captured the top generals and put them to death on the spot.

The second coup attempt took place in 1972. It involved the same high drama, but with fewer players. Again high-level military officials instigated the attempt: this time they were from the Air Force. When the king's plane entered Ribat's airspace, it was surrounded by Moroccan F-5 jets. Again, violence occurred: shots were fired but not lethal ones. The F-5s fired near the royal plane or at the peripheries of it, not at center where the king sat—entirely vulnerable in terms of firepower, but not in terms of cultural perception. Again one cannot help but suspect that the gunners themselves, when they had the reigning Prince of the Faithful in their sights, could not bring themselves to fire the lethal shots. No other interpretation makes sense. Again the precise details are obscure because the men involved were killed immediately thereafter, but what is certain is that the king and his plane managed to escape. Hasan II's pilot, under the king's direction, crash landed in a field next to the Ribat–Dar al-Bayda' highway (the same highway upon which the troops had gone marching in the 1971 coup attempt). The king climbed out of the wrecked plane, walked to the road where he waved down a passing truck, and calmly climbed in. He rode back to the capital city and ousted the coup leaders from the few positions they held. The throne was still his.

Most Moroccans were enormously impressed by the trajectory of the two coup attempts. All in all, Moroccans—like most humans—

tend to be a practical lot and, for many, the aborted coups were a concrete verification of the legitimacy of their ruler and their form of rule. A Prince of the Faithful who survives attacks by armies and planes must be taken seriously, and is.

Real practical problems exist in Morocco; some worsen by the day. The attempted coups themselves are testaments that Moroccans can contemplate—at least in the abstract—an overthrow of the sharifi prince. But the abstract contemplations have not been fully realized in practice. It appears that during the aborted coups, when the army privates and air force gunners had the sharifi caliph in their gunsights, more basic perceptions came to dominate. Deep-seated understandings infused all else. Communication took place from body to body that prevented the slaying. What could be contemplated as a mental option could not be carried out as a physical act.

I suspect that what the men saw before them was not simply a flawed man, the political ruler, but rather the powerholder whom the rituals continually present: the last caliph the world knows, the last ruling Prince of the Faithful, the center of Moroccan political identity for over a millennium, the definer of the nation, the definer of man, the great sacrificer who each year slays a ram on the population's behalf, the ruler in whose veins Muhammad's blood still flows, the ruler who is surrounded by truth's light and Qur'anic words. Seeing who was before them, the young men turned away and did not slay their king, but rather shot people and things near him, a physical action that echoes the trajectory of Moroccan political critique.

The king walked away from each attempted coup and back onto the age-old throne. He called emergency meetings of his cabinet and set before them the task of addressing the country's economic and social ills. Then later, in private, with only his closest confidants about, the king prayed deep into the night. The thirty-ninth-generation descendant of the Prophet Muhammad sang out prayers in the name of God the Merciful, the Compassionate and thanked him for the great sparing. And the caliphate endures, and a blood descendant still rules Morocco's throne.

Appendix A. Prophetic Blood Links: Patrilines Close to the Prophet and Political Inheritors

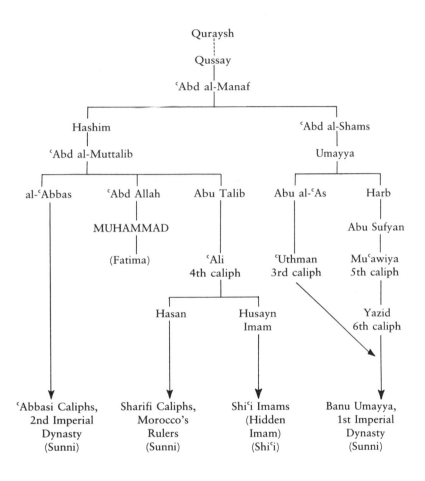

NOTES:

Not all members of the patrilines are depicted.

Fatima is the only woman shown in this patrilineal charter.

The exact patrilineal links between Quraysh and Qussay are unknown.

The first two caliphs of Islam, Abu Bakr and ʿUmar, come from more distant sections of the Quraysh and are not included on this chart.

Many Shiʿi believe that the Hidden Imam went into occultation in 874 (A.H. 260) and will return.

Appendix B. Partial Genealogy of ʿAlawi

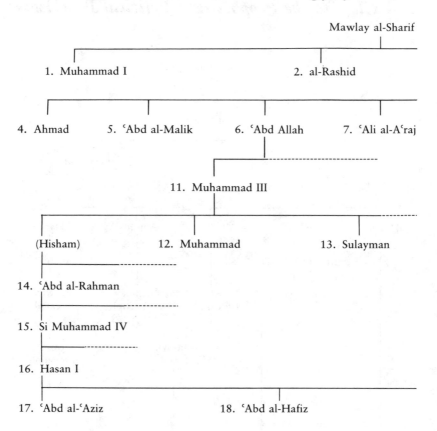

Mawlay al-Sharif

1. Muhammad I   2. al-Rashid

4. Ahmad   5. ʿAbd al-Malik   6. ʿAbd Allah   7. ʿAli al-Aʿraj

11. Muhammad III

(Hisham)   12. Muhammad   13. Sulayman

14. ʿAbd al-Rahman

15. Si Muhammad IV

16. Hasan I

17. ʿAbd al-ʿAziz   18. ʿAbd al-Hafiz

NOTES:

Numbers to the left of names indicate the order of dynastic succession.

- - - - indicates that the ruler had other sons who did not become monarchs.

Vertical connections are shown only for the patrilines that carried on the caliphate. For instance, ruler 12 and ruler 13 both had sons, but they are not indicated because they did not inherit the throne.

Family Showing Dynastic Succession

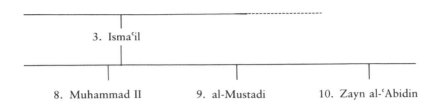

```
                                        |---------------------
        |                               |
        3. Isma'il
        |
  |-----------|------------------|-----------------------|
  8. Muhammad II       9. al-Mustadi        10. Zayn al-'Abidin
```

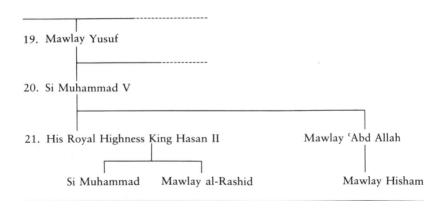

```
  |---------------------
  |        |
  19. Mawlay Yusuf
  |
  |--------|----------------
  |        |
  20. Si Muhammad V
  |
  |-------------------------------------------|
  21. His Royal Highness King Hasan II        Mawlay 'Abd Allah
  |                                           |
  |-------------|                             |
  Si Muhammad   Mawlay al-Rashid              Mawlay Hisham
```

Hisham ibn Muhammad III is shown even though he did not become caliph because his patriline carried on the monarchy; his son, grandson, and great-grandson became the country's rulers. Ruler 13 had many sons, but his nephew, ruler 14, Mawlay 'Abd Rahman, took over the caliphal throne upon his death.

preface

1. Japan's monarchy is older but does not actively rule the country; the reins of practical power are not in its hands.

2. Paul Friedrich made a statement to this effect at the meetings of the American Anthropological Convention, November 1986, in Philadelphia.

3. Important anthropological work has been done on local, regional, and transregional rituals focused upon saints or religious brotherhoods, for example, al-Boudrari (1984), Crapanzano (1973 and 1980), Eickelman (1976), Geertz (1968), Gellner (1969), Hammoudi (1980), Mernissi (1977), and Rabinow (1975).

1. argument

1. Braudel (1973) and Wallerstein (1974, 1979) do not examine the North African side of the 1500s age of transition. When they turn to Islam, they turn to the Ottomans. Yet the Ottoman case, when viewed

from the Ottoman center, is not illustrative of Muslim North Africa and the Middle East. Like the Iberians, the Ottomans came to power in the 1400s and 1500s as an expansionary northern Mediterranean regime. The Ottomans were crucial players in world history, but they do not exemplify the basic processes that characterize the Arab-Muslim heartland in the 600s-to-1350s age of domination and in the 1350s-to-1700s age of transition. That heartland lay to the south and southeast of the Mediterranean, not to its north. For that region, the Moroccan case is more illustrative. Morocco was the only North African country not to be incorporated into the Ottoman Empire.

2. See Domhoff (1974) for the rituals of the power elite, and see chapter 15, note 3 on Catholic communion and Jewish Rosh Hashanah.

2. *prism*

1. See Rutter (1984) and Cook (1984) on the establishment of sexually distinctive patterns of eye contact and spatial segretation.

2. Although avant-garde theater often shares with ritual the celebration of "real-life" experiences, it is not usually repeated in highly stylized form to large portions of the total population over time, a necessity for the systematic informing of collective meaning.

3. *Muhammad*

1. The Muslim calendar is based on lunar rather than solar reckoning. A solar year is approximately eleven days longer than a lunar year, hence *anno Domini* years are longer than *anno Hijrae* years.

2. Dresch (1984, 1986), Dunn (1977), Eickelman (1981:63–155), Lindholm (1982), Rassam (1974), Rosen (1979), and Salzman (1978, 1981) explore issues of patrilineality in the Muslim world.

3. Unless otherwise attributed, all quotations from the Qur'an are from Arthur Arberry's translation, *The Koran Interpreted* (1955).

4. Sacrifice need not have the offering and self-denial connotations that it has in Judaism and Christianity. Sacrifice is a dramatic connection to the divine made through dramatic action, in the Muslim case through the ritualized slaying of an animal that sanctifies it, allowing it to be eaten as well as given away. All animal slayings in the Muslim world are to be turned into sacrifices: the animal must be turned towards Makka, the name of God uttered, and the blood ritually spilled. Unsanctified meat should not be eaten. Yet the Great Sacrifice is different because the death of the ram gains sanctity not only for itself, but also for the humans on behalf of whom it is slain. The ram is a real substitute. It is a blood sacrifice that sanctifies humans, without humans having to die. The sacrificer sometimes delegates the act of slaying to another—a butcher, a servant, or sometimes even a son—yet he remains the authority under-

writing the sacrifice. The other is simply his instrument, his arm. In Morocco most heads of households themselves slay the great ram.

4. death and debate

1. At his farewell pilgrimage to Makka, the Prophet Muhammad gave a moving address which, as Mottahedeh notes, allows for a great diversity in Muslim opinion as to proper political authority (1980:7). According to one source, Muhammad said, "God has given two safeguards to the world: His Book [the Qur'an] and the Sunna [the Example] of His Prophet." According to another source, Muhammad said, "God has given two safeguards to the world: His Book and the family of His Prophet." (1980:7). In combination, Book, Sunna, Prophet, and family supply the undergirdings for the diverse political entities one finds in the Muslim world.

2. See Hodgson (1974a:280–498), Lapidus (1988:67–136), and Saliba's (1985) translation of al-Tabari on the ʿAbbasi High Caliphate. Al-Tabari wrote before the tension between the " 'legitimate' power, as represented by the caliphate, and the 'real' power, as represented by the military" resolved itself into a complementary mode of sharing authority (Saliba 1985:xii). On Islam's expansion as a whole, see Bulliet, *Conversion to Islam in the Medieval Period* (1979), and on the consequences of Islam's expansion into one particular city, see Bulliet *The Patricians of Nishapur* (1972).

5. Islam and potent glory

1. The importance of trans-Saharan trade, especially in gold, is addressed by Abitol (1980), Basha (1976), Bovill (1968), Bulliet (1975), Celerier (1923), Deverdun (1959), Hopkins (1973), Ibn Hawqal (1845 [900s]), al-Idrisi (1835–1840 [1100s]), Jacques-Meunié (1982), A. Lewis (1951), and Lopez and Raymond (1961). Udovitch's collection of articles (1981) on economy and society in the Middle East is relevant, as is Wakin's examination (1972) of what Islamic documents of sale reveal about economic, social, and judicial life. Saad's work (1983) on Timbuktu highlights the florescence of political and social life when trans-Saharan trade was rich and the plummet when that trade declined. The number of Islamic schools went from several hundred to a handful.

2. Galloway (1977) provides the summary of the role of sugar trade to the Muslim world and the consequences of its later transfer elsewhere. Berthier (1966) uses archaeological material to provide a thorough examination of the ancient sugar industry in Morocco, and Jacques-Meunié (1982) examines the economic dimensions of that trade and includes statistics. Ibn Hawqal (1845 [900s]) and al-Idrisi (1835–1840s [1100s]) summarize the sugar industry in the early eras. Mintz (1985) explores the dynamics of the sugar trade as it passes into European control.

6. bubonic plague

1. The economic and social repercussions of the bubonic plague have been explored in numerous works, including Deaux (1969), Dols (1977), Galloway (1977), Gottfried (1983), McNeil (1976), and Ziegler (1969).

2. On the Portuguese expansion into Morocco, see especially Boucharb (1984), Dos Passos (1969), Newitt (1973), Ricard (1955), Vogt (1979), and Eanes de Azurara (1936 [1450]).

7. sharifi resolution

1. Thirty percent of the merchants in the town in which I lived from 1976 to 1978 claimed to be direct descendants of the Prophet Muhammad. Most of the merchants were native Berber speakers. The number of Moroccans who claim direct descent from the Prophet Muhammad is truly astounding. Some make the claim with more effectiveness, some with less, but the extent of the claim shows the cultural potency of that connection. As to the objective foundations, doubtless there is some validity in some of the links claimed; somewhere, in some distant branch of the individual's genealogy, there may be a connection to the Qurayshi patriline of which Muhammad was a part (just as in the United States, if one explores all the kinship links in all their varied connections through time, we will find that many Americans are "related" to the family of George Washington). What is important for social organization is that some collectivities preserve and honor genealogical inheritance in such a way that it becomes a cultural and political asset in the present. This is the case for descent from Muhammad in much of the Muslim world.

2. For the rise and rule of the Sa'di dynasty, see especially Cornell (1983, 1986), de Castries (1921), al-Fishtali (1973 [1500s]), Harakat (1985), al-Ifrani (1889 [1700s]), Kably (1978), al-Nasiri (1954–1956, vol. 6), and especially Yahya (1981), as well as summaries in the general histories of Abun-Nasr (1987), Brignon et al. (1967), and Laroui (1977a).

3. King Hasan II and Queen Elizabeth II continue to hold the titles that al-Mansur and Queen Elizabeth I held, that is, respectively, "Prince of the Faithful" and "Defender of the Faith." Elizabeth II took the latter title upon her coronation. The title was bestowed on the British monarchy by the Catholic Pope before Henry VIII's break with Catholicism, and Henry kept the title after the break. On the personal correspondence between al-Mansur and Queen Elizabeth I, see *Gentleman's Magazine* 1810. For the popular tenor of the times, see al-Majdhub (1966 [1500s]).

8. Prophet's Birthday

1. The two other rituals with which 'Id al-Mawlid, "the Celebration of the Prophet's Birth," shares prominence are 'Id al-Kabir and 'Id al-

Saghir. 'Id al-Kabir means "the Great Ritual" (I translate it as "the Great Sacrifice") while 'Id al-Saghir means "the Little Ritual" and is the one that ends Ramadan's fasting. 'Id al-Kabir and 'Id al-Saghir are canonical rituals in Islam, while the Prophet's Birthday is not. Of the Prophet's Birthday, the Islamic jurist Ibn Taymiya states, "it belongs to those innovations [*bid'a*] which the early Muslims [*salaf*] did not approve of, neither did they practice them . . . but God knows best" (1321–1322:312).

2. A candle procession that resembles al-Mansur's great candle procession in Marrakush can still be seen in Sala (Salé; Brown 1976). For many Moroccans, especially members of religious brotherhoods such as the Hamadsha, the Prophet's Birthday has become an important occasion for ceremonies of ritual sacrifice.

9. 'Alawi blood descendants

1. On the historical foundations of the 'Alawi dynasty, see for example Aafif (1980–1981), Abun-Nasr (1987), Brignon et al. (1967), Cigar (1981), Eustache (1984, especially vol. 1), Geertz (1968), Julien (1978), Laroui (1977a), Levi-Provencal (1922), al-Mansour (1989), al-Nasiri (1954–1956, vols. 7, 8, and 9), and Sebti (1986). Jackson (1968 [1809]) gives an informative outsider's account of Morocco before the French colonial vision was established.

2. Not until the dahir of November 17, 1915 (A.H. 1334) did the 'Alawi dynasty add the five-pointed green seal of Sulayman (Solomon) to their pure scarlet-red banner. The addition was made on French instigation in order to distinguish Morocco's national flag from the plain red signal flag used in maritime communication.

3. There is an enormous amount of literature concerning Mawlay Isma'il, much of it written by foreigners during his fifty-five year reign. Not surprisingly, much of that work is enormously biased towards European perspectives (especially since some of it was written by captives), and yet as long as the biases are kept in mind, the work is informative; see especially the accounts of de la Faye (1726), Mouette (1683 and 1710), Pellow (1890 [1700s]), Saint Olon (1695), and Windus (1725). For an indigenous account of that era written by a man in the outlying regions, the book by al-Zarhuni (1940 [1725]) is excellent. Colin (1929) and Nekrouf (1987) provide twentieth-century accounts of the great monarch.

10. first marriage

1. My template for the marriage ceremonies was developed by first codifying, in schematic form, the sequence of words, actions, and events of each of the ceremonies described by Westermarck, observed by myself, and described by others, including Addison (1671), Aubin (1912), Chenier (1788), Davis (1983), Doutte (1909), Kramer (1970), Jamous (1981),

Joseph and Joseph (1987), Mernissi (1982), Mouette (1683), Naamane-Guessous (1987), Saint Olon (1695), Tharaud and Tharaud (1930), and Windus (1725). Over eighty ceremonies, drawn from throughout the countryside, were involved in the initial tabulation. The original purpose of my codification was to accent the variety that exists in Moroccan wedding ceremonies, and the original paper that emerged from it emphasizes those differences. Yet what was striking when the variety had been codified was the common underlying substructure. From the vantage point of that substructure, whether the groom breaks the bride's headdress, a vase, or violently lets down her hair upon entering the room does not matter; all are local variations on the common theme of male violence and domination as marking male entry. The sequence I discuss in the text illustrates the underlying substructure. Any given local ceremony will include that basic structure as well as many of the specific elements described and will elaborate both through local variations and local color.

Other works on the role of women that informed my analysis include those of al-Amin (1968), Davis (1983), Dwyer (1978), Howard-Merriam (1984), R. Joseph and T. Joseph (1987), S. Joseph (1986), Mernissi (1977), and Rassam (1980). Abu-Lughod's (1986) work on women's poetry also entered in, as did Altorki's (1986) analysis of women and change in Saudia Arabia, el-Guindi's (1981) work on women in Egypt, Marsot's (1979) study of women in medieval Islam, Salih's story *The Wedding of Zein* (1978), and Fernea and Bezirgan's *Middle Eastern Muslim Women Speak*.

11. bride's blood

1. See Alland (1985) for a discussion of phallic symbolism and procreation rituals elsewhere.

12. ram's blood

1. The practice of reading the future of the nation in the dying ram is long established and well documented in Morocco; for instance, see Chenier (1788:2:197), de la Faye (1726:91–92), Saint Olon (1695), and Westermarck (1911). The city in which the sultan performs the sacrifice has changed over the years because the capital itself has changed from Fas, to Maknas, to Ribat.

13. Ibrahim myth

1. The Qur'an does not mention the son's name in its sacrifice story, and yet in popular Muslim understandings, there is no question about which son was to be sacrificed. It was Isma'il. No Moroccan, nor any other Muslim I have ever met, thought any other son was to be put to the death. Isma'il's place in the sacrifice is so obvious that the query into

any other possibility is perceived as absurd. Nonetheless, scholars, particularly Western scholars brought up in Judaic and Christian traditions, where Isaac (Ar. "Ishak") was the son to be sacrificed, continue to debate the issue. Given the majority opinion of Muslim believers, it is ironic that the 1927 *Encyclopedia of Islam* includes the trial of Ibrahim's sacrifice under "Ishak" [Isaac] not "Ismaʿil" (vol. 2, p. 532). The 1960 revised edition has made some changes, and notes the story of sacrifice under both Ishak and Ismaʿil, yet still argues that there is some debate. It does however note that learned Muslim opinion supports the notion that Ismaʿil was the son to be sacrificed. Popular Muslim opinion has never been in doubt.

2. Mountains have also been linked with women. The cult of Aphrodite was associated with Mount Ida (Friedrich 1978:74). The Zulus associate the rain goddess with sacred mountains and consider young females to be the proper human intermediaries who commune with the goddess in order to make her rains fall. They are her caretakers and they fete her with beer, flowers, and singing. During the most sacred times, men stay away from the mountains so that the rain goddess will not be offended by them (see Berglund 1976:64–74).

3. Theoretical interest in rituals of sacrifice peaked in the late 1800s and was associated with evolutionary thought. In the span of a few years, Frazer (in *The Golden Bough,* 1890), Hubert and Mauss (1898), and Smith (1967 [1885], 1892) all put forward major theories of sacrifice. Local-level studies followed, including Westermarck's (1911) detailed survey of sacrifice in Morocco. Then for nearly three-fourths of a century, scholarly interest in sacrifice in general, and regional interest in Islamic sacrifice in particular, faded. (There were however a few important exceptions to the overarching trend, including Linton (1926), Chelhod (1955), and Evans-Pritchard (1956). Then in the late 1970s and 1980s, with anthropology's renewed emphasis on rituals in general, sacrifice has come once again into the limelight. Important recent work on sacrifice includes that of Beidelman (1987), Bolle (1983), Bourdillon and Fortes (1980), Burkert (1983), Das (1983), Girard (1977), Gose (1986), de Heutsch (1985), Jay (1981), Thurman (1983), Turner (1977b), Valeri (1985), and van Baal (1976). *Sacred Performances* brings the discussion of sacrifice to the Muslim world and offers an interpretation that extends beyond it.

For an analysis of a fascinating popular rite associated with the Great Sacrifice in some parts of Morocco, see Hammoudi (1988). In this rite, a young man dresses up in the sewn skins of sacrificed rams, and with other young male friends, goes running through the streets and countryside in a ritual of fun-making, rule-breaking, and sexual upheaval.

15. *sexuality and sacrifice*

1. Of late, the possibility of a sacred-sexual connection has begun to be explored again. In her novel *Oral History* (1984), writer Lee Smith creates it; "*Oral History* finds an intersection of sexual and religious experience in some interesting and important ways" (Jones 1986:17). As Hill (n.d.) notes of that novel, it is an intersection in which male and female participate, but which the man then denies. His denial is shown in his physical leaving of the mountains where the connection took place and his returning to the flat plains. As he finally drives away, a mountaineer shoots out the rear view mirror from his car—a sign of how momentous is the departure from the holy mountain where sex and the sacred were one.

2. Plays in ancient Greece held much the same role as myths in other societies. Greek deities existed in multiple forms, and so did their myths. Euripides and Aeschylus offer different interpretations of Iphigenia's sacrifice. In Euripedes, Iphigenia survives the sacrifice, while in Aeschylus, who uses a more patriarchal interpretation, she does not. Both are plausible renderings of the ultimate human dilemma of life and death that these myths address through their specific tellings of the father called upon to sacrifice his child.

3. Christian communion celebrates the sacrifice of Jesus, the Son of God, on the cross, an event that Christians interpret as bringing the hope of eternal life to all. The wine represents the blood that Jesus shed. In most rituals of Christian communion, male officiates oversee the dispensing of this blood, which can overcome the limits of earthly life and lead to everlasting life. Among Catholics, a celibate priestly caste controls this sacred blood; their capacity to dispense the blood of transcendent life is made directly dependent on their abstinence from natural intercourse and natural birth.

Jews celebrate their great sacrifice rite each year on Rosh Hashanah, the New Year. The first day of Rosh Hashanah focuses upon the story of Isaac's natural birth, which involves the female, the mother. But the second, the great day of Rosh Hashanah, focuses upon the father-wrought transcendent birth that emerged from Abraham's successful facing of the sacrificial trial, a sacred birth that overcomes the limits of the mother's natural birth. On the great day of Rosh Hashanah, the story of Abraham and Isaac and the sacrifice is read from the holy Torah and physically affirmed through the ritual blowing of the ram's horn, the shofar, a hundred times—the only occasion on which the great horn is so often blown (Beth Kissileff, "Rosh Hashanah," paper for Autumn 1988 seminar "Rituals and Anthropology," Department of Anthropology, Columbia University).

4. William Faulkner looks at what patriarchy does to men in *Absalom, Absalom* and what patriarchy does to women in *The Sound and the*

Fury. Of Caddy, the female protagonist in *The Sound and the Fury*, Faulkner said he could not tell her tale for he loved her so much, and so instead lets three white men and one black woman tell it. Caddy is venturesome, inquisitive, honest and, by the world, crushed. Faulkner wrote a short story, "That Evening Sun," about her and her brother Jason before he wrote *The Sound and the Fury*. The short story ends with a vivid icon of male dominance and female questioning. The son sits silhouetted on his father's shoulders, the vertical maleness backdropped by the evening sky. Jason looks down at his sister, and Caddy gazes up at him. Having finally figured things out, she calls Jason a "coward." Her father quickly and authoritatively intervenes on behalf of the son, rebuking his daughter with the angered utterance of "Candace." And thus the story ends. In *The Sound and the Fury*, this shielded brother grows up to be a banker who takes Caddy's "illegitimate" child from her, will not let her see the little girl, and steals the money that Caddy sends to the child. Faulkner is clear on Caddy's nobility, and equally clear that this world pushes her to tragedy. She is last seen in a Nazi staff car.

Contemporary novelist Lee Smith focuses on patriarchy's impact on women in *Black Mountain Breakdown* (1980), *Oral History* (1984), and *Fair and Tender Ladies* (1988). The first two books end with female tragedy; the third, and last, offers another way, showing the female actively recreating her life through the writing of letters to a sister who no longer lives. Through the letters, she remains a fair and tender lady, capable of surviving, and even thriving, in this world.

Anna Julia Cooper highlighted the problem of patriarchy at the turn of the century in *A Voice from the South* (1969 [1892]). She states, "While our men seem thoroughly abreast of the times on almost every other subject, when they strike the woman question they drop back into sixteenth-century logic" (p. 75). Cooper argues that times have changed and that the question for the woman is not now, "How shall I so cramp, stunt, simplify and nullify myself as to make me eligible to the honor of being swallowed up into some little man? But the problem, I trow, now rests with the man as to how he can . . . reach . . . women who demand the noblest, grandest and best achievements of which he is capable" (p. 70–71).

Critical analytical thinking on these issues is at the base of Carol Gilligan's ground-breaking book on the psychology of women, *In a Different Voice* (1982), and Griffin's poignant work, *Pornography and Silence* (1981). As Griffin demonstrates, the pivot of pornography has nothing to do with eroticism but rather with men's violent domination of women and nature. "The bodies of women in pornography, mastered, bound, silenced, beaten, and even murdered, are symbols for natural feeling and the power of nature, which the pornographic mind hates and fears" (p. 2).

In *The Woman That Never Evolved* (1983), Sarah Hrdy explores these issues from the perspective of biological anthropology, while Katherine

Newman explores their cultural and economic dimensions in *Falling from Grace* (1988:202–228.)

The problems inherent in historical Christianity's wedding to patriarchy and opposition to women and nature are addressed in Elaine Pagels' *Adam, Eve, and the Serpent* (1988) and in Matthew Fox's *The Coming of the Cosmic Christ: The Healing of Mother Earth and the Birth of a Global Renaissance* (1988). Fox is a Roman Catholic priest and describes his book as "My final statement before being silenced by the Vatican" (*New York Times*, "Review of Books," January 8, 1989).

16. colonial dichotomy

1. The immediate precolonial era is explored in depth by Burke (1976), Cigar (1981), Dunn (1977), Julien (1978), Hermassi (1972), Laroui (1977b), Lazarev (1981), Miège (1961, 1981), Pascon (1977), Sebti (1986), and Seddon (1977, 1981). Charles Issawi's more general work (1966) on the economics of the Middle East in this age is helpful in deciphering what transpired.

2. The colonial era itself is addressed by many including Abun-Nasr (1971), Combs-Schilling (1984), Damis (1970, 1983), Entelis (1989), al-Fasi (1948), Geertz (1968), Halstead (1967), Hermassi (1972), Julien (1978), Laroui (1977b), Leveau (1985), Moore (1970), Stewart (1964), and Swearington (1987).

3. For the religious and political foundations of precolonial, colonial, and anticolonial Tunisia, see Anderson (1986), L. C. Brown (1974), Combs-Schilling (1984), Hermassi (1972), Kraiem (1973), Lejri (1977), Ling (1979), Moore (1970), and Stone and Simmons (1976).

4. Bin Baraka was an ideologue of the leftist political party Union Socialiste des Forces Populaires (USFP), an offshoot of the more mainline Istiqlal ("Independence") party spearheaded by 'Alal al-Fasi. Because of his opposition to the king, Bin Baraka was kidnapped by Moroccan security agents in France in 1965 and subsequently killed (see Entelis 1988:65).

17. body and soul

1. Important works on the postcolonial era in Morocco include Abu-Lughod (1980), Eickelman (1985, 1986), Entelis (1989), Geertz (1968), Ihrai (1986), Leveau (1985), Munson (1984, 1986), Seddon (1977, 1981, 1984), Swearington (1987), Tessler (1982), Tozy (1979, 1984), Waterbury (1970, 1979), and Zartman (1964, 1982, 1987).

2. The foremost expert on the fundamentalist movement in Morocco is Mohammed Tozy (1979, 1984). Henry Munson (1986) has also done important work on it.

3. The Saharan conflict concerns that part of the Sahara that was col-

onized by Spain and then ceded back to the indigenous peoples in the 1970s. Morocco claims the western Sahara as its own, citing the long history of political linkage. The Algerian-backed Polisario claim the land as their own. For years, a war raged, but Morocco and Algeria have now reached a rapprochement and King Hasan II is talking to the Polisario. The most crucial event in the conflict took place in November 1975 when the king mobilized nearly half a million Moroccan citizens in a massive peaceful demonstration. Armed only with quotations from the Qur'an, they occupied part of the Sahara. This peaceful pilgrimage, called the "Green March," was an enormously popular event that garnered considerable legitimacy for the king (see Entelis' discussion, 1989:40). King Hasan II himself and his children participated. The foremost Western experts on the Saharan issue are John Damis (1983) and Tony Hodges (1983).

4. For a discussion of the 1971 and 1972 coups, see Coram (1972), de Wolf (1971), Entelis (1989:62–63), and Waterbury (1972). Coverage in *Le Monde, Jeune Afrique,* and *L'Express* was excellent. In 1983, another military plot was discovered, and senior officers were arrested. Once again the plot is alleged to have been spearheaded by a military man extremely close to the king, General Dlimi. He is officially reported to have died in a "car accident" (see Entelis 1989:63).

'Abbāsī. *Of and pertaining to* 'Abbās (uncle of Muḥammad). The second imperial dynasty of Islam, 749–1258 (A.H. 132–656), with capital at Baghdād.

'Abd. *Servant of.* Affixed to one of the ninety-nine names of God in forming names in the Muslim world.

'Abd al-'Azīz. *Servant of the Venerated.* Seventeenth 'Alawī monarch, 1894–1908 (A.H. 1311–1326), deposed by brother.

'Abd Allāh. *Servant of God.*

'Abd al-Ḥajj. *Servant of the Pilgrimage.*

'Abd al-Malik. *Servant of the King.* Fourth Sa'di monarch, 1576–1578 (A.H. 984–986).

'Abd al-Raḥmān. *Servant of the Merciful.*

'Abd al-Salām. *Servant of the Peace.*

'Abd al-Waḥīd. *Servant of the One.*

Abū. *Father of.*

Abū 'Abd Allāh al-Qā'im bi Amr Allāh. *Father of the Servant of God, Steadfast by the Command of God.* Founder of the Sa'di dynasty, died 1517 (A.H. 923).

Abū Bakr. *Father of Bakr.* Close companion, advisor, and father-in-law of Muḥammad. First of the Rāshidūn caliphs, he succeeded Muḥammad in 632 (A.H. 11) and died in 634 (A.H. 13). Father of ʿĀʾisha (see figure 4.1).

Abū al-Ḥasan. *Father of the Good.*

Abū Sufyān. *Father of Sufyān.* Member of Banū Umayya, leader of Makkan opposition to Muḥammad, then reached a compromise and was pivotal in Muḥammad's victorious entry into Makka. Father of Muʿāwiya, founder of the Banū Umayya dynasty, and of Umm Ḥabība, wife of the Prophet.

Abū Ṭālib. *Father of Ṭālib.* The uncle of Muḥammad who raised him after his grandfather died; father of ʿAli.

ʿAdnān. Legendary ancestor of the North Arabs.

Afughāl. Small town in southern Morocco where al-Jazūlī was first buried; to it the Saʿdī dynasty journeyed to garner al-Jazūlī's political-religious credit.

Aḥmad al-Manṣūr. *Aḥmad the Victor.* Fifth Saʿdi monarch, with glorious reign 1578–1603 (A.H. 986–1012). Instituted elaborate national ceremonies for the Prophet's Birthday.

ʿĀʾisha. Exuberant, childless, and favored wife of Muḥammad the Prophet; daughter of Abū Bakr.

ʿAlāl al-Fāsī. *ʿAlāl from Fās.* Leader in Morocco's independence movement.

ʿAlawī. *Of or attributed to ʿAli.* Ruling dynasty in Morocco from 1600s to present.

ʿAli. Cousin and son-in-law of Muḥammad and one of his closest companions; the fourth of the Rāshidūn caliphs, ruled from 656–661 (A.H. 35–40). The first Imām of the Shīʿī, father of al-Ḥasan and al-Ḥusayn; married to Fāṭima, daughter of Muḥammad.

Allāh. *God.*

Amīr al-muʾminīn. *Commander of the Faithful, Prince of the Faithful.* Title used for the caliphs of Islam.

ʿAql. *Intellect, reason.*

ʿArafāt. *Knowledge, mercy.* Mountain and adjacent plain, located four hours distance east of Makka, where the Makka pilgrims spend the ninth day of Dhū al-Ḥijja (month of the pilgrimage) seeking God's mercy.

al-Aʿraj. *The Lame.* Early leader of the Saʿdī movement.

Asfi. *Safi.* Moroccan port.

ʿĀshūrāʾ. The tenth day of Muḥarram, the first month of the Islamic calendar; voluntary fasting day for Muslims. The Shīʿī hold mourning rituals to commemorate the martyrdom of al-Ḥusayn at Karbalāʾ on the tenth of Muḥarram 680 (A.H. 61).

Asila. Port on Morocco's northwest coast.

Aṭlas. Mountain range which separates Morocco's heartland plains from the Sahara and the rest of North Africa.

Āyatullāh. *Sign of God.* A principal religious leader among the Shīʿī in the absence of the Imam.

al-Azhar. *The Brilliant One.* One of the oldest Islamic universities, in Cairo, Egypt, inaugurated in 972 (A.H. 359).

al-Badīʿ. *The Incomparable.* One of the ninety-nine names of God; name of the glorious palace built by the Saʿdī al-Manṣūr in Marrākush.

Badr. Crucial battle fought in 624 (A.H. 2), won by the Muslims.

Badr al-Dīn. *Full Moon of the Religion.* Distinguished name taken by some Muslims.

Baghdād. City situated on both banks of the Tigris. Founded in the 8th century (A.H. 2nd century) by the ʿAbbāsī dynasty as their capital, it continued to be a cultural metropolis of the Islamic world for centuries.

Banū. *Sons of.*

Banū Marīn. *Sons of Marīn; Merinids.* Berber tribesmen, third ruling dynasty in Morocco 1258–1420 (A.H. 656–823).

Banū Rustam. *Sons of Rustam; Rustamids.* A Khārijī dynasty who fled to northwest Africa and established a thriving political-commercial community 777–909 (A.H. 160–296).

Banū Umayya. *Sons of Umayya; Umayyads.* First imperial dynasty of Islam, capital at Damascus, 661–750 (A.H. 41–132).

Banū Waṭṭās. *Sons of Waṭṭās. Waṭṭāsids.* Sublineage of Banū Marīn that dominated parts of Morocco, 1420–1550 (A.H. 823–957); usually termed a regency, not a caliphate.

Baraka. *Blessing, benediction.*

Bayʿa (pl. bayʿāt). A political oath of allegiance rendered by some Muslims to their leaders.

Berbers. Inhabitants of North Africa prior to the Arab conquest.

Bidʿa. *Innovation, novelty; heretical doctrine.*

Bilād al-Makhzan. *Lands of government and rule of law.*

Bilād al-Sība. *Lands of dissidence.*

Bilāl. A companion of Muhammad who gave the call to prayers in the time of the Prophet; died ca. 641 (A.H. 20).

Bin. *Son of.* (Colloq.)

Bi'smi'llāh al-Raḥmān al-Raḥīm. *In the name of the God, the Merciful, the Compassionate.*

Caliph. (Ar. **khalīfa**). *Successor.* Central political position in Islam, established shortly after the death of Muḥammad in 632 (A.H. 11).

Ceuta, *see* **Sabta.**

Dāhir. *Legal ruling.*

Dār al-Baydāʾ. *Casablanca; White House.* Morocco's economic capital.

Dār al-Islām. *Domain of Islam.*

Dastūr. *Constitution.*

al-Dastūr. Tunisian political party.

Dhū al-Ḥijja. Month of the pilgrimage, the last month of the Islamic lunar calendar.

Dīnār. *Monetary unit, money.*

Fās. First imperial capital of Morocco, established ca. 789 (A.H. 172); center of learning, politics, and commerce for 1,200 years.

Fāsī. *People of Fās; of or pertaining to Fās.*

Fāṭima. Daughter of Muḥammad, wife of ʿAlī, mother of al-Ḥasan and al-Ḥusayn; icon of her became dominant in Islam.

Fāṭimī. Shīʿī/Ismāʿīlī dynasty in Egypt, 909–1171 (A.H. 297–567); derived their name from Fāṭima.

Filālī. *People of Tāfilālat; of or pertaining to Tāfilālat.*

al-Fishtālī. Scribe in the Saʿdī court.

Fitna. *Dissension, sedition; a beautiful woman.* Term used in Islamic sources to denote civil war.

Ḥāʾik. *Fine-woven, weaver.* Blanket used as an outer garment in some parts of Morocco.

Ḥadīth. An account of what Muḥammad did or said, which serves as a precedent for Muslims to follow. The Ḥadīth were told by his companions and transmitted by word of mouth; written down in the 800s and 900s, their lines of transmission were scrutinized before written recording. The most important compilations of Ḥadīth include those of al-Bukhārī, 810–870 (A.H. 194–256) and al-Muslim, 817–875 (A.H. 202–261); both collections of Ḥadīth were reedited and printed in Cairo in the 1200s and the 1300s.

Ḥafṣa. Wife of the Prophet, daughter of ʿUmar, the second of the Rāshidūn caliphs.

Hājar. Concubine of the Prophet Ibrāhīm, mother of Ismāʿīl.

Ḥajj. Muslim pilgrimage to Makka, one of the five pillars of Islam.

Ḥājjī. *One who has completed the Ḥajj.*

Ḥamadsha. A religious brotherhood in Morocco.

Ḥamīd. *Praiseworthy, laudable.*

Ḥanīf. *True (i.e., Islamic).*

Ḥaraka (pl. ḥarakāt). *Movement, military conquest.*

al-Ḥasan. *Good.* Elder son of ʿAlī and Fāṭima, grandson of Muḥammad. A political compromiser, he accepted Muʿāwiya as caliph in 661 (A.H. 41); the ʿAlawī dynasty of Morocco traces their descent from him.

Ḥasan II. Present king of Morocco, son of Muḥammad V, astute politician who skillfully led the country through the tumultuous postcolonial era to the present.

Ḥasan al-Wazzānī. Young Moroccan ideologue, important in the independence movement.

Hāshimī. *People of the Banū Hāshim clan of the Quraysh tribe.*

Hijra. *Abandonment, emigration.* The emigration of the Prophet Muḥammad from Makka to Madina in 632 (A.H. 1); marks the beginning of the Islamic calendar.

Ḥinnāʾ. *Henna.* Natural dye that leaves a blood-red stain.

Ḥūr. *Virgin of paradise.*

al-Ḥusayn. Second son of ʿAlī and Fāṭima, martyred by the Banū Umayya at the battle of Karbalāʾ in 680 (A.H. 61).

Iblīs. *Satan.*

Ibn. *Son of.*

Ibn Baraka. *Son of God's grace.* Political-religious leader in Morocco's Sūs in the 1500s; conferred legitimate authority on the Saʿdī movement.

Ibrāhīm. *Abraham.* Prophet of God, father of all believers (Muslims, Jews, Christians); withstood the trial when God demanded the sacrifice of his son Ismāʿīl.

ʿĪd al-Kabīr. *The Great Celebration.* The Feast of the Great Sacrifice, honors the Prophet Ibrāhīm and the Prophet Ismāʿīl's sacrificial trial. Instituted by the Prophet Muḥammad in 624 (A.H. 2), celebrated on the tenth day of Dhū al-Ḥijja.

ʿĪd al-Mawlīd. *The Birth Celebration.* The celebration of the Prophet's Birthday.

Idrīs I. First Islamic monarch of Morocco, founder of Morocco's monarchy and the Idrīsī dynasty; ruled from 789–791 (A.H. 172–175).

Idrīs II. Second Idrīsī monarch, ruled from 803–828 (A.H. 187–213).

Idrīsī. First Islamic dynasty of Morocco, 789–959 (A.H. 172–348).

Imām. *Prayer leader.* A prayer leader, or in Sunnī Islam a political leader with considerable spiritual authority; in Shīʿī Islam, the descendants of Muḥammad through the line of Fāṭima, the sole legitimate rulers of the Islamic community even when rejected by it. The Shīʿī hold them to have a spiritual function as successors to Muḥammad.

Imi-n-Tānūt (Berber). *Mouth of the well.* Town in foothills of the High Atlas Mountains.

In Shāʾ Allāh. *If God wills.*

ʿĪsā. *Jesus.* Important Prophet in Islam.

Islam. *Submission to God.* The faith of Muslim believers.

Ismāʿīl. *Ishmael.* Son of the Prophet Ibrāhīm who was almost sacrified at the demand of God; became a prophet, and along with his father Ibrāhīm built (or rebuilt) the Kaʿba.

al-Jazūlī. Moroccan political-religious leader in the 1400s (A.H. 800s), spokesman for sharīfī descent and leader of resistance against the Portuguese.

Jibrīl. *Gabriel.* Archangel who brought the Qurʾān to Muḥammad.

Jihād. *War in accordance with Islamic law against unbelievers.*

Jinn (pl. jānn). *Spirits.* Invisible beings both harmful and helpful who intervene in the lives of mortals.

Kaʿba. An ancient stone shrine that is the most famous sanctuary of Islam, called the temple or house of God, situated almost in the center of the Great Mosque in Makka.

Kanza. Berber concubine of Idrīs I, gave birth to Idrīs II in 791 (A.H. 175).

Karbalāʾ. Battle fought in 680 (A.H. 61), in which the Banū Umayya led by Yazīd I defeated the ʿAlawī army of al-Ḥusayn; al-Ḥusayn along with many of the descendants of the Prophet were martyred.

Kātib. *Secretary, scribe.* Specifically, one who serves in the government offices.

Khadīja. Muḥammad's first wife, a strong, dynamic commercialist, early convert to Islam.

Khalīfa. *Successor; see* **Caliph.**

Khārijī (also Khawārij). Members of a group of strongly egalitarian, democratically oriented Muslims, who protested ʿAlī's acceptance of arbitration at the Battle of Ṣiffin in 658 (A.H. 38); ʿAli was killed by a Khārijī in 661 (A.H. 40).

Kutubiyya. Mosque in Marrākush, built by the al-Muwaḥḥidūn.

Laʿb al-Bārūd. *Play of the gunpowder.*

Lāla ʿĀʾisha. Daughter of King Muḥammad V of Morocco who publicly went unveiled when she gave an important speech in Tangier in 1947 (A.H. 1366); pivotal in Morocco's women's rights movement.

Madīna. City in the Arabian Peninsula to which Muḥammad and the Muslims emigrated in 622 (A.H. 1), where the political community of Muslims was born.

al-Maghrib. The far west of the Muslim world, usually taken to include Morocco, Algeria, Tunisia, and Libya.

Maghribī. *People of al-Maghrib; of or pertaining to al-Maghrib.*

Mahdī. *The rightly guided one, Messiah.* A stellar figure who many Muslims believe will appear at the end of the age and bring about a reign of justice; for the Shīʿī, the twelfth Imām, from the line of ʿAlī and Fāṭima, who went into occultation in 874 (A.H. 260).

Mahārī. Camel bred for racing.

Makka. *Mecca.* The holiest city in Islam; Muslims turn to it five times a day in prayer.

Makkawī. *A person from Makka; of or pertaining to Makka.*

Malik. *King.*

Marrākush. *Marrākish, Marrakesh.* Moroccan imperial city in the south; a vast, spectacular oasis.

Mawlāy. (colloq. Mūlāy, classical Mawlāya). *My Lord.* Form of address to a sovereign, used in Morocco for the King and other prominent sharif; usually affixed to the first name, as illustrated below.

Mawlāy ʿAbd Allāh. Second Saʿdī monarch, ruled 1557–1574 (A.H. 965–982).

Mawlāy ʿAbd al-Ḥafiẓ. Eighteenth ʿAlawī monarch, ruled 1908–1912 (A.H. 1326–1330).

Mawlāy ʿArafa. Pretender put on the throne by the French in November 1953 (A.H. 1373) when they exiled the proper ruler Muḥammad V.

Mawlāy Ḥasan II. Twenty-first ʿAlawī monarch, 1961-present (A.H. 1380-present), astute politician who skillfully led Morocco through the tumultuous postcolonial era to the present.

Mawlāy Ismāʿīl. Third ʿAlawī monarch, ruled 1672–1727 (A.H. 1082–1139); one of the most forceful monarchs Morocco has ever known.

Mawlāy al-Rashīd. Second ʿAlawī monarch, ruled 1661–1672 (A.H. 1075–1082); proclaimed "Prince of the Faithful" in Fās in 1666 (A.H. 1077).

Mawlāy al-Sharīf. Founder of ʿAlawī dynasty.

Mawlāy Yūsuf. Nineteenth ʿAlawī monarch, ruled 1912–1927 (A.H. 1330–1346).

Minā. Valley near Makka where the sacrifice ritual for pilgrims takes place.

Mashwī. Whole roasted lamb.

Mīzān. *Scale.*

Muʾadhdhin (pl. muʾadhdhinūn). The person who gives the public Islamic call to prayer.

al-Muʾmin. *The Believer, the Faithful.*

Muʿāwiya. Fifth caliph after Muḥammad; sister Umm Ḥabība was a wife of the Prophet. First caliph of Islam's first imperial dynasty, the Banū Umayya; ruled 661–680 (A.H. 41–60).

Muḥammad. The last Prophet of God, the founder of the political-religious community of Muslims; died in 632 (A.H. 11).

Muḥammad al-Shaykh. First Saʿdī monarch, ruled 1548–1557 (A.H. 955–964).

Murābiṭ. *Saint, one tied to God.* Religious leader.

al-Murābiṭūn. *Those Who are Tied to God; Almoravids.* Berber tribesmen; second ruling dynasty of Morocco, 1073–1147 (A.H. 465–541).

Musallā. *Place of prayer.* In Morocco a consecrated place outdoors for performing the collective celebration of major ritual occasions such as ʿId al-Kabīr; in Morocco's wedding ceremonies, place where the groom is transformed into sulṭān.

Muslim. *Those who submit.* The people who believe in Islam.

al-Mutawakkil. *The One Who Relies on God.* Third Saʿdī monarch, ruled 1574–1576 (A.H. 982–984); ousted by uncle, then became a pretender.

al-Muwaḥḥidūn. *Those Who Believe in the Oneness of God; Almohads.* Berber tribesmen; third ruling dynasty of Morocco, 1147–1269 (A.H. 541–668).

Naṣr Allāh. *The Victory of God.*

Nikāḥ. *Marriage.*

Niya. *Intention, determination, will.*

al-Nūr. *The Light.* One of the ninety-nine names of God.

al-Qarawīyīn. Mosque-university complex established in Fās in 800s (A.H. 200s).

Qaṣīda (pl. qaṣāʾīd). Ode or poem. Written to honor the Prophet and his descendants in ʿId al-Mawlid celebrations.

Qaṣr al-Sūq. Town in northern Morocco where in 1578 (A.H. 986) the battle of Wādī al-Makhzan was fought.

al-Qurʾān. *The Koran.* The holy book of Islam, transmitted from God to the Archangel Jibrīl to Muḥammad.

Quraysh. The overarching patrikin corporation that dominated Makka when Muḥammad was born and from which he, as well as many other members of the early Islamic elite, came.

Quṭb. *Pole.* Pole of faith, a person who by his virtue and piety raises himself above his contemporaries and serves as their source of guidance. Ṣūfī term.

Ribāṭ. *Rabat.* Capital of Morocco.

Ramaḍān. The ninth month of the Muslim calendar; holy month of fasting and prayers.

al-Rashīd. *The Rightly Guided.*

al-Rāshidūn. *The Rightly Guided Ones.* Title given to the first four caliphs of Islam, Abū Bakr, ʿUmar, ʿUthmān, and ʿAli.

Rīf. Mountainous area in northern Morocco.

Ruqayya. Daughter of Muḥammad given in marriage to ʿUthmān, the third of the Rāshidūn caliphs.

Saʿdī. Fifth great ruling dynasty of Morocco, 1548–1641 (A.H. 955–1051); reestablished blood descent from Muḥammad as a necessary criterion of rule after six hundred years of its absence.

Sabta. *Ceuta.* Crucial Moroccan port on the Mediterranean, for a thousand years an outlet for the Sijilmāsa-Fās trans-Saharan trade. City through which the celebration of the Prophet's Birthday entered Morocco; first city occupied by Portuguese as they began their age of expansion.

Salā. *Salé.* City on Morocco's coast, important center of privateering in the 1700s (A.H. 1000s).

Salaf. *Predecessors, forebears, ancestors.* The early believers.

Ṣalāh. *Prayers.* The ritual worship performed five times daily, one of the five pillars of Islam.

Sawda. Wife of Muḥammad after the death of Khadīja.

Sayyid. Respectful form of address; also, descendants of ʿAli through his son al-Ḥusayn.

Sayyid Baraka. Ṣūfī mystic and brotherhood leader who enhanced Saʿdī credit.

Sharīf. Descendants of Muḥammad through Fāṭima and ʿAli. Morocco's present ruling dynasty, the ʿAlawī, like the sharīfi Saʿdī and Idrīsī dynasties before them, claim blood descent from Muḥammad through his grandson al-Ḥasan (see figure 7.1).

Sharīfi. *Of or pertaining to sharīf.*

Shaykh (pl. shuyūkh). *Leader.* Respectful form of address.

Shīʿī. *From Shīʿa ʿAli, or the party of ʿAli.* Partisans of ʿAli; Muslims (11 percent of the total) who believe that the only proper rulers of the Islamic community are direct patrilineal descendants of ʿAli, the Imāms. The Shīʿī lost the battle for historical dominance of the Muslim world;

the last Imām, the Mahdī, went into hiding and one day is to return to the world to bring about the reign of justice. Among the most famous Shīʿī groups are the Zaydī, the Ismāʿīlī, and the Imāmī.

Ṣiffīn. Battle fought in 658 (A.H. 38) between ʿAlī and Muʿāwiya in which the Khārijī withdrew from the camp of ʿAlī after he accepted arbitration.

Sijilmāsa. Major city built in the Tāfilālat oasis of Morocco by the Khārijī; crucial stopover in trans-Saharan trade, 700–1700 (A.H. 100–1100).

Silsila (pl. salāsil). *Chain, lineage, dynasty.* Lines of transmission from one generation to the next, can be spiritual or genealogical.

Ṣūfī. Mystic; the commonest term for that aspect of Islam which is based on the mystical life.

Sulaymān. *Solomon.*

Sulṭa. *Power, authority.*

Sulṭān. *Power, reign, authority.* Title for dominant political figures in Islamic history, used originally in the ʿAbbāsī period to denote non-caliphal rulers; title conferred upon groom in marriage rites.

Sunna. *Customary practices.* Particularly those associated with the time of Muḥammad; they are embodied in the Ḥadīth.

Sunnī. That majority of Muslims (88 percent) who accept the authority of the early caliphs of Islam, in contrast to the Shīʿī and the Khārijī.

Sūra. Verse(s) from the Qurʾān.

Sūs. Rich agricultural region in southern Morocco, south of the High Atlas Mountains.

Tāfilālat. Important oasis from which Morocco's current ruling dynasty comes; for nearly 1,000 years part of a main trans-Saharan trade route.

Ṭanja. *Tangier.* Important port in northern Morocco.

Tārūdant. Important city in the Sūs.

Tazerwālt. Important religious and cultural center in southern Morocco.

ʿUmar. Companion, father-in-law of the Prophet, who married his daughter Ḥafṣa. Second of the Rāshidūn caliphs, ruled from 634–644 (A.H. 13–23).

Umm Ḥabība. *Mother of Ḥabība.* Wife of Muḥammad, sister of Muʿāwiya, daughter of Abū Sufyān.

Umm Kalthūm. *Mother of Kalthūm.* Daughter of Muḥammad, given to ʿUthmān, the third caliph, in marriage.

al-Umma. *The Community of Believers.*

al-ʿUrs. *The Wedding.*

ʿUthmān. Companion, brother-in-law of Muḥammad, third of the Rāshidūn caliphs, from powerful Banū Umayya clan of the Quraysh. Married Muḥammad's daughters Ruqayya and Umm Kalthūm, ruled from 644–655 (A.H. 23–35).

Wādī al-Makhāzin. Location of 1578 (A.H. 986) battle between Moroccans and Portuguese.

Wazīr (pl. wuzarāʾ). *Minister, vizier.*

Yālaṭīf. *Oh My God, the Kind One.* A form of Islamic prayer uttered in times of calamity and crisis; became important in Moroccan resistance to the French.

Yawm al-Jamal. *Day of the Camel.* Battle of the Day of the Camel, in which 'Alī in 656 (A.H. 36) defeated the army of 'Ā'isha and other companions of the Prophet, who challenged 'Alī's ascension to the caliphate upon the death of 'Uthmān in 655 (A.H. 35).

Yazīd. Second caliph of the Banū Umayya dynasty, whose army defeated al-Ḥusayn, the son of 'Alī, at Karbalā'; son of Mu'āwiya, ruled from 680–683 (A.H. 60–64).

references

Aafif, Muhammad. 1980–1981. "Les harkas Hassaniennes d'apreš l'oeuvre d'A. Ibn Zidane." *Hesperis Tamuda* 19:153–168.

Abitol, M. 1980. "Le Maroc et le commerce transsaharien du XVIIe siècle au début du XIXe siècle." *Revue de l'occident musulman et de la méditerranée* 30:5–19.

Abu-Lughod, Janet L. 1980. *Rabat: Urban Apartheid in Morocco.* Princeton, N.J.: Princeton University Press.

Abu-Lughod, Lila. 1986. *Veiled Sentiments.* Berkeley: University of California Press.

Abun-Nasr, Jamil M. 1971. "The Independence Movement of the Maghrib." *Tarikh* 4:54–67.

—— 1987. *A History of the Maghrib in the Islamic Period.* Cambridge: Cambridge University Press.

Addison, Lancelot. 1671. *West Barbary, or, A Sort of Narrative of the Revolutions of the Kingdoms of the Fez and Morocco.* Oxford, England: Oxford Theatre.

Aeschylus. 1953. *Oresteia: Agamemnon, The Libation Bearers, The*

Eumenides. Translated by Richard Lattimore. Chicago: University of Chicago Press.

Africanus, Leo (al-Wazzan, al-Hasan). 1896 [1526; tr. 1600]. *The History and Description of Africa and the Notable Things Therein Contained.* Translated by John Pory. 2 vols. London: Bedford Press.

Ajami, Fouad. 1986. *The Vanished Imam: Musa Al Sadr and the Shia of Lebanon.* Ithaca, N.Y. and London: Cornell University Press.

Alland, Alexander, Jr. 1985. "Rituel masculin de procréation et symbolisme phallique." *L'Homme* 25(2):37–55.

Altorki, Soraya. 1986. *Women in Saudi Arabia.* New York: Columbia University Press.

al-Amin, Ahmed. 1968. "L'évolution de la femme et le problème du mariage au Maroc." *Présence africaine* 68:32–51.

Anderson, Benedict. 1983. *Imagined Communities: Reflections on the Origin and Spread of Nationalism.* London: Verso.

Anderson, Lisa. 1986. *The State and Social Transformation in Tunisia and Libya, 1830–1980.* Princeton: Princeton University Press.

Arberry, Arthur. 1955. *The Koran Interpreted.* New York: Macmillan.

Asad, Talal, ed. 1973. *Anthropology and the Colonial Encounter.* London: Ithaca Press.

Ashford, Douglas. 1961. *Political Change in Morocco.* Princeton: Princeton University Press.

Aubin, Eugène. 1912. *Le Maroc d'aujourd'hui.* Paris: Colin.

Auriol, Vincent. 1971. *Journal du septennat 1947–1954.* Annotated by Jacques Ozouf. Vol. 7, *1953–1954.* Paris: Colin.

Awn, Peter. 1984. "Faith and Practice." In Majorie Kelley, ed., *Islam,* pp. 1–27. New York: Praeger.

al-Bakri, Abu 'Ubayd 'Abdallah ibn 'Abdul-'Aziz. 1857 [1000s]. *Kitab al-mughrib fi dhikr bilad Ifriqiya wa 'l-Maghrib.* Arabic text with French translation. Alger: Imprimerie du gouvernement.

Barakat, Halim, ed. 1985. *Contemporary North Africa: Issues of Development and Integration.* Washington, D.C.: Georgetown University Center for Contemporary Arab Studies.

Basha, Najat. 1976. *Le commerce au maghreb du XIe au XIVe siècles.* Tunis: Université de Tunis.

Beidelman, T. O. 1966. "The Ox and Nuer Sacrifice." *Man* 1:453–467.

—— 1987. "Sacrifice and Sacred Rule in Africa." *American Ethnologist* 14:542–551.

Bel, Alfred. 1932. "La fête des sacrifices en Berbèrie." *Cinquantenaire de la faculté des lettres d'Alger, 1881–1931.* Algier: n.p.

—— 1908. "Notice sur l'ouvrage intitulé." In *Actes du XIVe Congrés International des Orientalistes, Alger 1905.* Troisième partie, pp. 160–167. Paris: Ernest Leroux.

—— 1938. *La religion musulmane en Berbèrie.* Paris: Geuthner.

Benedict, Burton. 1983. *The Anthropology of World's Fairs.* Berkeley: Scolar Press.

Berglund, Axel-Ivar. 1976. *Zulu Thought Patterns and Symbolism.* London: C. Hurst.

Berlin, Brent and Paul Kay. 1969. *Basic Color Terms: Their Universality and Evolution.* Berkeley: University of California Press.

Berque, Jacques. 1958. *Al-Yousi: Problèmes de la culture marocaine au XVIIe siècle.* Paris: Mouton.

—— 1969. *Les Arabes d'hier à demain.* Paris: Editions du Seuil.

Berrada, Mohamed. 1985. "The New Cultural and Imaginative Discourse in Morocco: Utopic Change." In Halim Barakat, ed., *Contemporary North Africa: Issues of Development and Integration,* pp. 231–249. Washington, D.C.: Georgetown University Center for Contemporary Arab Studies.

Berthier, Paul. 1966. *Les anciennes sucreries du Maroc et leurs réseaux hydrauliques.* 2 vols. Rabat: Imprimerie Français et Marocain.

Bettelheim, Bruno. 1954. *Symbolic Wounds: Puberty Rites and the Envious Male.* Glencoe, Ill.: Free Press.

—— 1976. *The Uses of Enchantment: The Meaning and Importance of Fairy Tales.* New York: Knopf.

Bidwell, Robin. 1973. *Morocco Under Colonial Rule: French Administration of Tribal Areas, 1912–1956.* London: Frank Cass.

Bloch, Maurice. 1974. "Symbols, Song, Dance, and Features of Articulation: Is Religion an Extreme Form of Traditional Authority?" *European Journal of Sociology* 15:55–81.

—— 1986. *From Blessing to Violence: History and Ideology in the Circumcision Ritual of the Merina of Madagascar.* New York: Cambridge University Press.

Bohannan, Laura and Paul Bohannan. 1953. *The Tiv of Central Nigeria.* London: International African Institute.

Bolle, Kees W. 1983. "A World of Sacrifice." *History of Religions* 23: 37–63.

Boucharb, Ahmed. 1984. *Dukkala wa 'l-istiʿmar al-Burtughali ila ikhla Asafi wa Azammur.* Casablanca: Dar al-Thaqafa.

al-Boudrari, Hasan. 1984. "La maison du cautionnement: Les shurfa d'Quezzane de la sainteté à la puissance." Ph.D. diss., Ecole des Hautes Etudes en Sciences Sociales. Paris.

Bouhdiba, Abdelwahab. 1985. *Sexuality in Islam.* Translated by Alan Sheridan. London: Routledge and Kegan Paul.

Bourdieu, Pierre. 1977. *Outline of a Theory of Practice.* Translated by Richard Nice. New York: Cambridge University Press.

Bourdillon, M. F. C. and Meyer Fortes, eds. 1980. *Sacrifice.* New York: Academic Press.

Bousquet, Georges Henri. 1949. *Les grandes pratiques rituelles de l'Islam.* Paris: Presses Universitaires de France.

—— 1957. *Les Berbères.* Paris: Universitaires de France.

—— 1959. "Quelques remarques sur la pratique rituelle en Afrique du Nord, principalement au Maroc." *Revue africaine* 103:324–345.

references

Bovill, Edward William. 1968. *The Golden Trade of the Moors.* 2d ed. London: Oxford University Press.

Braithwaite, John. 1929 [1729]. *The History of the Revolutions in the Empire of Morocco Upon the Death of the Late Emperor, Muley Ishmael.* London: Arno Press.

Braudel, Fernand. 1928. "Les Espagnols et l'afrique de nord de 1492 à 1577." *Revue africaine* 69:184–223, 350–410.

—— 1973. *Capitalism and Material Life, 1400–1800.* Translated by Miriam Kochan. London: Weidenfeld and Nicolson.

Braun, Frank. 1978. "Morocco: Anatomy of a Palace Revolution that Failed." *International Journal of Middle East Studies* 9:63–72.

Brignon, Jean, Abdelaziz Amine, Brahim Boutaleb, et al. 1967. *Histoire du Maroc.* Paris: Hatier.

Brockelmann, Carl. 1973. *History of the Islamic Peoples.* Translated by Joel Carmichael and Moshe Perlmann. New York: Capricorn.

Brown, Kenneth. 1972. "The Impact of the Dahir Berbere in Sale." In Ernest Gellner and Charles Micaud, eds., *Arabs and Berbers,* pp. 201–216. London: Lexington.

—— 1976. *People of Sale: Tradition and Change in a Moroccan City.* Cambridge, Mass.: Harvard University Press.

Brown, L. Carl. 1974. *The Tunisia of Ahmad Bey, 1837–1855.* Princeton, N.J.: Princeton University Press.

Brown, Roger. 1958. "How Shall Things Be Called?" *Psychological Review* 65:14–21.

al-Bukhari. 1862–1868 [800s]. *Kitab al-Jami^c al-Sahih,* vols. 1–3. Leiden: E. J. Brill.

—— 1907–1908 [800s]. *Kitab al-Jami^c al-Sahih,* vol. 4. Leiden: E. J. Brill.

—— 1903–1914 [800s]. *Al-Sahih: Les traditions Islamiques.* 6 vols. Translated by O. Houdas. Paris.

—— 1964. *L'authentique tradition musulmane: Choix de hadiths.* Translated by G. H. Bousquet. Paris: Bernard Grasset Editeur.

Bulliet, Richard W. 1972. *The Patricians of Nishapur.* Cambridge, Mass.: Harvard University Press.

—— 1975. *The Camel and the Wheel.* Cambridge, Mass.: Harvard University Press.

—— 1979. *Conversion to Islam in the Medieval Period.* Cambridge, Mass.: Harvard University Press.

—— 1981. "Botr et Béranès: Hypothèses sur l'histoire des Berbères." *Annales économies, sociétés, civilisations* 1981(1):104–116. Paris: Colin.

Burke, Edmund III. 1972. "The Image of the Moroccan State in French Ethnological Literature." In Ernest Gellner and Charles Micaud, eds., *Arabs and Berbers,* pp. 175–200. London: Lexington.

—— 1976. *Prelude to Protectorate in Morocco: Precolonial Protest and Resistance, 1860–1912.* Chicago: University of Chicago Press.

Burkert, Walter. 1983. *Homo Necans: The Anthropology of Ancient Greek Sacrificial Ritual and Myth.* Berkeley: University of California Press.

Caille, René. 1830. *Travels Through Central Africa to Timbuctoo and Across the Great Desert to Morocco, 1824–1828.* 2 vols. London: Henry Colburn and Richard Bentley.

Case, Sue-Ellen. 1985. "Classic Drag: The Greek Creation of Female Parts." *Theatre Journal* 37(3):317–327.

Celerier, J. 1923. "Le Maroc, pays du sucre et de l'or." *France-Maroc* 7:113–115.

Cenival, Pierre. 1925. "La légende du juif Ibn Mech'al et la fête du sultan des tolba à Fes." *Hespéris* 5:137–218.

Chelhod, Joseph. 1955. *La sacrifice chez les Arabes.* Paris: Presses Universitaires de France.

Chenier, M. 1788. *The Present State of the Empire of Morocco.* 2 vols. London: G. G. J. and J. Robinson.

Chronique de Santa-Cruz du Cap de Gué [Agadir]. 1934 [1500s]. (Anonymous). Edited and translated by Pierre Cenival. Paris: Paul Geuthner.

Cigar, Norman. 1981. "Socioeconomic Structures and the Development of an Urban Bourgeoisie in Precolonial Morocco." *Maghreb Review* 6:55–76.

Clark, Kenneth. 1956. *The Nude: A Study in Ideal Form.* Bollingen Series 35, no. 2. New York: Pantheon Books.

Colin, Edmé René [pseudonym Defontin-Maxange]. 1929. *Le grand Ismail: Empereur du Maroc.* Paris: Marpon.

Colson, Elizabeth. 1974. *Tradition and Contract: The Problem of Order.* Chicago: Aldine.

—— 1977. "A Continuing Dialogue: Prophets and Local Shrines Among the Tonga of Zambia." In R. Werbner, ed., *Regional Cultures*, pp. 119–139. London: Academic Press.

—— 1980. "The Resilience of Matrilineality: Gwembe and Plateau Tonga Adaptations." In Linda S. Cordell and Stephen Beckerman, eds., *The Versatility of Kinship*, pp. 359–374. New York: Academic Press.

Comaroff, Jean. 1985. *Body of Power, Spirit of Resistance: The Culture and History of a South African People.* Chicago: University of Chicago Press.

Comaroff, John L. and Simon Roberts. 1981. *Rules and Processes: The Cultural Logic of Dispute in an African Context.* Chicago: University of Chicago Press.

Combs-Schilling, M. E. 1981. "The Segmentary Model Versus Dyadic Ties: The False Dichotomy." *MERA Forum* 5(3):5–18.

—— 1984. "Islam, Power, and Change: Variation in North African Independence Movements." In Jack Glazier et al., eds., *Opportunity, Constraint, and Change: Essays in Honor of Elizabeth Colson.* Kroeber Anthropological Society Papers, no. 63–64.

—— 1985. "Family and Friend in a Moroccan Boom Town: The Segmentary Debate Reconsidered." *American Ethnologist* 12:659–675.

—— n.d. Abiding Constraints: Permanence and Change in a Moroccan Boom Town. Manuscript.

—— n.d. Sexuality and Sacrifice: God's Ascent and Woman's Fall. Manuscript.

Cook, Mark, ed. 1984. *Issues in Person Perception.* New York: Methuen.

Cooper, Anna Julia. 1969 [1892]. *A Voice from the South.* New York: Negro Universities Press.

Coram, A. 1972. "The Berbers and the Coup." In Ernest Gellner and Charles Micaud, eds., *Arabs and Berbers,* pp. 425–430. London: Lexington.

Cornell, Vincent J. 1983. "The Logic of Analogy and the Role of the Sufi Shaykh in Post-Marinid Morocco." *International Journal of Middle Eastern Studies* 15:67–93.

—— 1986. "Socioeconomic Dimensions of Reconquista and Jihad in Morocco: Portuguese Dukkala and the Sa'dian Sus, 1450–1557." 1986 draft of working paper. Von Grunebaum Center for Near Eastern Studies, University of California, Los Angeles.

Cour, Auguste. 1920. *La dynastie marocaine des Beni Wattas (1420–1554).* Constantine: Imprimerie D. Braham.

Crapanzano, Vincent. 1973. *The Hamadsha: A Study in Moroccan Ethnopsychiatry.* Berkeley: University of California Press.

—— 1980. *Tuhami: Portrait of a Moroccan.* Chicago: University of Chicago Press.

Crow, John. 1963. *Spain: The Root and the Flower.* New York: Harper and Row.

Cruse, D. A. 1977. "The Pragmatics of Lexical Specificity." *Journal of Linguistics* 13:153–164.

Cudsi, Alexander S. and Ali E. Hillal Dessouki, eds. 1981. *Islam and Power.* London: Croom Helm.

Damis, John. 1970. "Developments in Morocco Under the French Protectorate, 1925–1943." *The Middle East Journal* 24:74–86.

—— 1983. *Conflict in Northwest Africa: The Western Sahara Dispute.* Stanford, Ca.: Hoover Institution Press.

Das, Veena. 1983. "Language of Sacrifice." *Man* 18:445–62.

Davidson, Basil and F. K. Buah. 1966. *A History of West Africa: To the Nineteenth Century.* Garden City, N.Y.: Doubleday/Anchor Books.

Davis, Susan Schaefer. 1983. *Patience and Power: Women's Lives in a Moroccan Village.* Cambridge, Mass.: Schenkman.

Deaux, George. 1969. *The Black Death: 1347.* New York: Weybright and Talley.

de Castries, Henry Comte. 1921. "Les signes de validation des chérifs Saadiens." *Hesperis* 37(3):317–327.

Defontin-Maxange (pseudonym) *see* Colin, Edmé René.

de Heusch, Luc. 1985. *Sacrifice in Africa: A Structuralist Approach.* Translated by Linda O'Brian and Alice Morton. Bloomington: Indiana University Press.

de la Faye, Jean. 1726. *Relation on forme journal du voiage pour la rédemption des captifs, aux roiaumes de Maroc et d'Alger 1723, 1724, 1725.* Paris: Louis Sevestre et Pierre-François Giffart.

Deverdun, Gaston. 1959. *Marrakech: Des origines à 1912.* 2 vols. Rabat: Editions Techniques Nord-Africaines.

de Wolf, Jean. 1971. "Rabat: La mutinerie sanglante." *Jeune Afrique* (July 20), 550:19–33.

Di Piero, W. S. 1980. "Partisans." *Carolina Quarterly* 32(1):30–31.

—— 1980. Untitled. *Carolina Quarterly* 32(2):22.

Dols, Michael W. 1977. *The Black Death in the Middle East.* Princeton: Princeton University Press.

Domhoff, G. William. 1974. *The Bohemian Grove and Other Retreats.* New York: Harper and Row.

Dos Passos, John. 1969. *The Portugal Story: Three Centuries of Exploration and Discovery.* Garden City, N.Y.: Doubleday.

Doutte, Edmond. 1909. *Magie et religion dans l'Afrique du Nord.* Alger: Lemcke and Buchner.

Drague, Georges. 1951. *Esquisse d'histoire religieuse du Maroc.* Paris: Peyronnet.

Dresch, Paul. 1984. "The Position of Shaykhs Among the Northern Tribes of Yemen." *Man* 19:31–49.

—— 1986. "The Significance of Course Events Take in Segmentary Systems." *American Ethnologist* 13:309–324.

Dunn, Ross E. 1977. *Resistance in the Desert: Moroccan Response to French Imperialism, 1881–1912.* Madison: University of Wisconsin Press.

Durkheim, Emile. 1965 [1912]. *The Elementary Forms of Religious Life.* Translated by Joseph Ward Swain. New York: Free Press.

Dwyer, Daisy. 1978. *Images and Self-Images: Male and Female in Morocco.* New York: Columbia University Press.

Dwyer, Kevin. 1982. *Moroccan Dialogues: Anthropology in Question.* Baltimore: Johns Hopkins University Press.

Dziubinski, Andrzej. 1972. "L'armée et la flotte de guerre marocaines à l'époque des sultans de la dynastie Saadienne." *Hesperis-Tamuda* 13:61–94.

Eanes de Azurara, Gomes. 1936 [1450]. *Conquests and Discoveries of Henry the Navigator: Being the Chronicles of Azurara.* Edited by Virginia de Castro e Almedia, translated by Bernard Miall. London: Allen and Unwin.

Easton, David. 1965. *A System of Analysis of Political Life.* New York: Wiley.

Eickelman, Dale F. 1976. *Moroccan Islam: Tradition and Society in a Pilgrimage Center.* Austin: University of Texas Press.

—— 1981. *The Middle East: An Anthropological Approach.* Englewood Cliffs, N.J.: Prentice-Hall.

—— 1985. *Knowledge and Power in Morocco: The Education of a*

Twentieth-Century Notable. Princeton, N.J.: Princeton University Press.

—— 1986. "Royal Authority and Religious Legitimacy: Morocco's Elections, 1960–1984." In Myron J. Aronoff, ed., *The Frailty of Authority*. New Brunswick, N.J.: Transaction Books.

Elder, Charles D. and Roger W. Cobb. 1983. *The Political Uses of Symbols*. New York: Longman.

The Encyclopedia of Islam. 1913–1936. 4 vols. London: Luzac and Co.

—— 1960–1986. Rev. ed. 4 vols. Leiden: E. J. Brill.

Entelis, John P. 1980. *Comparative Politics of North Africa: Algeria, Morocco, and Tunisia*. Syracuse: Syracuse University Press.

—— 1989. *Culture and Counterculture in Moroccan Politics*. Boulder, Colo.: Westview Press.

Erckmann, Jules. 1885. *Le Maroc moderne*. Paris: Librairie Coloniale.

Erikson, Erik. 1966. "Ontogeny of Ritualization." In Rudolph. M. Loewenstein et al., eds., *Psychoanalysis—A General Psychology: Essays in Honor of Heinz Hartmann*. New York: International Universities Press.

Euripides. 1973. *Iphigeneia in Tauris*. Translated by Richmond Lattimore. New York: Oxford University Press.

—— 1978. *Iphigeneia in Aulis*. Translated by W. S. Merwin and George E. Dimock, Jr. New York: Oxford University Press.

Eustache, Daniel. 1970–1971. *Corpus des dirhams Idrisi et contemporains*. Rabat: Banque du Maroc.

—— 1984. *Corpus des monnaies ʿAlawites*. 3 vols. Rabat: Banque du Maroc.

Evans-Pritchard, E. E. 1956. *Nuer Religion*. Oxford: Clarendon Press.

Farid, Malik. 1969. *The Holy Qurʾan*. English translation and commentary. Rabwah, Pakistan: Oriental and Religious Publishing Corp.

al-Fasi, ʿAlal. 1948. *Al-Harakat al-Istiqlaliyya fiʾl-Maghrib al-ʿArabi*. Cairo.

Fernea, Elizabeth W. and Basima Q. Bezirgan, eds. 1977. *Middle Eastern Muslim Women Speak*. Austin: University of Texas Press.

Fischer, Michael M. J. 1980. *Iran: From Religious Dispute to Revolution*. Cambridge: Harvard University Press.

al-Fishtali, ʿAbd al-ʿAziz. 1973 [1500s]. *Manahil al-Safa fi ʾl-akhbar al-muluk al-shurafaʾ*. Rabat: Matbuʿat Wizarat al-Awqat.

Foucault, Michel. 1972. *The Archaeology of Knowledge and The Discourse on Language*. Translated by A. M. Sheridan Smith and Rupert Sawyer. New York: Pantheon.

Fox, Matthew. 1988. *The Coming of the Cosmic Christ: The Healing of Mother Earth and the Birth of a Global Renaissance*. New York: Harper and Row.

Friedrich, Paul. 1978. *The Meaning of Aphrodite*. Chicago: University of Chicago Press.

Gailland, Henri. 1905. *Une ville de l'Islam: Fes*. Paris: Phillippe Renouard.

Galloway, J. H. 1977. "The Mediterranean Sugar Industry." *Geographical Review* 67(2):177–92.

Garraty, John A. and Peter Gay, eds. 1972. *The Columbia History of the World*. New York: Harper and Row.

Gaudrefroy-Demombynes, M. 1923. *Le pèlerinage à la Mekke: Etude d'histoire religieuse*. Paris: Geuthner.

Geertz, Clifford. 1968. *Islam Observed*. New Haven: Yale University Press.

Geertz, Clifford, Hildred Geertz, and Lawrence Rosen, eds. 1979. *Meaning and Order in Moroccan Society*. New York: Cambridge University Press.

Geertz, Hildred. 1979. "The Meanings of Family Ties." In C. Geertz, H. Geertz, and L. Rosen, eds., *Meaning and Order in Moroccan Society*, pp. 315–391. New York: Cambridge University Press.

Gellner, Ernest. 1969. *Saints of the Atlas*. Chicago: University of Chicago Press.

—— 1981. *Muslim Society*. Cambridge: Cambridge University Press.

Gellner, Ernest and Charles Micaud, eds. 1972. *Arabs and Berbers: From Tribe to Nation in North Africa*. London: Lexington.

Gellner, Ernest and John Waterbury, eds. 1977. *Patrons and Clients in Mediterranean Societies*. London: Duckworth.

Gentleman's Magazine. 1810. "Queen Elizabeth to Mulay Abd el Melk, 1577." September, p. 219.

al-Ghazzali, Abu Hamid. 1953 [1000s]. *Le livre des bons usages en matière de mariage* (extrait de *Vivification des sciences de la foi*). Translated [into French] and annotated by L. Bercher and G. H. Bousquet. Paris. Maisonneuve.

Gilligan, Carol. 1982. *In a Different Voice· Psychological Theory and Women's Development*. Cambridge, Mass.: Harvard University Press

Girard, René. 1977. *Violence and the Sacred*. Translated by Patrick Gregory. Baltimore: Johns Hopkins University Press.

Gluckman, Max. 1963. *Order and Rebellion in Tribal Africa*. London: Cohen and West. (See especially chapter 3, "Rituals of Rebellion in South-East Africa," pp. 110–136.)

Goody, Jack. 1976. *Production and Reproduction: A Comparative Study of the Domestic Domain*. New York: Cambridge University Press.

Gose, Peter. 1986. "Sacrifice and the Commodity Form in the Andes." *Man* 21:296–310.

Gottfried, Robert S. 1983. *The Black Death: Natural and Human Disaster in Medieval Europe*. New York: Free Press.

Gould, Stephen Jay. 1987. "Life's Little Joke." *Natural History* 96: 16–25.

Green, Arnold H. 1978. *The Tunisian Ulama, 1878–1915*. Atlantic Highlands, N.J.: Humanities Press.

Griffin, Susan. 1981. *Pornography and Silence: Culture's Revenge Against Nature*. New York: Harper and Row.

el-Guindi, Fadwa. 1981. "Veiling Infitah with Muslim Ethic: Egypt's Contemporary Islamic Movement." *Social Problems* 28:465–485.

Halstead, John P. 1967. *Rebirth of a Nation: The Origins and Rise of Moroccan Nationalism, 1912–1944*. Cambridge, Mass.: Harvard University Press.

Hamidullah, Muhammad. 1960. "Le pèlerinage à la Mecque." *Les Pèlerinages: Sources Orientales* 3:117. Paris: Editions du Seuil.

Hammoudi, Abdallah. 1980. "Sainteté, pouvoir, et société: Tamgrout aux XVII et XVIII siècles." *Annales économies, sociétés, civilisations* 35: 615–649.

—— 1988. *La victime et ses masques*. Paris: Editions du Seuil.

Hanks, William F. 1986. "Authenticity and Ambivalence in the Text: A Colonial Maya Case." *American Ethnologist* 13:721–744.

Harakat, Ibrahim. 1985. *Al-maghrib al-tarikh*. 4 vols. Casablanca: Dar al-Rashad al-Haditha.

Hart, David. 1981. *Dadda 'Atta and His Forty Grandsons: The Socio-Political Organisation of the Ait 'Atta of Southern Morocco*. Cambridge: Middle East and North African Studies Press.

Harris, Lawrence. 1909. *With Mulai Hafid at Fez: Behind the Scenes in Morocco*. London: Smith, Elder.

Harris, Walter B. 1889. *The Land of an African Sultan: Travels in Morocco, 1887, 1888, 1889*. London: Sampson, Low, Marston, Searle, and Rivington.

—— 1895. *Tafilet: The Narrative of a Journey of Exploration in the Atlas Mountains and the Oasis of the North-West Sahara*. Edinburgh and London: William Blackwood.

—— 1921. *Morocco That Was*. Edinburgh and London: William Blackwood.

Hermassi, Elbaki. 1972. *Leadership and National Development in North Africa*. Berkeley: University of California Press.

Hill, Dorothy Combs. n.d. *The Female Imagination in an Age of Transition: The Fiction of Lee Smith*. Twayne's United States Author Series [in press]. Boston: Twayne.

Hodges, Tony. 1983. *Western Sahara: The Roots of a Desert War*. Westport, Conn.: Lawrence Hill.

Hodgson, Marshall G. S. 1974a. *The Classical Age of Islam*. Vol. 1 of *The Venture of Islam: Conscience and History in a World Civilization*. Chicago: University of Chicago Press.

—— 1974b. *The Expansion of Islam in the Middle Periods*. Vol. 2 of *The Venture of Islam: Conscience and History in a World Civilization*. Chicago: University of Chicago Press.

—— 1974c. *The Gunpowder Empires and Modern Times*. Vol. 3 of *The Venture of Islam: Conscience and History in a World Civilization*. Chicago: University of Chicago Press.

Hopkins, A. G. 1973. *An Economic History of West Africa*. London: Longman.

Howard-Merriam, Kathleen. 1984. "Women's Political Participation in Morocco's Development: How Much and For Whom?" *The Maghreb Review* 9:12–23.

Hrdy, Sarah Blaffer. 1983. *The Woman That Never Evolved.* Cambridge: Mass.: Harvard University Press.

Hubert, Henri and Marcel Mauss. 1964 [1898]. *Sacrifice: Its Nature and Function.* Chicago: University of Chicago Press.

Ibn Hawqal, Abu al-Qasim Muhammad. 1845 [900s]. *Description de Palerme au milieu du Xe siècle de l'ère vulgaire.* Paris: Imprimerie royale.

Ibn Hisham, Abd al-Malik. 1955 [1300s]. *Al-Sirah al-Nabawiyah.* 2 vols. Edited by ʿA. al-Shibli, M. al-Saqa and A. al-Abyari. Cairo: n.p.

Ibn Khaldun. 1969 [1381]. *The Muqaddimah: An Introduction to History.* Translated by Franz Rosenthal, edited and abridged by N. A. Dawood. Princeton, N.J.: Princeton University Press.

Ibn Tasabat. 1518. *Bibliography of Morocco.* No. 424. Rabat: Royal Archives.

Ibn Taymiya, Ahmad. 1321–1322. *Minhaj al-Sunna al-Nabawiya.* Cairo.

al-Idrisi, Abu ʿAbdullah Muhammad. 1836–1840 [1100s]. *Géographie d'Idrisi.* Translated [into French] by P. A. Jaubert. Paris: Imprimerie royale.

al-Ifrani, Muhammad al-Saghir ibn Muhammad. 1889 [1700s]. *Nozhet-Elhadi [Nuzhat al-hadi]: Histoire de la dynastie Saadienne au Maroc (1511–1670).* Translated and edited by O. Houdas. Paris: Leroux.

Ihrai, Said. 1986. *Pouvoir et influence: Etat, partis et politique étrangère au Maroc.* Rabat: Edino.

Issawi, Charles, ed. 1966. *The Economic History of the Middle East, 1800–1914.* Chicago: University of Chicago Press.

Jackson, James Grey. 1968 [1809]. *An Account of the Empire of Morocco, and the Districts of Suse and Tafileit.* London: Frank Cass.

Jacques-Meunié, D. 1982. *Le Maroc saharien des origines à 1670.* 2 vols. Paris: Librairie Klincksieck.

Jamous, Raymond. 1981. *Honneur et baraka.* Paris: Editions de la Maison des Sciences de l'Homme.

Jardine, A. 1789. *Letters From Barbary, France, Spain, Portugal.* Dublin: H. Chamberlaine and P. Byrne.

Jay, Nancy. 1981. "Throughout Your Generations Forever: A Sociology of Blood Sacrifice." Ph.D. diss., Brandeis University.

—— 1985. "Sacrifice as Remedy for Having Been Born of Woman." In Clarissa Atkinson, Constance Buchanan, and Margaret Miles, eds., *Immaculate and Powerful: The Female in Sacred Image and Social Reality,* pp. 283–309. Cambridge, Mass.: Harvard University Press.

al-Jazuli, Muhamad. 1976 [1400s]. *Dalaʾil al-Khayrat wa-Shawariq al-Anwar fi Dhikr al-Salat ʿala al-Nabi al-Mukhtar.* Rabat: n.p.

Johnson, Mark. 1987. *The Body in the Mind: The Bodily Basis of Reason and Imagination.* Chicago: University of Chicago Press.

references

Jones, Anne Goodwyn. 1986. "The Orality of *Oral History.*" *Iron Mountain Review* 3(1):15–19.

Joseph, Roger and Terri Brint Joseph. 1987. *The Rose and the Thorn: Semiotic Structures in Morocco.* Tucson: University of Arizona Press.

Joseph, Suad. 1986. "Women and Politics in the Middle East." *M.E.R.I.P. Reports* 16:3–7.

Julien, Charles André. 1951–1952 [1931]. *Histoire de l'Afrique du Nord: Tunisie, Algerie, Maroc.* 2 vols. Paris: Payot.

—— 1978. *Le Maroc face aux impérialismes, 1415–1956.* Paris: Editions J. A.

Kabbaj, Mohammed Mostafa. 1979. "Traditional Child Socialization and the Incursion of Mass Communication in Morocco." *International Social Science Journal* 31:429–443.

Kably, Muhammad. 1978. "Musahama fi Tarikh al-Tamhid li-Zuhur Dawlat al-Sa'diyyin." *Majallat kulliyat al-adab* (3–4):7–59. Rabat.

Kafka, John S. 1983. "Challenge and Confirmation in Ritual Action." *Psychiatry* 46:31–39.

Khalidi, Rashid. 1985. *Under Siege: P.L.O. Decisionmaking During the 1982 War.* New York: Columbia University Press.

Kierkegaard, Sören. 1983 [1843]. *Fear and Trembling.* Edited and translated by Howard Hong and Edna Hong. Princeton: Princeton University Press.

Kraiem, Mustapha. 1973. *La Tunisie précoloniale.* 2 vols. Tunis: Société Tunisienne de Diffusion.

Kramer, Jane. 1970. *Honor to the Bride like the Pigeon That Guards Its Grain Under the Clove Tree.* New York: Farrar, Straus and Giroux.

Lakoff, George. 1987. *Women, Fire, and Dangerous Things: What Categories Reveal About the Mind.* Chicago: University of Chicago Press.

Lammens, Henri. 1912. *Fatima et les filles de Mahomet.* Rome: Pontifical Institute.

Lan, David. 1985. *Guns and Rain: Guerillas and Spirit Mediums in Zimbabwe.* Berkeley: University of California Press.

Langer, Suzanne K. 1957. *Philosophy in a New Key: A Study in the Symbolism of Reason, Rite, and Art.* Cambridge, Mass.: Harvard University Press.

Lapidus, Ira. 1988. *A History of Islamic Societies.* Cambridge: Cambridge University Press.

Laroui, Abdallah, 1977a. *The History of the Maghrib: An Interpretive Essay.* Princeton, N.J.: Princeton University Press.

—— 1977b. *Les origines sociales et culturelles du nationalisme marocain (1830–1912).* Paris: Maspero.

Lazarev, Gregori. 1981. "Remarques sur la seigneurie terrienne au Maroc." *Structure et cultures précapitalistes: Actes du colloque tenu a l'université, Paris VIII.* Paris: Anthropos.

Leared, Arthur. 1891. *Marocco and the Moors: Being an Account of*

Travels, With a General Description of the Country and Its People. 2d ed. Sir Richard Burton, ed. New York: Scribner and Welford.

Lejri, Abdallah. 1977. *Evolution du mouvement national: Des origines à la deuxième guerre mondiale.* 2 vols. Tunis: Maison Tunisienne de l'Edition.

Lempriere, William. 1793. *A Tour From Gibraltar to Tangier, Mogodore, Santa Cruz, Tarudant, and Thence Over Mount Atlas to Morocco: Including a Particular Account of the Royal Harem.* 2d ed. London: J. Walter.

Le Tourneau, Roger. 1965. *La vie quotidienne à Fes en 1900.* Paris: Hachette.

—— 1978 [1949]. *Fes avant le protectorat.* New York: AMS Press.

Leveau, Remy. 1985. *Le fellah marocain défenseur du trône.* 2d ed. Paris: Presses de la fondation nationale des sciences politiques.

—— 1987. "Pouvoir politique et pouvoir économique dans le Maroc de Hassan II." *Les cahiers de l'Orient* 6:31–42.

Levi-Provencal, Evariste. 1922. *Les historiens des chorfa: Essai sur la littérature historique et biographique au Maroc du XVI au XX siècle.* Paris: Larose.

—— 1954. "Un nouveau récit de la conquête de l'Afrique du Nord par les Arabes." *Arabica occidentalia* 1:17–52.

Lévi-Strauss, Claude. 1962. *La pensée sauvage.* Paris: Librairie Plon.

—— 1970. *The Raw and the Cooked.* Translated by J. and D. Weightman. London: Jonathan Cape.

—— 1976. *Structural Anthropology.* Vol. 2. Translated by Monique Layton. Chicago: University of Chicago Press.

Lewis, Archibald. 1951. *Naval Power and Trade in the Mediterranean, A.D. 500–1100.* Princeton, N.J.: Princeton University Press.

Lewis, Gilbert. 1980. *Day of Shining Red: An Essay on Understanding Ritual.* Cambridge: Cambridge University Press.

Lewis, Wyndham. 1932. *Filibusters in Barbary.* New York: Robert M. McBride.

Lindholm, Charles. 1982. *Generosity and Jealousy: The Swat Pukhtun of Northern Pakistan.* New York: Columbia University Press.

Lindsay, W. S. 1874. *History of Merchant Shipping and Ancient Commerce.* 2 vols. London: Sampson Low, Marston, Low, and Searle.

Ling, Dwight L. 1979. *Morocco and Tunisia: A Comparative History.* Washington, D.C.: University Press of America.

Linton, Ralph. 1926. "The Origin of the Skidi Pawnee Sacrifice to the Morning Star." *American Anthropologist* 28:457–466.

Livermore, H. V. 1947. *A History of Portugal.* Cambridge: Cambridge University Press.

—— 1973. *Portugal: A Short History.* Edinburgh: Edinburgh University Press.

Lopez, Robert, and Irving W. Raymond. 1961. *Medieval Trade in the Mediterranean World.* New York: Columbia University Press.

references

McNeil, William H. 1976. *Plagues and Peoples*. Garden City, N.Y.: Doubleday/Anchor Books.

Maher, Vanessa. 1974. *Women and Property in Morocco*. Cambridge: Cambridge University Press.

al-Majdhub, Abd al-Rahman. 1966 [1500s]. *Les quatrains du Medjdoub le sarcastique, poète maghrébin du XVIème siècle*. Collected and translated by Jeanne Scelles-Millié and Boukhari Khelifa. Paris: G. P. Maisonneuve et Larose.

al-Mansour, Muhammad. 1989. *Morocco in the Reign of Mawlay Sulayman, 1792–1822*. London: MENAS.

al-Maqqari. 1949 [1600s]. *Nafh al-Tib*. Vol. 7. Cairo: n.p.

Marsot, Afaf L. al-Sayyid. 1979. *Society and the Sexes in Medieval Islam*. Malibu, Ca.: Undena Publication.

Meakin, Budgett. 1899. *The Moorish Empire*. New York: Macmillan.

—— 1901. *The Land of the Moors*. New York: Macmillan.

Mernissi, Fatima. 1977. "Women, Saints, and Sanctuaries." *Signs* 3: 101–112.

—— 1982. "Virginity and Patriarchy." In Azizah al-Hibri, ed., *Women in Islam*. Elmsford, N.Y.: Pergamon Press.

—— 1987a. *Beyond the Veil: Male-Female Dynamics in a Modern Muslim Society*. Revised ed. Bloomington: Indiana University Press.

—— 1987b. *Le harem politique: Le prophète et les femmes*. Paris: Albin Michel.

—— 1988. *Chahrazade n'est pas marocaine: Autrement, elle serait salariée!* Casablanca: Le Fennec.

Merton, Robert K. 1940. "Bureaucratic Structure and Personality." *Social Forces* 18:560–568.

Messina, Maria. "Henna Party." *Natural History* 97:40–47.

Michaud, Roland and Sabrina Michaud. 1981. *Mirror of the Orient*. Boston: New York Graphic Society.

Miège, Jean-Louis. 1961. *Le Maroc et l'Europe (1830–1895)*. Paris: Presses Universitaires de France.

—— 1981. "Le commerce trans-Saharien au XIXe siècle." *Revue de l'Occident Musulman de la Méditerranée* 32:95–120.

Miller, James A. 1984. *Imlil: A Morocan Mountain Community in Change*. Boulder, Co.: Westview Press.

Miller, Judith. 1986. "Moroccan Jews Talk of the King's Fate, and Theirs" *New York Times,* July 31, A2.

Mintz, Sidney W. 1985. *Sweetness and Power: The Place of Sugar in Modern History*. New York: Viking.

Molino, Jean. 1987. "La culture comme enjeu: Considérations intempestives—notes critiques sur la culture au maghreb." *L'Annuaire de l'Afrique du Nord* 1987:29–40. Paris: CNRS.

Montagne, Robert. 1930. *Les berbères et le makhzen dans le sud du Maroc*. Paris: Librairie Félix Alcan.

Moore, Clement Henry. 1970. *Politics in North Africa: Algeria, Morocco, Tunisia.* Boston: Little, Brown.

Moore, Kenneth. 1976. *Those of the Street: The Catholic-Jews of Mallorca.* London: University of Notre Dame Press.

Moore, Sally Falk and Barbara G. Myerhoff. 1977. *Secular Ritual.* Amsterdam: Van Gorcum.

Mortimer, Edward. 1982. *Faith and Power.* London: Faber and Faber.

Mottahedeh, Roy P. 1980. *Loyalty and Leadership in an Early Islamic Society.* Princeton, N.J.: Princeton University Press.

Mouette, Germain. 1683. *Histoire des conquestes de Mouley Archy, connu sous le nom de roy de Tafilet; Et de Mouley Ismael ou Semein son frère, et son successeur à présent régnant.* Paris: Couterot.

—— 1710. *The Travels of Sieur Mouette in the Kingdoms of Fez and Morocco. During his Eleven Years of Captivity in Those Parts.* London: St. Paul's Church-yard.

Munson, Henry, Jr., trans. and ed. 1984. *The House of Si Abd Allah: The Oral History of a Moroccan Family.* New Haven: Yale University Press.

—— 1986. "The Social Base of Islamic Militancy in Moroco." *Middle East Journal* 40:267–284.

Murphy, Robert F. 1964. "Social Distance and the Veil." *American Anthropologist* 66:1257–1274.

—— 1987. *The Body Silent.* New York: Henry Holt.

Murphy, Robert F. and Leonard Kasdan. 1959. "The Structure of Parallel Cousin Marriage." *American Anthropologist* 61:17–29.

Musallam, B. F. 1983. *Sex and Society in Islam.* New York: Cambridge University Press.

al-Muslim, Abu al-Hasan. 1283 [1800s]. *Al Jamiᶜ al-Sahih.* 5 vols. Cairo. (See especially book 16, *Nikah,* on marriage.)

Naamane-Guessous, Soumaya. 1987. *Au-delà de toute pudeur: La sexualité féminine au Maroc.* Casablanca: Soden.

Nash, June. 1981. "Ethnographic Aspects of the World Capitalist System." *Annual Review of Anthropology* 10:393–424.

al-Nasiri [al-Slawi], Ahmad ibn Khalid. 1954–1956. *Kitab al-Istiqsaꜥ li akhbar duwal al-Maghrib al-Aqsa.* 9 vols. Casablanca: n.p.

Nekrouf, Younes. 1984. *La bataille des Trois Rois.* Paris: Albin Michel.

—— 1987. *Une amitié orageuse: Moulay Ismail et Louis XIV.* Paris: Albin Michel.

Nelson, James. 1978. *Embodiment.* Minneapolis: Ausburg.

Nelson, Kristina. 1985. *The Art of Reciting the Qurꜥan.* Austin: University of Texas Press.

Newitt, M. D. D. 1973. *Portuguese Settlement on the Zambesi: Exploration, Land Tenure, and Colonial Rule in East Africa.* London: Longman Group.

Newman, Katherine S. 1988. *Falling from Grace.* New York: Free Press.

Ortner, Sherry. 1974. "Is Female to Male as Nature Is to Culture?" In Michelle Zimbalist Rosaldo and Louise Lamphere, eds., *Women, Culture, and Society*. Stanford: Stanford University Press.

Ossendowski, Ferdinand. 1926. *The Fire of Desert Folk: The Account of a Journey Through Morocco*. Translated by Lewis Stanton Palen. London: George Allen and Unwin.

Pagels, Elaine. 1988. *Adam, Eve, and the Serpent*. New York: Random House.

Paquignon, Paul. 1911. "Les mouloud au maroc." *Revue du Monde Musulman* 14:525–536.

Partin, Harry B. 1967. "The Muslim Pilgrimage: Journey to Center." Ph.D. diss., University of Chicago.

Pascon, Paul. 1977. *Le Haouz de Marrakech*. 2 vols. Rabat: Editions Marocaines.

Pellow, Thomas. 1890 [1700s]. *The Adventures of Thomas Pellow of Penryn, Mariner*. London: T. Fisher Unwin.

Peter, Emrys. 1984. "The Paucity of Ritual Among Middle Eastern Pastoralists." In Akbar S. Ahmed and David Hart, eds., *Islam in Tribal Societies*. London: Routledge and Kegan Paul.

Peters, F. E. 1982. *Children of Abraham: Judaism/Christianity/Islam*. Princeton, N.J.: Princeton University Press.

Rabinow, Paul. 1975. *Symbolic Domination: Cultural Form and Historical Change in Morocco*. Chicago: University of Chicago Press.

Radcliffe-Brown, A. R. 1965. *Structure and Function in Primitive Society*. New York: Free Press.

—— 1964 [1922]. *The Andaman Islanders*. New York: Free Press.

Rahman, Fazlur. 1979. *Islam*. 2d ed. Chicago: University of Chicago Press.

Rappaport, Roy. 1971. "Ritual Sanctity and Cybernetics." *American Anthropologist* 73:59–73.

—— 1979. *Ecology, Meaning, and Religion*. Berkeley, Ca.: North Atlantic Books. (See especially "Ritual Regulation of Environmental Relations Among a New Guinea People," pp. 27–42, and "The Obvious Aspects of Ritual," pp. 173–221.)

Rassam, Amal. 1974. *The Ait Ndhir of Morocco*. Ann Arbor: University of Michigan Press.

—— 1980. "Women and Domestic Power in Morocco." *International Journal of Middle East Studies* 12:171–179.

Ricard, Robert. 1917. "Le Printemps à Fes: Le Sultan des Tolbas." *France-Maroc*, March 15, p. 32.

—— 1955. *Etudes sur l'histoire des portugais au maroc*. Coimbra: Universidade de Coimbre.

Rodinson, Maxime. 1971. *Muhammad*. Translated by Anne Carter. New York: Pantheon.

Roff, William R. 1985. "Pilgrimage: Theoretical Approaches to the Hajj." In Richard C. Martin, ed., *Approaches to Islam in Religious Studies*, pp. 78–86. Tucson: University of Arizona Press.

Rosch, Eleanor, Carolyn Mervis, Wayne Gray, David Johnson, and Penny Boyes-Braem. 1976. "Basic Objects in Natural Categories." *Cognitive Psychology* 8:382–439.

Rosen, Lawrence. 1972. "Muslim-Jewish Relations in a Moroccan City." *International Journal of Middle East Studies* 3:435–449.

—— 1979. "Social Identity and Points of Attachment: Approaches to Social Organization." In C. Geertz, H. Geertz, and L. Rosen, eds., *Meaning and Order in Moroccan Society*, pp. 19–111. Cambridge: Cambridge University Press.

Rutter, Derek. 1984. *Looking and Seeing: The Role of Visual Communication in Social Interaction.* New York: Wiley.

Saad, Elias N. 1983. *Social History of Timbuktu: The Role of Muslim Scholars and Notables.* Cambridge: Cambridge University Press.

Sabbah, Fatna A. 1984. *Woman in the Muslim Unconscious.* Translated by Mary Jo Lakeland. New York: Pergamon Press.

Sahlins, Marshall. 1976. *Culture and Practical Reason.* Chicago: University of Chicago Press.

—— 1977. "Colors and Culture." *Semiotica* 16:1–22.

—— 1985. *Islands of History.* Chicago: University of Chicago Press.

Said, Edward. 1978. *Orientalism.* New York: Vintage.

Saint Olon, François Pidou de. 1695. *Relation de l'empire de Maroc.* Paris: Chez la veuve Mabre Cramoisy.

Saliba, George, trans. and ed. 1985. *The History of al-Tabari: The Crisis of the 'Abassid Caliphate.* Albany: State University of New York Press.

Saliba, George and David A. King. 1987. *From Deferent to Equant: A Volume of Studies in the History of Science in the Ancient and Medieval Near East in Honor of E. S. Kennedy. Annals of the New York Academy of Sciences,* volume 500.

Salih, Tayeb. *The Wedding of Zein.* Translated from the Arabic by Denys Johnson-Davies. London: Heinemann.

Salmi, Ahmed. 1956. "Le genre des poèmes de nativité (mauludiyya-s) dans le royaume de Grenade et au Maroc du XIIIe au XVIIe siècle." *Hespéris* 43:335–435.

Salmon, G. 1905. "Le culte de Moulay Idris et la mosquée des chorfa à Fès." *Archives marocaines* 3:413–429.

Salzman, Philip. 1978. "Does Complementary Opposition Exist?" *American Anthropologist* 80:53–70.

—— 1981. "Culture as Enhabilmentis." In Holy Ladislov and Milan Stuchlik, eds., *The Structure of Folk Models,* pp. 233–256. New York: Academic Press.

Schneider, Jane. 1977. "Was There a Precapitalist System?" *Peasant Studies* 6:20–29.

—— 1978 "Peacocks and Penguins: The Political Economy of European Cloth and Colors." *American Ethnologist* 5:413–447.

Sebti, Abedlahad. 1984. *Aristocratie citadine, pouvoir et discours savant au Maroc précolonial: Contribution à un relecteur de la littérature généalogique fasi (XVe–début du XXe siècle)*. Thèse de troisième cycle d' histoire, Paris VII.

—— 1986. "Au Maroc: Sharifisme citadin, charisme et historiographie." *Annales* 1986:(2)433–457.

Seddon, J. David. 1977. "Tribe and State: Approaches to Maghreb History." *Maghreb Review* 2(3):23–40.

—— 1981. *Moroccan Peasants: A Century of Change in the Eastern Rif, 1870–1970*. England: William Dawson.

—— 1984. "Winter of Discontent: Economic Crisis in Tunisia and Morocco." *MERIP Reports* (October):7–16.

Sehimi, Mustapha, ed. 1981. *Citations de S. M. Hassan II*. Rabat: Société Marocaine des Editeurs Reunis.

Sell, Edward. 1920. *The Faith of Islam*. 4th ed. London: Madras.

Shinar, P. 1977. "Traditional and Reformist Mawlid Celebrations in the Maghrib." In Myriam Rosen-Ayalon, ed., *Studies in Memory of Gaston Wiet*, pp. 371–413. Jerusalem: Hebrew University.

Silverstein, Michael. 1981. "Metaforces of Power in Traditional Oratory." Department of Anthropology, University of Chicago. Paper read to the Department of Anthropology, Yale University, February 1981.

Smith, Lee. 1980. *Black Mountain Breakdown*. New York: Ballantine.

—— 1984. *Oral History*. New York: Ballantine.

—— 1988. *Fair and Tender Ladies*. New York: Putnam.

Smith, William Robertson. 1892. "Sacrifice." In *Encyclopedia Britannica*, 9th ed., 21:132–38. Chicago.

—— 1967 [1885]. *Kinship and Marriage in Early Arabia*. Boston: Beacon Press.

—— 1972 [1889]. *Lectures on the Religion of the Semites*. New York: Schocken Books.

Les sources inédites de l'histoire du maroc de 1530 à 1845. 1905–1960. Henri Comte de Castries, general editor. Paris: Leroux. (Two incomplete series of unedited sources were gathered from European archives and published in Paris between 1905 and 1960. The first, "Dynastie Saadienne," concerns the Saʿdi; the second, "Dynastie Filalienne," concerns the ʿAlawi.)

Spellberg, Denise A. 1988. "Nizam al-Mulk's Manipulation of Tradition: ʾAʾisha and the Role of Women in the Islamic Government." *The Muslim World* 127:111–117.

—— 1989. "ʾAʾisha: Religious Image and Historical Reality: The Depiction of ʿAʾisha bint Abi Bakr in Medieval Islamic Society." Ph.D. diss. Department of History, Columbia University.

Stewart, Charles F. 1964. *The Economy of Morocco, 1912–1962*. Cambridge, Mass.: Harvard University Press.

Stone, Russell A., and John Simmons, eds. 1976. *Change in Tunisia: Studies in the Social Sciences*. Albany: State University of New York Press.

Stutfield, Hugh E. M. 1886. *El Maghreb: 1200-Mile Ride Through Marocco*. London: Sampson Low, Marston, Searle, and Livingston.

Swearingten, Will D. 1987. *Moroccan Mirages: Agrarian Dreams and Deceptions, 1912–1986*. Princeton, N.J.: Princeton University Press.

Tambiah, Stanley J. 1985. *Culture, Thought, and Action: An Anthropological Perspective*. Cambridge, Mass.: Harvard University Press. (See especially "A Performative Approach to Ritual," pp. 123–166.)

Taussig, Michael T. 1980. *The Devil and Commodity Fetishism in South America*. Chapel Hill: University of North Carolina Press.

Terrasse, Henri. 1949–1950. *Histoire du Maroc*. 2 vols. Casablanca: Editions Atlantides.

Tessler, Mark. 1982. "Morocco: Institutional Pluralism and Monarchical Dominance." In I. William Zartman, ed., *Political Elites in Arab North Africa*, pp. 35–91. New York: Longman.

Tharaud, Jérôme and Jean Tharaud. 1930. *Fez: Ou les bourgeois de l'Islam*. Paris: Librairie Plon.

The Thousand and One Nights. 1889. Translated into English by William Lane (as *Arabian Nights*). London: Chatto and Windus.

Thurman, Melburn D. 1983. "The Timing of the Skidi-Pawnee Morning Star Sacrifice." *Ethnohistory* 30:155–163.

al-Tirmidhi. 1292 [800s]. *Sunan al-Tirmidhi*. 2 vols. Cairo.

Toynbee, Arnold J. 1934. *A Study of History*. Vol. 3. London: Oxford University Press.

Tozy, Mohamed. 1979. "Monopolisation de la production symbolique et hiérarchisation du champ politico-religieux au maroc." *Annuaire de l'Afrique du Nord* 18:219–234.

—— 1984. "Champ et contre-champ politico-religieux au maroc." Ph.D. thesis, Political Science. Aix-en-Provence.

Trotter, Philip Durham. 1881. *Our Mission to the Court of Morocco in 1880*. Edinburgh: David Douglas.

Turner, Bryan. 1984. *Weber and Islam: A Critical Study*. London: Routledge and Kegan Paul.

Turner, Victor. 1974. *Dramas, Fields, and Metaphors: Symbolic Action in Human Society*. Ithaca, N.Y.: Cornell University Press.

—— 1977a. *The Ritual Process: Structure and Anti-Structure*. Ithaca, N.Y.: Cornell University Press.

—— 1977b. "Sacrifice as Quintessential Process: Prophylaxis or Abandonment?" *History of Religions* 16:189–215.

Udovitch, A. L., ed. 1981. *The Islamic Middle East, 700–1900: Studies in Economic and Social History*. Princeton, N.J.: Princeton University Press.

Valeri, Valerio. 1985. *Kingship and Sacrifice: Ritual and Society in Ancient Hawaii*. Translated by Paula Wissing. Chicago: University of Chicago Press.

van Baal, J. 1976. "Offering, Sacrifice, and Gift." *Numen* 23:161–178.

Vogt, John. 1979. *Portuguese Rule on the Gold Coast, 1469–1682*. Athens: University of Georgia Press.

Voll, John Obert. 1982. *Islam: Continuity and Change in the Modern World*. Boulder, Co.: Westview Press.

Von Grunebaum, G. E. 1976 [1951]. *Muhammadan Festivals*. London: Curzon Press.

Wagner, Roy. 1986. *Symbols that Stand for Themselves*. Chicago: University of Chicago Press.

Wakin, Jeanette. 1972. *The Function of Documents in Islamic Law: The Chapters on Sales from Tahawi's Kitab al-Shurut al-Kabir*. Edited, annotated, and with introduction by Jeanette Wakin. Albany: State University of New York Press.

Wallerstein, Immanuel. 1974. *The Modern World-System: Capitalist Agriculture and the Origins of the European World-Economy in the Sixteenth Century*. New York: Academic Press.

—— 1979. *Capitalist World Economy*. Cambridge: Cambridge University Press.

Waterbury, John. 1970. *The Commander of the Faithful: The Moroccan Political Elite: A Study in Segmented Politics*. New York: Columbia University Press.

—— 1972. "The Coup Manqué." In Ernest Gellner and Charles Micaud, eds., *Arabs and Berbers*, pp. 397–423. London: Lexington.

—— 1979. "La légitimation du pouvoir au Maghreb: Tradition, protestation, et répression." *Développements Politiques au Maghreb*. Paris: Centre National de la Recherche Scientifique.

Watson, Robert Spence. 1880. *A Visit to Wazan, the Sacred City of Morocco*. London: Macmillan.

Weber, Max. 1968. *Economy and Society: An Outline of Interpretive Sociology*. Translated by Ephraim Fischoff et al. New York: Bedminster Press.

Weir, T. H. 1904. *The Shaikhs of Morocco: In the 16th Century*. London: Simpkin, Marshall.

Wensinck, A. J. 1960. *A Handbook of Early Muhammadan Tradition*. Leiden: E. J. Brill.

Westermarck, Edward. 1911. "The Popular Ritual of the Great Feast in Morocco." *Folk-Lore* 22:141.

—— 1914. *Marriage Ceremonies in Morocco*. London: Macmillan.

—— 1926. *Ritual and Belief in Morocco*. 2 vols. London: Macmillan.

—— 1930. *Wit and Wisdom in Morocco: A Study of Native Proverbs*. London: Routledge.

Weston, Jesse. 1957. *From Ritual to Romance*. Garden City, N.Y.: Doubleday.

Whitehead, Alfred North. 1948. *Science and the Modern World*. New York: Mentor Books.

Windus, John. 1725. *A Journey to Mequinez, the Residence of the Present Emperor of Fez and Morocco, on the Occasion of Commodore Stew-*

art's Embassy Thither for the Redemption of the British Captives in the Year 1721. London: Jacob Tonson.

Wolf, Eric. 1951. "The Social Organization of Mecca and the Origins of Islam." *Southwestern Journal of Anthropology* 7:329–356.

—— 1982. *Europe and the People Without History.* Berkeley: University of California Press.

Worsley, Peter. 1980. "One World or Three? A Critique of the World System of Immanuel Wallerstein." *The Socialist Register,* pp. 298–338. London: Merlin Press.

Yahya, Dahiru. 1981. *Morocco in the Sixteenth Century: Problems and Patterns in African Foreign Policy.* Essex: Longman.

al-Zarhuni [ez Zerhouni]. 1940 [1725]. *La rihla du marabout de tasaft: Sidi Mohammed ben el Haj Brahim ez-Zerhouni.* Eighteenth-century text translated [into French] from Arabic and annotated by Colonel Justinard. Paris: Geuthner.

Zartman, William. 1964. *Morocco: Problems of New Power.* New York: Atherton Press.

—— 1982. "Political Elites in Arab North Africa: Origins, Behavior, and Prospects." In William Zartman, ed., *Political Elites in Arab North Africa,* pp. 1–34. New York and London: Longman.

—— 1987. "King Hassan's New Morocco." In I. William Zartman, ed., *The Political Economy of Morocco.* New York: Praeger.

Ziegler, Philip. 1969. *The Black Death.* London: Readers Union Collins.

index